Where the Gulls Are

Fishing with Joe

Bob Burroughs

With contributions by
Frank Miller
Tim Wakefield

AuthorHouse™
1663 Liberty Drive
Bloomington, IN 47403
www.authorhouse.com
Phone: 1-800-839-8640

© 2011 Bob Burroughs. All rights reserved.

No part of this book may be reproduced, stored in a retrieval system, or transmitted by any means without the written permission of the author.

First published by AuthorHouse   7/27/2011

ISBN: 978-1-4634-1720-8 (sc)
ISBN: 978-1-4634-1719-2 (hc)
ISBN: 978-1-4634-1718-5 (e)

Library of Congress Control Number: 2011908866

Printed in the United States of America

Any people depicted in stock imagery provided by Thinkstock are models, and such images are being used for illustrative purposes only.
Certain stock imagery © Thinkstock.

This book is printed on acid-free paper.

Because of the dynamic nature of the Internet, any web addresses or links contained in this book may have changed since publication and may no longer be valid. The views expressed in this work are solely those of the author and do not necessarily reflect the views of the publisher, and the publisher hereby disclaims any responsibility for them.

DEDICATION

This book is dedicated to the loving memory of Catherine Ann Burroughs (1934 – 2008) who never fished, hated fish and the water they swam in, but supported and encouraged me anyway.

I am indebted to the book's reviewers:

Father Timothy Scherer, Professor of Languages and world class scholar, at The Athenaeum of Ohio;

Ms Sue Ray, voracious and eclectic reader, who lent the perspective of a non-fisherman;

Rod Null, avid fisherman and Professor of Mathematics at Rhodes State;

Frank Miller, saltwater IGFA record holder, and early accomplice in ill-advised fishing adventures.

And I am especially indebted to contributors Tim Wakefield and Frank Miller.

But most of all, to the legions of Joes out there on the lakes, streams and seas of North America, over 50 million license holders at last count, according to the Fish and Wildlife Service, from whom came the inspiration, and for whom this work is intended.

Table of Contents

Chapter 1.	Fishing with Joe: *What it's about*	*1*
Chapter 2.	Getting Hooked *The terrible, contagious, incurable Icthyosis*	*6*
Chapter 3.	Learning the Hard Way *Boots and Bikes*	*10*
Chapter 4.	The Stuff Dreams Are Made Of *That Man, and That Fish*	*17*
Chapter 5.	Go North, Young Man, Go North *The Shortest Distance to a Straight Line*	*34*
Chapter 6.	Jockey Schwey *Impersonating a Crappie*	*55*
Chapter 7.	Wilderness On The Cheap *Canoes and Canvas*	*68*
Chapter 8.	Unnatural Lakes *Opportunities Everywhere*	*91*
Chapter 9.	Chaos at Coquina *Getting the Blues*	*103*
Chapter 10.	Coral Corral *Paradise Found*	*117*

Chapter 11. The Land of Kah-weh-teh-kon
Fishing Sacred Waters 140

Chapter 12. On Beavers' Wings
Fishing the Inaccessible 163

Chapter 13. Chasing Sunsets
California Crying Trout 184

Chapter 14. A Dose of Salt
Landlubbers Learn Lessons 204

Chapter 15. A Fish Named Sauger
Big Time on the Big O 234

Chapter 16. The Sweet Sea
Renaissance 256

Chapter 17. Pa-hay-okee
Fishing the Edge 276

Chapter 18. Meeting the Natives
Lions and tigers and BEARS, Oh, my! 304

Chapter 19. 61°N, 146°W
Yes, Virginia, There is a Salmon Claus 323

Chapter 20. Taman Negara
Fishing the Sungei of Malaysia 340

Foreword

Embedded in the population of our modern world there is a subclass. These have not evolved sufficiently to shed their hunter-gatherer tendencies. They are misfits in this age. They are categorized as "fishermen". Bob Burroughs is a member, in good standing, of this clan.

Should you be a non-angler, and have ever given a confirmed fisherman that "why would you ever want to do that?" look (I am a mathematician. I know "the look"), this work affords you some insights, and a rare opportunity to partake of stories that might otherwise only be experienced around a campfire after a full day on the water. They are stories to be savored.

For those who do love/live to fish, a word of caution. Recently, I shared but one chapter with a colleague at my college. Shortly thereafter, he was at my office door with numerous reminiscences, prefaced with phrases like "One time my Dad and I…" and "Next year, I plan to…". That said, pull up a comfortable chair, grab a good cup of coffee or perhaps a cold beer. You are going to enjoy this! I know you will find yourself saying, "I remember when…" and "I think I'll head over there next…" as Bob takes you on wonderful journeys to but a few of the waters he has plied.

I have had the singular pleasure of sharing time fishing with Bob. From brief excursions at a nearby stream to weeklong trips a thousand miles from home, exploring the wonders of an ocean, he demonstrates the same boundless passion for the sport. It is contagious.

It's time for me to give the author a call, and see if he needs someone to hold down the other end of his canoe this weekend. If he hasn't taken off midweek for the Outer Banks, or somewhere, I'm pretty sure I know what the answer will be.

Rodney Null

23FEB2011

CHAPTER 1
Fishing with Joe:
What it's about

This is a different kind of book about fishing....well, angling. The word *fishing* is generic. It can encompass trawlers and purse seines and the like. It means the pursuit of fish, commercial or sport, human or animal. Bears and otters and cormorants and kingfishers and ospreys *fish*. Commercial fleets *fish*. It is probably grammatically correct to say that sport fishermen *angle*. But that's not how we really talk. Ed and Charlie, meeting in the parking lot after work, don't say, "Let's go angling next Saturday."

So, here, that word, fishing, means rods and reels, and maybe even arrows and spears and trot lines and jugs. But mostly, rods and reels. (For some reason, we call rods without reels "poles". They're included.) The folks who sport fish we'll call anglers or fishermen, agreeing, of course, that the term *fisherman* is not gender specific. F*isherperson* is too long. The British use the term *fishers*.

There are more books about fishing than there are salmon in Alaska, going all the way back to the late 1500's. And they are not rare works in the libraries of a few scholars and enthusiasts. There are a great many of us, we anglers. And we read. We read a lot. Isaac Walton's *The Compleat Angler* is the third most printed book in the English language, behind only *The Bible*, and *The Complete Works of Shakespeare*.

There are scholarly tomes, written by graduate student English majors, on Walton and his contemporaries. There are classic books by the great outdoor writers, the likes of Earnest Hemingway. There are useful how-to books by guides and well-known tournament anglers. And, of course, there are those wonderful books and articles that use fishing as a vehicle for humor. And if you don't find some humor in this madness called fishing, you may wish to seek professional help.

But this book about fishing is different. For one thing, it begins with golf.

With the admission that I have never played golf, I will freely state that I love golf. I support and encourage golf. It is a thoroughly wonderful sport. It is played outdoors, on grass, among trees, ponds and streams, under the sky. It provides exercise. It fosters comradeship. Best of all, it keeps people off the water.

Golf is similar to fishing in many ways. Both began as pastimes for the upper classes. Ordinary folks, in the early days of the sport, were too busy trying to make a living to have time for golf. And, they did not have access to courses. And when it came to putting fish on the table, that was serious business, and they tended to use more efficient methods than rods or poles.

With advances in technology came advances in economic productivity, and there followed a general democratization of almost everything, including golf. Public courses appeared, and the game was no longer the sole province of the members of country clubs. The popularity of golf soared. Soon, the game was no longer just a recreational activity; it became competitive at a whole new level. The professional tournament player had arrived on the scene.

And so, to the casual observer, there appear to be three distinct groups of golfers. The first group: the tournament professionals. The second group:

those with access to the best courses, the best equipment and the best guidance and instruction. The third group: those with limited time and budget, who play when and where they can, for the pure enjoyment of it.

Let's briefly examine the three groups.

For the first group, golf is a business, a deadly serious business. As for a professional in any sport, practice is endless. Like a racing team trying to get that last 0.5 mph out of its car, the tedious pursuit of elusive perfection is the tournament golfer's way of life. And life is nomadic: from tournament to tournament, from appearance to appearance, from clinic to clinic. And then, there's sponsorship to worry about, and public image, upon which sponsorship and endorsements depend.

For the second group, by contrast, the sport can be a glorious thing. With the resources, the connections and the access, they can play the world's finest courses, in the world's most beautiful and exotic locations. And they can do so on their own schedule. Unlike the first group, they do not absolutely, positively have to be at a particular course on a particular day. And if they happen to have a poor performance one day, the television cameras are not there to tell the world about it. That story is very likely contained within the four walls of the club bar. A little good-natured ribbing, maybe a lost bet, but no disaster.

For the third group, golf can be equally glorious, but in, perhaps, different ways. The public links, a few miles from home, may be a little threadbare, and the weather may be cold, or raining, but four friends, none of whom will ever break eighty, are laughing, hooting at one another's mistakes, and having the time of their lives. The chores at home and the problems at work are forgotten. And in the lounge, after the last putt has finally been sunk, they are planning their precious, once-a-year trip to a really top-notch golf resort.

Golf with Joe.

Who is Joe? Or is it Joan? Well, he's John Q. Public; she's Jane Doe, or any of the myriad of names given to ordinary, do-your-work, pay-your-bills, mind-your-business folks. She's a neurologist, or a waitress, or a housewife, or an attorney. He's a banker, or a farmer, or a welder, or a professor. Neither can devote much time to golf. Both have other bells to answer.

Both have other financial demands. But both relish and treasure those precious hours on that grass, among those trees, under that sky.

Whether John or Jane, from here on, we'll call that famously anonymous, remarkably unremarkable person, Joe. You know who Joe is………because he's probably you.

Now the trouble with arbitrarily defined groups is that they always have a lot of overlap. But no matter. The concept is what counts.

But what does all of that have to do with fishing? Everything. Fishing has exactly the same three distinct groups. And while the mainstream outdoor magazines, and the overwhelming majority of books on the subject of fishing, pour most of their ink over the first and second groups, this book is about the third group.

Fishing with Joe.

And that's why this book is different.

Here's what it's about. It's about a lifetime of fishing with Joe ……actually, a number of Joes. It's all first hand, written by the guys who were there, sometimes, written right on the spot. And even though there are several contributors, it is, at least in part, a sort of fishing autobiography. It spans seven decades. It includes all of the errors, fumbles and ignorance, all of the disasters and near-disasters, and therefore, all of the learnings. After all, everybody's parents told them, at one time or another, "Learn from the mistakes of others". That is good advice. Learning from the mistakes of others is cost effective and time saving.

These are not the stories of the privileged or the sponsored, the negatives carefully edited out, to evoke an "I wish I could do that" response. These are the stories of the ordinary, the negatives purposely unedited, which may well evoke a plan, rather than a wish, or a knowing, "Yeah, I did that, too".

So…… you're going fishing with Joe, with Joe's time constraints, and on Joe's budget. You'll meet some characters. You'll share adventures, some wonderful and some frightening. You'll be fishing in backyard creeks, in rivers, great and small, in the tannin stained waters of the northern tier states and of Canada, in the remarkable TVA system, in the fresh-water seas called The Great Lakes, in the North Pacific, and in the Atlantic.

You'll be fishing in pristine wilderness, and in the shadows of skyscrapers. And Joe will take you on some once-a-years and some once-in-a-lifetimes, because that, too, is part of being Joe. You and Joe will fish in Alaskan glacial streams, over Bahaman reefs, in the Everglades, fresh and salt, on the surf-pounded Outer Banks, in the always surprising Gulf of Mexico, in steep Wyoming canyons, and even in the jungles of Malaysia.

The places are almost all beautiful, but sometimes the fishing won't be pretty. That's how fishing is. Otherwise, as someone once said, they'd call it *catching*.

Chapter 2
Getting Hooked
The terrible, contagious, incurable Icthyosis

My father had it. My grandmother was a carrier. My uncles had it, too. One of them, Uncle Bud, was in the advanced stages. It isn't hereditary, but it is extremely contagious. One close contact and you were infected. Several more, and you became incurable. Most of the victims were infected the same way: by well-meaning relatives. Their lives were changed forever by Icthyosis: Fishing Fever.

My own case is textbook. Millions of Icthyosis victims could tell almost identical stories. I remember the day vividly. It was yesterday.

The depression was winding down. My father, by virtue of two jobs, one as a salesman and another running a poultry farm, was able to trade in his ancient Nash on a brand new, shiny, 1940 Dodge. I can still see it. It was maroon, and had a gleaming, chromium-plated ram proudly charging from the front of the hood. With a new car, there is but one thing to do: go somewhere. And my uncles, Pete and Bill, had the perfect destination.

We lived east of Cincinnati – hardly the fisherman's paradise. But Uncle Pete knew somebody who knew somebody who knew the watchman at a gravel pit. And that pit had filled from the underground water table. Whether by human agency, or by inadvertent stocking by herons and kingfishers, it had developed a population of native species: bluegills, smallmouth bass, and especially, channel catfish. A few phone calls, and the plan was set.

I could hear my father and uncles debating, but I pretended not to.

"Oh, come on, let's take him along . He's almost six".

"He's five", Dad said, "and he can't swim".

"I've got a life jacket. He can wear that".

"It's too big".

"Well, we'll strap it up good and tight".

In the end, Dad lost the debate. The ratty, old kapoc life jacket was like being clamped between two boards, but it got me included, although I wasn't sure in what. I was outfitted with a steel casting rod (it's still in the basement) and a raspy level wind reel, filled with braided black line. The line extended through a balsa float, about the size of a longneck beer bottle, to a hook snelled with what looked like today's trimmer cord. I also got a full thirty seconds of instruction.

Dad at once removed the hook, and replaced it with one having no barb. Instead, where the barb would have been, the hook was bent into an S-curve, intended, apparently, to at least slow down the escape of a hooked fish. I haven't seen one of those hooks in sixty years. That's testament to how well they worked.

On the way, we stopped for bait – not at a bait shop, but at a grocery store. My uncles bought shrimp, bread, lunchmeat and beer. We already had plenty of chicken liver. No thought was given to soft drinks. Cincinnati was a German heritage town. Of course the kids drank beer….in those days.

The water in the gravel pit could not be seen until we walked to the edge of the steep bank. Dad insisted on carrying me down to the water's edge, where a narrow shelf of level ground extended twenty or thirty yards in each direction. He placed me up against the grade and strictly warned me to go no closer to the water. He looked at my uncles and shook his head.

The water was very clear, and green tinted. All I could think of were those jungle pools in the Tarzan movies, and half expected to see a hippo surface at any moment. Uncle Bill put a piece of shrimp on my hook, and cast the huge float about fifteen feet. Then, he baited his own hook with chicken liver, and sat down. We all sat down…for what seemed a very long time.

I remember that the sun was behind the high bank, and the sandwiches long since eaten, when Uncle Pete's float twitched. "Hey! Pete!" somebody shouted. There was considerable scrambling, and by the time Pete had rod in hand, the float was gone. I had no idea what to expect. But when I saw that steel rod become U-shaped, I was mesmerized. On the other end of that line must be some horrible monster of the deep.

The "monster" dragged up onto the gravel bank was a channel catfish of, perhaps, two pounds. But it was silver gray above and creamy white on its belly and was the most beautiful thing I had ever seen. Here was this creature, invisible and silent, unattainable deep in that green water, and now in our hands. This was a miracle.

Now, I became very serious about this enterprise. I watched my float intently, but it remained still. Dad and the others caught two more, but I was being ignored. Finally, Uncle Bill reeled in my line, removed the undisturbed shrimp, and draped a huge glob of chicken liver on the so-called hook. He cast it very gently, so as not to dislodge the chicken liver, not more than eight or ten feet. I resumed my intense watch. But nothing happened.

The attention span of a five year old is short, and soon began to waver. I recall Dad reminding me several times to watch my float. The third or fourth time I turned back toward it, I had trouble finding it. "Dad, I can't see it".

"You got a bite. Reel in until you feel something, then jerk up on the rod".

My execution of those instructions missed on all counts. But when the line came taught – even though I had been reeling in the wrong direction – there was this surge. There was something alive, dynamic, strong out there. I was connected to some unseen force, some mysterious power. But not for long. The barbless hook performed its intended function and came easily free.

My father and uncles cheered as if I had scored the winning touchdown in the Super Bowl. "But Dad", I whined, "he got away". Then Dad said something that I did not understand until later….much later.

"That's OK. That's not what it's about".

The genie was out of the bottle. All I wanted to do was to go back to that green water. Something wonderful lived in it. Movies, amusement parks and the like had instantly become insignificant as destinations. My father wisely turned my incessant pleadings to constructive advantage. Going fishing became the ultimate reward for exceptionally good behavior.

It took several more outings, outings not nearly so well remembered, before

I actually landed a fish. Strange. I don't remember that fish. But I'm sure that some radiologist, examining a scan of my brain, will be puzzled by the indelible, ghostly image of a magnificent two pound channel catfish.

Chapter 3
Learning the Hard Way
Boots and Bikes

My fishing education was interrupted by a cataclysmic event: World War II. It is said that everyone remembers exactly where they were, and what they were doing, when events of global magnitude occur. It's true. I was flat on my stomach on the living room floor, looking at the pictures in the comic section of the Sunday paper. My father, as usual, was reading the rest of that paper, listening to a classical music program on the Crosley. I think it was *The Longines Symphonette.* (Everybody in Cincinnati called a radio a "Crosley" – no matter who made it – because broadcasting pioneer Powell Crosley built those well-respected receivers there. The catalog houses specializing in nostalgia items still offer replicas of Crosley radios.) Those too young to have been there have witnessed the scene many times, in old movies, and on The History Channel: "We interrupt this program to bring you the following message".

And, the scene is a time-honored classic. A family is gathered around their radio. The announcer introduces a newsman, who describes the attack on Pearl Harbor. The children look puzzled. The parents exchange worried glances. That is exactly what happened.

The children had no clue as to what this all meant, but I could sense that it was very serious, and not good. Soon, Uncle Bill, Uncle Bud and my Cousin, Al – everybody called him "Moe" – were in uniform. Uncle Pete was working 12 hour shifts, seven days a week, in a machine tool plant. My father took on yet another job, in a factory making defense electrical components. All of my fishing instructors were either absent or otherwise occupied.

Everything was scarce. Even those not yet fifty years old already know the story. Rationed gasoline was too precious to use for fishing trips. Tires were extremely hard to get, and, in those days, average tire life was about one quarter of what it is today. Nylon, the new miracle fiber, was to be used for parachutes, not fishing line. Any daylight time that my father wasn't working at one of his jobs was spent working in the garden. The "Victory

Garden" was strongly encouraged to augment the nation's food supply, and that is what we called ours, although we had always had a garden. I still do.

Of course, I was conscripted to help in the garden. Every time my hoe would turn up an earthworm, I would reluctantly, but gently, return it – I had been instructed that they were good for the soil – thinking that it was a great waste of talent. Another of my assignments was to hand pick insects from the plants. Insecticides were scarce, expensive, and, in those pre-EPA days, highly toxic. The mainstay was arsenate of lead, and then there were other heavy metal compounds, like Bourdeau Mixture, and there was nicotine sulfate. The organic compound of choice was Rotenone – said to be less toxic to humans. DDT had not yet appeared on the consumer market. All of these would prove later to have negative impact on fish populations.

But for now, food production had priority, and my father had the manpower (me) to rid the garden of pests by hand. It was hard, boring, mindless work. But, there was an upside. Over the hill from the garden plot was a small creek. We carried water for the garden from it during dry periods. It had a few pools, most barely 200 square feet, and none of them much more than three feet deep. But there were sunfish in those pools. A trophy specimen was a full five inches long. As an incentive, Dad would allow me to fish those pools with the bugs I had collected – after he inspected the rows to see that none were left.

Dad stashed a pole – not a "rod", but a genuine cane pole – in the weeds. It was not originally intended as a fishing pole, but was an eight foot length of cane left over from some other use. It did not taper much. It was fitted with some of the braided black line from one of the reels, a cork, half split lengthwise, from a home-brew bottle, a small hex nut as a sinker, and a rusty hook, which by memory I would judge to have been a #6. Maybe a #4. I learned a lot with that rig.

Most of the time without guidance, I had the opportunity to experiment. When there had not been rain for a few days, the water was clear enough to see every fish in the pool…or so I thought. Naturally, I concluded that the nearer I could drop the bait to a fish, the more likely that fish was to bite. That strategy worked only a small fraction of the time. Usually, the disturbance caused by the falling rig would cause the target fish to streak away. My eyes would try to follow it, but it would, as if by magic, disappear. After a few "casts", there was not a fish to be seen, even though I could see every square inch of the bottom. Well, it was obvious. They had all gone to the next pool, too fast for me to see. What other explanation could there be?

After slogging through thick weeds – most of them stinging nettle – the same scenario played out in the next pool. And the next. But when I made my way back to the first pool, there they were again. So, I must have driven them in front of me on the way back. Child logic was no match for the observed phenomenon. I dropped the cabbage worm into the water, again the fish disappeared, and I sat down, frustrated. Kids bore easily. Up from the creek bank, where there was soil instead of gravel, I turned rocks over, hoping to find an earthworm without an agricultural assignment. Maybe the fish were afraid of cabbage worms.

Finally having captured a fat, red earthworm, I went back to the pole. But the cork was gone. On that rusty hook wriggled a sunfish. Aha! For Joe, fishing is a lifetime of Aha! moments. Were that not so, Joe would probably be playing golf.

When the fish disappeared, they weren't gone, only hiding. But where? I could see every rock. There were no holes or caverns, no undercuts or ledges. It seemed impossible. But the same tactic, cast, hide and wait, worked again and again.

Dad whistled and I stashed the pole. We left for the house. I told him what had happened.

"You're not the only one trying to catch those fish. There are kingfishers and raccoons and snakes and other things after 'em. If the fish couldn't hide from them, there wouldn't be any fish in that creek. The least shadow moving across the water could be a bird. The least splash could be a raccoon. When they're still, on the bottom, they don't need to be under anything. Their color and pattern hides 'em. Always remember, if you can see a fish, that fish can see you".

Continuing education.

When the creek was a bit murky, from recent rainfall, fishing was easier. But when it was bank full and muddy, fishing was terrible. More lessons.

Some of the insect pests were popular with the fish, others were not. And that preference changed from day to day. I didn't know why. Still don't.

It did not take very long to either exhaust, or educate, the fish population in those pools. There were very few other opportunities within walking distance. But during the next school year, it turned out that my grade school classmates did know of some. I found that there were lots of Joe Juniors, and fishing was the common bond made us all friends. (The word "all" needs to be taken in context. There were a total of thirteen people in my grade school graduating class.)

These opportunities were mostly farm ponds, created to water livestock, and never intentionally stocked. They were small, one quarter to one half acre, with their shorelines churned to deep muck by cattle hooves. Their fish populations were similar: sunfish, yellow-bellied catfish, and sometimes, an occasional bass or channel catfish, all stocked by whatever eggs clung to the bills or feet of itinerant herons or kingfishers. Access required braving poison ivy, stinging nettles, mud, and worst of all, that dread of all kids, *permission.*

Remember that this was all before the present age of pandemic litigation, in which a simple kindness can often make one a defendant. Still, there was, I suppose, the fear that kids, accidentally or intentionally, might do damage to the property. So, permission was not always obtainable. To Joe Junior, that meant but one thing: night fishing. To be included meant initiation into an exclusive, secret society.

The new kid was always suspect. The senior members of this band of guerillas – maybe ten or eleven years old - had to perform certain security checks to satisfy themselves that the newcomer was not a risk. These consisted of a series of crossings of the heart and hopings to die, and threats of eye blacking and arm breaking, until satisfied that the secret plans would never be revealed. "OK, now here's the plan", said Harry, the leader by virtue of being a head taller than anybody else. There followed a plan so detailed and comprehensive that Navy SEALs could not have carried it out. But we all felt better that we had a foolproof, even if irrelevant and unexecutable, plan.

Harry pointed at me. "You and Paul find out how we can get in there without going past the house. You know, the back way".

The back way? We don't even know the front way. This may involve several counts of trespassing. I put up my hand.

"What if somebody sees us?"

"Uh…say you're looking for your dog".

The plan was that we would all tell our parents that we were going fishing at Bergen's Pond, then going to one of the other guys' houses for dinner, and then listen to some radio shows. "Say you'll be home real late, like maybe nine o'clock." Boy, Harry thought of everything.

You could always get permission from the Bergens. The pond had been a goldfish farm, but that enterprise had been abandoned. The goldfish were by now eight to twelve inches long. Other species were few and far between. But, after all, a goldfish was a fish. And these weren't those fancy aquarium goldfish with the frilly fins and the sickly, streaked colors. These were raised as bait goldfish, a popular baitfish for big catfish in the larger local streams, including the Ohio River. They were hardy, prolific and looked like a real fish….only gold colored.

Paul and I started to reconnoiter the assigned area. We strolled innocently along, looking for some path from the road toward the target pond. And there it was. A trail left the road, looking as if it were generally in the direction of the pond. It ran adjacent to an occupied lot, with the residents tending their garden. "What kind of dog you got?" asked Paul.

"Airdale"

"Oh."

We seemed to have raised the interest of the gardeners. They were staring at us. But what could be more natural or innocent, on a summer afternoon, than two lads searching for a lost dog, one calling, "Here, Buster"……….and the other calling, "Here, Dale"?

The trail led right to the pond. Footprints were plain. We were obviously not the first raiders. What a surprise. But, mission accomplished, we turned homeward. Harry reassured us. "Don't worry. Indians made that trail years ago". Harry should know. He's a Big Kid. But I never knew that moccasins had heels.

On the appointed day, we met at Bergen's pond. Following Harry's instruction, we all wore the darkest clothes we had. We pretended to fish until the sun was over the horizon. Then Harry called us together. "Now listen. Put some mud on your face, and on your arms. No flashlights. If somebody shines a light on ya, just freeze. Don't move a muscle. They'll never see ya. Bait up by feel. And no talkin'". Harry had seen too many war movies. That part about baiting up by feel made me wish I had some of Dad's ineffective barbless hooks. Off we went.

The stage was set for an exciting adventure. But that curtain never opened. The first - and last – acts of the drama were about tripping in the dark, falling in the mud, struggling to thread a wriggling red worm onto an invisible hook, and trying to untangle backlashes you couldn't even see. No one had challenged us. It was as if no one cared that we had infiltrated this forbidden honey-hole. And for good reason. No one caught a fish.

We rinsed off the mud as best we could in the pond's outflow stream and trudged home. We had pulled it off; our stories held up. There was a learning in all of this. Just because a piece of water is hard to access, and few people fish it, does not necessarily mean that there is good fishing. But that was a lesson I would have to relearn many times in later years.

Learning the hard way began with tackle. The tackle of the era was difficult enough to master at high noon, much less in the dark. Casting reels had advanced to "level wind", that is, a guide geared to the reel's spool moved back and forth across the spool's width to evenly distribute the stored line. So, when the rig or lure splashed down, the reel continued to spin, unless thumbed to a halt at exactly the right moment. Too much thumb: shortened cast. Too little thumb: the dreaded backlash. It could take an hour to untangle, a sweating, finger-cramping, teeth-gritting hour.

The typical Third Group (Joe) freshwater casting rod was made from steel. The better ones were tubular, the cheaper ones were solid. Second Group rods were split bamboo. Hand made, and expensive, but with wonderful actions. And why not? Bamboo is a naturally occurring fiber composite. Typical Joe rod guides were "German silver", a nickel alloy. Second Group guides were ceramic rings retained in corrosion resistant metal mountings. At the high end were guides made from very hard gemstone – not jewelry grade, but very pricey, anyhow. (Remember, at this point in history, there was no First Group in fishing.)

Lines were braided, and large diameter for their load carrying capacity.

Nylon was scarce and new on the scene, so most fishermen were equipped with cotton line, which, if not carefully unspooled and dried after each use, would rot. Guide friction was high compared to today's monofilament and synthetic fiber braids.

Still, with enough practice, a skilled angler could begin to approach the casting proficiency of……. a novice using current technology gear. The whippersnappers don't know how good they've got it.

Learning the hard way meant getting to fishing sites on foot or by bicycle……if you were lucky enough to have a bicycle in the WWII years. It meant finding drop-offs and deep holes and sand bars with a lead weight, counting reel handle rotations, not just reading a sonar screen. It meant learning to read the current in a stream. It meant having a very small selection of old but precious lures, precious enough that climbing a tree or diving into cold water to retrieve a snagged one was the common practice. It meant finding a reef with a map and a compass, estimating speed and measuring time, and allowing for current and crosswind, not just plugging co-ordinates into a global positioning system (GPS) and letting satellites and computers do all the work.

It was minimalist fishing. And it is not altogether out of style. There are still places where simplicity is not only still successful, but is required in order to *be* successful. To fish places where access means that everything you eat, wear, live in, fish out of, and use comes in on your back, mastering minimalist fishing is very useful indeed. And there are *fish* in those places. Getting there and staying there is challenging. That's *why* there are fish in those places. We'll travel to some of them in later chapters. Learning the hard way is a good thing. It makes one appreciative.

Chapter 4
The Stuff Dreams Are Made Of
That Man, and That Fish

With the scarcity of real-life quality fishing opportunities, I went vicarious. The family dentist, Dr Harkrader, was a sportsman, and a world class pistol shot. His office was full of trophies, including a walnut plaque on which was mounted a gold engraved, presentation grade, M1911 .45 ACP. I was deeply impressed. And, it was good to know that my teeth were entrusted to so steady a hand. The waiting room table was strewn with magazines, Life, Time, Better Homes and Gardens, and…….wait…….what's this? The cover picture showed a man holding an enormous fish. There were pine trees and a lake of spectacular blue color in the background. The man was wearing a heavy, red and black plaid shirt, and on his belt, a large knife and a pistol! I could read now, so I quickly turned to the referenced page, and scanned the article as fast as my limited reading skills would allow.

The fish was something called a muskellunge. The article did not divulge the exact location, but the lake was in "northern Wisconsin". The man had been casting a live sucker along a weedy shoreline. He had used his Colt Woodsman pistol to dispatch the beast. Wow! Oh, Wow! I had no idea there were such a magazines as *Sports Afield*, *Outdoor Life* and *Field and Stream*. Yet here they were, right on Dr Harkrader's table.

Wisconsin! Why, Mom's family lives there! And next summer, we're scheduled to visit them. Little realizing how large and how varied a place Wisconsin is, I visualized them living in the forest, beside such a lake, with a canoe drawn up onto a sandy beach. That was nowhere near the reality, of course, but it was a pleasant dream that would last for several months. I begged to take that now long-out-of-date magazine home. The good doctor readily agreed, remarking to my mother that it would be good to encourage reading.

I read it cover to cover. No. I *studied* it cover to cover. I saved ice cream money to buy, instead, at the village pharmacy, current copies. We traded them among the Joe Juniors like baseball cards. Even the ads were exciting. There were lures and tackle that that I never knew existed. There were species of fish that I never knew existed. There were places that I never knew existed. And, there was an unintended consequence. My teachers began to tell my parents how much my reading proficiency, vocabulary and composition skills had improved. Not my fault. It was an accident.

An eternity later, the school year ended. Soon, Mom and I would be departing by train for that magical place called Wisconsin. Dad would join us later. He had saved enough gasoline ration stamps for the trip. He did this by walking, or bicycling, five miles, each way, each day that weather would permit, to the end of the street car line, in order to commute to his jobs.

Departure was now just a matter of days. No kid ever counted down to Christmas with more anticipation. And, it got even better. Mom and Dad were discussing plans for the trip at dinner.

"I'll get to Racine on the eleventh. We'll all leave to go up north the next morning", Dad was saying.

Up north? UP NORTH???

"Where's up north?"

"Well, we're going to drive up to Boulder Junction, to Fish Trap Lake. That's in Vilas County. You know, that's the Muskie Capital of the World. Or that's what they say. They all been there before. Bud says it's good fishin'. Yeah, we'll all go. Bud's home on leave, and Uncle Herman will be going to Racine with you."

I expected to wake up at any moment. Too bad. This was a terrific dream. I could see that magazine cover. I could see *that man*, and *that fish*.

Now, both the clock and the calendar seemed frozen. The story is told that Albert Einstein, in an attempt to simplify his notion of relative time, said, "If you sit down on a hot stove, a second seems like a minute. If you are talking to a pretty girl, an hour seems like a minute". Each minute to departure seemed like an hour. But each finally passed.

I had never seen, or imagined, such a place as Union Terminal, Cincinnati's railroad station. It was a huge quarter-sphere, the walls covered with vast mosaics depicting the history and industry of the City. And in the war years, the term "bustling" was a gross understatement. The enormity and frenzy of it were intimidating. Most of the experience was lost on me. I was destination-focused. I was going fishing.

Union Terminal, today, hosts no trains. It is a museum complex.

In the forties, by rail, it took five hours, door to door, to get from Cincinnati to Racine. Today, flying commercial jets, it takes seven hours. That's "progress".

I met Uncle Herman for the first time on the train. He wasn't really my uncle. He was Mom's uncle, Grandma Ruilman's brother. And he was, as they say, a character. Fishing with Joe, somehow, seems to involve contact with a lot of folks who qualify for that title. Uncle Herman, for reasons never fully divulged, was apparently of independent means. He didn't work, although he did not seem old enough to be retired. I never knew whether he was a bachelor or a widower, but he was single. He divided his time between fishing and what Mom referred to, in tones less than complimentary, as "the ponies". He was spontaneous and socially irreverent. I liked this guy.

As the train trip neared its end, Uncle Herman pointed out the window. "Well, we're in the land of cheese. This is Wisconsin." It didn't look any different to me than Ohio, Indiana or Illinois. Where were the birch trees and pines of that magazine cover? Where were the lakes? What a disappointment. There were the same cornfields and houses and roads and towns as in the last 400 miles. Where do you fish? That question would soon be answered. But not the way I had expected.

Uncle Bud met us at the station. He had just arrived himself, and was still in khaki uniform. If ever a kid could have an idol, Bud was it. He had been a pilot and flight instructor before the war, as well as a midget race car driver, bow hunter (before that sport was popular), and built short wave radios in the basement. He also built his own fishing tackle. He was now a pilot in the Army Air Corps, and although he could not then tell us, his upcoming assignment was to be in the India/Burma region. Had the adults known that, there would have been a lot more worry. To me, those were just the names of places. After the war, he added charter captain and photographer to his resume. And he always drove supercharged Studebakers or Dodge Hemi's. What was not to admire?

And he was a fisherman, devoted and fanatic. But he was a specialist. He was a walleye man. No other species mattered. He would not consider fishing during daylight hours, and usually did not wet a line before midnight. Never mind that Lake Michigan, practically at his doorstep, was then, before the invasion of lamprey eels, a spectacular lake trout fishery. Never mind that some of the lakes in the region held trophy northern pike. Walleyes. Only and ever, walleyes.

My maternal Grandfather was the antithesis of his son, Bud, and of his brother in law, Herman. He was a serious, conforming, rather humorless man, strict and straight. That was his heritage. His parents had come to Cincinnati from Prussia. He was a lithographer by trade, and lived in Racine after having been made unwelcome in Cincinnati for his role in organizing the printers' union. Wisconsin was a more tolerant union environment. He was, by any standard, a good man, active in many charities, and widely respected in the community. He, too, was a fisherman. But his fishing emphasis was meat for the family table. And that was another learning for Joe Junior: Bud had a target species; Grandpa sought targets of opportunity. Made sense to me.

I soon benefited. Grandpa asked me whether I would like to go fishing with him. That question was not quite finished before the answer came. The next morning, we went out to the frame, one car garage. Grandpa retrieved from the rafters two very long cane poles, each in three sections of about six feet, a minnow bucket, and an empty twenty gallon garbage can. Then we walked across the street. The neighbor sold minnows from his garage, and Grandpa bought ten dozen! There was barely room for any water in that bucket. "It's OK if they die", he said. I had, by now, my own life jacket, and was sent for it.

We drove only a few blocks to downtown Racine, where he parked the car in a municipal parking lot. All I could see were buildings and concrete. Not a single pine tree. No trees at all! Then we walked around the corner of the Racine Hotel and I had to catch my breath. There, a hundred yards away, was more water than I had ever seen! It stretched to the horizon to the east, and stretched to the north and south until the shoreline disappeared. It was a deep blue in the distance, and clear green closer in. The harbor was enclosed, except for an opening at the eastern end, by a breakwater, mostly concrete, but in some places, made of huge boulders. The top of the breakwater was well above the lake level, but there were swells of about four feet that morning which sent spray over it at a few locations.

I was awed, but eager to get a line in the water. I did not know what our quarry was…or care. Grandpa strictly ordered me not to run ahead, but to stay beside him. Grandpa's orders were absolutely to be obeyed. He would steady me over broken sections of the wall, and shield me from the spray where it broke over the wall. We were some distance from the beach when he set the garbage can and minnow bucket on the concrete surface.

"Alright", he said, "let's see if they're biting today". He showed me how to hook the minnows, emerald shiners, just below the dorsal fin. The poles had no floats. I thought that strange. How would I know when I had a bite? "Lower the line until you feel it hit the bottom, then raise it about this far". When a fish bites, you'll know. It'll feel like a tapping".

These poles had considerable taper and flex. It was hard to maintain "about this far". Within less than a minute, there was an unmistakable tapping sensation. Snapping the pole violently upward, I sent minnow, hook and sinker over my head and onto the concrete behind. "No, no", Grandpa was actually laughing, "ease it up until you feel some weight. Then, snap it. But not so hard. Oh!" He turned his attention to his own pole. I watched as he did just what he had told me. The pole bent downward, and Grandpa hoisted a fat, bright yellow and green, lake perch onto the top of the wall. I had never seen one. The colors were magnificent, but faded quickly. It was what I would later learn is called a jumbo perch, and, in those times, Lake Michigan was full of them.

Grandpa took a length of clothesline from his pocket and lowered the garbage can, filling it about half full. Then he laboriously hauled it up. He was a slight man, and there were eighty pounds of water in that can. He tossed the perch into it. For the next hour, the bite was non-stop. I finally got the hang of it, and began to contribute a few fish to the can. "You know when to set the hook on a perch?" he asked. I shook my head. "Just before they bite". He chuckled to himself. I didn't get it. I do now.

Then, the bite stopped, fairly suddenly. After a few fishless minutes, I guess I began to look worried. "It's OK", he said, "they'll be back." It took about two hours, but he was right. We added to the can with regularity, all of them between ten and thirteen inches. At one point, I hooked a larger fish. The pole bent dangerously when I tried to lift it free. Grandpa told me to work it over toward the breakwater, and he would grab the line and pull it up. This he did. The fish was bright silver, and about two pounds. "What is it, Grandpa?"

"Freshwater herring. Menominee, I think they're called".

"Can you eat 'em?"

"Oh, yah. Good, too."

After what seemed like a few more minutes, but was probably more than an hour, Grandpa drained the water from the garbage can to lighten it. Then he said, "Come on. We have a lot of work yet to do." The can was two thirds full of fish, and it was heavy. I carried the poles and the empty minnow bucket. The lake had calmed, now, and there were no more drenchings with icy spray.

We worked for hours cleaning those perch. I was given the job of scaling, not yet trusted with knives, which Grandpa kept razor sharp. It was a point of honor with him. And razor sharp meant exactly that to Grandpa. He considered that a knife which could not be used to shave was a knife sharpened without skill, care and diligence…..virtues he held in great esteem. He held that a dull knife was dangerous. "That's how you get cut", he said, "you have to use too much force with a dull knife". Another learning.

It had been a great day, full of learnings. Water bigger than I ever imagined. A species I had never seen. Poles without floats. Great fishing right in the middle of a city. Still, I was anxious to see what "up north" was like. *There was that man. And that fish……….*

A few days later, everyone was up at 4:30 AM to begin the trip "up north". The odometer distance was a little over three hundred miles, but in the forties, it took about nine hours of driving time, and a total of almost twelve. There were frequent stops, including a visit to a cheese factory. These folks were tourists.

Little by little, the flora changed. There were fewer hardwood trees and more pine and birch. Row crop farming was nowhere to be seen, and even the dairy operations became sporadic. After the town of Rhinelander, some of the roads were not paved. The last stop was in Boulder Junction, at a general store/bar/bait shop. The adults were buying staple supplies… coffee, bacon, onions, potatoes, and, of course, a cold beer.

But I was fascinated by the minnow tanks. They were galvanized troughs intended for watering cattle, and had been modified to allow water to circulate, by gravity, from a tank in the loft of the structure. That tank was pumped full, by hand, from a well. There were three troughs. One contained the common, garden variety minnows I was used to seeing in creeks. Another held chub minnows nearly as large as the smaller perch we had caught on the breakwater. But the third had about a dozen suckers, all of them bigger than any of those perch. This must have been what the man in the article was casting when he caught that muskellunge! Then, it's true! There really is such a place and such fish. And we are actually there.

Whatever my elders were doing, it seemed to take forever. *Come ON. Somewhere around here there's this lake .... Can't be far, now. Let's GO.* Of course, none of that was ever verbalized. I was already too smart for that.

Back in the cars. I rode with Uncle Bud. I knew he'd get there faster. The road soon became gravel. And narrow. Now and then, the tips of pine branches would brush the windows. This was more like it. Soon, we turned off the "main road" onto a sandy lane marked only by two tire tracks. Between them, knee-high weeds and grass grew, but there were, at least, no trees in it. The sky was not visible in this green tunnel, and even though it was late afternoon, it seemed dark. But after several hundred yards, brightness returned, and we rolled to a stop in a grass clearing.

There were three cabins visible, as well as a tool shed and an ice house. But I didn't see a lake. There should be a lake. And it should be ringed with pine and birch trees, and it should be the color I had seen in that picture. Outside the car, I began to look in every direction.

Uncle Bud smiled. "Over there", he pointed. I ran toward a shallow rise and on the other side, there it was! It was exactly like *that picture*. It was magnificent. There was a path down to the water, with sections of logs placed as steps where it was too steep to maintain a footing. At the bottom was a crude dock, perhaps 25 feet long, made from logs and rough cut boards. It tilted a bit, and some boards were missing, but it was clearly serviceable. Beside it, pulled up on the sand, were two wooden boats. A third boat was tied to one side of the dock. This boat had an outboard motor mounted on the transom, and a fuel can and a landing net inside. I did not go down to the water, but I had a plan.

The first part of the plan was to establish good will. No one was ever so willing a worker in getting the cars unloaded, and the luggage put away. Cheerful fetching and carrying was my hallmark, and my vocabulary was unusually full of polite and respectful responses.

"You can leave the tackle in the car", Grandpa said. "We'll get that tomorrow".

At length, Grandpa called everyone to the picnic table on the porch of the cabin. He went to the icebox, and chipped shards of ice into a bowl with an icepick, an implement hardly known today. He passed glasses around, and handed me a bottle of Coca Cola – the original, green, ribbed bottle. He filled the glasses with ice, and then produced a bottle labeled Old Overholt, and poured the amber liquid over the ice. Then, he proposed a toast. We all stood.

"To Saint Christopher for a safe journey, and to God, for allowing us to be here in this beautiful place".

I never forgot that simple expression of gratitude. It has been maintained as a family custom. To this day, every family fishing trip begins that same way. Sure, I have fishing companions with no particular belief systems. But I have observed that an aggressive bear in camp, or a boat taking water in a storm, have a decidedly mitigating effect on atheism, even if only temporary.

"Well, we had better think about getting supper started", someone said. Time for the second step of the plan.

"Can I help?"

"No. Go outside and play."

"I think I'll go down and look at the lake."

"Put on your life jacket."

"OK."

It worked! Now, for the third step of the plan. I had made sure that the trunks of the cars were not relocked after unloading the other items. I dashed to the dusty maroon Dodge and retrieved my rod. The reel and line were still in place. I had only one lure that I thought would look anything at all like a large minnow. It was a garish, chromium plated spoon set with gaudy red and yellow "jewels" of glass. I dashed for that dock. Then I remembered. I didn't have my life jacket. What a tragic error that would have been. All the good will building would have been wasted. By the time it was retrieved, I was out of breath, but here I was, on the end of the dock, and I just knew that a few yards away, just out of sight, were schools of huge muskellunge, just waiting to devour that outlandish spoon.

Forty or fifty casts later, I managed to hook a decent slab-side crappie. And, being late for supper, or having one of the grown-ups find it necessary to come and fetch me, would not be wise. So, disappointed that large muskellunge were neither as numerous, nor as eager, as I had hoped, I trudged up the hill with the slab-side. At least, it was something.

Back at the cabin, it got rave reviews. I knew it didn't deserve them. So did everybody else. But that's how grown-ups work.

Later that evening, we heard a car, making that unmistakable gravel-crunching sound, approach. George Lohman knocked at the porch door, and then immediately, before any response could be made, came in. George was a guide and the proprietor of the fishing camp. He knew Uncle Bud. The two of them had fished together before the war.

"Well," he boomed, "here safe and sound. Say, I got two clients in the third cabin. They're muskie guys, Bud, so you won't have anybody in the walleye spots. I'm takin' 'em out tomorrow to High Lake, other side of the cut. You'll have this lake to yourselves. Edge of that weedbed about 200 yards off the dock has been pretty good for walleyes this spring. Don't know about now."

"Help yourselves to the ice. Got plenty. Good winter for cuttin' ice. And there's plenty of red worms under that pile of last year's sawdust. Oh. There's a five gallon can of gas in the tool shed. I can get it without ration stamps for the camp. No oil to mix, though. You bring an outboard?"

Grandpa told him that we had. And that we had oil. "OK", he said, "you're all set. Prob'ly see you tomorrow night."

And George Lohman was gone. The day was gone.

The cabin was large enough to accommodate everyone comfortably, and, being road accessible, it was much better equipped than the fly-in outpost cabins I would later experience……and prefer. This was almost like being at home. Road weary, there was not much further talk from anyone. In what seemed like the next instant, I was conscious of a refreshing chill in the morning air, and that air carried the wonderful scent of a wood stove perking coffee.

Six decades later, the aroma of pine smoke and coffee still put that morning before my eyes in complete and marvelous detail.

No one seemed in a hurry to get the boats in the water…except me. Dad and Grandpa, at length, decided that they would try that weed bed mentioned by George Lohman for walleyes. Uncle Bud said that it would be a waste of time. He wouldn't do that until after sundown. He suggested that they pursue muskies by trolling the shorelines. Dad objected that they did not have proper tackle or bait for that enterprise. But in the end, that is what they did.

Grandpa intercepted George Lohman before he and his clients departed, and bought a few of those large suckers. He retrieved his outboard motor from the trunk of the car, and affixed it to one of the boats beached beside the dock. The boats were wooden, about 14 feet long, and it took all four of the men to drag one to the water, only about ten feet away, and to wrestle it into deep enough water to float it clear of the sand. It immediately began to leak. Grandpa said that would be all right. The wood would swell and seal itself. And it did. Sort of.

Uncle Herman winked at me. "You and me will go out and show 'em how to catch fish".

"Uh, before you gentlemen embark", he said to the others, "how about helping me and the boy get this other tub afloat". Then he went to the tool shed and came back with two sets of oars.

"Don't forget these", he said to the others, "You trust that contraption to get you back", he said, pointing to the outboard, "and you'll miss supper."

Uncle Herman had a great distrust of things mechanical. He did not drive or own a car. Flying was totally out of the question for him. And he did not even like the idea of the new, Diesel powered trains.

But I was fascinated by that outboard engine. It was a very early model Evinrude, single cylinder, 1 ½ horsepower, and weighed probably as much as a current technology model with ten times the power. It was started by winding a rope around a pulley on the flywheel. Spark advance and throttle were separate controls. The fuel tank, which held less than a gallon, was mounted atop the engine, delivering fuel by gravity. (But then, gravity is cheap and fairly reliable.) It was cantankerous and balky, with quirks that only Grandpa understood. But, to me, this was yet another miracle. This homely machine could take you fishing faster and farther than oars or paddles, and do it with no physical exertion on your part.

I had often gazed at it longingly, stored in Grandpa's basement, and yearned to dissect it to discover what must be the mysterious secrets that converted gasoline into propulsion.

Grandpa carefully measured one-half pint of engine oil and poured it into a can containing an equally carefully measured gallon of gasoline. This mixture he poured, then, into the engine's fuel tank. Everything careful. Everything precise. That was Grandpa.

Then he methodically followed a mental checklist, culminating in a sharp pull of the starting rope. A dozen or so pulls later, punctuated by taunts from Uncle Herman, there was a popping sound and a slight puff of smoke. On the next pull, there were a series of pops, and then a sustained staccato. They were off.

"Well, don't just stand there", grinned Uncle Herman, "help me get this stuff in the boat. No. Wait. Come with me". He went to the tool shed again, and emerged with a spade. Then he raided the trash barrel for an empty can. We went to the pile of sawdust used to insulate the ice in the icehouse through the summer. "Almost forgot what George said", he muttered to himself. Under the sawdust, in the damp soil, were hundreds of fat, glossy earthworms. In minutes we had several dozen.

"Now", he said. "Now we're ready. Heh, heh. We'll show 'em". We returned to the boat, and pushed free of the dock. Uncle Herman manned the oars and headed for what appeared to be nowhere in particular. But occasionally he would stop, look at the shoreline, look at the nearby island, and look overboard. Then he would change direction slightly and row again. Then he said, "hah", and lowered the classic fish camp anchor….a paint can full of concrete. This patch of water looked like the rest of the lake. But I was sure it was not. Uncle Herman never bet long shots.

"See?" he said as he prepared his tackle, "those guys are after big fish. They're betting on a big one…you know, home run, last of the ninth. Always remember that there are a whole lot more small fish in any water than there are big ones, so you got better odds. If our dinner is what those guys are likely to catch, it's gonna be beans. You and me gotta put something on the table. There's a rock bar here. And some weeds. Now, watch."

Uncle Herman rigged with just a hook, baited with an earthworm. He did not cast, but simply tossed the earthworm over the side with six or eight feet of slack line. He watched it slowly sink. When the line suddenly pulled taut, he reeled in a thick-shouldered fish, shaped something like a bluegill or sunfish, but more muscular, with a larger mouth, and about 9 inches long. "There you are," he beamed, "a loudmouth bass!"

Later I would learn that the fish was a rock bass, or warmouth. But to Uncle Herman, there were three species of bass: largemouth, smallmouth, and loudmouth. We went on to boat a dozen or so more….barely enough to feed seven. So, Uncle Herman moved the boat about 100 yards, to a weedy creek mouth. With worms and bobbers we added 14 perch to the larder. Not Great Lakes jumbos, to be sure, but edible 7 to 8 inches.

As he was stowing the oars at the dock, we began to hear the little Evinrude. "Now, don't say anything", he admonished, "they might have caught one. But I'll give ya eight to five on it".

The other boat came within sight around the island and docked. Expressions on faces told the story. "Come on", chirped Uncle Herman, "me and the boy here got dinner. Let's have a beer." We went to clean fish.

I never forgot that lesson. On any given water, on any given day, there are always more small fish than big fish. Of course, depending on the water, "small" and "big" are matters of degree.

That night, Bud and Dad anchored at the edge of the weedbed 200 yards off the dock. Before finally being driven off by mosquitoes, they had netted two walleyes. I was disappointed when I saw them. They were perhaps 15 inches. "Tomorrow night, we'll wait until later. The bugs will be almost gone by midnight. And here, I brought some genuine GI repellent. Stinks, but works pretty good". Uncle Bud was selling, but I don't think Dad was buying.

Neither did Uncle Bud. He pointed at me. "Well, how about you? Want to go with me?"

Me? He's asking me?

"Uh, sure. I'll go".

Wow! Going fishing with my idol. Staying up late. And who will say me nay if it's Uncle Bud asking? It wasn't the smartest decision I ever made, but then, most of my fishing adventures haven't been based upon the smartest decisions. That's how Joe is.

Next morning, I went out again with Uncle Herman, and we caught a few panfish. My mother had mandated that I be back in by noon to take a nap, "if you're going to stay up all night with my crazy brother".

The nap was pointless. I could not sleep. Visions of walleyes with golden skins and huge marble eyes danced across my mind. I saw myself catching the biggest fish and winning the praise of my hero. I saw us bringing to the cabin a stringer of plump walleyes too heavy for me to carry. I saw Uncle Bud and me frying some of them for breakfast, ready before the others got up, with enough left for dinner. I wasn't sleeping, but I was certainly dreaming.

We never saw George Lohman's clients come in on the previous day, and hadn't seen them all day on this day. Their boat was not at the dock when Uncle Herman and I left, which was not exactly at the crack of dawn. Uncle Herman enjoyed several leisurely cups of coffee after breakfast, and an extended stay in the little wooden building behind the cabin, before gathering his gear and heading toward the dock. Their boat was not at the dock when we returned, nor when I walked down the hill before supper. But, it was there when Uncle Bud and I departed, just before midnight.

He did not use the outboard motor, but the oars, instead. And no lights, he insisted. He had marked the edge of the weed bed with a white balloon, held in place by a lead weight. "We'll find it. Moon's still up. If I can find an air strip in the dark, this won't be a problem". And find it we did. He lowered the anchor slowly, quietly.

"Bait with one of these minnows", he whispered, "and just let it swim. No sinker. After you bait up, put some of this on." He handed me a small bottle. It was GI mosquito repellent. He didn't want that scent on the bait.

I did as instructed. The oily liquid in the bottle didn't smell as bad as I thought it would, and it didn't smell as bad as the mosquitoes thought, either. They formed clouds around us. And, like what is oft said of dogs, the incessant "bzzzz" was worse than the bite. Whoever discovered DEET, the current state-of-the-art repellent, is indeed a benefactor of humanity.

The mosquitoes were making me frantic, but Uncle Bud seemed oblivious to them. In the light of the kerosene lantern, which was strictly to be kept on the bottom of the boat so that no light fell on the water, I could see mosquitoes surrounding him, too. He showed no sign that they were at all a nuisance. He saw me staring and squirming. "Things only bother you if you let them", he said. I did not know how to not let them. But I remembered what he said. Good advice. Hard to do.

The moon was now disappearing behind the dark silhouettes of the pines and birch on the island behind us. The wind had died. There was utter, total silence. I don't think I had ever heard it before. Then, out of this silent darkness, another sound I had never heard before. A mysterious, maniacal sound, that brought chills, and an involuntary stiffening of my spine. "Just a loon", Uncle Bud whispered.

"What's......."

"Shhh. It's a bird. Tell you later".

I have heard many loon calls, in dark, lonely places, over the years. I will never forget that one.

By about 4 AM, Uncle Bud had boated three walleyes, all about 16" long. I had missed several bites, preoccupied with mosquitoes and whatever other unseen and unheard creatures might be lurking in the forest night. But he had been right. The mosquito hordes had thinned considerably. And it was, in spite of mosquitoes and my fear of the unknown, beautiful. The forest was sharply outlined against a sky illuminated only by starlight. And in the absence of any ground lighting, there were more stars than I knew existed. Four hours earlier, I could not wait to go in, but dared not say so. Now, I dreaded leaving.

As the sky began to brighten with the coming dawn, the time came.

"Getting light", said Uncle Bud. "No sense staying". He drew up the anchor and rowed toward the dock.

In the daylight, I was duly impressed by those fish, large by my standards, with their mahogany backs, golden sides and creamy white bellies, their huge, translucent eyes, and their curved needle fangs. Sure, forty years later, fishing Lake Erie, such walleyes would be released without even removing them from the water. But that morning, they were trophies.

We never saw the muskie men that day, either. Uncle Bud and I slept through most of it. At mid-day, Dad and Grandpa returned with nothing. Uncle Herman had a few panfish, small perch and loudmouth bass, as he called them. With the three walleyes, barely enough for dinner.

After a lunch of canned spaghetti, there was a discussion.

"It's pretty hot today", Grandpa was saying. "Not much point in fishing until evening."

"Hot? How long you been gone from Cincinnati?", demanded Uncle Herman. "Why, it can't be more than 84 or 85. You forgot what hot is. But it is awful bright. You're right about the fishing. Let's play cards."

And that is what they did. I went down to the lake, just to wade, catch frogs, or whatever else I could find to do. Bored and about to leave in late afternoon, I heard a distant hum. A boat, about a mile away, was approaching. In a few minutes, it was clear that it was heading for the dock, and that it was the camp's third boat. The muskie men! I had to see the monster fish that they surely had aboard.

Soon it was close enough to see that George Lohman was in the rear, running the motor, one far newer than Grandpa's. It was quiet and smooth, by comparison. The working parts were covered by a cowl, and the starting rope even rewound itself! I had seen that on the first day, when the boat was unmanned at the dock. The two other figures in the boat were wearing undershirts and facing aft to avoid the spray, as there was a light chop on the lake that afternoon.

As they secured to the dock, one of the men stood, picked up his shirt, and put it on. Sure enough, it was plaid…..red and black! And a hunting knife and a holstered pistol hung from his belt! It was *that man*! The one in the picture! It wasn't really, of course, but the scene would be complete as soon as they hoisted *that fish,* which I was sure was lying in the bottom of the boat. Maybe even *those fish.* "Well, fellows, I tried every trick I know," George Lohman was saying, "that's how it goes, sometimes."

"Yeah, we know. The fish of ten thousand casts, they say."

"That's muskies all right." Lohman lifted a fuel can onto the dock, and the three were gone.

I felt cheated. And, I felt cheated for those two men. By all accounts, they were in the right place. They had all the right equipment. They had the right bait. They had a good boat. They had a native expert. And they had no fish.

There was certainly a lesson here for a Joe, Jr.

I wandered back to watch the card game. It had degenerated into a listless routine. I didn't see Grandma anywhere. She was usually the one who kept things from becoming dull. "Where's Grandma?"

"Oh," someone said, without looking up, "taking a nap, I guess". But she was not. She was, in fact, nowhere to be found. I expressed some concern, but no one seemed worried.

Uncle Herman tried to reassure me. "Don't you worry about my sister. She can take care of herself. Probably just took a little walk. There's an old logging road that goes to a broken down bridge that used to cross the cut to High Lake. Road's still clear enough to walk on, and it's shady. Bet that's where she is."

He was right about location, but not about purpose. In about an hour, she came trudging up to the cabin with a weathered cane pole she had found in the tool shed, and two fat largemouth bass, 4 to 5 pounds each. "If you men can't put some fish on the table, somebody better", she teased.

"How'd you catch 'em, Mom?" asked Uncle Bud, in a decidedly meek tone.

"Just walked down to the old bridge, out on it as far as I could, and dunked some worms down between lily pads. The water's only about knee deep in the cut. I don't know what you men do all day and all night on the lake. There's nothing to this fishing business. Somebody hand me a knife. And a beer."

It was beginning to sting. Four men and a boy outdone by a grey-haired grandmother.

Next day, Uncle Herman and I went to the cut by boat. In the clear, shallow water, it was impossible to approach the weed beds, rowing a heavy wooden boat, without spooking the fish. The bottom was soft muck, impossible to wade. The old bridge wreckage was the only practical access. And that belonged to Grandma.

And so passed the rest of the trip. Uncle Bud clung determinedly to the pursuit of walleyes, with fairly uniform results. The rest of us changed target species to largemouth bass, in lily pad beds other than the cut, with limited success.

When fish were needed, Grandma walked to the bridge.

Chapter 5
Go North, Young Man, Go North
The Shortest Distance to a Straight Line

As soon as the last notes of Elgar's "Pomp and Circumstance" have died away, and the high school graduation parties have begun, we all think we're grown up. We also think that we already know, if not almost everything, then certainly a working majority of it. No, it's OK. That's just how it works. That is the normal scheme and sequence of things for the vast majority of us.

My classmate, Frank Miller, and I were certainly no exceptions to that rule. In fact, we may have been prototypes. Frank was an enthusiastic fisherman, and remains so. He is today, in fact, an IGFA record holder. But those are stories he himself will tell you in later chapters.

It was 1953, and we had convinced ourselves that we should take a week, before the burdens of adulthood smothered us, and pursue a truly quality fishing experience. We had beaten the local streams and ponds to a froth. Now it was time to put lines into the kinds of waters we had only read about. The major outdoor magazines of the times offered a smorgasbord of seductive locales: western trout streams, coastal surf hotspots, deep sea charters, north woods wilderness lodges, Great Lakes lake trout charters, TVA reservoirs. For us, there were two over-riding considerations, distance and cost.

We pored over maps, but knew nothing about potential destinations. Finally realizing that we did not, in fact, know almost everything, we decided to seek advice from people who had actually been to some of these wonderful places. But how would we know who, in our limited network, if anyone, had been where?

"Hey!" Frank said, "I know who to talk to, Jake Foxbauer. He talks to a lot of people who fish."

Jake was the local taxidermist, and an avid outdoorsman.

"OK. He's a friend of my Dad. I'll go see him tomorrow".

I was sure Jake would freely share information with me. This was part of the all-important intelligence gathering phase of fishing with Joe. Of course, we did not know that……then.

It was always a treat to go to Jake Foxbauer's shop. It was full of mounts of all descriptions, fish, fowl and furbearing. It was almost a museum of natural history. And Jake was a master craftsman. The specimens looked as if they were about to scamper away, or to attack, if you moved. One could not help but instinctively walk wide of the timber rattlesnake mount, so realistic that those gleaming, terrifying fangs always seemed a clear and present danger.

Of course, that mount had incorporated some poetic license. A coiled rattlesnake does not have its mouth open and its fangs extended. Nevertheless, there is something deep within us, indelibly written in some bio-chemical code, that triggers an automatic get-out-of-range response at the sight of a snake……even a long deceased snake.

Jake emerged from the back of the shop, wiping his hands on a towel. "What can I do for you, young fella?"

"Mr. Foxbauer, I'm Bob Burroughs, and…….."

"Oh, Yeah. Frank's boy. How's your Dad?"

"Oh, he's fine, sir. I was wondering if you could give me a little advice?"

"Sure. Free advice is always worth every cent you pay for it. What do you want to know?"

"Well, Frank Miller and I are planning a little fishing trip, and we don't have a lot to spend or want to go too far. Where's the nearest place we can do some real wilderness fishing….you know….camping? I've got a canoe."

"Tall order. There's not much wilderness left. You'd have to go at least 1200 miles west. Nothing east. Still some open country in the mountains southeast, but not great fishing this time of year. I'd say your best bet is north."

"How far would we have to go?"

"Oh, closest would be the Upper Peninsula of Michigan. About 600, 650 miles."

"Oh. Nothing any closer?"

"Well, not if you're looking for really secluded places with not much fishing pressure. I know that's far, and you'll have to take the ferry across the Mackinac Straights. It'll take you two days at least. They're gonna build a bridge across the Straights, I hear, but it's not there yet. Now…..hey….wait a minute. My deer hunting buddy, Norm – your Dad knows him – was to a place in Michigan not more than about 400 miles from here, just last year. One day drive, easy. It's some river. Mostly a trout stream. Runs into Lake Huron. Norm says it's pretty deserted between towns".

"Where is it?"

"I don't know. And I don't remember the name of it, either. Tell you what. I'll call Norm tonight and find out all about it. Call me tomorrow."

"OK. Thanks a lot, Mr. Foxbauer."

There was something remarkable about this. Here was a man, well on the other side of the "what's-the-matter-with-kids-today" demarcation line, willing to go to considerable inconvenience just to help two teenagers – neither having choir boy reputations - go fishing. And in a small town, *everybody* knows, and makes decisions by, your reputation. Whether or not that reputation was grounded in fact never seemed to be relevant. It was what it was, and would always be.

It vaguely bothered me that I could not define what that "something remarkable" was. But over the decades, a hundred, or maybe a thousand, similar incidents have shown that there is a transcendent spirit here. There is an undefined, unorganized, boundary-less entity, with no formal charter, no membership rolls, no qualifications and no monetary dues. (You pay your dues, to be sure, but with coinage far more valuable than currency.) There are no officers, no elections, no awards, and no annual dinners. The meetings are all impromptu, ad hoc, held on river banks, piers, boat ramps and sometimes under canoes warding off a sudden storm. Words like "club" and "association" and "league" admirably fit smaller groups, bound together by geography or by a common interest in a species or a method. Even words of broader scope, like "brotherhood" and "community", seem somehow to fall short. I didn't have a word for that over-arching entity, and I still do not. But I have met fellow members many times since……. principally when either they, or I, needed assistance, always freely given.

I related to Frank what I had learned. "Sounds good", he grinned. "Let's make a list of what we'll need".

It soon became apparent that the list was not a list of what we might need, but a list of what we had. And it wasn't much.

"Dad's got a good tent", Frank was saying. " We used to use it on trips to Florida when I was little. It's out in the barn. Let's have a look".

Under some chicken wire and spare barn siding we could see folded, mildewed canvas, and dug it out. It was, in fact, "a good tent", made of very heavy gage canvas, with a substantial steel framework, 18" long steel pegs and guy lines that looked as if they had been intended for Barnum and Bailey. There were a few small areas where mice had gnawed through the canvas, but they were not in the roof or high on the sides. The steel was a little rusty, but not to the point of compromising structural integrity.

"Hey, this looks great!"

Unrolling the canvas on the floor, the tent's greatness for our purpose rapidly faded. It was indeed a family sized tent, and for a large family. Frank had a brother, and two sisters. The tent was subdivided into men's and women's quarters. We realized that this was gross overkill for the minimalist adventure we had in mind.

"What we need is a pup tent".

"Yeah. Who's got one we can borrow?" There were no answers to that question forthcoming.

'Well, my Dad's got a tarp, pretty good one, nylon. It's about ten by twelve. We can tie a rope between trees for a ridge pole and tie down the corners". If it's raining, we can go to the side away from the wind." Seemed like a sensible plan to me. Of course, as we shall see, it was not.

"Well……..I don't like not having a way to close up the ends." Frank was not sold on the tarp idea, but given the alternatives, he finally said, "OK. Bring plenty of bug dope."

To keep things in perspective, it is useful to remember that this was taking place long before the back-packing craze had swept the nation. Camping gear tended to be military surplus, or to come from rather exclusive, and expensive, suppliers to well-heeled sportsmen and guide services. We were operating in the worst of both worlds: unavailability and ignorance. But…. we were seventeen years old, indestructible, and knew everything…..well, almost everything.

Neither of us had sleeping bags. But both of us had seen movies wherein cowboy heroes simply rolled up in saddle blankets, and cheerfully awoke warm and comfortable, even when they found themselves additionally insulated by five or six inches of new snow. So, what would be the problem? It was June, for heaven's sake.

Transportation was not considered to be a problem. I had a 1947 Studebaker Champion. It was practically new by our standards: only six years old and with only a little over 200,000 miles on it. It was the famous "both ways" body design, with a "hood" on both ends. In a few years, the rest of the industry would catch up with the little company in South Bend, but for now, the laughing-stock body style served us well. There was a lot of trunk space.

Abundance of cargo capacity is indeed a treacherous blessing. One must resist the temptation to take things along simply because one *can*, and not because one *should*. We resisted that temptation admirably…. because we were already taking everything we had.

The canoe? Simple, despite the fact that we had no car-top rack. One of my uncles was a mover, and had quilts that were used to prevent the scratching of furniture and appliances. A quilt over the roof, ropes from the canoe to the four corners of the vehicle, and where could it go? We would see that there was an answer to that question…..and it wasn't, "nowhere". The paddles fit easily into the trunk, and we used life jackets (PFD's) to fill in the "rattle spaces". (That's right. PFD's. We at least realized that we weren't THAT indestructible.)

It was mid-afternoon when one of us remembered to call Jake Foxbauer. In retrospect, it seemed ridiculous to go through all of the list and packing activities before we even knew that there would be a destination. But at the time, we *knew* that we were going *somewhere*. So nothing was wasted.

"OK, now, "said Mr Foxbauer, "you got a pencil? All right. Norm said that the name of the river is the Au Sable. No, I'll spell it for you. He said that a good run would be from a town called Mio down to Lake Huron. Two, maybe three, days. He said there're some dams along that stretch that back up small lakes, or ponds. Full of trout, some of 'em". Okay? Have a good trip."

"But, Mr Foxbau………." Click.

"OK, Frank. I'll tell you all I know. And it won't take long."

Armed with little knowledge of where we were going, what it would be like, and woefully under-equipped, we added food to the larder and prepared to leave early the next morning. The question of food supply was really a matter of what we could scrounge from the family pantries. Pork and beans was a reliable staple. There were cans of corn and lima beans, Bisquick biscuit mix, some coffee packed in a pint fruit jar, a small sack of flour (which we had no idea how to use) and what was left of a can of shortening, as we certainly knew we would need that to fry fish. We gave no thought to the obvious, like salt, sugar, soap, means of cleaning dishes, a means of purifying water, and the like. I seem to recall that we reassured ourselves that we would be so far into wild country that river water would be pristine and drinkable, and that fish, wild berries and nuts would be abundant. Ignorance may be bliss, but bliss usually has a very short life expectancy.

"We better get a map".

"Yeah. Hey! Dad's got a road atlas in here," said Frank, jerking his head toward the house. "Big one. I'll get it."

It was as Frank had said: large scale, lots of detail, and not many years out of date. "There! Right there! There it is. Mio". Frank was pointing with a nail from the workbench in the barn.

"Yeah, and there's the river". The map showed a thin, blue line undulating gently in a generally southeastward direction. "Look. There's the ponds he told me about. And there's no towns or roads or anything along most of it".

We looked at one another and grinned. At last, at long, long last, we would be stepping into those mesmerizing pictures, at which we had so often stared, in the pages of those outdoor magazines. We would be savoring the scent of the pine forest, dipping canoe paddles into a clear, cold, wilderness stream, feasting upon wood-fire-cooked fresh fish, and waking to the songs of birds and the chatter of squirrels. We would reset our calendars. It would be centuries earlier. On that river, slightly off to the starboard, would be other canoes, present but not visible, bearing bearded men, wearing tuques, bantering in French. Explorers and missionaries. Men the likes of Pere Marquette. Those strong and experienced voyagers would soon outdistance us, around the next bend, leaving only a wraith of a wake.

And then, of course, there is always ubiquitous and inconvenient reality.

Frank's countenance suddenly turned serious. "Let's check something. Hand me that tape there on the bench." He carefully measured the distance from Mio to Lake Huron, bending the tape to follow the river as best he could. Then he held the tape against the scale of miles in the corner of the map.

"How far you figure we can paddle in a day?"

"Well, we used to hike twenty miles in a day in Scouts. Paddle at least twenty. Maybe more."

"OK, then. Jake said two or three days, didn't he?. Sounds about right.

We only need to take enough food for two nights. Third night we'll be back at the car."

It was comforting that we had independently verified what we had been told. We were wordlessly smug that we had acted with such maturity. It was wonderful to know not only that we were right, but that we were sure we were right. We had learned in American History class that frontiersman/statesman David Crockett is alleged to have advised, "Be sure you're right, then go ahead". We were sure we were right, and we were certainly going ahead.

It would be another decade or two before the computer industry would invent the phrase that describes the dangers in accurate and careful manipulation of bad data: Garbage In, Garbage Out.

Les Voyageurs

The Interstate highway system, the great legacy of President Eisenhower, was in the planning stages; there were but a few stretches of limited access, four lane, divided highway in actual existence. For us, that was just as well. The old Studebaker was powered by an 80 hp (on a good day) in-line six. True, it would deliver 35 miles per gallon, but struggled with even moderate grades or headwinds. With the canoe on top, its top speed would likely have caused traffic jams where the speed limit was anything over 60 mph. All things considered, it made for a leisurely trip.

And that, too, was just as well. We had gotten the early start we had planned. The sky was only a faint purple when we cinched down the last lines holding the canoe aboard, firmly, we were convinced. On two lane state and federal highways, it was difficult to average forty miles per hour. Towns were frequent, and full of traffic lights – always red – stop signs, and twenty-five mile per hour limits. So, when we had crossed the Michigan border, on US 23, a four lane divided highway, we decided to make up some time. For a few miles, the experience was glorious. The day was bright, with a very blue, low humidity sky. I was admiring that sky when the two lines running from the canoe to the front bumper abruptly disappeared.

In the rear view mirror appeared our worst nightmare. The canoe had lifted off, and was gracefully soaring, upside down, along behind us, all four lines fluttering in the wind. Transfixed in horror, I watched it slowly roll keel down, and veer to the right. It landed in the grass of the berm, and skidded, on the still dew-wet, knee-high grass, in a direction exactly parallel to the road, seeming not to slow very much. I looked back at the road….. and at the apex nightmare: we were crossing a bridge, a bridge with a very substantial concrete abutment, directly in the path of the errant canoe.

Frank was dozing, but snapped wide awake in the tire-squealing panic stop.

"Frank! Frank! We lost the canoe!"

Our fond plans instantly evaporated. Our most important fishing implement was destroyed, and five or six hours into the trip. There would be nowhere to go but back home; nothing to do but abandon the odyssey, and in shame for our incompetence. It was a disaster.

"Well", Frank said at length, "let's go look".

It was a short bridge, but a very long walk. Now, anticipation was not so much fun. Both of us visualized the splintered pile of kindling we would find on the other side of that two foot thick, steel-reinforced concrete structure, hard, fixed and immovable.

Reaching it, we peered gingerly around the corner. The canoe was still in perfect alignment with the road edge. We could only see as far forward as the front seat from where we stood, but what we could see appeared intact. We looked at each other, and took the final forward step. The bow was against the concrete, and was, to understate, a bit aft of where it should have been, but the gunwales had not fractured, and the keel was sound as far forward as the point of impact, where it was broken, but cleanly, and about a foot above the ground. The canvas skin was torn at that point, but the rip extended only about 6 inches in either direction.

"If we're careful not to bump its nose, I think it'll work. The tear is above the water line. If we stay out of rough water……yeah…it'll be OK." Frank may have been trying to convince himself, but he sold me.

"All we need is a can of flashing sealant. That'll flex enough to stay watertight. The rest of it is roofing tar anyhow. Flashing sealant will stick to that just fine." Four years working in a hardware store after school had some residual values, as I have found countless times since.

By that time, a Michigan State Police cruiser had pulled up. The trooper, who looked not very much older than we, rolled down the right hand window.

"Oh, great," mumbled Frank, "just what we need."

"You guys OK?"

"Yeah. Our canoe's got a bloody nose, though".

"I should cite you guys for an unsecured load. That canoe could have hit another vehicle….caused injuries".He looked at the canoe, and shook his head. "Well, no harm done…… looks like you guys got enough trouble. Just make sure you don't lose it again." He waved and wheeled away.

"Let's get that canoe back on top and get out of here before some by-the-book cop comes along."

"Right."

The quilt was easily recovered, huddled in the ditch about 50 yards back. None of the lines were broken or cut; they had simply worked their way over the outer ends of the bumpers. This time, we lashed them together, so that the incident could not recur, and ran another line over the belly of the canoe and through the rear windows, secured by a tautline hitch inside the car, where it could be constantly monitored for tightness. First lessons in a principle that every fisherman should employ: redundancy.

In a hardware store on the outskirts of Ann Arbor, we bought a quart of roof flashing sealant and a cheap putty knife. In minutes, we had generously slathered the canoe's wounds with healing asphalt balm. The remainder of the run was blessedly uneventful, although precious daylight had been lost.

The river was found exactly where Jake's hunting buddy said it would be. There was no easy access. The canoe and gear had to be wrestled down a fair slope adjacent to a bridge, where loading and boarding were complicated by a very respectable current. There was a general store/filling station/bait shop nearby, and we bought a cardboard ice cream container of red worms, on the theory that one can catch anything with red worms, and made arrangements with the proprietor to leave the car there. We had asked him what would be the best way to get back from the mouth of the river at Lake Huron. He merely shrugged and held up his thumb, indicating a mode of transport not unfamiliar to us. But we failed in a very important duty. This was, in part at least, a bait shop, a key source of intelligence to fishermen everywhere, and we didn't even ask the most obvious of questions. There would be a price for that failure.

There were just a few things we didn't know. What were the predominant species? How were they typically caught? Where? At what times of day? What were the locally favored baits or lures? And there were some fairly important questions not relating to fish. Was there dangerous white water downstream? And the most obvious question of all: was the water safe to drink?

Armed with such overwhelming ignorance, but ignorant even of the extent of our own ignorance, we pushed the canoe out into the current. In most places, the current was swift enough that returning over any significant distance by paddling back upstream was not a practical option. I reminded Frank that we were now committed. He shouted back over his shoulder, holding his paddle aloft like a spear, "Remember from latin class? Alia jacta est".

"Oh, yeah. The die is cast. Caesar wasn't it?" Frank didn't answer.

There were deadfalls almost blocking the stream from place to place, especially in narrows. Some of them had collected other floating debris, and acted almost as wing dams, pushing the current to one side of the channel, intensifying the flow rate, and scouring the bottom into deeper holes. Off toward the slack current side of one of them, behind a sunken log, were a half dozen fish, hugging the bottom, facing upstream. They were easily visible in the clear water.

"Frank! Look at that. There they are. Just like they said. "

"What?"

"Under those trees back there. There's a bunch of trout. And they're big!"

By that time, the current had taken us 30 or 40 yards downstream, and into a relatively still pool. We tied off to an overhanging branch to rig our tackle. The plan was to then paddle back upstream on the slack side, and to cast small spinners into the group of fish. This would have to be done stealthily to avoid spooking them, and the casts would have to be precise in order to avoid the obstructions.

"Ready?"

"Yeah. Quiet, now."

We were more successful at a stealthy approach than I expected we would be. We were within 20 feet, and the fish were still there. Frank's first cast fell exactly on target. I could see the spinner's blade shimmer as it sank within inches of one of the fish......which paid absolutely no attention.

"You're in the best position, Frank. Try it again."

Again, no response from the fish. On the fourth cast, the lure fluttered down directly onto the back of one of the fish, which exploded upstream, scattering the rest. Several darted under the bow of the canoe and into the deep slot on the current side of the obstruction.

"You know what's wrong with those trout?" Frank asked.

"No."

"They're CARP, that's what! I got a clear look at those two. All this way and this river's full of carp." Whether they were, in fact, carp was never confirmed.

"There's gotta be trout. Jake said so. Just because there were carp in this hole doesn't mean that's all there are. Let's go on."

It was, of certainty, a beautiful stream, as secluded as the map had suggested, and paddling was a pleasant occupation. We fell into the trap of looking for fish, rather than reading the river for promising, fish-holding locations. My father's advice of a decade earlier, "Remember, if you can see a fish, that fish can see you", was forgotten. So novel for us was water of this clarity that we became hunters, not fishermen. And that is seldom fruitful.

The day was seductively pleasant, moderate temperature, low humidity, and a light westerly breeze; perfect for comfort. But clear water and a "bluebird" day rarely result in aggressive feeding on the part of fish, especially freshwater fish. There are exceptions to that rule, of course, especially on big water, but this day was not one of them. So bright was the sky that we did not pay heed to the sun slipping quickly toward the edge of it. The long, tapered shadows of pine trees now bridging the river finally gained notice.

"Hey! It's gettin' late, and we haven't got any fish for dinner."

"Yeah. Well, maybe we can find a still pool and catch some bluegills or perch on some of those worms."

"Let's try it. I'd settle for yellow-bellied catfish right now."

But this was not the sort of stream we were used to, at least, in that immediate vicinity, it was not. The streams we knew consisted of series of riffles, or rapids, with pools between them, sometimes deep, sometimes shallow, sometimes wide, sometimes narrow, and we knew how to read those. But this stream was much more consistent in depth, flow and width. And it had weed growth on the bottom. Sunlight could penetrate to the bottom at practically all of its depths, in contrast to the stained, silty streams we knew, where plant growth was limited to edges, and to shallows of a foot or less. We could not find, in 30 minutes of maximum effort paddling, backs vigorously bent against our paddles, a pool that looked promising. This was not our experience base, and we were stumped.

Finally, we resolved to tie off upstream of the next stretch that appeared at least relatively deep, and to drift worms, under light bobbers, through it, setting the depth shallow enough to avoid snagging weeds, sunken logs or other obstructions. Sure that this strategy would produce some species or other, enthusiasm returned. We payed out line so as to maintain a drift as nearly equal to current speed as possible. This, we reasoned, would be the most natural presentation, and we sat, wound like coiled springs, ready to react to that certain and inevitable strike.

It never came. After five or six drifts, each covering 75 or 80 yards, it became clear that this was not going to work, either. Frank shook his head. "Gettin' dark. We better make camp."

Finding a campsite, for the simple camp that we could equip, should have been easy. All we needed was a reasonably flat place with two trees of adequate size, 12 to 18 feet apart......approximately. And one other thing: there needed to be a place to beach a wounded canoe. The river's banks were not, generally, rocky, and the land along the river was forested with tens of thousands of trees. It turned out, however, to be frustratingly difficult to find a site. It was very nearly dark before we finally had the canoe unloaded, and the tarp hung and staked, partly because we had forgotten the stakes, and were forced to manufacture some from driftwood. The initial stake design failed because the stakes were driven into light, sandy soil, not the heavy clay soil we were accustomed to, and pulled loose almost immediately. There was an upside. We had more than enough by-product driftwood for the fire.

It had been a long day, filled with physical exertion. We were tired, and very hungry, as late-teen males almost always are, even under far less exertive circumstances. Two large cans of pork and beans vanished in seconds. The campfire biscuits, made from a commercial pre-mix and powdered milk, were listless balls of soggy dough, burned black on one side, but none escaped. The beverage du jour was classic fish camp coffee, boiled in a well abused aluminum pot, complete with ashes and a substantial content of solids.

There was little in that crystal sky to restrain heat loss from the earth, and when the sun had set, the air quickly developed an almost autumnal bite. I put on the World War II surplus bomber jacket that Frank had laughed at, asking me if I thought we were going to Alaska. That jacket was fleece-lined, high-collared, and very welcome. It, or something equivalent, has accompanied me on every fishing trip north of the fortieth parallel, regardless of season, ever since. We had under-equipped ourselves on the blankets as well. We had also neglected to bring anything to serve as a ground cloth, preventing soil moisture from making the blankets damp and therefore even colder, but nature had kindly provided a thick layer of dry pine needles on the woods floor. Nevertheless, it was a long, shivery night, not without its learnings.

The tarp-tent was black in color, so that the sun's first light did not penetrate it. The open ends told us that dawn had come, but we had decided, without discussion, that we would wait for some warming solar radiation before abandoning our blankets. There was no wind, and the black tent warmed quickly, deceiving us as to the temperature outside. Breakfast was oatmeal and coffee, and the second helpings consumed the rest of the oatmeal supply.

"You think that river's safe to drink?"

"I don't know. My canteen's about empty."

"Well, let's boil some and refill our canteens. Maybe we'll find a spring or a little feeder stream that doesn't have anybody living around it."

In less than an hour, we were back on the river. Another beautiful day, an idyllic stream flowing through pine woods, and the "hope springs eternal" anticipation that we would unlock the secret to catching fish today, buoyed our spirits. We reverted to reading the river for likely spots, but again failed to arouse any response from any fish of any species. We determined that, since we had been totally unsuccessful in the stream, we would paddle at flank speed to one of the ponds shown on the map. Perhaps there, in deeper water, we would find conditions better matching our experience.

The river's meanderings seemed so pronounced that I put my compass between my feet on the floor of the canoe. Sure enough, the needle swung from southeast to northeast, to northwest, to north, to northeast, and to southeast again in only a few minutes of paddling. This was nothing like the gentle undulations suggested by that map in the road atlas.

"Hey, Frank. This river's wandering all over the place. It's gonna be a lot further than we thought."

"Yeah. I been watchin' my shadow".

We had not yet reached the first pond as daylight began to fail, abetted by the gathering of some clouds, benign enough looking. Having learned from the previous day, we allowed ourselves more daylight to pitch camp, and even found a very small tributary, clear and cold, that we surmised was spring fed. We convinced ourselves that it would be safe to drink. We set up camp within about fifty paces of it.

We had paddled with great diligence for most of the day, ignoring lunch. Supper that evening seriously depleted the remaining larder, so much so that, around the campfire, we discussed alternatives. We had depended upon fish as a diet mainstay. I have never done that again, despite the fact that every such trip since has yielded more than enough fresh catch to meet each day's needs.

Twice, so far, we had ignored the principle of redundancy, a failing which has likely ruined more fishing outings than all other causes combined – including weather. Perhaps fishermen in Groups One and Two need not be so cognoscent of the principle; sponsors, outfitters and charter captains may provide needed back-up. But in Group Three, Joe is wise to continually ask himself, "What happens if...?" Those fishing with Joe for a while have no doubt noticed some statistical anomalies: If Joe has a spare transom plug, he never misplaces the first one; If he has the auxiliary engine on the transom, the main propulsion engine always runs like a Swiss watch; If he dons his rain gear while the approaching cloud bank is still on the horizon, it never rains; and so on. Ignore redundancy at your own peril…..sometimes, grave, life-threatening peril, not just an inconvenience or a ruined trip.

After some discussion, we decided to stick with the original plan: make for the first pond and eat whatever we could catch. We would leave before breakfast…because there wasn't any breakfast, at least none which could be considered anything close to "normal". We shared our last two cans of provisions, eaten cold: lima beans and apple sauce. Then we paddled downstream at the highest rate we thought was sustainable. We didn't even bother to crush the cans, as we had the others, in order to save space in the trash bag. That was to prove providential.

In less than a half hour, the stream began to slow and widen. Soon we could see an open expanse of water. The pond! It had been so close. The turbidity of the water began to increase. There was phytoplankton in this water; it was green, and it was warmer than the river, but it was still alien. We decided on a broad spectrum approach; we would employ our entire repertoire, and all with red worms, the universal freshwater bait. We started by drifting with the waning current, bait close to the bottom, where a perch, walleye, or catfish…..even a carp….might be waiting. Next, we cast shallow-set worms, below light floats, to the shoreline, where bluegills, bass or crappie might feed. Nothing we did elicited any response.

Einstein's ideas about the relationship of space and time may or may not have anything to do with this, but Joe is well aware, by anecdotal evidence, that the earth spins faster, taking clocks and watches with it, when one is fishing. We looked up to see that the sun was high…..and so was the wind. Even though the pond was relatively small, a nasty little chop was rising, high enough to reach the canoe's wounded nose. The patch was being flexed with each wave, and the inevitable result was that it began to leak; at first a trickle, then a stream. In minutes, the bottom was ankle deep, serving only to bring the breach in the hull nearer to the trough of the waves.

"Hey! We're sinking. We better get to shore as fast as we can." Frank answered by seizing his paddle.

"Did you bring that black goop?"

"No."

"We need to bail this thing. What have we got?"

"Nothing. Wait. There are some empty cans in the garbage bag. You keep paddling. I'll bail."

Ankle deep, there is a surprising amount of water in a canoe. It was soon obvious that Frank could not keep up with the inflow. It felt as though I were paddling a coal barge. But, foot by foot, the canoe was finally within wading distance of the shore line. We rolled over opposite sides to avoid capsizing, and pulled the sodden craft ashore, removed our gear, and overturned the canoe to drain it. We hauled it clear of the water, and carried it to an open area where the sun would help dry it. Then we hung our blankets on a rope between trees, and began to sort out the rest of the gear. Everything was wet. We had not yet come to grips with the reality that, without the canoe, we were stranded.

Each of us had packed belongings in surplus US Navy duffel bags. They were cheap, plentiful, and strong. They were a foot or so in diameter, and about 3 feet long, made of heavy white canvas, and had some WW II sailor's name stenciled on the side. Mine had belonged to a Charles Stinson. I do not remember the former owner of Frank's bag. I was always bemused by the fact that WW II US Navy duffel bags were not waterproof……not even water repellent. Both were soaked, as were our clothes and gear. The food was not affected. There was none.

We laid all of the contents of those bags out in the sun to dry. One of the items I had packed, with absolutely no logical reason for having done so, was a light, single shot, take-down 22 rifle. Frank looked at it intently.

"Hey – I didn't know you had that. That's *dinner*! There's got to be a rabbit or some squirrels, or something around here."

There were some administrative issues….like licenses, seasons, etc, but we were hungry....really hungry. People don't have much body fat at our (then) age. We did not know that starvation, even for the young and lean, is a matter of weeks, not of days. We were convinced that our lives were at risk, and that we would worry about administrative matters later.

"You go hunting", reasoned Frank. "I'll dry out this stuff. Shoot anything you can."

My hunting was every bit as successful as our fishing had been. There was not a sign of anything edible. There were plenty of pine squirrels, only slightly larger than chipmunks, and tiny song birds, but no rabbits, quail, grouse, doves, or gray or fox squirrels. After about four hours, I returned to camp, exhausted and discouraged. We sat down on the bank beside the canoe and considered how we might repair it. The afternoon was warm and the sun was delivering the proverbial "noon, June, in Yuma" radiation. The black surface of the canoe was too hot to touch, and the heavily applied flashing sealant was beginning to sag and flow downward under its own weight. We stared at it for a few minutes, wordless and helpless.

"Cloth!" Frank shouted, "Yeah. Cloth. Just like fiber-glassing a fender."

Without further explanation, he seized a T-shirt from the line, where our clothes were drying, and tore it into strips. With a piece of driftwood, he pressed the strips into the soft, tarry sealant, over the tear in the canvas.

"Come over here. Quick. I need some back-up from inside."

The sealant seeped into the strips, and stuck to the driftwood "tools". The operation rapidly became a black, gummy mess. But it worked. We gently lowered the bow into the water, holding the stern as high as we could in order to submerge the torn area. It did not leak. In fact, I used that canoe for another decade with no further repair. Its final demise came from being carried off by a flash flood, never to be found. It was replaced by an aluminum canoe, a heavy duty model, designed for use in rocky rivers. It is today dented and pock marked, after 45 years of abusive service, and still does not admit a single drop. It is a tough and reliable fishing platform. But it lacks the precise handling, the easy glide, the lines and grace, of the hand crafted, wood-and-canvas Old Town.

Removing the sealant without the benefit of soap or solvent took some time, and was never fully accomplished. We sat beside the fire pit, scrubbing vigorously with a slurry of ashes and water. It was a slow war of attrition. Then Frank tapped my arm, and whispered, "What's that?"

"Where?'

"Out there. Swimming. See that?"

There was indeed a v-shaped wake, 60 yards out and closing, behind what could only be a head. Turtle? Too fast. Beaver? Too small. Snake? Too big. By the process of elimination, it could only be either an otter, or a muskrat.

"If that's a muskrat," hissed Frank, between closed teeth, "shoot it. Wait 'til it's in shallow water, in case it sinks."

We dined that evening on roast muskrat, finding it to be much like rabbit, although flavor would not have mattered. No scraps, including organ meats and skull muscles, were wasted. Vultures never picked a carcass so clean.

The consensus was that the pond, too, had been unproductive, and that the best plan was to stow fishing gear and to paddle for Lake Huron, recover the car, and to seek other fishing waters. The remainder of the river run was happily unremarkable. Portages around the dams were relatively easy, and well before sundown, we were ashore in Tawas City.

Getting back to the car was easier than expected. In those days, before pervasive, everyone's-out-to-get-me paranoia gripped the society, travel by means of outstretched thumb, especially on largely deserted rural roads, was entirely practical. Before dark, we were re-provisioned, if not re-equipped, and our selection of food items was wiser than before. We spent that night in a primitive campground, whether state or National Forest campground, neither of us recall. After an early, and this time ample, breakfast, we headed north again; no defined destination, just a direction.

Wisdom is a step-wise, incremental thing. It is not an epiphanal leap. Our intelligence gathering was unsophisticated, but we now, at least, were aware that we needed it. At diners and at gas stations that looked as though they had been moved, intact, from Mayberry, and at which we guzzled grape

Nehi if we had no other reason to stop, we never failed to ask, "Where's a good place to fish around here?" That question never failed to elicit a response, which, in turn, required evaluation. There were listless, go-away-boy-you-bother-me answers, there were sincere, but not knowledgeable answers, there were even answers intended to deceive. And then there was the gold standard answer: accurate, knowledgeable, and seriously intended to help. Even though our discernment could not even qualify for a Learner's Permit, one such answer led us to a small, out-of-the-way lake, which I will not identify in the futile hope that it remains so today.

There was road access to that lake, which led to a fish camp, owned by a Mr. Rasmussen, a husky, jolly fellow, with a deep accent, which we guessed, clued by the name, to be Scandinavian. His camp consisted of four cabins, and seemed deserted. The lake was shallow and weedy, and Mr Rasmussen appeared to occupy the only portion of the shoreline that was not marshland, occupied by reeds, cat-tails, and a raucous host of red-winged blackbirds.

"Yah," he said, "You boys better stay with me. All swamp, all over." He waved his arm expansively. "I make good deal, Yah? Got empty cabin here." He pointed to a small A-frame. "Two stories even. Hot and cold water running up and down the stairs".

We conferred privately, concluded that we had enough cash to stay two days, with enough left to fuel the Studebaker home. We relied heavily upon its stinginess. But we wanted to be sure we were making a sound investment.

"OK, Mr Rasmussen, are there really fish in this lake?"

"Yah, sure". (I never thought that I would hear that ethnic cliché in real life.) "Pikes. Lots pikes. Hey, I even show you how to catch pikes. Right now. Come."

He immediately walked toward his dock, where he boarded an aluminum rowboat, about 12 feet long, motioned for us to do the same, and rowed no further than about 150 feet, into a thick bed of weeds. He took a large, nearly round, oval copper spoon, with a single hook, from a box under the seat, and attached it to the line on a cane pole, about 12 feet in length, which we had assumed was for perch or bluegill. He dropped the spoon over the stern, laid the pole in the bottom of the boat, and placed his foot upon it, with an accentuated firmness, and continued to row. The spoon skittered across the weeds, dropping here and there into small, open holes. About one time in every three, water would explode from that hole, and once in about every three such explosions, Mr Rasmussen would boat a northern pike. They were not trophies by any means, in fact, they were scarcely large enough to avoid the epithet, "hammer handle". But they were more fish than we had seen, and they were of eating size, albeit marginally.

After boating and releasing just two, which took perhaps ten minutes since leaving the dock, he said, "See? Easy." Then he simply rowed back to the dock, disembarked, and went about his business.

This was the ultimate in intelligence gathering: a live demonstration. We spent two days, caught a number of pike, and released most of them, hoping for something larger. We could see the advantage of the single, rather than treble, hook, and of the stiff pole, which lifted the fish vertically, rather than reeling it horizontally through an aquatic jungle. "When in Rome......"

Time and money exhausted, we headed home. During a long and boring stretch of highway through the pool-table-flat cropland of northern Ohio, Frank suddenly exclaimed, "Hey! I figured it out!"

"What?"

"He meant that there was hot and cold running water on both floors."

Chapter 6
Jockey Schwey
Impersonating a Crappie

Learning at the (Artificial) Foot of the Master

For eight years, my wife and I lived in a small village along the Little Miami River, called Camp Dennison, so named because it had been a Union army camp during the Civil War. It was my wife's girlhood hometown. We were newly married, and, as a more literate exposition might say, impecunious. But since this is a book about Joe, we were broke. I was a student, we already had one son, and so, anything that added to the larder was a positive. We raised a garden, and I fished the river. After all, a channel catfish was one night's entrée, and that helped.

Jockey Schwey lived in Camp Dennison. I had met him before; he was a friend of my wife's family. His given name was George. He had lost a leg, just below the knee, in a construction accident. He was still employed by the same construction company as the "gopher"…….the guy who picked up and delivered parts and materials needed at the job sites. That's how he got the nickname "Jockey". He always wore an old time railroader's cap. It was his trademark. I had never seen one outside of western movies.

The artificial leg barely slowed him down. He was fully functional, up to and including playing on the local softball team. And, as happens, one disability led to a compensating over-development. Jockey had incredible upper body strength. He could do one-handed pull-ups, something I, twenty years his junior, could not do. He could drive a softball further than anyone on the team. He had to. His base running ability was limited. And he could wade on the slippery, moss-covered limestone of the river bed with a surefootedness that not many two-legged fishermen could match.

Jockey had not been born in Camp Dennison. He was from an equally small town on the banks of the Ohio River. He referred to himself as "an old river rat". And he knew how to catch fish. Not elegantly, perhaps, but efficiently. He never spoke of it, but he wisely perceived that I was fishing for food, and he told me, "Tomorrow night, I'll show you how to catch some fish. Tonight, we'll catch some bait".

About an hour after dark, I could hear the jingling of valves in Jockey's 1937 Chevy in the driveway. "Come on", he grinned, "we're goin' to the graveyard". The Township cemetery was only few hundred yards away. Some of the headstones in it dated back to the late 1700's. It was well cared for, and uniformly mowed. And it was full of night crawlers.

Jockey produced a carbide miner's lamp from the back seat, and lit it. "Them flashlights is too bright. Scares 'em." I had gathered night crawlers before, of course, but always with a flashlight. He was right. The carbide lamp worked much better.

We had five or six dozen, when I asked, "Don't we have enough?"

"Nah. We're gonna bait a lot of hooks. And we're gonna bait 'em heavy".

It was late May, and the river was stained, but not muddy, and running about a foot over pool stage. Jockey had an ancient wooden boat chained to a sycamore tree on the bank. It was only about ten feet long, but was unexpectedly heavy. When Jockey built a boat, it was built to last. It could endure the abuse of rocks at either end of the rapids that river folks called "riffles". And Jockey knew that those rocks are where river fish forage after dark.

The next evening, an hour or so before dark, we boarded his boat. He had an old picnic basket, no longer presentable at church socials, that now served as his tackle box. In it was a muskmelon-sized ball of cotton twine, a metal box full of 1/0 Aberdeen hooks, a knife and a rusty ice pick. The ice pick would serve the function of what yachtsmen would call a fid, a tool to help untie knots.

As crude as that boat may have been, Jockey's oars were splendid. They were carefully varnished, with the tips faced in copper, salvaged from roof flashing scraps from some construction site. This was intended to prevent splitting the ends when the oars were used to pole the boat over shallows, as they often were. The oar locks were secured to the oars with the usual clamping arrangement, but augmented with brass wood screws driven into the oar on both sides of the oarlock to prevent any slippage, so that the working lengths of the two oars were always exactly equal. He saw me admiring them. "You aint got good oars, you aint got a good boat", he said.

"Now, while I'm rowin', you cut some of this twine into one foot and two foot pieces. Don't have to be exact. Then, tie these hooks onto one end. Just run the twine thru the eye, and loop it and pass it through like this. Won't pull loose, but unties pretty easy. Hang 'em over the side of the boat...... hooks out. We don't wanna hook two suckers...heh, heh."

The pool Jockey intended to fish was about 200 yards long, with an enticing deep hole on the west bank, near the center. But he rowed by it. "Good hole", he said, "but kids swim there. Don't wanna hook them, neither." Just south of the incoming riffle, Jockey pulled ashore. He handed me the ball of twine. "Tie one end of this off to that willow right there, and then pick up a couple of rocks about brick size".

"OK".

Back in the boat, I held the ball loosely so that it could rotate, paying out line. On the opposite bank, Jockey pointed to an exposed sycamore root. "Not too tight, now. We aint gonna do no tight rope act. Look here. Here's how you tie 'em on."

Jockey showed me how to loop the main line, and attach the hook leader in a sort of a bowline-like knot. Again, it was intended to hold tight, yet be easy to untie. The hooks were not tied at uniform intervals. Jockey placed more hooks in areas he thought would be productive and fewer where he did not. "Them store-bought trotlines has got all the hooks same space apart. Waste of bait", he snorted.

Once the hooks were secured, we baited them with the nightcrawlers. From time to time, Jockey would nod in my direction and say, "Use two on that one". There was no obvious reason. It wasn't where the hooks were close together, or far apart. It seemed to be random. But he was the master. I was merely an apprentice.

"Now", he said, "where's them rocks?"

"Got 'em right here."

"Well, tie 'em on short leads, and we'll sink this line where it needs sunk."

Without the use of oars, we pulled the boat along the line, the current stretching it downstream.

"One right here."

"Now, the other one".

It was done. The line was set. The boat was beached and secured to the tree with a huge, rusty padlock that smelled of Diesel fuel. (Diesel is always capitalized. It's a man's name.) "Soak 'em in coal orl and they never freeze up", he explained.

"Well, we won't check it in the morning. You gotta go to class and me to work. We'll get it tomorrow after supper." And so we did.

Checking a trotline is an exercise in anticipation, like making that first cast to the edge of a promising weedbed, or dropping a jig in the middle of a school of breaching stripers. You just *know* that you are mere seconds from a fish. Or not. We picked up the west end of the main line, and it hung as static as a telephone cable between two poles on a calm day. Bait was still on all of the hooks that we could see. What a disappointment. The preparations….bait gathering……setting the line……attaching the hooks…..baiting them….and now, checking the line. Why, I thought, if

I had invested that many hours with rod and reel, I would surely have at least one or two fish. This was a bad idea.

Then we came to the first of the sinker rocks. It was wedged between two large slabs of limestone in about four feet of water. We couldn't see it in the stained, swift water, but we knew. Jockey waved a thumb toward the water. The message was unspoken, but clear. The apprentice was going in to free it. Made sense. He didn't have his waders, and the artificial limb definitely didn't belong submersed in river water.

The evening was cool for late May, but not cold. I had slipped on an old jacket that I wore for hunting and chores. In my haste to get to the business of checking the trotline, I had paid no attention to the fact that there was still a full box of 12 gage, number six shot, rounds in the left pocket, and a pair of fence pliers in the right. When I went over the gunwale on the downstream side of the boat, I sank, like a six ounce snapper jig, into a hole scoured out by the current exiting the riffle…..as rivers will do. Never trust them.

The river had the element of surprise, a box of 12's, and a two pound tool on its side. It also had fear. I knew that there had been several drownings in this pool, over the years. On my side was youth - I was twenty-two – and some reasonable swimming skills. During high school years, my classmate, Lowell Langfeld, and I swam two miles every Wednesday afternoon during the summer break. Then why can't I get to the surface?

Every one has heard the "grasping at straws" saying. That is what I instinctively did. The water was not so deep that I could not reach beyond the surface, where a crushing grip closed on my wrist. Without ever releasing the main line, Jockey pulled me up to the boat, and clamped my hand to the gunwale. "Work around to the shallow side. Now, get that rock loose". Jockey was not easily distracted from the task at hand.

Once the sinker rock was dislodged, the main line was no longer static. "See there? I knew there'd be some in that eddy current." That is where he had placed hooks closer together. Now it made sense. It wasn't random at all to an experienced river rat.

"They don't want to fight that current all night waitin' for somethin' to drift by. They'll lay just off to the side of it, in that slow back current".

The catch was not a bonanza. Three nice channel catfish and what Jockey called a white perch.

It was not a white perch, but a fresh water drum, what folks in the Great Lakes region call a sheepshead. In the Ohio and Mississippi valleys, though, that fish is a white perch. Don't call it otherwise, or you will be immediately corrected by the nearest river rat. Vigorously. River folk hold that it is, at least, a separate subspecies from the fresh water drum found in the northern lakes. And it indeed seems to be somewhat slimmer in shape. The most important difference is that is colored differently, bright, iridescent silver, rather than dingy bronze, and the river variety is far better table fare. It makes no sense that a drum from warm, muddy river water should be superior in flavor and texture to one from a clear, cold lake, but that is the fact. Joe learns early on that fishing is full of counter-intuitive experiences.

(There is some very upscale academic support for the strongly held opinion of the river rats. Milton B. Trautman, Emeritus Professor of Zoology at The Ohio State University, states: "In the past 100 years much has been written concerning the marked differences in edible qualities between drums from Lake Erie and those from the Ohio River. More than a hundred years ago, Kirtland voiced the general opinion that drums from lake Erie were "hardly eatable" whereas those from the Ohio drainage were "always fat, tender and delicious". Prof Trautman also states that: "Since 1932, white perch was the name almost universally used in the Ohio River drainage, and sheepshead about Lake Erie". Trautman goes on to say that there is also a marked difference in the size of drums in the two water systems. Lake Erie drums seldom reach 10 pounds, while river system drums are commonly caught in the 25 pound range, and that he himself had caught a specimen weighing 36 pounds. However, he stops short of calling them separate subspecies.) (*The Fishes of Ohio*, Ohio State University Press, 1981)

I told you that fishermen read a lot.

Struggling to unhook the first channel catfish, I learned why Jockey used the special knot that he had taught me. "No time for that. Just pull the leader right here". It came instantly free. "Tie another one on, and bait it up." In minutes, the fish were boated and the line reset.

"Let's go", Jockey said, "I hate cleanin' fish in the dark". It had been an experience. I was soaked, and cold. While Jockey rowed, I unloaded my jacket pockets. Jockey shook his head. "Why don't you just tie a tow chain around yer neck?" There was a learning here. The human body, in near-naked condition, floats – sort of. It doesn't take much weight to shift that balance. That lesson should have lasted, and didn't. Years later, I caught myself wading chest deep in the surf at Cape Hatteras……with one pocket full of four ounce bluefish spoons and the other full of pyramid sinkers.

PFD has two meanings: a) Personal Floatation Device; b) Protection For Dummies. When you see a guy wading a treacherous river (and they all are), without one, it only means that he's a few learnings short. It is not my intent to drown. At least not until the very last fish on earth has been caught.

We ran that trotline on an inconsistent, when-we-felt-like-it basis. But the fact that we were so doing got to be common knowledge around the village. One April, the river had been high and muddy for an unusual number of weeks. Drift and debris made keeping the main line in place impossible. We waited for better conditions.

The Fish Fry

My next door neighbor, Jim Miles, had married a woman from the area of Somerset, Kentucky. She had relatives there, and each spring, the Miles family would spend a few days visiting her kinfolk, and crappie fishing in Cumberland Lake. They would routinely come back with more than one ice chest full of crappie fillets. Jim would hold a neighborhood fish fry. It became a well anticipated tradition. Jim was always a bit evasive about exactly where and how this abundance of crappies had been caught, with answers like, "Oh, in this general area", waving his hand over several thousand acres of map. Bait? "Minnows and things." Daylight or dark? "Yeah." We abandoned the interrogation.

When the Miles house was dark for about a week in late April of that year, we knew where they were. A day or two after their return, Jim came over one evening. He was wearing a polo shirt…..and a sheepish grin.

"You know….this fish fry……well, we didn't do too good this year. You guys run a trotline. Uh…you got any fish?"

"No. Water's been too high all month."

"Well….uh…you think you could catch some? I don't want to disappoint anybody."

A challenge!

"I'll talk to Jockey. See what we can do." What I didn't realize was that "see what we can do" became a promise the instant it reached Jim's ears. "OK," he beamed, "I'll get the invitations out!"

"Now, wait a minute, Jim. I said we'd………."

"No, no. That's OK. I have faith in you guys", as he was hastily retreating out the back door, ending any further discussion.

What had I done?

I drove over to Jockey's house. A phone call didn't seem appropriate. I related what had happened.

"This ain't our problem. Where we gonna get any crappies around here? Hell, he couldn't even get enough down at Cumberland. We can't even catch any catfish. Well, he's just gonna have to serve 'em hamburgers."

"Yeah, but you know how everybody looks forward to Jim's fish fry. Can't you think of anything?"

Jockey was one of the kindest hearts I have ever encountered. "Well, there's that little lake over at the state park. It's only about 200 acres, but there's a few crappies in it. They're small."

"A few is right. Few and far between."

"Well, there's gotta be somethin' in it. They been catchin' some nice bass. 'Course, we can't catch enough of 'em in the time we got. If we ran a line over there on Friday night…you know….set it just at dark….. and run it just at dawn, nobody'd see us."

"Is it illegal?"

"Not far as I know. I just don't want all them campers and swimmers hangin' around. We'll catch us some small crawdads and minnies and make up some doughballs. Bait for everything. We'll take your old canoe.

Damn boat's too heavy. I'll take the boss's truck. That's why we'll do it Friday. He don't need it on Saturday." Jockey was clearly warming up to the idea.

My "old canoe" certainly was. It had belonged to the father of a high school classmate of mine. It was a good canoe, an Old Town. But it had been neglected. The canvas covering was cracked and fragile. So, I had painted it with roofing tar. Ugly, but didn't leak. One end had been damaged in an accident on the way to a float trip on the Au Sable, but it still worked.

Friday evening, we loaded the Old Town on the 1 ½ ton stake body 1949 Ford truck. We had seined some craws and minnows, collected some night crawlers and made some dough balls from Jockey's formula…involving Wheaties and vanilla. "Breakfast o' champions," he chuckled.

At the lake, we followed a pre-existing road that had been submerged, by the impoundment, at a bridge. The superstructure of the bridge was still visible.

Jockey pulled off the road near the water's edge, and we launched the canoe. "Never liked these damn things. Too tippy."

"Over there", he pointed, and we made for a brushy bank. One end tied off, we let the ball of twine wander about the canoe bottom as the line payed out. "Looky there. See that old fence post out in the water? That's where we'll tie 'er off".

"But, it's on the same shoreline. Let's take it across."

"Nah. They'll be feedin' along the bank. This here's the place." In short order, now that I was at least partially trained, the line was set. We alternated baits: nightcrawler, doughball, minnow, crawfish. The shoreline was fairly shallow, so no sinker rocks were needed.

Back on shore, we tied a tarp across the tops of the truck's stake sides, as a rain shelter. Crawling under it, we spread out an old carpet as a sleeping mat. Then, Jockey produced a box of doughnuts. "You know, doughnuts need coffee. There's an old pot up there in the cab, an' a little coffee in a bag. Jump down an' get' em, will ya?"

I found the items he had mentioned, and gathered a little wood. Dry box elder wood, plentiful in the bottoms of the creek channel, burns like gasoline. In a few minutes, water was boiling in the dented, blackened coffee pot. "Pour it all in there. One thing I hate, it's troubled water".

The canoe could have been patched with that coffee. It was thick, black, strong and bitter. The grounds had not entirely settled, and gritted on the teeth. But it was hot, and the sugar from the dunked doughnuts made it almost pleasant. A taste for this stuff could be acquired. We laid down on the carpet, but no one slept.

The Creek Bottoms Symphony Orchestra was holding its annual late spring concert. From the tree frog piccolo section to the bullfrog bassoons, and a hundred creatures in between, the woods was full of sound….including a solo by a soprano owl. And, carpet or no, that truck bed was hard. Around midnight, Jockey shook me. "Here", he said, "have a little river rat sleepin' medicine." He offered a flask of blended Bourbon whiskey, firey and harsh, but all we had. It was light when I awoke.

What struck me was the stillness. There was no wind. The air was damp and cool, and a bright mist hung over the bottoms. Not a fog, and there is a difference, but a mist. Is it a matter of droplet size? I don't know. But I know the difference between a fog and a mist. Every Joe does. And that air was laden with the smell of native wild honeysuckle and of that little ground-covering plant, whose name I don't know, with the tiny purple flowers and the distinctive, pungeant aroma. It grows in the bottoms and endures only until the really warm days. Recent high water had deposited silt along the shoreline, and it has a trademark smell. Wonderful smells. Wonderful, earthy, watery smells.

Jockey already had the canoe afloat. "Well', he said as I got aboard, "we'll see. We'll see." Still 50 yards from the line, we saw. The line was thrashing violently. "At least one big one", Jockey said, not necessarily to me. We recovered hooks starting at one end of the line, rather than going directly to the fish.

"You got a big fish on, you don't want a bunch of hooks flailin' around while you're tryin' to boat it. That's how you hook suckers. And stow them hooks, 'cause there's gonna be a lot of floppin' in here." River rat wisdom.

Jockey bypassed the fish, not even raising them to the surface, until all the other hooks were recovered. Most of them still were baited, totally undisturbed. I hadn't even seen the fish. There were only three for the night's work, but it was clear that they were large. We went back along the line to collect them.

"Now, watch it. We don't want to tip this thing over." Jockey leaned forward to get the weight of the fish as close to the canoe's centerline as possible. He untied the leader, then gently raised the fish's head. In one motion, he seized the gill cover, and flipped the fish into the canoe. He had been right.

There was, in fact, "a lot of floppin'".

The fish was a carp, ten to twelve pounds. The other two were nearly identical. "That orta do it. There's enough here to feed the neighborhood," Jockey grinned. "Now, let's get outta here".

"But….those are carp. Those people aren't gonna eat those. They're expecting crappies."

Jockey smiled. "By the time I'm done, they'll *be* crappies." I wasn't sure what he meant, but I was anxious to find out.

Jockey filleted the fish in the usual manner. Then he soaked the fillets in a mild brine for about an hour, while we cleaned and stored the gear. He honed a very thin-bladed knife until, as he demonstrated proudly, he could shave his forearm with it. Most of the blood in the flesh of the fish had been removed by the salt solution. Any remaining red meat he carefully excised. Then he sliced the two inch thick slabs into half inch slabs. These he cut into pieces about six inches long, four inches wide at one end, two inches wide at the other, and placed them in a plastic bucket. He put a small stone on the top of them, and covered them with milk.

"Where'd you learn to do all this?"

"Oh, when I was a kid, I sold fish to the American Legion for their fish fry. Learned how to fix carp from an old guy in New Richmond. Whenever anybody asked me what kind of fish they were, I'd say 'fresh'. I wouldn't say no more. Never heard no complaints. And they'd look me up every month."

"They're gonna know it's not crappie."

"Shoot. Let Miles get a few beers in 'em, and they'd eat Jonah's whale. Don't you worry."

After a few hours, he floured them. "Can't see the big flakes," he explained.

The fry was scheduled for Sunday evening. Jockey and I got there early. "Now, listen, Miles," Jockey admonished, "fry up the crappies you got first. Then we'll cook these".

"Tell him," Jim said, pointing at me. "He's gonna be doing the frying". That was news to me. I hadn't counted on spending the evening in a cramped, hot kitchen. But on second thought, no one else would be handling the fish. That was a positive.

Jim looked at the dishpan full of pre-floured fish. "What kind of fish are they, Jockey?"

"Fresh. And don't ask no more questions."

Jim Miles went off to be a host. Jockey and I prepared to fry fish.

"Hey, Jockey. Let's not fry one and then the other. Let's mix 'em. See what happens."

He started to shake his head, then he frowned and finally broke into a broad and mischievous grin. "Yeah. OK."

We could not keep up with demand. Jim returned every few minutes with an empty platter. "Out of crappies yet?"

"Uh…..no." It was a true statement.

Jim shook his head. "Must have had more than I thought," he said, carrying away another full platter.

Bottom line: before Jockey and I had a chance to eat, all of the fish were gone. Jockey winked at me. "See? I told you." We got rave reviews.

But no fish.

Neighborhood kid admiring a Jockey Schwey "crappie".

CHAPTER 7
Wilderness On The Cheap
Canoes and Canvas

Several different groups of us returned, just about every year, for seven or eight years, beginning in the mid-1960's, to a place called Whitefish Lake, in the Algoma District of Ontario. We came to know it fairly well, and always caught bounties of fish, which is how learning a piece of water normally rewards. But eventually, it became too well visited, roads got paved, new camps appeared, and it no longer presented an aura of wilderness.

Wilderness is not necessary to good fishing. There are waters bordering highly urban landscapes that reliably yield excellent fishing, areas that seem almost immune to fishing pressure – if properly managed by the authority responsible. But wilderness is pre-requisite to a wilderness fishing experience, and smaller, fragile bodies of relatively infertile, cold water do respond fairly quickly to fishing pressure. Many of the small, northern lakes fit into that category. So, our circle of fishermen set out to find wilderness fishing….. that we could afford to access on limited budgets.

The easy options are remote lodges, and fly-in services, both of which we considered to be outside of our budget constraints. Our alternative was to find wilderness, with lakes and rivers which we could access on our own, on foot and/or by canoe. Even fifty years ago, wilderness was becoming increasingly scarce….and distant. Once again, our northern neighbor showed the most promise. The western United States has a significant amount of vacant land, much of it owned by the federal government – "public land" – but most is leased to ranch operations, and access to it is certainly not unlimited. And there is another problem: it doesn't rain very much. Unless a lake or stream is fed by mountain run-off, or unless a lake is created by way of damming a stream and creating a reservoir, there is relatively little water to fish. The average ratio of water area to land area is small.

By contrast, the Province of Ontario, alone, contains one third of the entire world's fresh water. Of course, approximately one half of four of the five Great Lakes is within the borders of Ontario, which contributes heavily to that statistic. But a glance at a map reveals that the land north of the Great Lakes is literally peppered with lakes and rivers. And, about 90% of its human population resides within about 100 miles of the international border, leaving the interior wonderfully lonely. Similar patterns apply to other provinces as well, especially Manitoba and Quebec. So, the compass point of choice was fairly apparent. Jake Foxbauer's advice had been sound.

Mae West is said to have remarked that, "Too much of a good thing is wonderful." Not always. The land is so vast, and the opportunities, at least as suggested by maps, are so many, that zeroing in on a specific destination is difficult. Risking your once-a-year on a dart thrown into a map is not wise. We needed reliable intelligence.

Bud Sroufe was a programmer/software writer who, by a tremendous stroke of good fortune for us, worked with Tim Wakefield and I. He annually, usually in July, fished the waters around an Ontario town called Chapleau, like a buffet – first one lake and then another, sampling a different lake every day. He fished alone. He did not camp, he stayed in town, and some of these lakes were three to four hours away, each way, not counting the portages into them. So, his time on the water was limited. Still, he had seen a lot of lakes, knew where they were, and how to fish them. What a resource! For the price of a few lunches, we got a lot of information – disorganized and a bit random – but a lot of it.

Tim and I agreed that Bud's style involved too much traveling and not enough fishing. We would prefer to select a promising lake, or set of nearby lakes, based upon Bud's information, and stay there. We posed this question: "Bud, if you had to pick just one lake, as the only place you could fish for the rest of your life, which one would it be?" I had expected a lot of qualifications and conditions, but there were none. After reflecting but a few seconds, he gave us the name of the lake (which I will not share, in the hope that it remains reasonably remote and unspoiled) and complete and detailed directions for how to get there. He also shared with us the names and locations of at least another dozen of what he considered "good" lakes. We didn't "collect" intelligence; it was poured over us like syrup on a pancake.

But the following summer, events beyond our control prevented a trip into that area. We had ignored one of the commandments: "Never let your marriage or your career interfere with your fishing." Most Joes, however, do allow such interference, for, to cite another cliché, "Discretion is the better part of valor." I was not able to get away until mid-September. Tim was unable to go even then, but another co-worker, a Wisconsin native named Arnie Griswold, eagerly volunteered for the venture. Arnie was a veteran outdoorsman, expert canoeist, and not unfamiliar with northern climes. Waiting longer, to accommodate people's schedules, was risky. Winter comes early and stays late in that part of the continent.

We asked Bud whether the lakes he had described were accessible without a 4X4 vehicle. "I do it in a Cadillac," he answered. Nevertheless, we chose an International Harvester Travelall. It was a 4X2, but was heavy and strong..... what is commonly referred to as "bulletproof". (It wasn't). The trip was long – nearly 800 miles - which we did overnight, non-stop. The last sixty, or so, miles took nearly four hours. The road was so rough that the globe of a gasoline lantern, in its case, and wrapped in a sleeping bag, was broken. The frame of the Travelall was cracked, but did not fail. We remained steadfast in the faith that it would be worth it.

The lake Bud had recommended was located in what is known as "Crown Land", that is, land belonging to the government. Most of northern "Northern Ontario" is Crown land, but not all, so free-lance camping, outside of established parks and private campgrounds, requires some homework, to avoid trespassing, or other embarrassing misdeeds. A camping permit is required of non-residents of Ontario, and so, we had to wait until the Ministry of Natural Resources office opened, before proceeding into the bush. The amount of legally accessible land - as opposed to physically accessible land – is enormous, millions of acres. But simply because one MAY go to a certain fishing location does not necessarily mean that one CAN go there, that is, actually get there, over land.

Overland access was typically via logging roads, some abandoned, some active. The longer abandoned, the worse the condition, since there was no reason to maintain them. Sometimes a logging road would lead to some place that had a reason to exist beyond logging, a mine, a park, or the like. Such roads would be maintained. Active logging roads were usually wide enough to allow two logging trucks to pass in opposite directions, and, if traveled on a weekend, were good transit, rough but sound. When the log trucks were running, they could be intimidating. There were usually large signs, posted at the main, public road, warning that the logging road was private, that you used it strictly at your own risk, and that the logging company was not responsible for anything that happened to you, no matter whose fault. Fair enough. After all, it WAS their road, and I thought it very generous that others were permitted to use it at all. Still, an 80,000 pound log truck, approaching at high speed on a twisting, undulating gravel road, with very little clearance, was………thought-provoking.

It was mid-day when we arrived, on a long abandoned and nearly overgrown lane, at the "wide spot in the road just past the creek ford" that Bud had described. It took very little searching to find the trail – on the right was a marsh, on the left, a bluff – not many real choices. It was overcast, but relatively bright, as autumn days often are, and in the low 50's. We walked the trail to the lake before unloading any gear, just to be certain that there was, in fact, a lake, and that there were no insurmountable barriers. The distance was shorter than I would have expected, maybe 75 to 100 yards; the trail was one of alternating muck and boulders….. and that I would have expected.

From the water's edge, at the end of the trail, we could not see the whole lake, but that was just as well. It might have been terminally overwhelming. There was shoreline that was relatively steep, and thickly wooded, beyond the marshy area to our right, which extended down lake less than 100 yards. This meant, to us, that deadfalls near the shoreline would fall into the lake, and that the underwater shoreline slope was likely to be similar to that which we could see above the water line. In turn, that meant a deep shoreline with abundant cover. Perfect for pike, an ambush predator.

There were rocky points visible, and small, oblong islands with long, shallow slopes on two opposite sides, and steep walls on the other two. These features shouted "walleye" at the top of their lungs. We could see a small, offshore weed bed within less than ten canoe lengths, and so, surely there must be more…..and bigger. The water was clear, but not crystalline. Visibility was perhaps four to six feet. In the distance was a large bay. We could tell from the slight change in color – a bit more green in the blue – that it was full of reeds and lily pads. It was perfect. It was absolutely perfect. It was the lake from heaven.

We had been so busy looking that we had forgotten to see. The deciduous trees were preparing to shed their summer raiment, which was, by now, autumn's joyful/sad scarlet and amber. Many of the low-growing plants, already anointed with frost, were brown, in a spectrum from blonde to russet. There were geese overhead, and beaver were more than their clichéd "busy". One of the great benefits of this sport called fishing is that it often takes one to magnificent and beautiful places…….places much like they might have been in the First Book of Genesis. I remembered that my father had told me, thirty years earlier, that fishing was not about fish. I was beginning – just beginning - to grasp what he had meant.

We lost no time getting the canoe, and gear, to the water's edge. It was always interesting to me that what we thought was the absolutely necessary, bare minimum, gear for two guys, for a week, could completely fill a seventeen foot canoe, well over the gunwales, and with enough weight to reduce freeboard alarmingly.

The first item on the agenda was to find a campsite. Arnie opined that an island campsite would be best. We checked out the islands. Only two of them had enough near-level space to pitch a tent, and those two were fairly barren and totally exposed to wind. The light breeze was chilly enough in mid-day. We could imagine what it might feel like after dark. A mainland camp, in the dense woods, would provide wind shelter, but would also be more prone to visits by those "shy, woodland creatures" you read about as a child…………………..especially bears.

But a woods camp is what we selected. We had noticed an area, on our way to the islands, that appeared to be reasonably flat. We paddled towards it. At one point was a small cove, perhaps twenty feet wide at its mouth, and forty feet long. There was but one place to scramble ashore, over a boulder, and there we found a barely defined trail, apparently made by beavers…. we hoped. Fifty or sixty feet along that trail was a site where the trees were just far enough apart that we could erect the tent. There was abundant firewood in every direction. "Close enough for government work," said Arnie. I readily agreed. There were fish out there waiting for us.

The gear was wrestled from the canoe. We pitched the tent. Everything else could wait. The rest of the camp could be established after dark; we had the gasoline lantern. We were not yet aware that it was no longer serviceable. Back to the canoe, where we assembled tackle. I wanted to re-engage with northern pike, but Arnie, Cheesehead that he was, voted for walleye. There must be something in the water in Wisconsin. "Bud said that he caught all the walleyes he wanted trolling around the island," Arnie remarked.

"Which island?"

"I don't know. We'll try 'em all."

"OK".

Paddle trolling from a canoe is a very good technique for such waters. It is silent and unobtrusive, which means that behind-boat distance can be shorter, minimizing snags, and shortening the radius in which a turn can be executed without the two lines coming into contact. It also provides enough activity to help keep the paddlers warm on a chilly fall day. We had made two passes around all of the islands but a very small one, alone in the middle of the lake, before the first hook-up. This was not as easy as Bud's glowing reports had caused us to expect. The fish was a walleye, perhaps a pound and a half. The trolling continued, in that same area, for another half hour without results.

"Well" Arnie suggested, "let's try the little one." There were submerged boulders visible on opposites sides of the island, a rocky ridge of which only the peak extended above the surface. It tailed off gradually into deeper water, being perhaps only eight to ten feet deep fifty yards from the island. The depths off the other sides of the island were unknown, but appeared to increase rapidly.

"What did Bud say he used?" I asked.

"Number 5 Mepps", Arnie answered, "got one?"

"No, but I got a number 3."

Mepps is the trade name for a rear weighted spinner, with a relatively long, cylindrical brass body. I could never understand why they were so popular and allegedly successful. They bore no resemblance to any natural prey item. Perhaps it was the flash of the spinner blade, or the particular sound pattern created in the water. In any case, I attached it, and we resumed our trolling pattern, shallow ellipses parallel to the rock ridge. Bud had been right. Hook-ups were regular, but size was consistent. We kept four of the virtually identical fish for supper.

"Hey, Arnie. Let's get camp set up before dark. A fire and some hot coffee would go pretty good right now."

"Yeah. I'm startin' to shiver. But look at the bright side....no mosquitoes!"

We cleaned the fish on the exposed boulder that was the island. Wet hands were suddenly uncomfortably cold, but walleyes clean quickly and easily. In five minutes, the chore was completed, not to fish market standards, perhaps, but as Arnie had said, "close enough for government work". The paddle back to camp was not more than a mile or two, but served to drive off the shivers. Earlier, the tent had gone up fairly easily. Arnie had used it often, and was practiced at erecting it. Some brush had to be cleared, and there was no avoiding the many boulders that protruded through the peat, or perhaps pre-peat, soil. Our clothes and sleeping bags were deposited in the tent; we didn't expect rain, but it was cloudy and that was threat enough. In collecting rocks to build a fire ring, we noticed that there seemed to be but two sizes of rocks: golf ball and school bus. But, finally, that task was completed, and we built a fire, fetched water, and brewed coffee.

That fire felt good: the summer sun, stored in cellulose fiber and resin. That "there is something about an open fire" is timeless and universal in our species. After thousands of years, we have completely domesticated fire. We enslave it in boilers and furnaces, in engine cylinders, in jet combustion chambers, but even now, we yearn for the color and dance of visible flames and the sun-like feel of radiant heat. So, like a favored retriever, or loyal herd dog, we bring it indoors, to lie at our feet and warm our souls, from stove or fireplace, even if the flames are artificial.

The coffee was strong, bitter and hot, as fish camp coffee is supposed to be. All we really needed it to be was hot. We fried the fish in oil over an enthusiastic fire, and only once set the oil ablaze, quenching it with a sheet of aluminum foil. The woods was damp, and presented no risk of forest fire, but we had the obligatory bucket of water at standby anyway. We boiled one of those packaged rice dishes, but not long enough, and the grains were definitely *al dente*. We didn't care. We had burned a lot of calories, and had not slept in 36 hours. Unrolling our sleeping bags, we discovered the broken lantern globe. At the moment, we didn't care about that, either. We were not going to need it that night. Goose down sleeping bags are wonderful. We were asleep before darkness fell on the forest floor.

The following day was dry and clear. The unimpeded sun brought temperatures up quickly. We had not arisen with the sun, and by the time we had finished the breakfast clean-up, even the fully shaded forest floor was beginning to be shirt-sleeve comfortable. Attention turned to the broken lantern. These devices had been a mainstay of life beyond the power grid for decades. The principle of operation was the same as that of the gas lights of the late 1800's: a gaseous fuel was burned catalytically on a grid of the mineral remains – ashes – of a small, silken sack, called a mantle. The catalytic reaction produced a brilliant white light. But, designed to be used beyond gas lines, the lantern had an additional step: it converted liquid fuel – gasoline without additives, or "white gas" – to a vapor before combustion.

Mantles, once burned to produce the ash that acted as the catalyst, are extremely fragile. The slightest breeze or bump could destroy them. So, the lanterns are fitted with a glass globe, more to protect the mantle than to prevent it from igniting other things. Users commonly carry spare mantles, but not spare globes. The lantern case is supposed to protect that. "You know," Arnie said, "these things will work without a globe. You just have to be careful about the mantles. You got some spares haven't you?"

"Yeah. Six. But both of the ones in the lantern are broken now. Replace them, and we've got four…..to last a week. And all it takes to break one is a little puff of wind".

"Yeah. Hey, how bad is the break it the globe? Can we wire it back together or something?"

"Nah. It's totaled."

"Well, worst case, we can paddle back to the truck, go into town, and get one."

"That will blow a whole day. Arnie, I didn't come here to go shopping."

Arnie stared at the fire. Then he turned to me. "OK. Here's what we do. We take foil and make a three quarter shade – you know, leave a 90 degree window for light to get out. That'll give us a lot of wind protection. We'll have to be real careful lighting it, but I think it'll work."

"But we won't be able to see anything out behind it."

"Are we sure we want to?"

Arnie had a point. And it turned out that his improvised repair worked perfectly well, all week. Arnie was very good at improvising. He was so oriented early in his career, as an aircraft mechanic in the USMC. He served in the South Pacific during World War II, as a crew chief, maintaining F4U Corsairs. With the lack of parts and materials common in that place and time, Arnie said that they kept planes in the sky "with toothpicks and paperwads". His squadron was commanded by the legendary, flambouyant ace, Greg "Pappy" Boyington. It was obvious that Boyington was no hero to Arnie, but he never disclosed why.

"I'm going down to the canoe and get my tackle organized", Arnie announced, and walked off toward the water. In seconds, I heard shouting. "Hey! Oww! What the….Oww….Get away!"

Arms swinging wildly, he ran back towards the tent. "Hornets! Hornets! Nest of 'em right on the trail!". I expected to see a swarm of them following him, but they did not. Seeing that they did not pursue, Arnie calmed a bit. He took me back along the trail to show me where it was. From a safe distance, we could see them entering and leaving a hole in the ground, not two feet off the trail. "Ground hornets. Worst kind," observed Arnie. We went back to the tent, found the first aid kit, and put some topical anesthetic on the stings. There were only two, but they were obviously painful.

"Didn't see 'em yesterday because it was too cold. They weren't active. We're gonna have to make a new trail, or beach the canoe somewhere else. You can't get by 'em." Arnie was right. We did cut a new trail, but the hornet nest was so close to the canoe that it was not really a safe alternative. A serious attack, with many stings, could be life-threatening; a schoolmate of mine had died from a reaction to bee venom. And, there was no other canoe dockage within practical distance. "What I do at home," I told Arnie, "is wait until after dark, then pour some gasoline down the hole and light it off. Works every time." We agreed that we would stay on the lake until dark, then employ that technique. For now, fishing was the objective of the day.

Now convinced that we knew where and how to catch "grocery" walleyes, we decided to pick a fight with big pike. A sunny, bluebird day was not a deterrent. Pike are ambush predators, lying beneath logs, rocks or in weeds, in the shade, waiting for a prey item to be outlined against a bright sky. We decided to start casting the shoreline from right where we were, and to cover the entire periphery of the lake, if daylight would last long enough. The cover, depth and water clarity were perfect. In every canoe length were a dozen prime ambush locations to cast to. The wind was gentle, and dependable, so that we could drift the shoreline with little paddle disturbance in the water. This was the pike water of dreams.

But those dreams failed to come true. We had worked shoreline for three hours, using the surest of all pike lures: red and white spoons, without a strike; not even from 20 inch "hammer handles". Arnie turned to me and shrugged, palms up, in the classic I-don't-know gesture. We switched to crank baits and surface lures, without results. We paddle-trolled the shoreline with a variety of lures, running at a variety of depths. Nothing worked. This was impossible. We were in the Garden of Eden and couldn't find any fruit. I don't recall exactly how many times, during those three hours, one or the other of us said, "I don't believe this!" I suspect that it was well into three digits.

At length, Arnie surrendered. "Look. This water's pretty cold. I would guess maybe fifty or fifty-five degrees. Lets go down to that stretch that looked like a shallow bay. Water will be warming up fastest there. Maybe that's where they are."

"Have you noticed…..we haven't seen a minnow or any kind of baitfish, or a craw, or a leech, or anything?"

"Yeah….like it's already winter."

The bay was more distant than it looked. We both shed our jackets on the way. The sun was warm and welcome, and made being in the open very pleasant. It was almost summer again. Water clarity was much diminished in the bay, to about two feet. Reeds covered an area of perhaps 100 acres, but they were sparse, averaging about six feet apart. Depth, as determined by canoe paddle, was three to four feet, and the bottom was not visible. We did not have a thermometer, so Arnie's theory went untested. This venue, too, proved unproductive.

We were drifting and casting, and inevitably, the wind brought us to shore, near an inflowing small stream. The water was shallow, twelve to eighteen inches, and full of lily pads. It would be impossible to cast a crankbait or spoon here. So, I attached something called a Beetle-Spin, the commercial name for a "safety pin" type spinner bait. Imagine an open safety pin, with a jig attached to the clasp and a spinner blade attached at the point, tied to the line at the loop of the safety pin. They were relatively snag resistant, and they were also cheap, so that loss to a snag was not a serious matter. The jig portion could be dressed with a live minnow, worm, leech, or a plastic grub or tail. Having no live bait, I chose a white plastic tail. Tossed into six inches of water, and retrieved through dense weeds, it immediately produced a violent strike, but not a hook-up. I held up the Beetle-Spin. "Hey, Arnie! Got one of these? Put it on."

In minutes, we had boated a dozen pike, all small, but pike nonetheless. Surely, in this congregation, there had to be a big one. Another false assumption. But it was an interesting afternoon. We probably caught and released fifty pike, but none over three pounds. And none caught in water much more than knee deep. "I knew it," gloated Arnie, "I told you. This shallow is the warmest water in the lake. Got to be!"

"Then, where are the big ones?"

"Uh……I don't know….Florida. Let's get some walleyes for dinner."

"Plenty of time. Remember, we can't go in until dark."

"Oh….yeah….that's right. Well, let's do some exploring, then."

The lake offered tremendous variety. We found another, and larger, bay full of reeds, these denser, and in places, almost impenetrable. We found, by sounding with a large lead sinker, holes more than fifty feet deep, and they weren't where we would have expected. They were often very close to shorelines and islands. By contrast, the depth in the middle of an open expanse of water was often only six or seven feet deep. We began to create a mental hydrographic map. No one had remembered to bring a pencil, and we vowed to never make that mistake again, as we found that mental maps are not of archival quality, and lead to spirited discussions.

We found rocky shallows, certainly off points, as would be expected, but also where the land topography gave no clue. We found more wooded shoreline with abundant cover from deadfalls and from beaver cuttings. We found five different beaver lodges, each surrounded by submerged, freshly cut small branches and twigs…..a sheltering magnet for small fish, and therefore, for predators. Each of these sites got red-circled on the mental map.

What we did not find were deep weedbeds. The one near our launch site seemed to be unique in this lake, with the exception of a few sparse, tiny patches, occupying less area than our tent. Aha! So, this wasn't the perfect lake, after all. Here was something to blame. Fishermen always need something to blame. Failure is never, ever, the result of a lack of skill or diligence. Ever.

Rather than going back to the island successfully trolled the previous evening, we decided to set up just off one of the rocky points. We collected a boulder for use as an anchor, paddled to the windward side of the bar, and quietly lowered it. If this spot turned out to be unproductive, we reasoned, we could always go back to the island just before sundown. We had twisted some aluminum foil around a branch near our cove, so that we could find it in the dark. But it was pleasant here. The wind was from the west, and so we could face eastward to cast the rock bar, faces away from the sun, which delivered welcome warmth to our backs. For an hour or so, there was no action. But that was of no consequence. We didn't <u>need</u> to catch fish here, there was always the island. And that is when it usually happens.

Whether by sun angle, or by some mysterious phenomenon that we will never understand, a switch was thrown. We caught a walleye. And after that, we caught a walleye on every cast, without regard to what lure we used, as long as it ran below the surface. Occasionally, a small pike would be boated, but for the most part, the fish were what we came to refer to as "standard walleyes" – fifteen to seventeen inches long, thick shouldered and solid, dark brown fading through bronze to ivory bellied. Then, on one cast, no fish was hooked, nor did any subsequent cast produce a strike. I have seen this behavior many times, by many species, in many places, fresh and saltwater. I do not understand why it occurs. There should be some maverick individuals, some stragglers. Nature is usually not so binary.

We had wisely kept the first four fish boated, on the "bird (fish) in the hand" principle. It was nearly sunset, and the island was 20 minutes' paddle away. Camp was at least an hour away. We stroked towards camp, stopping at an exposed rock face to clean the fish. Cleaning fish in, or near, camp is tantamount to sending a dinner invitation to every bear in the area. Remains were dumped in open water, making sure that all of the air bladders – the fish's bouyancy control – were punctured, so that the carcasses would sink. Before re-embarking, we put our jackets back on; as soon as the sun had disappeared, a chill rolled quickly across the landscape. There was no difficulty in finding the cove.

Carefully, we approached the hornet nest, using flashlights to seek out the hole….while as far from it as possible. There were no hornets entering or leaving. Apparently, the combination of cold and dark had them inactive, exactly as planned. In camp, I poured out about six ounces of lantern fuel into a paper cup. About to creep up to the hole, I was stopped by Arnie. He handed me a mosquito net. "Just in case", he said.

I delivered the gasoline to the hole without incident. I held a lighter to the opening, and there was a "fwooof" sound. I jammed the cup into the hole, and walked back to the fire ring. "Well, that's that," I said to Arnie. It wasn't.

We spent some time that evening around the fire, warming ourselves against the night air. The temperature had plummeted under the cloudless sky. There was no moon, but what little of the sky we could see through the forest canopy was strangely bright. Arnie walked down to the cove, and yelled for me to join him. "Look at that," he said, "northern lights! Can't see much from here. Let's douse the fire, and take the canoe out in the open lake….just at the edge of the cove."

The display was not spectacular, but worth seeing, especially for those who never see aurora borealis in their own latitudes. Finally, cold soaked, we decided to return to those warm, down-filled sleeping bags. Arnie sniffed the chill air. "We didn't douse that fire well enough. I can still smell smoke." So could I, but it didn't smell like pine or birch. It smelled like tea. We secured the canoe, and started towards the tent. In a few paces, the flashlight beams became visible cones of light. Smoke! It was seeping from the ground in the vicinity of the hornet nest. The "soil" wasn't the silt, clay and sand we were accustomed to, it was largely plant debris and moss, and we had ignited it!

"My God!" Arnie gasped, "grab the bucket and the biggest pot we have! Hurry!" We spent the next hour carrying water and saturating the area. It did not seem to help. Smoke continued to roll out of the ground. We consoled ourselves that the fire could not go deep; the ground was only a foot or two above lake level. But there was no limit to how much it could spread horizontally. We decided on a strategy of containment, pouring water at the periphery of the smoking-emitting area. There seemed to be no limit, either, to the amount of water that the ground could absorb; it was weirdly impossible to make wet. We longed to see mud.

Gradually, the smoke abated, but we continued to saturate the now boggy ground. After ten smoke free minutes, we rested. We were no longer cold, at any rate. We retired to the tent, but resolved to check the area again in an hour. If there was no more smoke, it would probably be safe, we reasoned, to go to sleep. In the meantime, I was entertained by Arnie's stories of his adventures in the South Pacific, and by a bottle of cognac we had acquired at the duty free store. At the end of the hour, there was no further sign of smoke. We sought welcome refuge in the sleeping bags. At least, we agreed, there would be no more problem with hornets.

The next day was a *déjà vu* day, exactly like its predecessor, except for hornets. We never were able to connect with a worthy northern pike, but could take walleyes practically at will. On the fourth night, sometime between midnight and dawn, we both awoke…..simultaneously. And we both knew that the other was awake. I was thinking how low the probability of that was, when the reason became clear. There was a rustling in the debris on the forest floor, behind the tent. Then came footfalls. We had seen snowshoe rabbits around the fire in the evening, and we knew that beavers work nocturnally. But these footfalls were no beaver or rabbit. They were heavy. And they were close. I felt the same cold sensation as I had many years before, when, like all small children, I was convinced that there was a monster under the bed.

Back at the MNR office, when we were obtaining the camping permit, we learned that the rules, for the area in which we were, prohibit any kind of weapons, not just firearms. No thought was given to that at the time, but there was thought being given to it now. I began to crawl out of the sleeping bag, to at least get a flashlight, but Arnie pushed me back down, and put his index finger over my mouth in the universal sign to keep quiet. We could feel, as well as hear, something heavy walking around the side of the tent, across the front, and then off to the right. The sound faded, then was gone.

"I didn't want you to spook it, if it was a moose," Arnie explained, "and have it dash into one of the tent guy ropes, get tangled up, and drag a bag of people off into the bush at forty miles an hour. Or, if it was a bear, have it feel threatened. That's something else I learned on the islands over there. Keep your head down." I understood. But I didn't get back to sleep for a while.

In the morning, the identity of the visitor was clear; we found moose tracks and droppings. I expressed surprise that a moose would approach so boldly. The camp had to be reeking with human scent. Arnie looked up from the griddle, which was laden with browning pancakes. "Do you know where a half-ton moose goes in this woods? Anywhere he wants to!"

It poured, and, alternately, drizzled rain most of the day. That did not deter us from the lake, but eventually, every rain suit leaks, and even a few drops can dampen the clothes beneath, stealing their insulation value. Worst, though, is the water that collects in the hull of the canoe, which, even though kept shallow by bailing, acts as a very efficient medium to transfer heat from feet to lake. Inactive lower extremities generate little heat, and conduct little from the body's core. Boots may be waterproof, and insulated, but ultimately, an aching cold seeps through all of them. It has been said that the difference between a good boot and a cheap boot is about two hours. We kept four standard walleyes, and returned to the shelter of the tent.

That night, we cooked supper over a gasoline stove, and in the tent, something we were reluctant to do. The canvas retains cooking odors, and acts as an olfactory neon sign that reads "DINER" to bears. But there was little choice. The rain had soaked the forest, and even the "squaw wood", the lower, dead branches of pine and spruce, usually dependably dry, were too wet to burn. We had brought the stove in case weather conditions were dry, and the risk of forest fire too great for open, wood fires. The MNR posts notices prohibiting open fires under high risk conditions, and the penalty for violation is steep, as it should be. And a patrol aircraft can see smoke, even from a cooking fire, for a very long distance.

But, we had not seen a bear, or sign of any, and had, so far, kept a "bear clean" camp. That meant that odor emissions were minimized. No fish were cleaned in camp, no food stored except in sealed containers, any leftovers were burned, dishes were scrupulously washed, and any non-burnable leftovers were taken to a distant, exposed rock, for the benefit of the gulls. Even the sealed containers were placed in a duffel bag and hoisted, out on a fairly slim branch, at least ten feet above the ground. Despite the cooking in the tent, this one lapse of discipline resulted in no incident. Unfortunately, that spawned some nearly disastrous over-confidence for later trips.

Luckily, the weather improved at the end of the week, and we packed out dry. The freight is lighter packing out – food has been eaten and fuel has been burned – but packing out, as opposed to packing in, is always onerous drudgery. It is physically impossible that the weight of an object can be increased by the mind….but it is. Back home, we cornered Bud Sroufe and interrogated him about the glowing descriptions he had given us regarding the quality of the pike fishing. He defended his descriptions vigorously. "Oh, you guys must have been doing something really wrong. Why, you can't help but catch pike in that lake, and big ones, too. I don't fish for 'em myself. Who wants those ugly damned snakes? They pester me when I'm tryin' to catch walleyes. You can't avoid 'em. Doesn't matter where you fish, either. They're just everywhere." He shook his head and walked away.

"Yeah, right", grunted Arnie.

Over the next decade or so, various members of our loosely defined circle made many return trips to that lake, and to neighboring ones in the general area. Bud had been right. During June and July, that lake produced northern pike in great numbers and often, of trophy size. In testimony, a framed Molson Big Fish Contest Award certificate hangs, not six feet from where I write this, for a forty-six inch northern pike, yielded by that very lake in 1983. Fishing in that area was not always fantastic, not even always great, but was never less than outstanding. And some of the experiences were, to say the least, interesting.

We re-used our forest campsite on subsequent trips. It was convenient, sheltered, already had some crude amenities, like the fire ring and a rough table, and…..we knew where it was. The downside was that, in the summer months, the moist, cool woods was a mosquito paradise. Members of the circle had been in some renowned mosquito infestations: Arnie in the South Pacific jungles, Wally Armstrong in Alaska muskeg, Tim in Malaysia, I in the Everglades – all agreed that our snug camp in the woods was as bad as it gets….. and maybe the worst any of us had ever seen. It was unpleasant at mid-day. In the evening, it was unbearable.

Repellents were now available containing a chemical called DEET. A product called Muskol was available in Canada, containing 95% DEET. It actually worked. Mosquitoes would absolutely not bite skin treated with Muskol. Nothing else worked. But preventing the bites was not the whole battle. The thick clouds of them, in your eyes, inhaled with each breath, all whining that maddening frequency in your ears……. Muskol did not affect. Mosquito nets controlled the inhalation, and kept them out of the eyes, but did not stop that terrible whine. One weapon, of some temporary benefit, at least, was a fogger. It created, by means of a propane heater, an aerosol (smoke) fog of a natural insecticide – or so advertised – called pyrethrin. This meant extra freight: propane cylinders and cans of insecticide, in addition to the fogger itself – about the size of a submachine gun. It was worth the weight.

Each morning, by turns, one of us would arise, slather on Muskol, being careful to not miss a single square inch of skin, and step quickly outside the tent. There, he would start the burner to pre-heat the fogger, necessary before it could be used. To those inside the tent, this step took two or three minutes. To the fogger operator, in a sandstorm of mosquitoes, it was an hour. When the vaporizing coil glowed red, the foggerman would saturate the camp area with insecticide fog. This would suppress – not eliminate – the hordes for about a half hour. The breakfast team would then dash into action. Using dry tinder and firewood collected the day before, and stored in the tent, they would brew coffee and boil water for packaged instant oatmeal, eaten from foam cups. The window provided by the fog did not allow time for more traditional breakfasts. Then, on to the lake, and open water, away from the wooded shoreline. There were plenty of mosquitoes there, too, until the sun – if any - was high, but only a small fraction of the on-shore density. The fogger was left at the canoe site, so that the first man ashore at the end of the day could clear the area. Before supper was prepared and eaten, and the housekeeping done, it was usually necessary to fog again. All of us had considerable exposure to the fog. The fogging chemical was advertised as being safe to humans and livestock. But, I still have this twitch………..

It took only one June trip to learn that the combination of black flies and mosquitoes was invincible. The fishing was fantastic, but not so much so that we ever used the forest campsite in June again. By July, the back flies were all but gone, and the fish were nearly as active. It was a classic matter of the cost/benefit ratio. We thought we had it figured out.

The next year, we tried a different lake, in the same area. It was not far from a bush road, although not visible from it, and was fed by a stream that was navigable by canoe, with a few short, easy portages over beaver dams. Better yet, there was a convenient tent site close to that road, along the stream, which meant that transporting all of the gear by canoe was not necessary. The site was open and airy, with few mosquitoes, at least when we set up, in mid-day, with a brisk breeze blowing. We pitched the tent, just below the last rapids, at the beginning of the still water, created courtesy of the beavers, and went fishing.

The cast of characters on this particular expedition included the elder two of my five sons, in their early teens, and Jim Santangelo. Jim and I have been fishing together for more than forty years, beginning on Whitefish Lake trips. Jim is a great fishing companion, one of those guys that nothing bothers, with a dry and quick sense of humor. He shrugs off cold rains, ignores hordes of mosquitoes, and always answers the proposal of some dicey adventure with his trademark, "Why not?" And Jim owned the ideal vehicle for this purpose, an International Harvester Scout, four wheel drive and built like a bank vault. We have driven that tough little machine into places from which we had no right to escape. He remarked that he had noticed that the primary feature of four wheel drive was that you could get stuck in ever less accessible places. He kept meticulous records of every trip; these narratives would have been impossible, or at very least, much less accurate, without them.

The lake was a picture post card. It was dotted with small, low islands, and consisted of a group of narrow fingers, suggesting that it was relatively shallow. It had no name, on the map. Action was furious. The lake was full of hungry, aggressive pike, most of them small, three to four pounds. They attacked any lure we could present with the proverbial reckless abandon. The boys were having the time of their lives, but learned, as had we all, at one time or another, that the forward end of a northern pike deserves great respect. Before we paddled back to camp, there were numerous, minor splatterings of blood at their ends of the canoes. The blood had not come from fish.

By the time we had reached the camp site, the sun was low in a sky that was harvesting clouds from the moisture of Lake Superior, a hundred miles to the west. There was no evening chill, in fact, the air was warm and still and humid. It felt good…..but….what was this? That air was filled with swarms of black flies! It did not make sense. It was July….mid-July. The fogger was in the Scout, and we used it to buy enough time to cook supper and get into the shelter of the tent, which we had thoroughly fogged, and allowed to ventilate through screened windows. What we had not known is that black flies, unlike mosquitoes, hatch in <u>running</u> water. The next day was overcast and fairly still, and we had the pleasure of the company of black flies all day at the camp site. Once on the lake, we were spared that torture. The next morning, we broke camp and moved on, seeking another venue…..one with a good lake, and a livable island, not favored by either species of insect. Virtually all of the lakes in the region are "good", and most have islands. By early afternoon, we were exploring new waters, with the usual breathless anticipation. Each new lake, at least during the first half hour, is always going to be the ultimate experience.

But since that is never actually the case, we would return to the original forest camp site about every other year. It was reliably outstanding, often great, and sometimes fantastic. On one such reprise, Arnie was again among the group. It happened that, while he and I were about as far from the campsite as was possible on that lake, a strong wind, of course blowing in the worst possible direction – directly from the campsite – arose, surprisingly quickly. A chop, approaching the freeboard of the canoe, soon followed. Against the possibility that conditions might worsen, we struck out for home. After about a half mile of maximum effort paddling, it became clear that the attempt was futile. Arnie pointed towards the thick reed patch near shore, where the vegetation was at least suppressing the wave height. We made for it.

The reeds retarded the drift rate of the canoe, and we were out of danger of being swamped or capsized. Arnie observed that, since there was nothing else to do, we had might as well fish. But we were moving at a brisk pace, the water was shallow, full of reeds, and the chop had turned the water turbid….almost muddy. Snagging would be frequent and inevitable. But Arnie held up a shallow-running crankbait called a "Big-O", attached it, and fed it out over the side, only ten or fifteen feet. On such a short leash, he could guide it between reeds, steering it with his rod tip. I chuckled silently to myself, "This is silly."

We had not drifted fifty feet when Arnie hooked a fairly heavy fish. "Well, there's always one dumb pike", I thought. But Arnie boated a really nice, four pound walleye, the largest we had ever taken in that lake. "Man, what a fluke", I mused. I made a mental note to never play poker with a guy with that kind of luck. Then, he hooked another. And another. I happened to have a Big-O, acquired for largemouth bass fishing in Florida. It was a wide-bodied, balsa wood crankbait, of a style just beginning to gain popularity at that time. I attached mine, and immediately began to hook thick, muscular, four to five pound walleyes. When we were blown ashore, we paddled back to the beginning point by staying in the shelter of the shoreline, in four to eight inches of water, another advantage of the canoe as a fishing platform. We repeated the drift with the same result. We kept our limit that day, on the theory that the others had probably been driven to camp by the wind, and had no fish. And, that was so.

By then, we had fallen into the practice of dinner in late afternoon, avoiding the mosquitoes that always appeared at sunset. Then, we would go back onto the lake for the evening walleye bite, finally to be dispatched campward by the gathering throngs. So, about 4 pm, the cocktail hour began. We had fastened a gallon thermos bottle to a tree, and filled it with one of those sugarless, citrus-flavored drink mixes, on the (mistaken) belief that, without sugar, there would be no attraction for the bears. Arnie was using that mix to dilute 151 proof rum, in a tall foam cup. Every time Arnie would put the cup down, one of my mischievous sons would covertly top it off…..with rum. Arnie was leaning, back to a tree, when someone said, "Hey, Arnie, how'd you catch those fish, again? I'd like to try that."

"Big-O……..Big-O," chanted Arnie, slowly sliding down the tree, "…….Big-OOOO". He slept through dinner, peacefully, at the base of a friendly spruce. Ever since, that has been a saying, a mantra, in our circle: "Big-O, Big-O, Big-O" is used to describe, interchangeably, an extraordinary fishing, or drinking, experience. Over the years, we caught many, many "standard" walleyes from that reed patch. But never again did we catch the larger specimens. We do not know why, except that it may have been the unique weather pattern……which we never experienced again.

The forest camp was visited several times by a "shy, woodland creature", most often a bear, who would ransack the food containers it could access, upset everything in camp, and knock down the tent, but was really no mortal danger. No amount of shouting or beating on pots and pans ever had any effect on these visitors. On one occasion, we tried throwing rocks. Pelting the bear with rocks did cause it to back out of the camp clearing, but not to go away. And, there was always the risk that a hostile act might be reciprocated. So, we were careful to keep a clean camp, hoist the food pack, and to simply stay out of the way while bears trashed the camp. If they did not find food, they usually did not come back.

We finally stopped using the forest camp after Tim had an unusually spooky, and terrifying, experience with a bear. But that's another story, in another chapter.

If, we reasoned, fishing was as good as it was in these lakes, with relatively easy access, what must it be like in lakes far from roads, deep in the bush? We pored over maps – we now had official topographic maps – looking for a promising lake that was difficult, but not impossible, to access in a day trip. Just because the topo showed a stream, it did not mean that it was canoe-navigable. Just because the lines of constant elevation showed no mountain or precipice blocking the way, did not mean that the country was not strewn with house-size boulders. But, at least, these maps gave some useful information. We made a selection from the smorgasbord of opportunities, and set out from our base camp at dawn.

We drove bush roads to as near as we could get to the route we had planned. There was no mark or feature by the roadside. The jumping off place was located by taking compass headings to visible topographic features and from clues taken from turns in the bush road, stream crossings, and the like. (Consumer GPS was not yet available.) The target lake was less than a mile from the point we had identified on the map, but a mile through virgin bush, extremely rough and extremely overgrown on the forest floor, with no established trail, even a game trail, is a very difficult hike, indeed. Add the burden of packs and canoes, and the difficulty increases many fold.

Given that, we decided to scout ahead, before carrying that load into a dead end. The hike was not as difficult, nor as far, as we had expected. We twisted pieces of aluminum foil around branches as we went. We had all been read Hansel and Gretel, after all. Once we could see the lake, we did not bother to go to the water's edge. It was there, and that's all we needed. We retraced our steps, picked up our gear, and headed back towards the hidden, secret, wilderness, never-before-fished lake. The distance was not so easily covered, now. A canoe, in thick bush, becomes a "Swedish Compass", not willing to change direction among close-set trees. Unbalanced by unfamiliar weight, footing over mossy boulders, large and slippery, becomes treacherous. But, at long last, the sky opened, betraying the lake ahead. As we continued down a long slope towards the water, we saw an obstacle we had not seen on the scouting patrol. The entire shoreline was obstructed by fallen trees and driftwood. To get a canoe to the water was going to require a great deal of effort. We had brought no ax or saw.

We tried to drag the deadfalls ashore, but these were not saplings cut by beavers. These were substantial trees. Their bleached trunks were often over a foot in diameter, and the portion submerged had had years to absorb water. Some of them weighed tons. Finally, we adopted an "if you can't lick 'em, join 'em" strategy. We used the trees as a bridge to the water, rather than trying to dislodge them. It resulted in slips and dunkings, but at great length we were finally afloat on a lake whose residents had never seen a fish hook. We mentally rubbed our hands together….oh boy, oh boy, oh boy.

The lake was nearly round. There were no islands. The water was very clear, visibility eight to ten feet. The shorelines were rich with forest debris, sunken whole trees and driftwood, still bleached white. The bottom was gravelly and there were no apparent weeds. The map had shown no streams connecting to the lake, and so, we had assumed that it was spring fed. The water temperature supported that assumption. It felt much colder than our "home" lake. "You guys go that way. We'll go this way".

"OK".

In the next hour, the two canoes combined to boat a total of exactly no fish. We were stunned, disappointed, and disillusioned. How could this be? Then somebody said that the explanation was simple: this was a trout lake. The clarity, the temperature and topography all pointed to it. We were just using the wrong techniques and lures. The rest of us, eager to grasp any straw, agreed that of course, that was the explanation, and we immediately attached small spinners and began to work deeper water..... rocks where we could find them. Anticipation bubbled over...... and over...... and over. Then, dreaded, unwelcome reality began to set in. This was not Nirvana, nor Valhalla, nor Shangri La. It was just a large, barren pool that just happened to be in a very remote place. Remoteness, of itself, does not guarantee great fishing. Let's see, how many times have I learned that, now.........?

Sadly, over time, that world began to change. Logging companies began to restrict access to logging roads. Not to all of them, but to enough that the menu at this buffet of lakes began to be limited. Permits are required to harvest forest on Crown lands. New regulations required that, at the conclusion of the harvest, the permit-holding logging company had to dynamite the bridges and block the roads. Whether this was brought about by political pressure from outfitters and resort owners, or to avoid litigation by parties injured on those roads, or both, is not important. So, access, as new timber harvesting permits are issued, will be lost to more of Crown land.

Joe's low budget wilderness paradise may be shrinking, but there is still a vast amount of it. In that same area, we have fished many, many excellent lakes, easily accessible from main roads. Budgetary restraints need not keep Joe from outstanding fishing experiences.

If he is willing, and able, to paddle and carry.

Sometimes, independent ventures into the wilderness can be a bit intimidating. The destination river was still 77 miles away. Best advice: remember the Boy Scout motto - **Be Prepared.***)*

Chapter 8
Unnatural Lakes
Opportunities Everywhere

Throughout most of the North American continent, especially that portion south of the Canadian border, natural lakes are *relatively* scarce. Minnesota, Wisconsin and Michigan are blessed with a relative abundance of them, and other northern states have natural lakes, but much south of the northern border states, they are few. Only in Florida do they regain significance as a major element of the fishing waterscape. ("Landscape" didn't seem appropriate.) Fortunately for Joe, water presents certain problems, and problems with water create fishing opportunities.......in lakes that weren't even there.

Water has this property: it runs downhill. When too much of it at a time runs downhill, it may cause severe loss......even loss of life. That phenomenon is called a flood, universally dreaded. At the same time, water flowing downhill contains energy; energy is valuable. And water is fickle. There is usually either too much, or not enough, of it. The flood is too transient an event to harvest the energy it contains, and most of the precious water flows away. So, the obvious solution is to constrain the rate at which the water flows downhill, storing it in reservoirs, allowing use of that water for drinking, irrigation, industry, and, where conditions allow, power. Sometimes, water is constrained for none of those uses, but simply to provide deep water for navigation. In any case, all of these reservoirs create fishable waters. And they are ubiquitous. Opportunity is everywhere.

There are estimated to be 75,000 major dams in the United States, creating over 600,000 linear miles of blocked stream, with well over a million miles of shoreline, and that only takes into account the major reservoirs. There are reservoirs in all fifty states; even lake-rich Minnesota has 17 of them. California has 138. Where does Joe fish in the dry, dusty center of the continent? Well, Kansas has 31 major reservoirs, Colorado has 12, and Utah has 28, just as examples. Reservoirs are easily found. Every state has a Division of Wildlife, or a Department of Conservation, or an agency of some such title, that will give Joe, upon request, not only the locations, but in most cases, detailed instructions on how to access them, resident species, and even, sometimes, popular lures and methods. This information is usually free.

The undisputed Granddaddy of reservoir systems was created by the Tennessee Valley Authority during the Great Depression. There are nine lakes on the Tennessee River itself, and 22 more on its direct tributaries. The Authority manages a total of 49 dams to assure the flows and depths needed for the multiple purposes it was set up to serve. There are 650,000 acres of fishable reservoir in the system, with 11,000 miles of shoreline. Think about that. That is a distance nearly halfway around the world, a very great deal of fishing opportunity indeed.

By contrast, Lake Erie has about 6,362,000 acres of surface area, and 850 miles of shoreline. So, while the total water surface area of the TVA system is only about 10% of that of Lake Erie, the smallest, by volume, of the Great Lakes, the total shoreline of the TVA system is about 13 *times* that of Erie. And Joe knows that, on balance, shoreline is where the fish are.

The TVA does not include other reservoir giants like Cumberland, Kentucky and Barclay lakes, but those are waters of the same genre, rivers flowing from the Appalachian highlands, detained for a while on their way to the Gulf of Mexico.

Species fishing waxes and wanes in just about any water, and the reservoirs are not exceptions. The hot crappie lake may not remain hot for very many years, while another lake in the system may be blossoming. The striper bonanza may shift from a given lake to, perhaps, the next one upstream….. or downstream. These declines and ascendancies may occur over years, or in a single season. This knowledge is a vital part of Joe's intelligence gathering. The typical Joe doesn't have the opportunity to try a different lake next week. He likely has but one week, or perhaps only a weekend, and he has to get it right the first time.

Falling heir to some apparently reliable intelligence, by accident, is what brought George Mallott and I to Watts Bar reservoir on the Tennessee River. A neighbor had a friend who was an artist, self-employed, in command of his own time. He spent much of each spring in the mountains of Kentucky and Tennessee, as a kind of itinerant angler. He had reported that Watts Bar was *the* crappie lake that spring, and that now was the time. A three day trip was organized in less than an hour, which is some measure of how much thought went into it. Domestic relations were also handled in a cursory manner. My wife always believed that Watts Bar was really a drinking establishment. As always, Joe will mend fences when he gets back. It is easier to ask forgiveness than permission.

The month was April, and the year was 1962. It was a Thursday, and immediately after work, we left for Watts Bar. We were not exactly sure where it was, but we had a road map of Tennessee. We had not gathered intelligence as to exactly where, on this large reservoir, our contact had caught these alleged crappies…..or how. We had no accommodations for the night, but were sure that there would be a campground, or fish camp, or somewhere that we could establish a base. Anyway, we planned to fish all night. We would find a place to rest tomorrow.

We had the ten foot car-top boat. We had an old, green Elgin 5 horsepower engine, We had a tent, a lantern, a cook kit and some bacon, eggs and bread. We had raingear and sleeping bags. We had tackle, including a minnow bucket. We had a Studebaker station wagon whose deck was big enough to sleep on, if necessary. Our confidence reminded me of that proverbial, fully computer- controlled airliner, on which the robot pilot told the passengers, "Nothing can go wrong…can go wrong….can go wrong….can go wrong…."

It took longer than we had expected to reach Watts Bar. Several false starts had been made from the main road in what we thought was the direction of the lake. They resulted in long and fruitless tours of the dark countryside. Finally we followed a sign advertising a bait shop. The sign was even lighted. This must, we figured, be a big time operation – relative terms indeed – and certainly must be near, or on the way to, the lake.

And, in fact, it was not only near the lake, but on it. It was bait shop/general store/campground/marina. And, to our surprise, it was not only open at one o'clock in the morning, it was busy. The campground was nearly empty, so these had to be locals. This was indeed a good omen. If these folks were willing to give up a weeknight's sleep, there surely must be something going on. We bought minnows, and fishing licenses, and the next morning's breakfast: candy bars,. All of this was taking far too much time.

Boats, motors and gear are not heavy until they are being removed from the water, so we were afloat in short order. Another boat, bearing three local fishermen, had beached, bought minnows, and was about to return to the lake. They were just climbing aboard as I was clamping the outboard to the transom. "Hurry up!" hissed George in a stage whisper. "We'll follow those guys. They just came back for more minnows. They have to be on to 'em!" Haste was not necessary. They seemed to be in no particular rush. Our engine was started and idling before they pushed clear of the shore.

George's plan was sound. We had no idea where to fish, and here were people who obviously knew the lake and where to fish it…….after all, they had run out of bait. But the soundness of a plan, and the ability to execute it, are different things. We followed them easily until clear of the marina area; then, within a minute, they were out of sight.

"Did you see where they went?"

"No."

"Where do we go, now?"

"Let's head to shore and find a tree in the water, or some brush." It was the classic crappie methodology: submerged cover, darkness, live minnows, April. It had always worked for me in other reservoirs, especially Cumberland. But there, I had the benefit of a neighbor who had married a girl from the Cumberland Lake area, and who knew the water. "Well," I asked myself, "how different can it be?" The answer to that question was, "a lot."

We puttered along the shoreline for at least a mile without the flashlight beam revealing a single fallen tree in the water. From the outline of the shore against the sky, we could see that the steep banks were wooded. But the beam of the light was not powerful enough to see more than forty yards or so, in the misty night air, beyond the waterline. We did not know whether we were near the dam, or well up the lake. The water was somewhat turbid, so we concluded the latter. We could see no anchor lights or navigation lights on other boats, and so also concluded that this was not "the place". But we could see distant lights on the opposite shore. "Let's try that shore", suggested George.

Probing with a lead weight showed that the water was not the typical depth expected of a hill country impoundment. So, we proceeded at idle towards the opposite shore, confident that the depth would be increasing. Idle speed had been the right choice. Several times, the propeller struck something, but kept turning. Whatever it was seemed relatively soft….not like a boulder. Then, smoothly and gracefully, the bow rose and forward motion stopped, engine still running. I shut it down, and tilted the engine up. Using the oars, we were able to push the boat free. But every attempt to get back under way resulted in another collision in just a few yards. George peered intently into the water with the flashlight. "Stumps! A whole field of 'em."

"Well, OK. Let's just tilt up the engine and row out of 'em." That did not work either. Some of the stumps were but inches below the surface, and the boat was continually grinding to a halt on them. Trying to escape in the dark was not practical.

"Well," George sighed, "we're here 'til daylight……at least. Might as well fish. Who knows?"

That was a good decision. There was a very light breeze, and it moved the boat slowly, bouncing it gently from stump to stump, like a pinball machine in slow motion. With minnows suspended about 18 inches below small bobbers, we began to hook into nice slabside crappies. The action ended with dawn, but by then, we had quite a respectable stringer.

Daylight made our situation clear. The lake level was obviously low. The normal waterline was some distance up the bank. At normal level, the stump field would have been far enough submerged that passage over it would have been quite safe. The original river channel was against the far shore, which was an outside bend of the river, leaving a secondary bottom that had been forested by the trees that were now stumps. Even in the light, navigating the boat out of the obstructions required some effort, but was readily accomplished. It was time to clean fish.

After breakfast, we set up camp and slept most of the day. At dusk, we would go back to the stump field. If the wind picked up, we reasoned, we could anchor. By noon, a cloud cover had formed and by mid-afternoon, it had become dense and threateningly dark. But there was no rain by late afternoon, and we prepared to return to the stump field….equipped with rain gear. But we had forgotten one important item, and we should have known better.

The anchor, a concrete block scrounged from the edge of the parking lot, was not necessary. There was no wind at all. The air was humid and heavy, ordinarily ominous signs, but there was no precipitation, and the cloud cover did not seem to be increasing. The radio in the vehicle could have given us a local forecast, but we had not bothered. Other boats were leaving the marina, and surely, if the weather were about to turn hostile, these local folks would know that. Surely.

We set up somewhere near what we thought was the center of the stump field, not knowing which way we might drift. The one emotion that always reliably precedes the first cast is anticipation. It is often short-lived. But George observed that it would likely be well after dark before the fish would feel safe enough, in this shallow water, to become active. A number of boats passed in the deep water of the old river channel, the procession continuing until well after dark, their green, starboard navigation lights tracing horizontal lines against the dark shorelines. We boated two or three specimens, not worth keeping, over a period of several hours. We began to doubt that we were in the same place we had been the previous night. Then we noticed a boat traversing the channel, with engine noise characteristic of wide open throttle, but with the red, port side navigation light visible. In minutes, there was another, then groups.

"Hey, George. Everybody's headin' in."

"Yeah. Must've limited out already."

"I don't think so. Look at that."

The western sky, just above the barely discernable horizon, was periodically ablaze. Simultaneously, the still air began to move, and to turn chill. It quickly rose to a level arousing a nasty chop. The boat began to pinball against the stumps again, this time with alarming impacts.

"Let's get out of here. That's a really ugly storm, maybe only ten or fifteen minutes away."

"We can't. Not in the dark."

"Then, get that anchor overboard. We're gettin' beat to pieces."

The anchor finally caught on something, and held. But the boat swung like a kite's tail, striking stumps with frightening force. We tried to get a loop of rope around a stump, to at least restrain the swaying, but without much success. The stumps were submerged, and the rope was made from polypropylene, a plastic which, unfortunately, floats. The rain had begun to pelt us with considerable vigor before we were finally able to wedge an oar between the roots of a stump, and snub the boat's side-to-side motion. Now all we had to worry about was lightning …..and one other thing: The boat was filling with water, more from the chop than from the rain, and we had forgotten an essential piece of gear: something to bail with.

Hats and hands are not efficient bailing tools, but we stayed afloat, and thunderstorms are usually reasonably brief. It blew over after about forty-five minutes. We were wet; few rainsuits are totally effective in rain driven by strong winds. But, even though the storm drove the temperature down in its passing, we were reasonably comfortable. And, after the storm had passed, we were beginning to take a few good fish. By dawn, we again had a very acceptable catch. Shakespeare had been right, "all's well that ends well".

Fishing reservoirs is challenging. Because they are not natural lakes, fish are often not where they would naturally be. We had been lucky. The stump field was an accidental find. Even if we had known it was there, we probably would not have chosen it. It was not conventional wisdom for this kind of reservoir. But far more significant than that, no one was fishing it, and given the number of trailers parked at the marina, it wasn't because no one was on the lake. Once as much local intelligence as possible has been collected, my favorite time-proven, on-water methods for finding fish, in descending order of effectiveness, are: 1) gulls; 2) boats; 3) sonar. The stump field met none of those criteria.

Gulls are not a reliable indicator for benthic species, or for low-in-the-water-column feeders. But for pelagic predators, especially those that feed co-operatively as schools, they are infallible. A flock of gulls, in the typical vortex pattern, is over shallow prey, with predators almost certainly in the vicinity. And when the gulls are making contact with the water, those baitfish are being driven to the surface, or are being fragmented, by feeding predators. That does not necessarily mean that the game fish will strike at baits presented, but if the lure is a good imitation of the prey species, or preferably is one of them, the odds are very good. And, if the predators are breaching, the odds are as favorable as they will ever be. In those cases, the lure need be "not even close". Given the choice, I will always fish *where the gulls are.*

In the incredible, glory days of the Lake Erie walleye phenomenon, in the 1980's, when limits were often caught in minutes, not hours, all one needed was a "Lake Erie Fishfinder" – a pair of binoculars. Scan the horizon, find a fleet of boats, and simply join them. It was not uncommon to join a group numbering hundreds of boats, drifting a reef, or sometimes, open water with no distinguishing feature, with everyone catching limits of fine, fat walleyes. But that, too, is another story, for another chapter. It is a story of nature's resilience and of wise resource management; a story of good news for Joe's grandchildren. Ecological success stories don't seem to get much press….it's the other way around.

Joe needs to be ever mindful of courtesy and angling etiquette, but a group of clustered boats, especially if local folks, can be a very valuable clue in trying to unravel an unfamiliar reservoir. But there is a caveat. There is something our circle refers to as "the nucleation effect". It is best illustrated by an example.

One autumn morning, Jim Santangelo and I were out for a catch of yellow perch. Not only do I consider lake perch to be the ultimate seafood – I wouldn't trade them for lobster, dorado or yellow tail snapper – they freeze well, and in the dreary days of mid-winter, are a most welcome dinner. At the launch ramp, we struck up a conversation with another party of fishermen, and they asked us for advice, as they had never been in the area before – just as Joe should do. We replied that we had not been there recently either, and would have to do some searching, as the schools are constantly moving. They asked if they could just tag along with us, and we welcomed them. Perch are bottom huggers for the most part, and, at that particular time of year prefer mud or marl bottom, seeking gravel or rock bottoms later on in the season. A fish whose body may be only two or three inches deep, close to a resilient bottom, thirty or forty feet down, is difficult for the typical Joe-price-range sonar to resolve, so that instrument was of little help. It was early in the day, and no other boats were visible. We went to a spot that had been productive in earlier years, set anchor, and began to fish, as did our new acquaintances. We caught nothing. But in less than an hour, there were fifteen boats clustered around us: the nucleation effect.

Reservoirs offer varied opportunities. Winter, in states much south of the northern tier, does not offer a great deal of fishing opportunity. Ice, if any, is usually not sufficiently safe, and most of the native species are relatively dormant. Temperatures undulate back and forth around the freezing point, and most days are a dreary gray. But one January, I got a call from Jim Santangelo. He had just attended the local boat show. "Hey," he said, "you gotta get down there and see this. There's a guy down there – a guide on Norris Lake – who's got a big cooler of stripers, fresh, just caught, and they hang over both ends of a really big cooler!"

Yeah, yeah, I thought, I've heard this song before. But I had a business meeting in the vicinity the next day, so I took in the show. Jim was right. Those stripers were spectacular. The guide said that winter was the best time to fish for stripers, and that they were in peak activity right now. (Oh, sure, I thought, this is your slow season.) He said that he hadn't brought any of the big ones because they wouldn't fit in the largest cooler he could find. (Right. That ranks right up there with "The check's in the mail".) But when I bluffed that we'd like to charter him for the next weekend, he told me he was booked solid for the next three weeks. That shot down my slow season theory. Besides, Clyde was a good ol' boy, who looked you straight in the eye, and had an aura of sincerity about him. We booked him for his first available date. We *wanted* to believe.

His available day was a Friday. He had other clients for the weekend. So, we towed our own boat to use for those two days. A Grady-White offshore center console boat, heavy and seaworthy, bought for rough and treacherous Lake Erie, was gross overkill for Norris Lake. And it was no fun to tow over the steep, narrow, twisting roads on the map our guide had furnished. It was no fun to launch either, but we would not learn that until the next day. Today, we would fish from his bass boat.

Stripers are an example of fish that weren't there in lakes that weren't there. "Striper" is a slang term for Atlantic striped bass, also called rock bass or rockfish, Native to the Atlantic coast of North America, but widely introduced elsewhere. The striped bass, like a very few other species, notably certain salmon, is anadromous, that is, tolerant of both fresh and salt water. Another anadromous fish is the nasty bull shark, which has been found in fresh water rivers, sometimes hundreds of miles from the sea, and which has a taste for people meat. I am old, and I got that way by never swimming with predators larger than myself.

We met Clyde as planned, at the marina, just after daylight on a cloudy, 35 degree morning. The marina was populated by two kinds of boats: bass boats and houseboats. His boat was the classic bass boat, open, low, sleek, and powered by an engine that looked several sizes too large. The boat was half the weight and twice the horsepower of the Grady, and we knew how fast the Grady would run, and so prepared ourselves for a very chilly ride.

We were not disappointed. Once outside the marina, the bass boat accelerated like a 1960's muscle car, and 35 degree air at 60 mph is…… invigorating. But the ride did not last long, for which we were grateful. We coasted to a stop at the mouth of a small, narrow bay, a flooded "holler" in Appalachian terminology. (That's a good, honest word – no confusion with something that has no interior: hollow.) Clyde then surprised us. We had expected baiting with large, live shad, or at least with six or seven inch crankbaits. Instead Clyde produced from his pocket one quarter ounce, white Dollflies, basically a jig dressed with a hair tail. This was a tiny lure given the huge fish Clyde had displayed at the show. We were beginning to wonder if this was some sort of prank on the gullible greenhorns.

Clyde told Jim where to cast. "Rat agin th' bank and reel slow. No. Not that other bank. This'n rat cheer." In less than a dozen casts, Jim was onto a "small" striper….only fifteen pounds or so! "Turn that'n back" Clyde instructed, "ye don't wanna use yer limit up 'cept on big 'uns." Now, we were well and truly impressed.

That turned out to be the only bad advice we got from Clyde. We only boated one larger striper all day. Clyde had shown us how to fish during the mid-day period, when the stripers sought deeper water – not the sixty to one hundred foot depths of summer, but twelve to fifteen feet. For this he used small minnows, the size ordinarily used for crappies, free swimming under a small bobber, with no sinker. If fish were observed breaching, or if a flock of gulls gathered, he would return to the Dollflies. "Rockfeesh don't want nothin' big to eat in cold water", Clyde explained.

By the end of the day, we were cold-soaked, but had limited out. The marina had a lighted fish cleaning table, and there was a queue to use it, so we retired to the cabin we had rented. No sense standing there in the cold if we didn't have to. That was a mistake. Getting used to warmth, abetted by a generous martini, has a negative effect upon willingness to go clean fish in finger-numbing cold, but it had to be done. "Well, let's go do it" was said three or four times before we actually went and did it.

The next morning was as cold and gray as its predecessor. Launching the Grady proved to be a challenge. The launch ramp was located in another narrow, flooded holler, and by the time the trailer was deep enough so that the craft was afloat, the propeller was against the rocks on the far bank. We had to withdraw the trailer and push the boat away from the bank with a pole in order to start the engine, and very carefully navigate it out to the marina so that Jim could board. The lake was at its low, winter pool stage, in anticipation of spring rains, and the ramp was never intended for boats of the length and draft of the five thousand pound Grady.

We thought that it would be discourteous to go to the places Clyde had taken us. After all, he probably had taken his current clients to those spots. Anyway, we knew what kinds of water to look for….we just didn't know where those were. Long boat rides are not for cold days in an open, center console configuration. We chose the nearest likely looking spots, and learned that likely looking is not enough. Stripers were not everywhere. But, making enough casts, and soaking enough minnows, in enough places brought us to within one fish of the limit by day's end. By that time, we were shivering uncontrollably.

Sunday morning, we fished only until noon, keeping no fish as we did not want to spend time cleaning them, facing a six hour period of re-trailering the boat and towing it home. But it had been an interesting adventure. Our circle made winter trips to Norris for a number of years after that, until a waning cycle in striper fishing there made it unattractive. On one of those trips, we had to shovel snow out of the boat before we could launch. That day was best day of striper fishing we ever experienced, with several fish in the 30+ pound class. I liked winter striper fishing. It was uncomfortable…. but uncrowded.

Reservoirs are a huge part of the fishable waters inventory. There may be 75,000 major reservoirs in the US, but there are hundreds of thousands of smaller ones: municipal water supply reservoirs, park lakes, retention ponds, golf course lakes, and, after all, farm ponds are reservoirs. In just about every state, just about every year, at least one of the "fish of the year" awards is produced by a farm pond. Reservoirs are admittedly harder to fish than natural lakes; each is different. There is a 2000+ acre reservoir a few minutes from my house. It produces a lot of good fish every year….. but not for me. I haven't solved it yet.

Reservoirs present Joe with three wonderful benefits: they produce a tremendous number of fish; they are a challenge; and they are ***everywhere***.

Chapter 9
Chaos at Coquina
Getting the Blues

In the mid 1980's, someone in our circle of fishermen, I don't recall who, had heard about a phenomenon that took place each fall on the Atlantic coast. The story went that schools of bluefish migrated south along the coast as water temperatures dropped, as far south as Cape Hatteras, in the Outer Banks of North Carolina. And these were the largest of the categories of bluefish. Smaller bluefish, found all along the coast, and into the Gulf of Mexico, are called "snappers" or "tailors". But these migrating bluefish were the "choppers" or "jumbos", weighing up to twenty pounds or more. And, the story went, they migrated in great schools, encircling enormous pods of baitfish, and herding them against the beach, in a maneuver called a "blitz". And not even a boat was needed; they could be caught in the surf.

At that point in time, we didn't have a boat that anyone not bent upon suicide would put into the Atlantic. A chance to catch large, saltwater fish from the surf was, to understate, attractive. Time to gather intelligence. A call to the Kitty Hawk Chamber of Commerce produced some leads, bait shops, guides, and the like, and given that such contacts had an agenda

– to attract visitors to the region – we sought disinterested parties. I think it was Tim Wakefield who called a state-run aquarium in Manteo. The story was confirmed.

With no experience base to fall back upon, we tried diligently to do our homework. For surf fishing novices, and we certainly were, there is a really excellent, concise "how to" book by Joe Malat, a professional surf fishing guide, called simply "*Surf Fishing*", published by Wellspring. We obtained a copy. We read everything we could lay hands on about this fabled place and this fabled fish. I had been to the Outer Banks before, on a family vacation, in June, and had done casual fishing in the surf and from piers, for spot and whiting and the like. I had not been impressed, and was disinclined to believe the incredible accounts we were reading. One of my father's many wise sayings was "If it seems too good to be true, it's probably not." And these stories were certainly too good to be true. But……. what if…… they were?

A boat may not have been needed, but a beach-worthy 4X4 certainly was. And Jim Santangelo had one. His I-H Scout was ideal: short wheelbase, high ground clearance, all mechanical four wheel drive, with no fancy electronic gee-gaws to go awry, no complex automatic transmission to fail……with the tide coming in. It may not have been the most comfortable Interstate cruiser, but it was perfect on the beach. Our later vehicles were good: two Diesel Suburbans and a full size Ford Bronco, but none quite so agile in chasing bluefish schools, trying to get *where the gulls are,* as that little Scout.

Our investigations seemed to indicate that late fall, between Thanksgiving and Christmas, offered the best chance of encountering a "blitz", the term used to describe the feeding hyper-frenzy of chopper blues. Accordingly, we left the week after Thanksgiving for Kitty Hawk. We had read about bluefish blitzes, about how aggressively bluefish feed, about how baitfish, and any other fish caught in the melee, including large speckled trout, beach themselves to escape the choppers' choppers. But until you have "been there, done that", all descriptions fall short. We had experienced fish feeding frenzies before and thought that we knew what to expect. We did not. Nor did we have any appreciation for the frenzy that occurs on shore when the jumbo blues are about.

December on the Outer Banks is reliably, constantly, endlessly windy. That is, after all, why Orville and Wilber chose it as their test site. Standing chest deep in cold water, on a forty degree day, in a 25 mph wind, from daylight to dark, may not sound like a pleasant occupation, but we would find out that legions of Joes, from all over the United States, some of them driving thousands of miles, did exactly that. It is something more than a fishing outing. It is an event, a meeting, a reunion. A blitz, or even the rumor of a blitz, will have 4X4's parked three feet apart, up and down the beach, as far as one can see. And upon the report, whether or not true, that blues are being caught somewhere else, that same beach will be deserted in less than five minutes. Very, very few bluefishermen pick a spot and wait for the fish. We would learn that the accepted practice was basically road hunting......... with a surf rod.

Bluefish devotees were easy to spot, even off the beach. The typical ensemble: a 4X4 SUV or pick-up truck, rod rack on the front bumper, driver and passengers dressed in chest waders, and a CB radio antenna. The latter was as essential to the style of fishing practiced as was the surf rod. Many of these vehicles bore vanity plates attesting to their purpose. Several of these were memorable: "2D BLITZ" , "BIGBLU", and "BLUS BROS". So ubiquitous were the chest waders that it was common garb in restaurants, shops, and, when we attended church on Sunday, several attendees were so attired. Waders were worn just in case there was news of a blitz. And when that news broke, even those whose duties required other clothing poured onto the beach, as they were. We saw one individual, dressed in a business suit, shed his shoes while running toward the surf, and wade into the numbing water waste deep. Blitzes don't happen every day, and he was not to be denied.

There is a bit of madness in all fishing. Normally rational people will stand shivering in ice water, or cling for dear life to a boat in rough seas with one hand, while casting with the other, or endure a blazing hot sun in an open boat on a one hundred degree day, or carry heavy packs and canoes through mosquito bogs, all in quest of that surge of unseen power, somewhere out there at the end of a tiny filament. But bluefishing in the surf seems to elevate that dementia to total and utter insanity, as we shall see.

The Outer Banks of North Carolina is a unique place. There are other barrier islands along US coasts, Atlantic, Pacific and the Gulf of Mexico, but none having the extent of access, nor the offshore hydrology, of the

Banks. The sea floor off the Banks is treacherous. There are more than 500 shipwrecks, some dating to colonial times, in the waters just offshore, earning the area the dubious name, "Graveyard of the Atlantic". Diamond Shoals, at Cape Hatteras, extends a shallow finger far out to sea, creating what is likely the finest red drum (aka channel bass, redfish) surf fishery in the entire world. And trophy red drum fishermen may be even more dedicated than the bluefish fraternity. They tend to fish at night, in winter, at Diamond Shoals, in piercing winds, and bone-chilling temperatures. The water at Diamond Shoals is rough even on calm days, but the spray and the wind do not deter these stalwarts. And for good reason. A Hatteras red drum may weigh well in excess of forty pounds. The world record is 94 pounds, 2 ounces. Joe Malat calls them "King of the Surf".

Offshore, there are billfish and tuna to be caught. The surf yields flounder, kingfish (whiting), weakfish (which are anything but weak), speckled trout, croaker, spot, spanish mackerel and pompano. Off the piers, king mackerel may be encountered in addition to the surf fish. Occasionally, sharks are hooked, usually sand sharks, but sometimes a hammerhead, which might be the size of a small canoe. Striped bass were few in the years our circle fished the OBX, but not absent, and that, as we will also see later, may be significant. But for all of this smorgasbord, our interest, and that of most of the fishermen on the Banks in December, in those days, was the powerful, aggressive chopper blue.

One of the most attractive features of the Outer Banks is that the Hatteras National Seashore, administered by the National Park Service, has spared vast areas of beach from the ravages of development. The beach and dunes are in their natural condition, save for a few villages that pre-existed the creation of the National Park. Vehicles are permitted on these beaches, with only a few areas prohibited in December, while many beaches are closed during the spring and summer months to protect nesting wildlife. This made the pursuit of bluefish, by the method used by most anglers at that time, possible. North of the National Seashore, towns like Kitty Hawk, Kill Devil Hills, and Nagshead required a seasonal permit to drive the beaches, too expensive to make sense for a few days' visit. In those areas, the beach had to be accessed on foot and only from official "beach access" sites. But frenzies are frenzies, on both sides of the water's edge, as the following incident illustrates.

First, it is necessary to understand the accepted methodology of those times. As soon as it was light enough to see birds aloft, Route 12 was crowded with vehicles, of the type previously described, both directions, with at least one passenger scanning the sky with binoculars. Most vehicles patrolled from the town of Corolla on the north end to the town of Hatteras on the south end, as no ferry crossings are necessary in that stretch, about 90 miles. Parties having more than one vehicle communicated via CB radio, switching channels according to a pre-agreed plan, to achieve as much security as possible. It was futile. There were so many ears, on so many channels, that private communication was impossible. As soon as someone spotted a flock of gulls, concentrated over some location along the beach, everybody knew. That commenced a race, on sand or pavement, to the place *where the gulls are*, no matter how cleverly the observer thought he had encoded his message. At that site, there would be traffic jams, illegal parking, trespassing, altercations and the like. Altercations were few. Everyone had the same goal: get to *where the gulls are*.

North of the National Seashore, the beach area is well developed. Except for the Beach Access points, private property prevails. Pursuing a school of bluefish between public access points is a very athletic endeavor. Sprinting in heavy clothing, wearing waders, is exhausting, and fishermen who do so need to be in excellent condition. The older, and usually heavier, anglers, like us, would try to determine in which direction the school was headed, and would drive to the next access point to ambush them. That does not always work. The schools would often leave the beach before reaching the next access point. So, getting to the place where the blitz was actually in progress was much to be desired, as a blitz may last only a few minutes.

One afternoon, we sighted a large flock of gulls, in the typical tornado-shaped feeding behavior. Stopping at the nearest access point, we could see that the blitz was occurring in the middle of a fairly long stretch of private beach. We decided to drive to the location, in the hope of finding some way to get to the water. We were not alone. The local streets were jammed with vehicles, but there was no access. The neighborhood was one of luxury beach houses, very, very upscale. One group of fishermen could stand it no longer. Rods in hand, they dashed up a driveway, vaulted a fence, and headed for the beach. The homeowner knew what to expect. He was on his balcony, shouting threats at the trespassers. One of them, not even slowing down, shouted over his shoulder, "It's OK! Bluefish rules!"

With that, the floodgates were opened. Dozens more followed. But it was too late. The blitz was over. We learned that bluefishing the Banks was pretty much the same as the rest of life. Success was a matter of being in the right place at the right time. Strategy plays a role, but luck plays the lead.

On that first three day trip, we caught but one jumbo blue. We had arrived at Cape Point, following a distant flock of gulls, just as a blitz had concluded, and the beach was clearing of anglers. Having no idea where else to go, we stopped and cast cut mullet into the surf. A four ounce lead sinker takes little time to reach the bottom in five or six feet of water, but mine never did. Almost simultaneously with the splash of the rig, a violent strike nearly toppled me forward into the surf. The cliché, "nearly took the rod out of my hands" may be trite and over-used, but it was an accurate description. The ferocity and tenacity of a chopper blue makes one an instant believer, ready to join the cult. And it was not even a particularly large specimen, perhaps twelve or thirteen pounds. I was a convert….no…. an addict, seduced by this straggler.

Every first week in December, for a number of years after that, our circle fished the Outer Banks for bluefish. Bluefish are a very cyclical species in terms of numbers. In the late eighties and into the nineties, we seemed to be riding the crest, but on the descending side. In 1997, came what is perhaps the single most interesting incident of my fishing life, and possibly that of any of our group, and memorable only partly because of fish.

The cast of characters included Jim Santangelo, Jeff Burroughs (one of my sons), Jim Reese and his brother, Tim, and Randy James. Jim Santangelo and I had planned to spend a week at the Banks that year, to improve our odds of encountering a blitz. They do not happen every day, and certainly do not occur where one may happen to be on any given day. Bluefishing is similar to the way my fishing buddy, Frank Miller, described his job as an airline pilot, flying the route from Miami to Quito, Ecuador: "….hours of boredom punctuated by a few heart-pounding moments". It was not unusual to stand on the cold, windswept beaches for days at a time without any sign of bluefish. Then, from out of nowhere, sometimes even without a telltale flock of gulls, the surf would boil with bluefish, attacking anything that moved.

Jim Santangelo and I arrived at Nags Head on Saturday morning. The others, three of whom were colleagues at The Ohio State University Hospital, would join us the following Wednesday night, as none were able to arrange an entire week absent from their duties. By then, Jim and I were to have scoped out where the most promising locations were. That, of course, was an exercise in futility, as the locations of blitzes, if any, are different from day to day. But we did try to determine if there was any pattern to reports picked up on CB radio, at bait shops, and from other fishermen. There was not. In fact, there didn't seem to be much going on anywhere. We knew that this would not be what our friends would want to hear.

It was very late on Wednesday night when they arrived. They were equipped with a Ford Explorer, suitable for the beach, and the usual complement of tackle. They were not equipped with a CB radio, but Jim and I had a spare unit, which could be quickly jerry-rigged to provide a serviceable, if not very neat, means of communication. They were anxious to fish, and so, they opted to trade sleep for daylight, and we all set off before dawn on Thursday. Since our scouting had produced no results, we determined to send the vehicles in opposite directions. But, in our haste, we had forgotten to rig them with the spare CB unit. That omission, as it turned out, set the stage for a bizarre and unforgettable sequence of events, still twenty-four hours into the future.

Jim retained his CB handle "Tonto", even though the faithful Scout had been, by then, retired, replaced by a sand colored, Diesel Suburban. Its huge capacity meant that we no longer had to pack light. We didn't have to pack at all....just throw things aboard. There was always room for more. Jim played his ethnicity to the hilt. He maintained that the vehicle was insured by "Mutual of Sicily" and inside one of his gear containers was a plaque reading:

> *Give a man a fish, and he will eat for a day.*
> *Teach a man to fish, and he will eat for a lifetime.*
> *Send a man to sleep with the fishes, and he ain't your problem no more.*

Jim and Tim Reese, and Randy James, weren't exactly sure, at first, how to take all of that.

Jeff and I boarded the Suburban, idling, lights off, in the pre-dawn. It wasn't hard to find, probably to the chagrin of our neighbors in the condo complex. Just follow the loud grung-grung-grung-grung sound. The others followed a few minutes later. We did not see them for the rest of the day. We were cruising Route 12, when someone said, "Birds!" The chase was on.

Jim took the next access ramp onto the beach some distance south of the Oregon Inlet bridge, and drove toward the flock. The gulls were definitely in feeding mode, and not fifty yards off the beach, but there was something not quite right here. There were only a half dozen vehicles on the beach, and there were only three fishermen in the water, casting to the school. We could see feeding fish breaching the surface. But no one was hooked up. What was going on here?

Whatever it was, we were going to be part of it. We dashed from the vehicle toward the beach. A man leaning against a pick-up truck yelled at us, "Hey! Don't bother. Fat Alberts."

Jeff never broke stride. "What?" he shouted back.

"Not blues," the man shouted. Then, at the top of his lungs, "FAT ALBERTS!"

Seeing that we had no intention of stopping, he shook his head and turned away. Of course, we had no idea, then, what "fat albert" meant. We could see feeding fish, in range, under an armada of greedy gulls. Not fish? Ridiculous. All three of the initial casts splashed down directly in the midst of the school. Everyone steeled against that certain, violent strike, white-knuckled grips on rod handles. All three of the four ounce, chrome plated spoons returned unscathed to the rod tips. Not possible! Repeated casts also yielded nothing. Whatever these fish were preying upon, they were apparently not interested in bluefish spoons. But then someone had a strike. The fish out there was certainly not a bluefish, or if it was, it was a very small one. The fish had not struck, but was snagged near its tail. The very next wave to break over us was one of disappointment.

The fish released on the beach was small, dark blue, and nearly football-shaped. It proved to be a false albacore, also called a "little tunny" or a "fat albert". They are a member of the tuna family, but are oily, bloody and fit only to be used for bait for larger predators. That was why the admonishment, "Don't bother". A misadventure? Not at all. This is how Joe learns.

Later that day, we had stopped at Oregon Inlet to compare notes with a group of other fishermen, who were standing on the beach, sipping coffee and chatting. No one was in the surf, casting. Their experience for the day mirrored our own: no action. There were birds, well off shore, circling a fairly large area, but not feeding. The consensus was that they were over a school of baitfish, but that the baitfish were not being driven to the surface by predators. At length, one of the men said, "Well, I guess somebody ought to have a bait in the water", and he began to cast the edge of the tidal outflow of the Inlet. His companions just shook their heads. "Keeps him busy." observed one of them. The rest of us had turned our attention to the possibility of catching sea trout on the sound side of the Inlet when we heard an exclamation from the lone angler in the surf: "Hey!"

All eyes focused on his surf rod, now a quarter circle arc, but our eyes did not dwell there for long. There was a unanimous dash for the surf. There were only a half dozen hook-ups among the twelve or fifteen anglers, but each of the three of us were lucky enough to find ourselves fast to strong and determined adversaries. By the time they were beached, the flurry was over. This event was not really a blitz, just a small school of stragglers looking for a fortuitous meal drifting seaward in the tidal flow. But, we asked ourselves, why wouldn't that sort of event recur over the rest of the afternoon, as long as the tide lasted? We thought we should contact the other vehicle, and let them know of our success, however limited. Repeated calls failed to produce a response. Jim discovered why. The spare CB unit was still on the cargo deck of the Suburban. There followed resolute pledges to correct that situation.

We had been wrong. There were no recurrences. Casting a heavy spoon as far as possible is a tiring business, and we switched to bottom rigs – something called a "fireball", which consisted of a foam ball at the hook, painted fluorescent red, and intended to keep the bait, cut pieces of mullet, off the bottom and away from crabs. This, too, was unsuccessful, but spared exertion. It was dark when we finally gave up and returned to the condo. When our friends discovered that we had caught fish, they were not happy with our failure to equip them with the CB unit. I said that I would immediately attend to that.

"Here's the keys. Lock it up when you're finished. Our tackle's in there."

"OK"

It took thirty minutes, or so, to install and check out the unit. The others were cleaning fish and seeing to dinner, but not before the traditional happy hour, which I realized I was missing. I concluded the task, relocked the Explorer, and thrust the keys into my pocket. By the time I got back inside, the place was filled with the aroma of broiling bluefish, and a group of fishermen who were already fairly happy. The Columbus group was short on sleep, and decided that they would not participate in a dawn patrol. Jim Santangelo, too, decided that some additional sleep would be welcome. So, Jeff and I would take the Suburban in the morning, but would not range very far from base, so that communication could be maintained. It was agreed that we would go only to the nearest beach access.

Friday morning, December 5th 1997, well before daylight, Jeff and I walked out onto the porch. The sky was lightly overcast, only a few stars were faintly visible. The wind was down, and the air was fairly warm, in the middle fifties. It held the promise of a nice day, maybe even a good day. But then, that's how dawns are for fishermen….always full of promise. We drove to the first access ramp on the National Seashore, a place called Coquina Beach. Driving the beach in the dark has its hazards, and so we stopped a short distance from the ramp, probably several hundred yards. It was still far too dark to see birds anyway. We rigged with four ounce Hopkins spoons, the local favorite, according to the bait shop, and walked toward the water's edge, still invisible, but given away by the sound of breaking waves. We waited for that first glimmer of dawn, facing the eastern horizon.

The faintest glow in the eastern sky revealed something amazing, at least to midlanders like us. As the ocean-borne swells rose and began to break, they were a transparent blue-green, looking through them into the light, with the rest of the sky still dark. And in them were hundreds of fence posts, all oriented in the same direction, facing the beach. We stared at that vision, trying to resolve what we were seeing.

"Bluefish!" Jeff shouted and launched the Hopkins eastward over the surf. He was instantly jolted by a violent strike, and I lost no time in putting a spoon in the water, with identical results. As soon as these two fish were beached, they were unhooked and left in the sand. We wanted to get lures back into the water as soon as possible. This school might move off at any time, especially with the brightening of the sky. As yet, at least, there were no gulls, and not a vehicle as far as we could see in either direction. This was a private bonanza, and we were determined to make the most of it.

These fish were incredibly aggressive. If a fish failed to be hooked in a strike, another fish would attack in seconds. Lines were broken as a hooked fish, lure still visible in its mouth, would be savagely struck by another bluefish, the combined load too great for the tackle. And the strikes were sledgehammer blows; a rod not tightly gripped would be gone. A hooked fish would be followed all the way to the beach by other fish, and we learned to back out of the surf, with a hooked fish, to avoid painful "kicks in the shins", collisions by those pursuers. Tackle was taking a beating. Fifty pound test, braided, stainless steel leaders would be shredded after beaching a few fish, and the heavy, treble hooks on the Hopkins spoons, the points normally equally spaced, would be compressed into a single plane by the crushing power of bluefish jaws. They don't call them "choppers" for nothing!

We had beached perhaps a dozen fish when Jeff suggested, "Hey! We ought to let those guys know!" I was reluctant to do anything but fish; this was a once-in-a-lifetime moment. Anyway, I tried to raise them, without success, and returned to the water. There were still no birds, and we marveled at that. But there were vehicles pouring onto the beach. How they knew was a mystery. There was no intercept of radio messages. We hadn't sent any. There was no telltale flock of gulls. Within minutes, there were 4X4's parked for hundreds of yards, up and down the beach. And there were hook-ups over all of that distance. This was an enormous school.

And then, from nowhere, there were gulls, countless gulls. The surf was littered with menhaden fragments. Menhaden which had avoided being chopped in half were driving themselves up onto the beach by hundreds and thousands. Gulls were brushing our faces with their wings, diving for baitfish pieces. The water began to betray the scale of the carnage with a red tinge. I had never experienced anything even remotely like this, and, likely, never will again.

Back at the condo, our friends had observed the massive flock of gulls, realized what was happening, and made for the Explorer, in what can be grossly understated as….haste. There, they stared at one another in disbelief. No one had the keys! A frenzied search of the condo did not turn them up. Then dawned what had happened, and I am sure that that my name was taken in great vain.

Jim and Tim Reese, and Randy James, summoned a taxi, to at least get them to the Coquina Beach ramp. The taxicab could not negotiate the beach, so Tim and Randy crossed the ramp on foot. Jim stayed with the driver, to be sure that they had a way to get back. Randy stayed near the ramp, in case we would return there from another direction, while Tim jogged south along the beach. At length, he found us. Both of us had fish on. Tim waded out to me, and asked, as politely as the circumstances would permit, whether I had, by any chance, his keys in my pocket. (Those were not his exact words). I was greatly embarrassed to discover that, in fact, I did. Seeing that we were some distance from the ramp, and knowing how anxious they were to get in on the action, I said, "Take the Sub. Keys are in it", jerking my head beachward. I gave the matter no more attention. I was otherwise occupied.

What I did not know was that there was a tan Jeep Wagoneer parked on the beach, almost directly behind me. I was vaguely conscious of somebody, four or five fishermen down the beach from me, yelling, "Hey! That's my truck!" but neither Jeff nor I were interested in the used car business at that point. Upon beaching the next bluefish, I noticed that the Suburban was still where we had left it, and concluded that Tim had decided to return to the ramp on foot. I also noticed that three or four vehicles were headed towards the ramp at unusual speed. It struck me as odd that anyone would leave the scene, with this mother of all blitzes still in full swing, but….whatever.

It was not until later that Jeff and I found out what happened next. Tim, in the inadvertently stolen Jeep, was making tracks towards the ramp. Behind him, in a friend's truck, was the enraged owner and his wife/girlfriend. Following them were two other vehicles, occupied by indignant vigilantes, intent on bringing this desperado to justice. As Tim approached Randy, he wondered why Randy seemed to be looking past him. He stopped, got out, and approached Randy.

"Where's the Suburban?" Randy demanded.

"Why, it's right……..Oh, my God!"

Now, Randy James is a big man, about six feet four inches and, I would guess, at that time, about two hundred sixty pounds…none of it flab. And that was a very good thing. The owner was, in Randy's words, "ready to kill" as he approached Tim with his impromptu posse. But the sight of Randy, standing between the owner and Tim, was sufficient to make them a bit more….thoughtful. By then, a group of ten or more people had collected. Randy recalled that it reminded him of the outraged townsfolk in the Frankenstein story. There were no clubs and pitchforks, but the wife/ girlfriend was holding a filleting knife. As Randy tried to calm the waters, the cab driver ran up. "I'm an official cab driver", he said, "and I saw the whole thing."

"That defused the lynch mob," Randy recalled, "and they finally calmed down and went back to fishing." The group returned in the cab to the condo, and I have to think that the cab driver got one of the best tips of his career. At least I hope so. I never asked. In fact, as the cause of this fracas, I was pretty quiet and humble for the rest of the trip.

That blitz, incredibly, went on all day. Jeff and I returned to the condo about noon, exhausted. We returned to the beach about mid-afternoon, and the beach was still shoulder-to-shoulder with fishermen (you will recall that the term is not gender-specific), all of them leaning backwards against arched rods. There was a wide band of baitfish fragments on the beach above the waterline, being ignored by engorged gulls, no longer flying, but waddling along close to the dunes.

Our observation was that at least 95% of the bluefish caught were released. They are not locally prized as table fare; they are oily and strong. But I love them. They taste like a by-God fish, not some white, bland, chicken-like, over-battered, sauce-smothered entrée in an upscale seafood establishment. The circle eventually stopped making the long trip to the Banks as the bluefish migrations declined. The last two trips resulted in not a single jumbo blue being caught, neither by our group nor by anyone we talked to. We do not know why. Perhaps no one really knows, despite a considerable amount of research having been done on the matter. There are several theories. Perhaps the striper fishery, resurging along the Outer Banks as a result of diligent and successful management, has presented bluefish with untenable competition for prey.

Bluefish populations are known to be cyclical, and maybe someday the migration will return to the Banks in the grand scale of those days. I hope so. A bluefish blitz, breathless, heart-pounding, exhausting, is unique among fishing experiences.

Or, for that matter, among any experiences.

Chapter 10
Coral Corral
Paradise Found

It is said that even a blind squirrel finds an acorn once in a while. This was one of those instances of being in the right place at the right time. To avoid the necessity of having to relocate, I had just changed jobs. I had joined a company which built custom manufacturing systems, and its customers were the best known names in consumer durable products: automotive, appliance, furniture, and the like. The marketing strategy of that company was what is known as "relationship selling", that is, building long-term, personal relationships with the buying decision makers in customer companies. One of the practices used to foster that strategy was to host a winter fishing outing for a select group of customers.

I was new, and unaware of that tradition; I was still trying to avoid getting lost in the plant. One morning, my boss, the president of the company, came into my office. "I've got an assignment for you. I need you to host a group of customers for a week". I assumed that he meant while they were in town for equipment try-out, or contract negotiation.

"OK. When will they be arriving?"

"They're not coming here. You'll meet some of them in Atlanta, and the rest in Fort Lauderdale".

"What's going on in Fort Lauderdale?'

He was becoming unable to contain a grin. "Nothing. From there, you'll fly them to the Bahamas. We have some cottages rented there, and a guide hired, on a little island called Green Turtle Cay. You have to help them catch fish, and whatever else they want to do. You play poker?"

"On occasion."

"Do you win at it?"

"Sometimes."

"Well, not on this trip. You will be playing customer poker. Your job is to lose, and lose big. Here's how it works. Their companies require that they pay their own expenses, and show receipts for everything. Your job is to be sure that they win all their money back, and that everybody's happy, all of the time. The fishing is great, so keeping them happy on the boat won't be a problem. Off the boat, just keep the liquor flowing, and make stupid bets."

The words that flashed across my mind were, *"Aw gee, do I really have to?"*

The cottages and the guide were reserved for two weeks. For each of those two weeks, two company representatives would host four to six customers. The first week, the company guys were to be Otto Perry and myself. The second week, my boss, and another person, would take over the hosting duties. Otto was the top sales executive of the company, and was a veteran of these soirees. Good thing. I didn't have a clue. The names of the customer people will be aliases, for the obvious reason given above.

Prior to departure, Otto briefed me on a few items. We would take with us several reels of 0.030" stainless steel weld wire……which was to be used for fishing line! Good Lord, I thought, how big *are* these fish? Otto assured me that we would need it. Break-offs were common! We would also be taking two cases of frozen, prime quality steaks, and some marine engine parts.

"Otto," I asked, "if the fishing is so good, why do we need steaks?"

"To bribe the customs officers."

"Why do we need to bribe them?"

"To get the engine parts into the country…..for Joe Sawyer, the guide."

He explained that the Bahaman import duties on manufactured items were outrageously high, and that Joe Sawyer would be very appreciative of the gift of these genuine, US built, Caterpillar parts. "It pays to keep Joe happy. If Joe's not happy, nobody's happy, and on this trip, you and I are in the happy business".

"Why don't we just bribe the customs guys with cash?"

"Oh, no. Can't do that. We'd be arrested and they'd be beheaded, or something. This way, they just confiscate the steaks, for not being officially inspected by the Bahaman equivalent of the FDA. Everybody's happy. See how it works?"

"Done this before?"

"Every year."

On the appointed day, we met Andy and Bill at the Atlanta airport, and Charlie, Dave, Ed And Frank at Fort Lauderdale. There we boarded an ancient DC-3, operated by a local flight service, not US-based, for the trip to Abaco. This operation was, to say the least, casual. The pilot – there was no co-pilot - wore a uniform, of sorts, and did his pre-flight, walk-around inspection with a cigarette dangling from his lips, being careful to avoid the oil dripping from the front main seal of the port engine. Perhaps the best description is to imagine the actor, Lee Marvin, as cast in one of his seedier roles, in the cockpit of a very well-worn airplane, starting the engines, then turning around, grunting, "seat belts", through the missing cockpit door, and firewalling the throttles.

From a fisherman's point of view, the scene below, as the islands appeared, was nothing short of a beatific vision. There were vast areas of dark green grass flats. There were beaches, gently sloping into turquoise crystal water, some of which plummeted abruptly into deep blue troughs surprisingly close to shore. There were mangrove thickets bordering narrow channels between islands. And, there were coral formations, large and abundant, with displays of color easily visible from the air. To the east of Abaco

Island, beyond its barrier reefs, was the open Atlantic, blue water, and the color declared that it became very deep, very quickly. There was no habitat lacking here for any of the warm water species.

At customs, everything happened just as Otto had said that it would. From the Treasure Cay air strip on Abaco, one small metal building, but an international airport nonetheless, it was necessary to take land transport to the water-taxi dock. Like the English, Bahamans drive on the left side of the road, but the vehicles were all, at least in the early 1980's, American cars with steering wheels mounted on the left side. It all seemed very clumsy, but it also seemed to work perfectly well. The water-taxi was a simple, open boat, benches on both sides, with a canvas top, high enough above the deck that there would be little shelter in a wind-driven rain, but it did provide shade….more important in this climate.

As the boat was being tied to the dock at Green Turtle Cay, mangrove snappers of about fifteen inches could be seen loitering around the pilings, along with unidentified smaller fish. Andy, who had been here before, saw me looking at them. "You know what they call those snappers down here?'

"No."

"Bait! You'll see what I mean tomorrow."

We were met on Green Turtle Cay by a man with a very compact pick-up truck, so small that he was able to drive it out onto the wooden dock. All of our gear went into the bed, into the cab, and onto the hood, of the truck, and we walked the several hundred feet, up an easy grade, to the two cottages. "Cottage" is not an accurate word. These were houses, one the size of typical, suburban, ranch style house in the states, the other a bit smaller. And they were well equipped, including two Bahaman women who had been retained to attend to cooking and laundry. I had been instantly catapulted, however briefly, into Group Two!

Joe Sawyer came by early in the evening to make sure that our tackle was in working condition after a year's storage in a closet in the cottage. He observed that most folks do not adequately clean tackle used in salt water, but it appeared that last year's party had done a good job. Normally, a charter service would furnish tackle, but Sawyer was not a charter captain; he was a lobster fisherman. He had been convinced, primarily by Yankee dollars, to charter his boat to the company for two weeks each year, in February, when the sea temperature was at its lowest. Joe, his brother, and their associates, caught lobsters by diving – no scuba gear, just mask and fins – and didn't care all that much for the chilly waters of February. So, the charter was truly what is popularly referred to as "a win – win deal". And the lobsters were not "lobsters" in the Maine lobster sense, they were langouste, or spiny lobsters, also called "goosters" by local folks in the Florida Keys. They lack the huge claws of Maine lobsters, and so, harvesting them by hand is a bit easier. All one needed was to be a superb swimmer, and to be able to dive to thirty feet and stay there for two or three minutes!

The Sawyers had been on the islands for generations, descendants of English settlers. That was typical of the caucasian residents of the island, many of them, like Joe Sawyer, tracing ancestors back into the 1700's. Sawyer's speech was neither British nor American.

It was English language, but accented differently than any I had heard before, and spiced with phrases that were Elizabethan. He sounded a bit like a Shakespeare play, and was not easy to understand. Moreover, he did not appreciate having to repeat himself. The pressure cycles of diving had taken their toll, and he did not hear well, further impeding the communication process. He had been off the islands only once, and that to pick up his boat in Florida. Green Turtle Cay had a great deal of local color. Joe Sawyer was vivid.

After two glasses of Bourbon, which he by no means sipped, Sawyer rose and solemnly announced, "Be on the dock at 8 o'clock, for I shan't wait."

Travel is tiring. The poker game that evening did not last long. I was able to lose only about a hundred dollars. I resolved to do better on succeeding evenings, but it requires a great deal of self-discipline to fold with four queens.

At exactly eight o'clock the next morning, Sawyer, always barefoot and usually attired lightly, no matter the weather, was tying off his thirty-seven foot , twin Diesel, Fliteline cruiser at the dock. This was a serious boat. And it was clearly a working craft, clean, but with little attention paid to the spit-and-polish cosmetics of the typical charter boat. We may have leased him for two weeks, but Sawyer's demeanor sent the unmistakable message that he was absolutely the captain. He issued orders as if we were seamen, or, at best, ensigns, in the Royal Navy. This guy was the real-life Captain Quint. I had to lean over the transom to be sure that "Orca" was not emblazoned on it. We would see some things later that would not have made that name inappropriate.

The boat was equipped with outriggers, but they had obviously not been used in a very long time. They were corroded and salt-encrusted to the point that they could not be deployed without a lot of reconditioning. Without them, only two of the eight of us could fish at a time. I was very disappointed at that situation. It meant that one's turn came around only on every eighth fish. I would learn two facts: 1) strikes were only minutes apart, sometimes seconds, and 2) every eighth fish often didn't provide enough rest between fights.

Sawyer gave us some cursory instruction. The bait to be used was a small fish called a balao, or ballyhoo. It looked something like a miniature marlin, with a pronounced bill, which extended from the bottom, rather than the top, jaw. He showed us how to hook the ballyhoo on the trolling rig, which consisted simply of a braided steel leader attached to a small hook, for attaching the baitfish, and two very large hooks which rode beside the baitfish. The ballyhoo was then split from the tail almost to the head. "Keeps it from spinning," he explained.

Sawyer issued orders to cast off, pointing at one or another of us and rasping, "You!" preceding each command. He started only one of the Caterpillar Diesel engines. Both of them, he explained, even at idle, resulted in too high a speed for negotiating the narrow channel out of the harbor. "Wake disturbs these fine gentlemen", he sneered, waving toward a group of yachts moored in azure water along an ivory beach. Green Turtle Cay was a popular stop for the cruising community. And, it turned out, was also a popular transfer point for certain "entrepreneurs" importing Central American agricultural products into the United States. Sawyer would never allow his boat to be out of the harbor after dark for fear of encountering them. "They run without lights, and will slay you without thought."

Once outside the harbor, the other engine was started, and I settled in for what I expected to be a long run. It was not. Within a few minutes, Sawyer throttled back, but only to a speed that allowed the hull to come down off plane. Then he called back another command: "Fish."

Andy and Bill were first up in the two rear-facing fighting chairs. At what

I considered a ridiculous trolling rate, the ballyhoo skipped and danced across the water. Jagged coral structure was visible about ten feet down, but no detail could be discerned, despite the clarity of the water, because of the speed. I had just concluded that this technique could not possibly work when Bill's heavy boat rod doubled over and the sizable Penn reel, its drag set just below the breaking strength of the weld wire, shrieked. "Fish on!" somebody yelled. I expected Sawyer to throttle back to idle, or go to neutral. He did not. He increased both throttles. The sudden and unexpected increased drag on the already heavy fish pulled Bill out of the chair, to an awkward and unbalanced standing position, at which point Dave grabbed his shirt, and thrust him back into the seat. If there had ever been straps on these fighting chairs, they were long since gone.

Sensing our surprise at his unexpected maneuver, Sawyer shouted back, "Had to pull 'im up out of the rocks. Otherwise, you would never get 'im up." He shook his head. "Nay. No chance". It made sense, and we were prepared for the technique after that. Once Bill had worked the fish to within thirty or forty yards of the boat, Sawyer did throttle back to idle, and shifted to neutral. Then he scampered to the transom, pulling on a pair of heavy, gauntleted, leather gloves. Bill was standing now, both hands on the rod, lifting. "Keep 'im up, now......up......UP!" screamed Sawyer. Bill was doing all that he could. He had extended one hand up the shaft of the rod, almost to the first guide, to improve his leverage. He was perspiring, and his face had the teeth bared, muscles tense, appearance of a weight lifter. We could see a dark but reflective shape in the water, a deep-bodied fish, side turned against the line, pulling hard for the shelter of the coral. "Ah," Sawyer grinned, "nice mutton snappah."

As the leader appeared, Sawyer grasped it. I saw a gaff hook in a cradle at the transom, and handed it to him. "No! No! No! Put that away," he growled. "I want no blood in the water....nor in the boat, neither. Do ye wish to reel in nothing but heads?" He heaved at the leader, and over the transom tumbled a pewter colored fish, with faint vertical bars, and the classic snapper shape. I could tell it was snapper family, but it was otherwise unfamiliar. In fishing the Florida Keys, I had seen a variety of snappers, yellowtail, red, mangrove, vermillion, but never one like this. It was not only different in color, but was the largest snapper I had ever seen in real life. We were all staring at it....all except Andy and Otto, both of whom had been here before. "Mutton snappah." Sawyer was pointing just below its dorsal fin. "See that black spot?"

The fish was neither weighed nor measured. I had expected a large chest filled with ice to be somewhere aboard, but Sawyer seized the fish under a gill cover, unhooked it, and dropped it into a wooden crate lashed against the transom. Everyone knows that a fish should be iced down, or gutted and gilled, or kept alive, if it is not to spoil. Everyone knows that a fish in a dry, closed box, in the sun, on an 80 F day, for six or eight hours, would be rejected even by vultures. And what everyone knows is wrong. According to Joe Sawyer, the best way to preserve the flavor of a saltwater fish until the end of the day is to keep it warm and dry. I did not believe that. But it was so; seven straight days of undeniable proof.

Charlie took Bill's place in the port side fighting chair. The weld wire line had to be paid out, by hand and with care, to avoid kinking. A kink irreparably weakened the wire, and kinked wire had to be discarded. The procedure was to loosen the drag and strip wire off against a light drag – not to do it with the reel spool disengaged. Charlie was about to show us why. He had no doubt concluded that it would be easier to unreel the wire with no additional drag, and so he disengaged the spool. The ballyhoo was only about thirty feet behind the transom, still in the propwash of the port propeller, when the wire was torn from Charlie's hands by a vicious strike. Almost instantly, the free-spooling wire was a stainless steel Gordian knot. The reel could neither release, nor retrieve, "line", which meant that the load on Charlie's arms and back could not be limited by the reel's drag mechanism. The wire hadn't broken, and, at length, Charlie expressed the wish that it would. But Joe Sawyer would not hear of it.

"Ye shan't cut that line! This matter is of his own making, for I told all of ye how to do it. Let him learn. Rest of ye, too." Sawyer turned his head forward and resumed the troll. He did not back off on either engine.

Charlie was beginning to look as though he was in real distress. We decided that the only sensible way to land this fish would be to cut the wire at the rod tip and attach it to a spare, empty reel. Someone would have to hold the line, until it could be fed onto the spool of the spare reel. This we would do with a pair of rusty vice grip pliers that was one of many sundry items on the top of Sawyer's console. Dave was just about to borrow it, without permission, when Charlie gasped, "Unh!" in a tone that brought all of us to the fighting chair.

The wire line was nearly slack, much to Charlie's relief. The fish was clearly gone. "Must've snagged a big rock back there. That broke the wire. Look at my shoulders. Is there an arm on each one of 'em? It felt like that snag yanked 'em both off!"

We assured Charlie that both arms were still in place, however useless they might seem at the moment. Then we began to recover the wire, hand over hand. There seemed to be too much drag on that wire for it to have broken. We concluded that the terminal tackle must still be attached. Only the fish had escaped. That conclusion was not entirely correct. The terminal tackle was, in fact, still attached. Also attached was the head of another large mutton snapper......cleanly sheared just behind the gills. "Shawk!" muttered Sawyer. "Dom them."

Captain Sawyer

The tangle of wire would have to be cut away from the reel. We just stowed that rod, to be dealt with later, and substituted another, which had been respooled with new wire the previous evening. Dave took his place in the port side fighting chair, and did not make the mistake that we had so dramatically witnessed.

The ballyhoo rigs were not trolled very far behind the boat. Distance wasn't necessary. These fish were not in the least intimidated by the boat. I marveled at that. Before Dave had unspooled enough wire to be at what would have been considered normal trolling distance, Bill shouted, "Strike!"

Again, Sawyer accelerated for a short distance, then turned to watch. Bill was sure he would be scolded for some misdeed or other in handling the fish, and periodically glanced over his shoulder at our captain. But Sawyer was apparently satisfied with Bill's technique. Bill was what my river rat friends would have described as "a big ol' boy", and he muscled that fish away from the jagged and abrasive coral structures with some considerable authority. And again, Sawyer dashed to the transom, gloves donned, and drew over it a fine yellowtail snapper. I had caught yellowtail in the Florida Keys, but nothing like this one. The Florida record is a bit over seven pounds. Bill's fish was at least that. But Joe Sawyer did not seem impressed. He simply tossed it unceremoniously into the wooden box, and returned to the helm.

Both Ed and Frank, in their turns, boated equally nice yellowtails. Then, I took Frank's place.

I had never used tackle of this nature before. The rods were equipped with roller guides, useful because the sharp bend of the wire over a static guide was avoided. These rods were clearly intended for heavy fish. The reels were affixed to the reel seats with four bolts, and had no level-wind mechanisms. It was up to the fisherman to distribute the line relatively uniformly across the spool, not easily done with a powerful fish at the other end of that wire. The fighting chairs were equipped with a gimbaled socket just below the front of the seat, and I made sure that the butt of the rod was securely seated in it. I could just imagine the tongue lashing that Sawyer would mete out if I allowed a fish to take that rod away from me. And I had seen the violence of the strike that had left Charlie with nothing but a snapper head. But, I was not at all prepared for what was about to happen.

We had trolled the extent of a relatively small coral reef, and Sawyer was moving toward another. He turned and announced, "No fish for a while. We're over a barren bottom. But keep the baits in the water. May be a school of dolphin anywhere." Ed and I relaxed a bit, but we both still held those rods in a death grip. The reef that Sawyer next intended to fish was less than a mile away. It would take less than seven minutes to get there, but with the early pace of action, it seemed a long time without a strike. Its bottom was featureless white sand, gleaming aquamarine in the sun. Nothing here. We were lulled into admiring the lush islands, most uninhabited, to starboard, and the purple-blue open sea to port. Then, from behind, someone hit my rod with a baseball bat. It was a sharp, stinging blow, an electric shock. "Uh….strike", was all I could manage.

Sawyer advanced the throttles, even though there were no coral structures here to avoid. But instead of the increased load I expected, the tension on the wire decreased. And it no longer trailed out behind the boat. It was off to starboard. This fish had run parallel to our course and was in front of us, opening the distance.

Sawyer saw what was happening, and turned sharply to port. He feared that the fish might cut across the bow, double back, and foul the propellers in high strength steel wire. When the wire came taught, it felt as though I was fast to a Sherman tank in full retreat. The drag clutch uttered a screaming objection. Then Sawyer eased back and shifted to neutral. We were over clean bottom. The fight was on, one on one. The 600 horsepower boat was no longer a participant. My companions watched, anxious to see what had been where no fish should have been. This was not like the previous hook-ups, tug-of-wars with strong, constant resistance. This was an affair of mad dashes, interspersed with moments of slack wire. This fellow, whatever he was, behaved like a northern pike. A northern pike on steroids, but a northern pike… complete with charges towards the boat. By the time the leader began to show, we were both exhausted. Sawyer was at the transom, and seized the leader. Then he spat. "Dom bah-cuda". There was to be no sparing of the gaff on this fish.

It was indeed a barracuda. Again, I had caught barracuda in the Keys. And again, not like this one. It was half again the length of the largest I had seen in Florida waters. Sawyer cut it open with a large knife, and threw it overboard. "Food for the shawks", he growled. "Keep the lines in the boat. We're movin'. No use for bah-cuda."

Sawyer ran at cruising speed for several miles, to another coral reef complex. Then, he throttled back and commanded that we resume trolling. Otto replaced me in the fighting chair. He was a veteran of this venue, and I was interested in his technique, but he appeared to do nothing that any of us had not done. Five or so minutes passed without a strike, then ten. Otto began to relax in the warm sun and gentle pitch of the boat. I saw Sawyer glance back at him and smile. He tightened a thumbscrew to lock the helm. Then he crept to behind Otto's chair and gave a sharp chop to the lower shaft of the rod, bounding back to the helm and looking straight ahead. Otto snapped awake and vigorously set the hook on a phantom fish. "Damn! Missed him."

Otto fixed his attention on his bait, back behind the boat, then began to frown. He glanced at the rest of us, all of whom stared innocently out at the horizon. Then he looked at Sawyer, who was unusually intent on the course of the boat. Otto broke into a grin. "That son of a bitch", he chuckled. "I'll get you for that, Joe", he shouted over his shoulder. Sawyer did not move his head. "Ye shan't", he chirped back. The gauntlet was down. Otto was a one-upsman. This would be interesting.

For the rest of the day, every species but yellowtail snappers were released. Yellowtail are fine table fare, easy to clean, and not so large that the fillets were inconvenient to fry, as frying was the preferred cooking method of our two cooks. The only foods they did not fry were pies and bread. The wooden box on the fan tail was too full to retain its lid as Sawyer maneuvered to the dock. I pulled Otto aside. "Eight guys are never gonna eat all these fish!"

"I know. We give 'em to the cooks, who sell or trade 'em in town. You want fresh key lime and coconut pie, you give 'em fish. Understand?"

"Oh. Yeah."

Sawyer drew a weatherbeaten 2 by 10, about 4 feet long, from the boat's sleeping quarters, now used as a storage bin. He placed it diagonally from a gunwale to the transom, then opened a fantail hatch and retrieved a long, curved knife. In minutes, he had deftly filleted the whole days catch, dumping the offal overboard at the dock. Now I saw why those mangrove snappers loitered there. They, and the smaller fish, immediately began to dissect the carcasses.

"Eight O'clock, now. Don't be late."

Sawyer cast off, and headed towards his own slip in the harbor. With one engine, idling, the boat, despite its size, left scarcely a ripple in the blue mirror water of the harbor. It was moving away towards the sun, setting despite the early hour, in the short days of February. Here was an idyllic scene, in this bay ringed by palm trees, blanketed by cloudless blue…..one to remember. I always will.

There followed showers and martinis, not necessarily in that order. As bartender, I made sure that the drinks were generous, and that no glass was ever empty. The strategy was that very relaxed poker players would not perceive that nobody could play as ineptly as I planned to play.

The dinner prepared by the Bahaman cooks was ample and superb. Appetizers were conch (pronounced "conk") fritters, the flesh of the conical shellfish pounded thin, and, of course, fried…..crisp. These were followed by candied yams and platters of fresh yellowtail. The fish had been marinated in the juice of native oranges, large, a beautiful, deep orange color, but utterly inedible in their raw form. They were far more tart and acid than a lemon, but perfect for the present use. They were referred to as "sour oranges" - totally appropriate. Desert was coconut pie, from coconut harvested and hand shredded that afternoon.

Overwhelming.

Otto and I served brandy and passed out Cuban cigars, unobtainable in the United States, but available in the Bahamas. The inevitable poker game ensued, and I was successful. I lost $240. It broke up fairly early. A day on the water and a heavy meal sent the group to bed before 11 PM.

We were all on the dock at 7:45. At precisely 7:55, down the harbor, we could hear the burbling exhaust of one Cat marine engine. It was barely light, but Sawyer was on his way. He seemed clearly pleased that we were all assembled and ready, but said nothing. The sky was overcast, for the most part, high thin clouds, but here and there, a black blister below the cloud deck. The bay surface was no longer a mirror. There were visible serrations of a light chop. "Everybody have a good, hearty breakfast?" We all nodded. "That's fine," said Sawyer, "There'll be a wee roll on the hocean today. A full belly prevents seasickness." We were not convinced of this bit of folklore.

Out of the harbor and around the point of the island, we could see what he had meant. There were swells, but not breakers, rolling from the east, that indeed caused the boat to roll, and not exactly gently, when trolling abeam of the sea. But the fish were not inhibited by the action of the water, and, before day's end, we had boated over thirty large fish, of a variety of species. Sawyer lamented that no dolphin (or dorado, or mahi mahi, whichever you prefer) had been taken. Most of the fish were released, but the wooden box was as full as on the previous day.

Sawyer had been right about the seasickness. Whenever any member of the party began to feel queasy, Sawyer insisted that they eat a sandwich. It worked like magic, even though it is, to say the least, counter intuitive. Sawyer also insisted that we stay well hydrated. We had brought no water aboard, and so, the only agent of hydration was beer. This, too, was counter intuitive.

But this, too, worked. Learning never ends.

The day's end program was the same: showers, copious libations, a great dinner, and the poker game. I erred seriously. The dealer specified a game that was replete with wild cards, pot matching, and the like. It was a game of luck, not of skill, and I ended up winning a huge pot. It was terribly embarrassing.

The following day, the wind was up. The sky was crystalline, and upon rounding the point of the island, whitecaps were prominent on the open ocean. Fishing again defied description. About mid-day, Sawyer announced that we were going to troll outside the coral reefs for dolphin. Despite the rough seas, the bottom was discernable in 60 feet of water. It was slate colored, and featureless. "More line," ordered Sawyer, "let out more line." We dutifully obeyed. Sawyer kept looking over his shoulder. Then he pointed. "There. Bull dolphin following!"

Hard to see, but not impossible, was a form, glowing neon blues and greens, a few feet behind Dave's balao. Sawyer then did an unexpected thing: he firewalled the throttles. As the balao accelerated away from the bull, he charged and seized it. Dave had a solid hook-up. Then Sawyer pulled back to idle, and shifted to neutral. "Don't bring him aboard," he screamed, "the rest of the school will stay with him." We had not seen any "rest of the school", but, sure enough, the boat was almost immediately surrounded by dolphin.

"Now," cackled Sawyer, "just drop yer ballyhoo overboard." In seconds, everyone was fast to a dolphin. It was, to use the old expression, a Chinese fire drill. Chaos reigned. Falling over one another, trying in vain to keep lines untangled, trying to keep fish out of the propellers and rudders, trying to bring heavy fish to boat, we must have looked like, not the three, but the eight, stooges. Sawyer was leaning on the console, roaring with laughter. "There. There, now. Is that enough excitement for ye?"

The eight of us finally managed to bring six dolphin aboard. And they were huge, none under three feet in length. The bull looked to be nearly five, but no one measured. "Aye, now there's some eatin' for ye," chortled Sawyer. The two not captured escaped because wire lines became entangled, and two anglers, on opposite sides of the boat, ended up in a tug of war with one another, while both fish, with the terminal ends of the lines slack, slipped the hooks.

One of the tangled lines was cut, and retrieved with the other line. Sawyer inspected the remnant carefully, and, convinced that all of it was accounted for, and not a hazard to his propellers, re-engaged the clutches. After an hour, in which no more schools of dolphin were encountered, Sawyer returned to the certainties of the coral reefs. Again, action was non-stop, and the wooden box was filled. It was as if these coral structures were fish pens…corrals….into which fish had herded like cattle.

That evening, one of the guests suggested that the local nightlife be explored. Nightlife? This was the far end of the continental shelf, a small island in the middle of nowhere. There was one tiny town. It occupied perhaps twenty acres, thirty at the outside. I looked at Otto. He nodded. "Okay," he said, "let's go to the Blue Bee".

The full name of this establishment was "Miss Emily's Blue Bee Bar". I had no idea, but it was internationally known. At one end of the bar was a huge glass bowl, containing thousands of business cards, in every imaginable language, some from countries I had never heard of. The cruising/sailing community had obviously been patrons of this rustic, semi-open-air watering hole for some decades. And it was popular with locals as well as tourists. It was crowded, and noisy.

Miss Emily was holding court behind the bar. She was black skinned; whether of African ethnicity, or some other, I could not tell. She was weathered looking and of what age I could not determine either, except that it was not young. But she was animated and dynamic, and engaged in one-liner repartee with customers, always giving better than she got. I told you that this madness called fishing exposes one to a lot of characters. Miss Emily was certainly one of them.

The speciality of the house was the Goombay Smash. There are today many imitators, but Miss Emily claims the origination of this delicious, but extremely potent, beverage. It was served in a styrofoam cup; no Waterford crystal here. The exact formula is Miss Emily's secret. One would have greater success trying to obtain the formula for Coca Cola. It clearly contains rum and some extract of coconut, but beyond that, the ingredients are a mystery. The house rule is that if a patron can drink four Goombay Smashes and leave the premises on two feet, unaided, the drinks are free. Folklore is that less than a dozen have ever accomplished that feat.

Bill was, as I have told you, a "big ol' boy". He calculated that, with his body mass, and his experience as a hard-drinking, auto industry Detroiter, if anyone could do it, he could. And so, he set out to so prove. The evening was warm, and the Goombay Smash cold and sweet. The first two are easy. With the third, one becomes a bit more thoughtful. Not Bill. He ordered a fourth. By this time, a ring of patrons had gathered to see this Olympic event. It took some time for him to drain the fourth foam cup, but he did it. "Now," he announced, lurching to his feet, "I'm gonna walk out of here."

And he did. But not unaided. He upset drinks on two tables on his way to the door, and had crashed into a post before sagging onto one knee. Two of us propped him up and got him safely outside. But the walk back to the cottages was about a half mile, uphill, on a jungle trail. If Bill went down, we were not sure we could get him home. We decided to rest a while and let him metabolize some of the ethanol. After about an hour, given Bill's solemn declarations that he was perfectly able to walk, we started up the trail. Bill had overestimated his abilities. He walked directly into a tree. Of and by itself, not a catastrophy. But this tree had been split by a hurricane, and its wound was covered in a slimy ooze of fungus or bacteria of unknown description. Bill's face was lacerated and was awash in this noxious, evil smelling goo. Otto and I had unspoken visions of a business disaster that we would have a very hard time explaining away.

We got Bill into the cottage as quickly as we possibly could. There, we began to scrub the slime from Bill's face. The stuff was sticky and not easily removed. It had to be painful, and we were all aware that Bill might not be totally conscious of why we were doing what we were doing, and that he might react, let us say, defensively. Bill had several unkind things to say about us during this process, but Otto, also a fairly big man, engaged him in conversation using the same tone and terminology as Bill, certainly unfit to relate, containing a number of four letter admonitions, to which Bill finally responded grudgingly, but favorably.

Andy had a tube of antibiotic ointment among his personal gear, and we slathered Bill's face with it. In the morning, Bill's face was a kaleidoscope of red, purple, blue and black, but there was no sign of infection. Bill's demeanor was contrite, and he did not feel well, internally, but he emphatically stated that he was going fishing. And he did, boating the largest mutton snapper of the trip. He declined to have his picture taken with it, however.

Incredibly, we returned to Miss Emily's that evening. We were much more moderate in our consumption of her featured beverage, but moderation in Goombay Smashes is almost an oxymoron. As my river rat friends would say, "They aint no sech thing." Nevertheless, the evening passed without incident, and we returned to the encampment at quite a respectable hour. Otto and I somehow felt guilty.

Morning exploded upon us bright, clear and breezy. At exactly eight o'clock, Sawyer was lashed to the pilings. "Well, let's be about it. Going to be bumpy today." That was an understatement. The boat writhed in a building sea. It was a symphony of roll, pitch and yaw. Within an hour, everyone was feeling the effects of the previous evening, and there frequent offerings of abdominal content to the sea. Sawyer was not affected. Strangely, neither was I. Sawyer was a veteran seaman, but I was not. Why was I spared? I got in a lot of fishing that day, as one after another declined their turns in the fighting chair. It seemed that the rougher the sea, the better the fishing. The box was again filled, almost singlehandedly. As usual, a number of fish came aboard with nothing aft of the gills, and displaying a truly frightening bite radius. What a great day!

My companions gratefully climbed onto the dock, its firm and motionless nature a refuge from the endless disorientation of the rolling, pitching, twisting sea. In an incredibly short time, their *mal de mer* was extinguished. Feeling sorry that they had lost a precious day in paradise, I bounded onto the dock to offer my regrets at their misfortune. But as soon as I stood upon firm ground, I was instantly nauseous, and threw up three times on the 200 foot walk to the cottage. I could not explain that. Still can't.

The next morning, Sawyer showed up at breakfast. He had walked from the harbor. His boat was still moored. "Bad news for ye," he began. 'The hocean's in a rage today. No wind here. But there's of certain a storm off to the east. Not going out. Couldn't keep ye aboard. Waves this high." He reached as far as he could over his head.

I could see that the waters of the bay were flat. "How about any inshore fishing?" I did not want to spend the day serving drinks and playing poker.

"Well, now. Do ye mind getting' yer feet wet? We could do some bonefishin' over on the grass flat between the islands."

"Sounds great!" I had only ever heard about bonefish. I had never even seen one. I had no idea what this was about, but whatever it was, it was better than being indoors.

"Well, I'll bring m' rowboat over in about an hour. Don't wear anything ye don't want wet."

"Wait. I don't have any light tackle."

"I'll loan ye mine."

I turned to the group. "Who's going?" There were no responses. I felt guilty. It was my job to entertain these guys. But this was the chance of a lifetime, and I was not about to let it pass. I had given them the opportunity, and they had declined.

Fishermen are great at rationalization.

I met Sawyer at the dock. He was equipped with an aluminum jon boat, powered by a 5 horsepower outboard. I was comfortable with this. This was more Joe style. Sawyer handed me a five and a half foot spinning rod with a small, Penn open faced spinning reel, spooled with six pound test monofilament line. He saw me staring at the reel. "Ye buy anything but a Penn reel, ye're throwing yer money away." That was Sawyer's opinion, and I would find that this day would test it.

Sawyer motored around to a sandy beached cove, ran the boat up on the beach, and jogged along the upper edge of it. He dropped to all fours and began digging furiously, like a dog recovering a cached bone. He dropped something into the pocket of his shorts, then continued along the beach.

Four times he stopped to dig. Then he returned to the boat. "Here. This is the bait." He held up four small, white crabs, about the diameter of a fifty cent piece. "Ye hook 'em in the corner of the shell, like this. Don't hurt 'em. Ye want 'em live and scamperin' along the bottom."

Then, he motored to a narrow pass between two small islands. He beached the boat. "Now, out with ye. Wade over that grass flat, quiet as a mouse. When ye see a tail out of the water, cast about ten feet ahead of it. Let that crab walk. And when a bone picks it up, let 'im run. Oh, maybe fifty yards or so, bail open. Then, set the hook. Don't tighten that drag none, ye hear me?"

I was barefoot, and shells in the sand really hurt my feet. But I did as Sawyer had instructed. In a few minute's time I saw a tail, just as he had said. My cast overshot the fish's path, and I reeled the crab into what I thought was his trajectory. I opened the bail, and waited. With a soft whoosh, line began to unspool from the reel. Fifty yards. How far is fifty yards? Heart pounding, I waited as long as I could stand. I snapped the bail closed, and whipped the rod vertical. Line screamed from the reel as if tied to a bullet. And the run went on and on and on. I glanced at the spool. Line was disappearing at an alarming rate, and would soon be gone. This fish was heavy for this light tackle, and something had to be done. I reached for the drag clutch.

Sawyer was watching. "No, dom ye!" he shouted from the boat. I could see spool through the line as the run finally slowed. The fish turned to the left, and was well over 100 yards away. I was able to recover some line, but then the fish suddenly turned to the right and ran again, but this time in an arc, taking only ten or twenty yards of line. Again, I could recover some line, against a determined sidewise pull, pumping the rod. I might have gained forty or fifty yards when the fish ran again, almost emptying the spool. But then, I began to recover more than I lost in each run. This fish was not easily run out of fuel. It was nuclear powered. And it was still a football field away.

But, with patience, and faith in Sawyer's instruction, ultimately, it was in my hands. Sleek, silver and beautiful, I cradled it and waded back to the boat, stopping often to wet its gills so that it could be released unharmed. Sawyer would have none of that. "Ah, Momma will cook that up for ye. They say they're not edible, but if ye know how to cook 'em, some of the best meat in the hocean. Turn any more ye catch loose. This one's enough."

I caught three more that day. This living torpedo has more horsepower per pound than an Indy car. I could only hope that the "hocean" stayed in a rage. This was far preferable to catching forty pound fish on a heavy boat rod and wire line. This was a challenge; a test of skill and finesse. And you didn't need a twenty thousand pound, 600 horsepower boat.

All you needed were unspoiled waters and a great coach.

Shortly after noon, Sawyer called me back to the boat. "Let's pick up a few conch for fritters." It was just as well; stalking tailing bonefish across the grass flats, trying to position for a cast, was tiring. They are alert and spooky, and always bolt just as you are finally within a few yards of casting range. So, spot another tailing fish, and begin a slow and cautious approach, vectoring on where you think that fish will be in the time it will take to quietly cover the distance. The quarry is a fish, but this sport is, in reality, hunting.

Sawyer maneuvered the boat into a sandy cove, beached it, and waded into the water, motioning me to follow. He was always shoeless, and his calloused feet seemed impervious to the many broken shells on the bottom. Mine were not. That pleasant little beach had a floor made of barbed wire. But large conch were plentiful, and we soon had a dozen or so on the bottom of the jon boat. The animals had all retreated, out of sight, into the massive shell. The shells looked empty, but the weight of them betrayed the presence of the conch inside. "Let's get back. I'll show ye how to get 'em out."

The jon boat tied to the dock, Sawyer went into the cottage and returned with a plastic five gallon pail. It took two trips to deliver all of the conch to the cottage yard. There, Sawyer produced an implement called a conch hammer. It resembled the tool often seen in the hands of archeologists or geologists; a handle bearing a head with a blunt face on one side and a curved point on the other. "These shells are stout," Sawyer began, "but there's a thin place right along this row of bumps. See there?" With a light blow, the pointed end of the head penetrated the shell. "Now ye work along this row 'til it spirals into the center. Try it." It wasn't as easy as Sawyer had made it look, but at length, the animal was exposed.

Just then, one of the cooks walked by, with an armload of sour oranges. "Hey Sawyer," she taunted, "you sure doin' it the hard way, mon." Sawyer looked up and snorted, but said nothing. When she had gone, Sawyer leaned over to me. "Ye know how they do it? They take a fish hook on a wire and reach up in the shell and hook the meat and hang it up in the sun for a day or two. Then the shell falls right off….aye, when the conch's half rotten! Is that what ye want to be eatin'?"

The blunt end of the conch hammer, upon closer inspection, was not really blunt. It had a cross-cut pattern – like a miniature waffle iron. This Sawyer used to pound the meat into thin strips. "There, now. Have those cooks fry these up," he said, handing me half of the strips. "And don't let 'em use any but these." Once again, Sawyer had been right. That evening's conch fritters were far superior to those we had eaten earlier.

Otto had not used all of the steaks in clandestine international trade. He had wisely saved enough to compensate for a day of poor, or no, fishing. Seven of the group dined that evening on corn-fed Midwestern beef. I ate bonefish, prepared by Mrs Sawyer in thin, boneless slices, under a sauce made from a fruit I did not recognize. It might have been citron. The bonefish flesh was very good……..but it was no Great Lakes perch. I resolved that if I ever had another chance to fish for bonefish, it would be strictly catch-and-release. Somehow, it was wrong to remove such a fish from the sea.

The next day, the group split up, half of us going with Joe Sawyer, the other half with his brother, Ian. I opted for Ian, who was not going to fish the coral reefs, but troll the outer edges of them for pelagic predators, such as king mackerel and dorado. "Might even hook a billfish," he had half promised. That was irresistible. Besides, Ian's boat was a twenty, or so, foot Boston Whaler, completely stripped, no upholstered seats, no console, powered by an Evinrude 150, steered by a long tiller which had been crafted by the local blacksmith.

Now, this was a Joe-style fishing boat!

Two of the four of us could troll at a time, the others sitting on the deck, against the curve of the bow. There were no gimbals to secure the butts of the rods, and Ian had no rod socket belts. This meant that the trollers, bracing themselves against the gunwales, had to hold the rods in ways they thought best minimized potential damage to their bodies resulting from violent strikes. Heavy rods and wire line offered little shock absorption. Each of us secretly backed off on the drag clutch settings. This was all backwards. Open water trolling should have been done in the large boat. But, this was the way the Sawyer boys had decided to do it.

Ian was younger than his brother by, it appeared, a decade. He was also a great deal more talkative. He kept up a constant stream of tall stories, local gossip, and jokes, all in appropriately salty language. Where his elder brother would tolerate no profanity aboard his vessel, Ian was a fountain of it. But he was a competent sailor, as we were trolling in four foot seas without a drop of sea water coming aboard. One advantage of the tiller over a conventional helm was that Ian could execute lock-to-lock steering corrections almost instantly. But shifting to neutral or to reverse was clumsy, accomplished via a home-made lever extending through a slot hacked into the engine cowl. Ian didn't use it much.

The first hook-up was a "chicken dolphin", a female dorado of moderate size. Dave boated it without Ian's help. "Glad it wasn't any bigger," he muttered, rubbing his side just below the rib cage. That gave us all pause. Because the fish had not been the bull, the leader of the school, the others did not follow it to the boat. But, Ian observed, there were dorado in the neighborhood, and that we should all be prepared. "Careful how ye hold yer rods," he admonished, "or they'll make a soprano out of ye!" Andy had an idea. He strapped on a life jacket, upside down and backwards, his legs through the arm holes. That idea quickly caught on, and we all mimicked it. I remembered that my cousin, tail gunner in a B-17 during WWII, had told me that that was how the ball turret gunner had worn his flak jacket. One has to prioritize.

We boated some fine dorado that day, but no kings. Some of the dorado, of course, came up only as heads. Andy was fast to a good dorado when one of the sharks took the entire fish, and Andy was now connected to a very heavy adversary. "Five, six hundred pounder," Ian offered. It was no contest. We did ultimately cut the wire. The next morning, Andy's midsection, despite the cushioning of the inverted life jacket, was a patchwork of storm-cloud colored bruises, and he complained of aches in his wrists and fingers. "I'm sticking to the big boat," he announced. That resolution was unnecessary. Ian was otherwise occupied, and so, there were no choices to be made. But Ian had been an adventure. I had been fortunate to be aboard.

We continued these trips for the next few years. But changing business conditions, and the fact that the owner, from whom we had rented the cottages, had retired and decided to live in one of them, ended these wonderful adventures. The last evening of the last trip, I went to stand alone on the dock. It was dark by then, but there were two star-emblazoned skies – one above, one in the mirror of the harbor. There was no moon, but the cumulative light of innumerable stars backlit the palm trees and mangroves. I could keep this image.

It would be unbearable to leave this island, but, by accidental, and incredible, good fortune, I had been here. Once again, fishing had taken me to a beautiful place, taught me lessons, introduced me to colorful characters, and gifted me with indelible memories.

It was well said by some screen writer, whose name I do not know, but whose work I admire, in the great, classic film, *"Grumpy Old Men."* The grandfather, mid-nineties, played by Burgess Meredith, is addressing his son, played by Jack Lemmon, in front of an ice shanty on a frozen lake in Minnesota:

"…….it's the experiences, son. It's all you've got. It's all there is."

Chapter 11
The Land of Kah-weh-teh-kon
Fishing Sacred Waters

About 90 miles east of International Falls/Fort Frances, on the north side of the US/Canadian border, there are 1.18 million acres of carefully preserved wilderness, accessible only by canoe. Stringent rules protect its pristine and spectacular beauty. There is no development. There is no logging. There is no mining. No power equipment of any kind is permitted. With a few precisely specified exceptions, no bottles, cans, or non-burnable containers may be taken inside its borders. There are no roads. Access is by permit only, with the number of permits carefully limited. And so, in this lake-dappled, river-strung sanctuary, primeval wilderness is alive, and well, and living in Quetico Provincial Park.

And the Canadian Provincial Park managers, bless them, intend to keep it that way. Canada's resolve to maintain the quality of the Quetico experience is serious.

And so it should be. To the original inhabitants, this was sacred land. So breathtaking was its beauty and so abundant its wildlife, that the Ojibwa considered it the birthplace of creation, the analogue of the Garden of Eden of Judeo-Christian tradition. This was the dwelling place of the Great Creator Spirit, the benevolent giver of life, and omnipotent constructor of the universe. It is thought by some historians that for centuries, Ojibwa neither lived, nor hunted, inside the area. They visited this land only for religious ceremonies, and to paint sacred pictographs on its cliffs and rock faces. These are still visible. These granite structures were the Sistine Chapels of an ancient faith. They were acts of worship offered to, as nearly as the name can be decoded, Kah-weh-teh-kon. Over time, the name was contracted to K'weh-teh-ko. English speaking explorers made it Quetico.

As Jim Massey, fishing buddy, and geologist by profession, remarked, "They may well have been right about this being the birthplace of earth. This *is* the oldest rock on the planet."

Our circle had heard of this place, I do not recall how, whether in print, or spoken word. I doubt if that knowledge came electronically. It was a bit too early for that. I suspect that somebody knew somebody who had been there: the anglers' grapevine. In gathering intelligence for a planned trip, we found that the process of obtaining an access permit had greatly enhanced odds of success if done through a Canadian outfitter. So, we determined that we would rent canoes through such an agency, rather than to cartop our own for a 2200 mile round trip. That decision was confirmed when we learned that the outfitter's canoes weighed twenty-five pounds less than our heavy-duty, rock-banging, river freighters. With many portages of canoes and gear, that was a worthwhile incentive. Not hauling canoes also meant that we could fly commercially to International Falls, submitting to airline indignities, but saving a day on each end of the trip. The plan was cast.

The group spent months refining our kit. We bought, modified, or built, and tested, ever lighter approaches to everything. We had set a specification that no pack could exceed 40 pounds. That, plus a 65 pound canoe, would be about the limit that inexperienced, no longer young, overweight, and out of shape fishermen could carry. We had intended to be conservative in that specification. We learned that we had been optimistic.

The eldest members of the group, Jim Santangelo and I, decided that we would paddle at least 50 miles in preparation, and that we would hike, carrying a pack containing forty pounds of ballast, at least a mile a day.

We actually approached the paddling goal, but found that carrying a forty pound pack for a mile was so easy that we abandoned that portion of our training. Later, we would find that solid and level ground was far less a challenge with a forty pound load than a log-strewn, steep, slippery trail, or a portage through knee-deep, sticky muck. And we were young then – barely 60 years old.

The other members of the group were my son, Jeff, reassuringly, to Jim and I, a cardiologist, and his colleague, Jim Reese. (You met him in the chaotic adventure at Coquina Beach.) Their thrust was to get as far as possible, as soon as possible, into the remotest possible area of the park. Jim and I, on the other hand, had accumulated enough bitterly purchased wisdom to know that remote, hard to access areas were not necessarily the best fishing. And, after all, wasn't fishing why we were going?

We contracted with Canoe Canada Outfitters, located in the nearest town to the park's access points, Atikokan, Ontario, to put us up in their bunkhouse the first evening, as the flight schedules got us to Atikokan quite late in the day. They also provided transport from I-Falls (the local contraction), canoes and paddles, permits and licenses, and, most important of all, a paid consultation. That consultation was the most cost-effective investment we ever made, on any fishing trip, in any venue, in our collective lives.

In the consultation, Jim Clark, partner in Canoe Canada Outfitters, provided a detailed map, marked with W's, B's, T's and P's. These cryptographs stood for walleyes, bass, lake trout and pike. He told us which waterways on the map were passable and which were not. Referring to one of them, he said, "This is blocked with a lot of deadfalls, but you guys can just blast through there, and save some paddling." We were to find that to "blast through" that spot would have required a Royal Canadian Navy icebreaker. But as to the fishing spots, he was always dead on. Towards the end of the session, he made a remark that we did not really understand. He leaned back from the map table, removed his glasses, and regarded each of us for what seemed a very long time. Then he said, "Enjoy the paddle. Fishing here is almost silly."

We were then directed us to a local restaurant called The Diversion. "Tell 'em you'll be there for breakfast at seven. Order in advance. We're haulin' you out of here at eight, eh. You're gonna burn a lot of calories tomorrow!"

The Diversion wasn't a restaurant, it was a history classroom. The walls were enlarged photos depicting the diversion of the Seine River to drain Steep Rock Lake, an enormous and ambitious project in the 1940's. There were huge deposits of high quality iron ore beneath that lake, and that was nothing short of a national treasure during WWII. Antique mining and earthmoving equipment was displayed about the place, and once the staff and the local folk saw us studying those and the murals, they were happy to treat us to an extended history lecture, not only regarding the mine, but the park as well. A summary is worth retelling.

The ore deposit had been discovered in 1897 by a geologist, William McGinnis. But no action was taken until 1929, when a Duluth mining company was convinced to undertake the job. The magnitude of the task was underestimated. Unfortunately for the war effort, no ore was recovered until after the war had ended. But the mine was active until the 1980's, and its ultimate shutting down worked great economic hardship on the boom town of Atikokan. And boom town it had been. Before the project, real estate along Main Street sold for $10 per acre. Shortly after the project was announced, the price rocketed to $100 per frontage foot!

The story told to us about Quetico was fascinating. The ice age had left a land crowded with lakes, oriented in roughly the same east-west direction, and connected by rivers. That is why it is possible to canoe for long distances with few, and short, portages. (We would find that "few" and "short" were relative terms.) This topography shouted "northwest passage" to the government in Ottawa, and several plans were proposed to open the waterways for larger craft, to develop dams and locks, and to bring commerce to the country to the northwest, connecting it to the Lake Superior port of Thunder Bay. To the native population, this was sacrilege to the land of Kah-weh-teh-kon. An uprising ensued. The government conscripted a militia to put down the uprising……from among prison inmates. There were such numerous atrocities that public opinion began to turn against the policy, and the "militia" was disbanded.

On the other side of the border, Theodore Roosevelt, conservationist and great proponent of national parks, assumed the Presidency in 1901. He strongly encouraged the Superior National Park, and in 1913, Ontario established Quetico Provincial Park as its adjacent Canadian twin sister, with similar restrictions on development and similar commitment to preservation of pristine wilderness. The Ojibwa, convinced that the Land of Kah-weh-teh-kon would not be desecrated after all, abandoned resistance. Quetico has been treated with reverence and respect ever since.

We also learned that every species of mammalian wildlife found in Canada resides in Quetico, except for polar bears. The name Atikokan is Ojibwa for "caribou bones". And, we would soon find, to our dismay, that the "shy woodland creatures" are not very shy in Quetico. Of course, no weapons of any kind are permitted…and that means ANY kind. Everyone has heard the expression "defensive driving". We adopted a strategy of defensive paddling, defensive camping and defensive fishing. That strategy's value would be later confirmed by an incident which was……memorable.

Jim Clark had given us the usual greenhorn advice: never run from a bear; never look a bear in the eye; group together to make yourselves as large an entity as possible….all the conventional wisdom. Then, he gave us some unexpected advice. "Don't hang your food packs in a tree. Two reasons. Bears can climb like squirrels, and the higher off the ground, the more the wind carries scent. Pull the canoes up on shore, eh, turn 'em over, and put the food packs underneath. Keeps scent down and makes a lot of noise if you do get raided. Don't pitch your tents near the canoes. That way, nobody gets surprised, eh." Our eyes must have been pretty wide at that point. He seized upon it. "Besides," he grinned, "we've had very few bear attacks this spring."

We got little sleep in the bunkhouse that night. Between anticipation of the coming strenuous adventure, and contemplating the statistics of Clark's "very few", deep and restful slumber was elusive. It was the first week of June, and daylight came early and chill. We loaded on carbohydrates and red meat at the Diversion. We expected to be scolded by our cardiologist companion, but his menu choices were worse than ours. "It's OK," he said, brandishing a fork loaded with pork sausage, "you're gonna get plenty of fish oil omega 3's to balance it out." And that, we certainly did.

At eight o'clock, we loaded our gear into the outfitter's van. We were amazed at how easily our driver singlehandedly lifted the canoes onto the van's racks, six and half feet, at least, off the ground. Of course, he only made it *look* easy. He was about twenty years old, and did this every day.

But we were duly deceived, and imagined that we would soon be handling them with equal deftness. It was a fairly short run to a wide spot in the gravel road, where our driver pulled to a stop. "OK. Here's the portage. You're on your own from here on. See you at French Lake in a week, eh? About four in the afternoon." He stood aside, clearly signaling that getting the canoes off the rack was our job.

It took two of us to remove each of the canoes, and that was embarrassing. Once we had the gear offloaded, with no further instruction, he was gone. There was no water visible, but there was a trail. Most of it traversed a mucky swamp, but a primitive boardwalk had been built, and the portage to Nym Lake, which we considered to be demanding, was the easiest that we would see. There were two options, according to the map. The shorter of the two was a trail to a small lake, crossed by canoe, followed by another portage to reach Nym Lake. The longer was to portage directly to Nym by another route. We chose the shorter. We would later learn that we had made a bad choice: loading, boarding, debarking and offloading required more time and effort than the extra distance would have.

Across Nym Lake, large, and choppy that day, was another portage to Batchewong Bay. From there, the map showed that we would travel by water for quite a distance. At that time, we had no GPS. But I had a topographic map, and I had a compass, and a former orienteering merit badge counselor should know how to use them. That was not my worry. My concern was that we would try to go too far, too fast, and be caught with daylight fading, trying to find a campsite, with a tired, hungry party.….all of the ingredients of haste and carelessness, potentially leading to injury. Or worse.

But good sense prevailed. With a good four hours of daylight left, we found a pleasant campsite at a narrows. To the north were broad stretches of shallow, weedy water. To the south, a small bay and a narrow cut, which opened to provide access to a number of lakes. To the east was a long lake, connecting to still other waterways leading east and south, to yet other waterways, and so on…..and on…..and on. It was decided that "the old guys" should establish camp, while Jeff and Jim Reese sought to catch supper. They paddled north into the shallow, weedy bays, and, before we had a fire ring built and a fire started, they returned with four large smallmouth bass – two each.

"This enough? We can get plenty more." We thought that their catch was more than sufficient, but were anxious to get in on the action. "String 'em to that root, and show us where all of this is going on."

"Not a hundred yards from here. Come on."

It was hard to believe. A surface plug cast over any hole in the weeds instantly produced a violent strike, followed by an aerobatic exhibition. And these smallies were biggies. I do not think that we boated one fish under 2 ½ pounds, most running much larger. All were released. Then, someone observed that the sun was free-falling towards the horizon, and that we had better do the rest of the task of pitching camp, and of cooking dinner. Then we all remembered that there was, in fact, a gnawing hole in our stomachs. We had, as Clark had said, burned a *lot* of calories. We stroked towards the campsite with considerable vigor.

Highly motivated, the group established a serviceable camp in very little time. While none of us had visited Quetico before, all were veterans of the outdoors, knew what to do, and did it quickly. The stringered bass were taken to a distant exposed rock and filleted, while a fire was built and utensils retrieved from the 30 gallon plastic trash container that had been modified into a back pack. We called it "the utility module". It contained the tent, tarp, saw, axe, cooking gear, dishes, and the non-food grocery items, such as paper towels, soap, and the like, as well as rope, twine, and the most essential of all supplies, duct tape. And, it was heavy. Try as we might, we could never even come close to the forty pound limit. It was at least sixty pounds, perhaps seventy, but once strapped on, a feat virtually impossible to accomplish alone, it was, surprisingly, not all that hard to carry. And it was, in those few minutes that evening, virtually emptied.

We used an extravagant amount of precious cooking oil to semi-deep-fry those fillets. It was worth it. The fillets were tender, succulent and sweet – the characteristic of the bass/bluegill/crappie family – with that also characteristic hint of pleasant mustiness. We ate all of them, probably twelve pounds of fish, live weight. Two of those packaged rice dinners, alleged to serve four each, also vanished. One of the party, I think it was Jim Reese, suggested that we recapture the oil by filtering it through paper towels back into its plastic bottle. A foil funnel was constructed, lined with a paper towel, and the operation proceeded, with some limited degree of success, and considerable spillage. We feared that all we had succeeded in constructing was a bear lure.

The party soon yielded to leaden limbs and sandy eyelids. Nor was there any enthusiasm for a dawn reveille. Spots of sunlight, animated by a light breeze, danced on the tent walls, and from a steep angle, before anyone arose. The night had not been cold, but departing the sleeping bags still resulted in a short-lived chill, which the sun outside the tent quickly dispatched. Jeff was already starting a fire. "What kind of fish do you want for breakfast?"

Knowing that bass were apparently readily available, I tossed out, "Walleyes".

"OK. Come on, somebody." Jim Reese accepted that invitation, and the two were quickly in the water and on their way. Santangelo and I relaxed, put the coffee pot on the grate, and planned to brew coffee, have a cup of it, and then go consort with smallmouth bass, while awaiting their return. The water had not yet boiled when we heard the scraping of a canoe bottom on the rocky shoreline. Walking over to the edge of the bank, I could see that there was no stringer attached to any of the thwarts. "Give up already?" I taunted.

"Uh….no", said Jeff. He reached into the bottom of the canoe and withdrew a foil package. "Here". He tossed it to me. Inside were the fillets of four walleyes, all ready to cook.

"That didn't take long! Where'd you get these?"

"Oh, we just started casting Rapala crankbaits on these rocky points." He waved generally eastward.

At breakfast, we agreed that we were beginning to see what Clark's cryptic remark had meant. At least for these two species, fishing here *was* "almost silly". Someone suggested that we do as Clark had suggested: "Enjoy the paddle", that is, break camp and travel. I objected. "Wait a minute. What more could you ask? These smallmouth are big, and they're all over that bay. You guys just proved that the main channel there is full of walleyes. It's like Frank Miller always said: 'Never leave fish to find fish'". Jeff argued that we had layed out a route and a plan, and that we should follow it. That was countered with the observation that the plan had not come down from Mount Sinai, and that it could be altered, if we pleased. At length, the decision was to spend the rest of the day at this camp, and to move on tomorrow.

I do not know how many smallmouth bass we released that day. I am sure that the number was in three digits. In mid-afternoon, Jim Reese turned around in the front seat. We had decided at breakfast that the canoes should be manned by one each of the younger, and of the older, members of the group. That conclusion grew from the fact that Jeff and Jim Reese were constantly outdistancing Jim Santangelo and I. Not only did we have an age disadvantage, but a weight disadvantage as well. This change helped to achieve a certain balance of power. "I've never caught a lake trout", Jim said. "Want to see if we can find one?"

"Sure."

As we paddled towards deeper water, where Clark had placed some T's on the map, I related an earlier lake trout adventure story. I omitted the fact that those were the only lake trout I had ever caught. Jim seemed to be listening with rapt attention. At least, he murmured, "Wow," several times. I didn't know whether that meant, "Wow, what an incredible pack of lies!" or, "Wow, I hope that same thing happens today!"

Clark had told us how to paddle troll for lake trout. They would still be shallow, he had said, this early in the season. That was one of the reasons we had opted for early June, balancing that positive factor against the negatives of black flies, mosquitoes and the possibility of cold, wet, weather at the end of the spring transition. I had fished in snow flurries this same week at Whitefish Lake. The technique was simple. Rods were not to be extended outward from the canoe, but were to be laid along its gunwales, parallel to the direction of motion. Reel drags were to be set with very little resistance, so that rods would not be pulled overboard by a hard strike. Clark had recommended crankbaits having a red, or orange, belly. This made no sense to me. A fish attacking from below, in this clear water, looking into a bright sky, would see only a silhouette. Why should color make a difference? But, in deference to his experience and knowledge, that is what we used.

Pursuit of lake trout turned out not to be "almost silly". We paddled a long distance before the first strike, and lost that fish. But, before the end of the day, we had boated two lake trout in the four to five pound range.

Where the Gulls Are

We released one of them, and planned to smoke the other, over alder wood, plentiful along every shoreline. From then on, lake trout lines were always behind the canoes while travelling, whether or not the waters being traversed had been marked with T's. You never know…….

Experiments with identical lures not having red or orange bellies proved Clark right. We clearly did not understand much about lake trout vision. We automatically assumed that it was similar to our own. It obviously was not. On a later visit to Quetico, following an unusually warm spring, we encountered early June temperatures in the high 90's, water warm enough to bathe in comfortably, and lake trout which could be taken only by vertically jigging in 100+ foot depths. There, the only successful lure colors were white or silver. Hook-ups were infrequent. There were better things to do.

Back at the campsite, we jerry-rigged a miniature smokehouse from aluminum foil, and smoked the lake trout. It turned out well. The oily meat of the salmonid family of fishes is well adapted to the smoking process. It was a fair sized fish, but it disappeared quickly, and had to be supplemented. The other canoe had kept no fish, and was dispatched to bring back two bass. That did not take long.

The plan to travel on the following day was cancelled by weather. A frontal system brought a heavy, all-day rain, punctuated by thunder storms. Jim Reese and I had paddled to the northwest corner of the weedy bay, when we saw that we were directly in the path of a very ugly storm. A well defined black edge, with impressive electrical activity and a gray curtain of rain, was approaching at an alarming rate. There would certainly not be time to get to the shelter of the campsite, at least a forty-five minute paddle away. We made for an overhanging rock face, about a half mile to the south. Shelter from the rain was not the objective. Avoiding being the highest object on the horizon, sitting in a metal shell, grounded by water, was the goal. Our teaming strategy had been wise. Having a young, strong, fear-motivated person in the forward seat was certainly an advantage. Rain, however torrential, will never drive me off the water. But mega-joule electrical discharges certainly will. And without delay.

We sat out the storm at the base of the cliff, bailing furiously with drinking cups. Our light, flimsy, back-packing rainsuits did not prevent our being drenched. And by late afternoon, the temperature had become a damp, chill, 58F. But we had boated some very respectable smallmouth bass, as well as several large northern pike, and counted the day a success, however uncomfortable.

The other canoe had similar experience. They were equally wet and cold, but grinning as we met at the campsite. "Storm didn't shut 'em down," Jeff enthused, " But we need to get these clothes dry." There were no objections to that motion. Rounding up birch bark and squaw wood, there was soon a most welcome fire dancing and crackling under the tarp used as a dining fly. As is usually the case, excessive impatience in the drying process resulted in minor scorching of some garments, but there was no damage that impaired usefulness.

The rain abated towards evening, to a chill drizzle. Preceding dinner, fresh, hot coffee, fortified with the rectified essence of Kentucky corn, as scripture says of wine, "gladdened the hearts of men". Enthusiasm to push on into deeper regions of the park , on the morrow, returned.

Breakfast the next morning was abbreviated: coffee and instant oat meal. Camp was hurriedly broken, and the gear loaded into the canoes. The laden craft were not nearly so nimble as those we had fished from on the previous day. But, with a steady, measured effort, an average pace of four miles per hour, in calm conditions, was possible. The objective was to reach a campsite on Rawn Lake, recommended to us by Jim Clark as a very good lake trout location. It was but 16 kilometers – 10 miles – but a determined headwind caused the paddle to require a full six hours of strenuous effort. Worse than that, we found the subject campsite occupied. We retreated to Rawn Narrows, a brief backtrack, given the wind velocity, and found a usable campsite. Here, seeking fish for dinner, we found that fishing was again certainly not "almost silly". It took serious effort to capture a meal. On balance, the change was almost welcome. It *should* be a challenge.

The campsite was on a small island, and we noticed that the trees were all completely covered with insects. Upon closer observation, they were dragonflies, swarming by the millions in this one, particular location, some at rest, some airborne. The constant drone of their wings was not just audible, it was loud, intrusive, irritating. But in return, there was not a mosquito on that island. The favorite prey item of the dragonfly, at least in that limited area, had been the victim of insect genocide. We were indeed grateful.

On this, and many following visits to the land of Kah-weh-teh-kon, we noticed that mosquitoes were not nearly the scourge that they always seemed to be in the bush in the country on the eastern side of Lake Superior. Part of the reason may have been that Quetico's forests were mature, original growth, with a dense canopy, and relatively little undergrowth. The forest floors were open, as opposed to the dense, impenetrable brush of the second and third growth forests where logging had been long practiced. Or, perhaps it was the climate, drier and windier than that on the eastern, leeward side of the Great Lakes, where lake effect precipitation prevailed, keeping the forest floor a soggy mosquito nursery. Whatever the reason, we were always delighted that, at Quetico, mosquitoes, while certainly present, were not the level of torment to which we had become accustomed.

We had expected that the steady, driving wind of the day would bring a weather change, and it did. The next morning, the thermometer which we used to determine water temperature told us that the temperature inside the tent was 35F. No one doubted its veracity. But the wind was still, the sky was clear, and we knew that the sun would soon remind the forest that it was, after all, summer. And so it did. By the time a breakfast of pancakes had been cooked, and the camp put in order, the air was still brisk, but pleasant. It was heavy with pine scent, and the water, in areas windward of the light breeze, was yellow with pine pollen, dislodged by the recent wind. The dragonfly hum was suppressed until the temperature had risen a bit, but then began in earnest. We decided upon a day trip to Art Lake.

Art Lake, an easy five miles distant, with only a short portage, and that done with only fishing gear, had been described by Clark as an excellent lake trout venue. With four days of paddling behind us, the requisite muscle complexes were beginning to learn the drill.

The portage to Art Lake paralleled the lake's outflow stream. The brief pool above the rapids, defining the difference in elevation between Art Lake and Rawn Lake, was full of visible fish. At first, we thought that they were whitefish, and there was gleeful hand-rubbing at the prospect of a baked whitefish dinner. But, they were suckers, at a distance, roughly similar enough to whitefish to be mistaken. Nevertheless, they were a species furnishing a forage source for the largest of northern, freshwater predators. This was a good sign.

Afloat in Art Lake, we could not help but to rest the paddles across the gunwales and stare. There are things and places that hold words and pictures in contempt; things and places that cannot be described by any word, or imaged by any medium; things and places that must be experienced. The land of Kah-weh-teh-kon abounds in such places. This was one of them. This language of the Angles and Saxons, refined over centuries, is among the most facile in descriptive power. But it is not equal to this task.

Jim and I began to troll what appeared to be a deep slot between two sheer granite faces, gray as slate, but sparkling with flecks of quartz, interrupted here and there by streaks of pink. The slot yielded four fine, fat lake trout, in the eight to ten pound class, certainly not trophies for a species whose official world record tops seventy pounds, but good fish indeed. In the upscale lodges of the Northwest Territories, or on a Great Lakes charter, they may even have been scorned. But this is Joe's world.

Three of them were returned to the clear emerald, cold and deep. The fourth would be salted, and incensed with alder smoke.

The other canoe had gone to the headwaters of the lake. There, in shallow weedbeds, they had boated twelve smallmouth bass of exceptional size. They kept only one. It was enormous. We guessed it at six to seven pounds. Jeff was shaking his head. "The thing is, these are as big as the biggest bass caught off the humps east of Kelley's Island in Lake Erie….but instead of two a day, it's two an hour. It's incredible…..it's fantastic….it's…it's……" Jim finished the sentence. "It's martini time".

At the portage, the canoes did seem lighter. We were able to shoulder them singlehandedly, just as our young driver had done. The paddle back to camp was, as they say, a walk in the park. No one leaned hard into the strokes. We were beginning to "enjoy the paddle", just as Clark had said. This was a place of such magnificence that it had to be absorbed, almost osmotically. It could not justly be remembered simply as a matrix of pixels on the retina. This was why a camera was utterly inadequate. We were beginning to "get it."

Recounting the day's events around the campfire, it was unanimous that moving camp again, to find something better, was not logical. It was difficult to imagine what "better" meant, unless it meant more secluded. We had, after all, seen several canoes. We had even encountered an occupied campsite. It wasn't the absolute and total isolation we had expected. In many subsequent visits to Quetico, we learned something. The human presence, in terms of people per square mile, need not be very large in order to encounter them, depending upon one's location. Several lakes and rivers in the park are virtual highways to hundreds of waterways leading off to a myriad of other rivers, lakes and campsites. Camp and fish on those main routes, and the odds of encountering voyageurs, however few, are near certainty. And that, on this first experience in Quetico, is exactly what we had done. Later experiences taught that seclusion is relatively easy: choose a dead end lake, one that is not a route to somewhere else.

But there is another lesson. We began to realize that perhaps the least fished waters were exactly those on the popular routes. We observed that everyone was paddling; no one was fishing. In a herd mentality effort to get to the most remote regions of the park, "where no one ever goes", most visitors ignored the waters nearest the access points. It was the old story of the two fishermen who lived in cabins on the opposite sides of a lake. Each morning, each of them would dash across the lake at full throttle…..to fish around the other's dock. Or, consider it fulfillment of the old proverb, "The grass is always greener………"

Not always.

The following dawn illuminated a forest basking in a mild 50 degrees. After the breakfast fire was doused, and the articles needed for the day were being rounded up, we discovered that the map was missing…..*THE* map – the one encrypted by Jim Clark. We had other topographic maps. There was no danger of being lost. But the fishing spots, the key intelligence item, the chart to the treasure troves…..gone! It could only have been lost at Art Lake, we reasoned. We had it when we arrived there; it was not in, or under, either canoe; it was not anywhere in camp; therefore, it must have been dropped during the portage out. Had it been blown overboard, unlikely because it was always kept on the bottom of the canoe, in a waterproof plastic bag, that would not have escaped notice. It would have floated, and would have been recovered. Backs strained against paddles, sprinting for Art Lake.

A tedious and careful search of the portage trail did not yield the missing map. Nor did a search of the windward shoreline. Nor did a search of the site where we had eaten a shore lunch. The search was abandoned; there was nowhere else to look. But, we had committed the unthinkable. We had littered this sacred place. The campsites we used had clearly been used before, and campsites we passed by had been used before. But nowhere was the least sign of carelessness. Not so much as tiny scrap of paper, not so much as a minute shard of plastic or foil was to be seen. People who used this land obviously respected it. And we, though not by intent, had now defiled it. That, not the information on that map, was the real loss.

High, thin clouds repainted the sky a milky blue. The mild morning temperatures, and the gathering moisture aloft, told us that foul weather was a likely forecast. The question, as always, was when. Tomorrow would be a long day of paddling, as we were scheduled to meet our driver at the pick-up point, the ranger station on French River, the headwaters of French Lake. There were several long expanses of open water to be crossed, and big water, stormy weather, and laden canoes are not a happy combination. But for now, there were fish in this liquid, emerald crystal, and to keep them waiting would be impolite.

We followed the protocol of the previous day. The bass enthusiasts kept only one bass, the trout fishermen did likewise, and we met at the appointed time for a shore lunch. More lake trout and more bass were released that afternoon. I could never have imagined that lake trout could be taken in mid-afternoon, trolling flat lines, with lures running no more than eight feet deep, yet that is also exactly what had happened at Wiggly Lake those many years before. I wouldn't believe that, either, except that I was there. One of the fascinations of fishing is that conventional wisdom so often fails. The mind must remain open to what is, and not run aground on what ought to be.

Trailing lures on the paddle back to camp, several northern pike and walleyes were boated in the narrow channel at the entrance to Rawn Lake. All were released. We had one trout and one bass already aboard, more than sufficient for dinner. But except for fish, food supplies were running short. We would have to rethink carbohydrate provisions for future trips. We were at that point that everyone who has ever tried the popular low carbohydrate diet eventually reaches: we would trade a magnificent, fresh lake trout fillet for one donut!

Dawn comes early at this latitude, and we were up with the sun. Breakfast was cooked, camp was struck, gear packed and loaded, and canoes launched, by 6:30. Bows were swung eastward, into a brisk wind. It seemed, in Quetico, that every paddle was against the wind, and every portage uphill….in both directions. We would learn, that day, that a tail wind was not necessarily a blessing.

Of course, tackle was not packed for travel. The trolling lines were always deployed. Estimating that we had sufficient time, a brief excursion was made to another promising looking lake on the north side of the main thoroughfare, Pickerel Lake. It produced a few, disappointingly small, bass and northern pike. The wind calmed, and then shifted, building steadily, from the southwest. Then came distant thunder. We headed for the south shore of Pickerel Lake for shelter, to a place called "The Pines". It had been marked on the map we had lost, but we remembered the location. Crossing Pickerel Lake was unnerving. The water had been elevated to whitecaps, and wind gusts, in the quartering sea, that is, waves coming from the stern at an approximate 45 degree angle, made it very difficult to hold course. This is where the sternman in a canoe earns his salt.

A single, small lake trout was boated in the crossing, and it provided lunch at The Pines. This place seemed *out* of place. It belonged on an atoll in the South Pacific. A gentle, wide beach sloped up to a glade surrounded by enormous, original growth pines. There was no undergrowth, but a mulch carpet of pine needles, decades, or perhaps centuries, deep. It was on the windward side of a bay, and windswept clear of mosquitoes. There was an awe to this place. These massive trunks were the living pillars of a great cathedral, whose windows were stained in a hundred shades of green, and in gold. Its dome was the sky, and its floor was luxuriously soft and aromatic. There is good reason why this land is called The Land of Kah-weh-teh-kon. There is good reason to forever preserve and cherish it.

The plan was to eat lunch while the wind and rain subsided. The rain ended. The wind continued to build. The generally quartering wind was our benefactor through narrow lakes and channels, but our enemy in the open water of French Lake. The canoes became almost impossible to control, and to allow one of them to be turned abeam of the waves would be disaster. Yet, that is exactly what the force of the wind constantly strove to do. But by this time, the canoe teams were working in concert, anticipating moves and reacting to unspoken signals. In less than two hours of fear-driven, maximum effort paddling, both canoes gratefully entered the mouth of the French River.

The river's current was considerable, but after the battle with the wind, it was nothing. The canoes were beached and unloaded at the ranger station. Our driver was summoned by telephone through co-operation of the ranger on duty. While awaiting his arrival, we availed ourselves of the displays depicting the history of the park, and of a brief movie on the same subject. These generally, but not completely, confirmed what we had been told by the local folk at the Diversion. On balance, in deciding whether to believe a government, *any* government, or the folks, I'll go with the folks every time.

The van arrived, heard before seen, crunching gravel on the road. This time, we, not the driver, single-handedly loaded the canoes on the van's racks. He looked pleased. "Made friends with 'em this week, eh? That's what usually happens." In the van, he had a small cooler, and opened it. "Don't suppose anybody'd like one of these?" He held out ice cold bottles of Molson's Canadian. It was ambrosia, malt nectar, *eau de vie,* to weary bodies. Canadians made jokes about thin, weak, flavorless American beer. The jokes were hard for Yanks to laugh at, because the theme was accurate. I once asked a bush pilot if the water in the lake we had just reached was safe to drink. "Tastes just like American beer", he grinned.

The outfitter's base offered one more luxury: hot showers. A week's worth of campfire soot, entrapped in the sticky residue of insect repellent, fish odor, and sweat disappeared in a welcome, soapy, torrent, amid swirls of steam. We slept much more soundly in the bunkhouse that night than we had a week before. This had not been merely a fishing trip. There had been something profound about this experience.

Members of our circle have returned to Quetico every year since, and will likely continue to do so. We are already into the third generation. Jim Santangelo and I have grudgingly accepted time's inevitable toll, and recognized that we are a liability to the group. Worn bodies are statistically more prone to injury and illness, becoming a serious, perhaps life-threatening, burden to the others. So, each June, with envious and heavy hearts, we wish good luck to those embarking, and eagerly await their reports. Despite surgical repairs to joints and tendons, in key areas like knees and elbows, I like to believe that I am still equal to the rigors of the Quetico experience. But the odds are against me. It is, I suppose, the price of survival. But that toll has purchased priceless memories.

On one excursion, our group numbered eight persons. The park limit to group size is nine. We would learn that there was wisdom to that rule. Fishing with Joe sometimes – no, usually - involves errors. Our first, in the interest of cost effectiveness, was to rent a 27 foot RV, and to drive to Atikokan. The rental cost, plus fuel, which the 460 cubic inch engine consumed in prodigious quantities, was still about one third the combined cost of air fares, transport from I-Falls to Atikokan and back, and room at the bunkhouse. Besides, we reasoned, we could sleep en route, arriving fresh at CCO. The drive took 24 hours…. and no one slept. RV suspensions are designed for slumber only when parked. The following day's paddle ended, not at the target destination, but when we simply were too exhausted – even Tim Wakefield's lean, fit, college age sons – to paddle further.

We discovered that most campsites were a bit tight for a group of eight. Campsites were typically on small spots of level ground, and dry, level ground is indeed scarce in this region. Logistics were also a problem. Cooking enough food, fast enough, with cooking gear designed for backpacking, is difficult, especially when three of the group were late teens males, burning huge amounts of calories. Now we began to understand the park rule. Group size was the second mistake.

Half of the group returned to Art Lake. The other half sought to find a way to Howard Lake. There was no portage shown on the map, but there was a stream that bore some promise of navigability. This was a lake that surely saw little fishing pressure. That made it irresistible, despite the fact that we had learned and relearned many times the lesson that remoteness does not necessarily mean good fishing. After much strenuous effort, we learned it again. The third mistake.

For the latitude and the season, the weather was unusually hot. Most days saw temperatures in the mid-nineties, and before the week was out, incredibly, 100F. These temperatures made the portages even more difficult, and on our planned route were portages of class 3, class 4, and class 5. (Portages, like rapids, are assigned classes of difficulty.) We were bound for Bud Lake. According to our "trip consultant", this time not Jim Clark himself, but a young man named Trevor, Bud Lake was the current smallmouth bass hot spot. The first portage, a long, steep class 3, began at Rawn Narrows . Pouring sweat, which, incidentally, rinsed away mosquito repellent, we finally launched at Bisk Lake, crossed it, and portaged to Beg Lake. Both lakes were unremarkable. From Beg, we portaged to

Bud, a "six man carry", that is, the canoes were carried, loaded and right side up, by six men. Once afloat on Bud Lake, which, without wetting a line, appeared to us to be unimpressive, a discussion – more accurately an argument – began.

The question was whether to give the highly recommended Bud Lake a serious try, or to paddle and portage on to Pickerel River/Sturgeon Lake, which involved a class 5 portage to Fern Lake. And it was already late in the day. The "grumpy old men", Jim Santangelo and I, argued for camping at Bud Lake – after all, it was the pick of the local expert. The real reason, of course, was that we were tired. But Jim and I were a minority, and lost the vote. On the far side of Bud Lake was what we thereafter lovingly referred to as "the portage from hell". It was narrow, steep, and, in places, hugged the edge of a precipice, far below which boiled a frothing rapids. The surface varied from huge boulders to knee-deep muck. At its end, at Fern Lake, even the young bodies had little left to give. The decision, unanimous, was to pitch camp at Fern Lake.

But camp sites on Fern Lake were not where Trevor had said they were, and those few places we found in which a tent might be pitched would have to be fresh-hewn out of the bush, an energy-intensive enterprise in which no one was, at that point, interested. The decision was to move on, however bone-tired the group was, to Olifaunt Lake, which involved only one short portage. Olifaunt was a large lake, and the likelihood of finding a place to sleep – all anyone cared about at that moment – was good. The portage was around short, but very swift, rapids. Fatigue clouded judgment, and we decided to run them. Capsizing any of the canoes would be a disaster, as all of them carried essential food and gear.

As the canoeist with the most mileage, I, and bowman Jim Reese, were elected by acclamation to go first. As I have said to myself so many, many times; *"Boy, this is stupid….but I'm gonna do it."* Reese and I paddled back upstream, and back and forth across the river, trying to read the current. On the near side was a pronounced "V", telling us that boulders on either side of it were forcing the flow between them. There was no "rooster tail" in the point of the "V", telling us that there was likely no shallow obstruction there.

An aircraft without enough airspeed is impossible to control. A watercraft without speed relative to the water is likewise helpless. "Jim! Right down the "V". Paddle hard and don't stop. Ready? Go!"

Jim was strong, even after the exertion of the day. We were able to keep the canoe aligned with the current, and shot out of the lower end of the rapids with an ease that surprised us. The others saw what we had done, and followed suit. It had been "a piece of cake", and therein was the danger that we would underestimate future rapids. We had met one of CCO's guides on the "portage from hell" and he had said that Olifaunt Lake had good fishing for all four species, but that Dore Lake (Dore is another name for walleye) was a better trout lake. We were far too exhausted to move on. We sought the first site on Olifaunt Lake on which we could pitch a tent. It was a small, flat area, high atop an enormous boulder, a single stone the size of a barn. It was exposed to the wind, had little firewood, and the tents had to be secured by placing large rocks at the staking points, and at the lower ends of the guy lines. But rocks were plentiful, the wind exposure discouraged mosquitoes, and the panoramic view was breathtaking. At least for the moment, we were home.

It was dinner time and we needed fish. Jim Reese and I trolled for Lake trout. The other canoes went after bass, walleye and pike, each on a different point of the compass. We had not trolled for more than a mile when Jim's reel screeched. He had hooked a really nice trout. That fish was a challenge on the tackle we were using. Finally, it was subdued enough for Jim to surface it at the stern of the canoe. Knowing that lake trout are extremely slippery, I seized it behind the gill covers with as hard a grip as I could muster, and lifted it from the water. "Wow! Hold it up. I want to get a picture of this guy." Jim fumbled for his camera. My arm was becoming fatigued. Here were the ingredients of disaster. This was mistake number four.

"OK. Hold it a little higher. Got it!" At that instant, the fish thrashed violently. It had been hooked by the rear treble hooks of a crankbait having two sets of trebles. It slipped downward, driving one of the front treble hooks into the joint of my right thumb, deep and between the bones. The pain was unbearable, and I dropped the fish, still thrashing, onto the floor of the canoe, trying desperately to clamp it under my boot.

Anything to stop the blinding pain induced by the motion. Jim saw what was happening. "Oh, my God!"

He crawled carefully to the stern of the canoe, and , with a pair of pliers, cut the hook from the lure by severing the split ring attaching it . He knew that the cutters would not cut the hardened hook itself. He then carefully unhooked the fish and, in attempting to stringer it, the slippery fellow escaped. He returned to the bow seat. "Can you paddle at all?"

"Yeah, a little. But only on the right side. Let's get back."

When we arrived at camp, no one was there, or in sight on the lake. We had expected that. Jim fetched a bottle of 151 proof rum and rinsed the wound site. "We'll wait for Jeff. He'll know what to do." He moved to return the bottle to the tent.

"Uh….don't run off with that".

"Oh. Yeah."

There was little daylight left when our companions got back to camp. Jim apprised Jeff of the situation. "OK," he said, "here's what I need. Somebody get the med kit. Anybody got a good set of cutters that will cut a hardened hook? OK. Now, somebody pour a half cup of scotch and bring it here. Somebody stand on his wrist. I can't afford to have any movement." Jeff injected lidocaine around the wound. "While that takes effect, drink this." He handed me the half cup of scotch whisky. "Dad, if that hook is in a tendon, or a nerve, lidocaine is not gonna do it. This may hurt a little." A little? That's what doctors always say.

In the light of a flashlight, Jeff cut the embedded hook from the remaining two on the treble. Then, with needle-nose pliers, he pushed the point, in a very particular direction, through the skin and directed someone to hold it with another pair of pliers. The precaution of having someone stand on my wrist was wise. It did "hurt a little". He then clamped the point of the hook in the needle-nose pliers, and pulled the hook through the joint and clear. "Now," he said, "I need another half cup of scotch. For me!" Antibiotic ointment and a band-aid were applied, and life went on.

There was no feeling in that thumb for two years. But after that, it has been completely normal. No strength or range of motion was ever lost. The younger members looked a bit queasy after watching the procedure, but it did not seem to affect their appetites. What it did affect was the care with which fish were handled. And that, perhaps, was worth the ordeal. I was not impaired for the rest of the trip; there was no pain, but tying knots in fishing line with a numb thumb was frustrating. Olifaunt was a very good lake, with excellent catches of all four species, the campsite was good, but the grass is always greener……

We struck out next morning for Dore Lake, 100 feet higher elevation, over a class 4 portage. Dore had an outlet stream, but no inlet that we could find. It had to be spring fed. Bass fishing was good. Trout were elusive. We fished for a few hours after daylight, then hid from the sun. Everyone was constantly thirsty. The thermometer at 4 pm registered 97F. Very, very unusual for this latitude. But it should be noted that the very next year, the very same week, temperatures rarely exceeded 60F, with some bone-chilling overnights.

Jeff got impaled on a hook himself, boating a bass at Dore Lake. He returned to camp, and had to surgically remove it, unaided. I would have liked to have been there to see the technique. I could have learned something potentially useful, as we will see in a later chapter.

Another incident at Quetico involved a "close encounter of the worst kind", with a very brazen black bear, who regarded humans with, at best, contempt, and at worst, as lunch. That is also a story for another chapter.

We broke two carbon fiber composite rods that year. Wonderful actions, but too brittle. Fiber glass rods handle big fish, relative to rod size, with impressive toughness. We also broke both camp shovels….surplus NATO issue. We hoped that US GI's had something better. We learned that polycarbonate is the only polymer material from which truly survivable bottles are made.

Gradually, with the learnings of every trip, the circle got the drill fairly well perfected. There is always the unexpected. On a very recent visit, the circle experienced its first canoe capsizing. It happened far from shore, in a high wind, in water cold enough to produce life-threatening hypothermia in a very short time. There were no casualties. There was considerable discomfort. And there was a restoration of the respect for wind, water, and the limitations of that wonderful and ancient craft called a canoe.

Quetico is an almost ideal venue for Joe. It is perhaps, on the basis of quality of fishing per unit cost, the finest fishing on the continent. Yes, Quetico requires physical effort and intelligent preparation, but the rewards are great. Quetico is more than a fishing trip. Quetico transcends that. At Canoe Canada Outfitters headquarters, there is a canoe paddle displayed on the wall. On the blade, are words inscribed by the pastor of a church in Illinois:

"The Lord is my PFD, I shall not want; He maketh me to lie down in dry tentage;

He leadeth me upon calm waters; His creation restoreth my soul.

Yea, though I portage through the valley of dark muck, I shall fear no evil, for thy map and thy compass, they comfort me.

Thou providest for me a feast of fishes in the sight of thine eagles, thou anointest my head with Muskol, my canteen overflows.

Surely, goodness and mercy shall follow me all the days of my life, that I may return, to dwell for a time,

in the land of Kah-weh-teh-kon."

Chapter 12
On Beavers' Wings
Fishing the Inaccessible

As overland access to wilderness lakes became more and more limited, for reasons described near the end of Chapter 7, those lakes still accessible were visited, of course, by more and more fishermen. No longer could we count on seclusion. The fishing did not seem to degrade, but the *wilderness experience* certainly did. And so, we began to look for alternatives. Mike Shepherd, a former colleague, and friend of both Tim Wakefield and of Bud Sroufe, stayed in touch, even though we were both on different business tracks, now. Mike had told us, in glowing terms, about some adventures he had experienced, using a wonderful fishing tool, new to us......called a bush plane. He gave us contact information connecting us to the flight service he had used. His sagas of fishing success were irresistible. We were sold.

There are a wide variety of fly-in packages available, and a wide variety of flight services, using a variety of approaches and equipment. One may opt for a high-end fly-in lodge, running water, electric power, with meals served, guides provided, fish cleaned, and every service expected of a luxury hotel. At the other end of the scale is the simple outpost camp, with a spartan cabin, sometimes only a permanent tent, where the only difference between it and the do-it-yourself camps we were accustomed to was the means of getting there. Of course, the latter was our choice.

The term, bush plane, instantly evokes an image. It is an image you have seen a thousand times…..in commercials and travel brochures, films and magazines. That image is of a single engine, high wing monoplane. It is fitted with pontoons. The wide wings seem too large. Its nose is not streamlined and sleek; it is round, and seems disproportionately large. It is homely and slow. It is legendary. It is the icon. It is the De Havilland Beaver.

There are many other aircraft which have been fitted with pontoons, and which fly to and from remote places. But the Beaver is special. It is not a land based plane fitted with floats; it was designed as a float plane….which was sometimes fitted with wheels. De Havilland Canada's design partners in its development included the Ontario Department of Lands and Forests. They wanted a float plane. They wanted it simple, strong and extremely reliable, even in the harshest winter conditions. They wanted short take offs and landings. They wanted huge cargo capacity. And they got all of that with the DHC-2 Beaver.

The story of this remarkable machine is fascinating, but too long to recite here. Beavers were built from 1947 until 1967, and of the 1657 built, most – except those that were unrecoverably lost, or placed in museums – are still flying. Cruising speed was traded for lifting capacity. But as one veteran bush pilot told the design team, "It only has to be faster than a dog sled." The DHC-2 Beaver is officially recognized as one of the top 10 engineering achievements of the 20th century by the Canadian government. And the Royal Canadian Mint enshrined the Beaver on a special edition quarter in 1999.

Why is all of that important? Well, I'm particular about my fishing equipment, whether owned, rented or chartered. Failure of that equipment can ruin Joe's once-a-year. And in the case of vehicles, land, air or sea, failure can ruin Joe. So, the first question asked when our circle is scheduling a fly-in is always: "Is the plane a Beaver?" We have yet to charter a flight service that answered, "No". But it's not just the safety/reliability factor. It's part of the adventure. It's fastening a seat belt to history, to a legend.

It's a ride on a wilderness Pegasus that has flown into the most forbidding places on earth. And back.

The first trip was eagerly anticipated. After an all night drive, we arrived at the outfitter's base about dawn. It was located on a beautiful, fairly large lake, connected to other lakes, and there were cabins and a lodge. We parked quietly and tried to sleep a bit until some observable activity began. It was of no use, of course, everyone was far too excited to sleep. Soon lights appeared in the lodge, which also served as base for the flight operations. We went inside, sure that we would be first in line for the first outgoing flight. We found that it did not work that way with this particular outfitter. There was a schedule of departure times for the various parties flying to various lakes, prepared in advance. We were nowhere near the top of that list. But, there was hot coffee, the lodge was pleasant, and we got all of the necessary paperwork out of the way. We settled in for a long wait.

The cast of characters for this particular foray included many of the usual suspects in our circle: Jim Santangelo, my son, Jeff, Tim Wakefield and his teen-age son, Tom, Gordon "Butch" Allen, a neighbor, experienced outdoorsman and rifleman of some note (locally referred to as "The Groundhog Assassin"), and me.

In late morning, the proprietor of the enterprise appeared and engaged us in conversation, or, more accurately, talked to us. Very few words passed in the other direction. He was not exactly the iconic picture of a wilderness bush pilot. He was more reminiscent of a 1960's era hippie, complete with long pony tail and a number of chains adorning a long-unshaven neck. And, he was an American…..here, hundreds of miles into Canadian bush country. And, he was, to describe him as politely as possible, loquacious. We were subjected to an unabridged autobiography. He had been everywhere and done everything, and was always the best at it, whatever it was. He had flown everywhere, and had managed to survive the most blood-curdling hazards. The lake we were to be flown to, he said, could not be found on any map. He had discovered it, and kept its location secret. (This was before the days of satellite mapping. The lake can certainly be found on current maps. But it is still unnamed.) However true any of this may or may not have been, we were becoming weary of it. At length he announced that, unfortunately for us, he would not be able to break away from other duties to personally fly us into this secret place, but that one of his young pilots would be assigned to the task. No tears were shed at that news.

Around noon, we went back to the truck to fetch some sandwiches, stretch our legs, and give our ears a rest. At the dock, an incoming party was unloading their gear from a Beaver. We stared in disbelief at how much equipment and supplies lay stacked on that dock, and with the unloading process not even yet complete. Neophytes that we were, we had packed as frugally as if this were another paddle-and-carry expedition. The outgoing party, about to board, had assembled their gear on the opposite side of the dock. It, too, was voluminous. I was standing next to Jim Santangelo. Jim had spent his life in the aerospace industry, and surely he would confirm my doubts. "Jim, those four guys and all that stuff are never gonna go into that airplane."

"Sure it will," he said, turning away, "that's a Beaver." And he was right.

We had not yet applied any repellent, and, rather than watching the departure, had returned to the lodge to escape the mosquitoes. In a few minutes, a young man came into the lodge, looked around the room, and then approached us. "Hi. I'm Bart. I'll be taking you next, just as soon as I drop those guys off. About forty minutes. Better get your gear down on the dock and weighed in." None of us knew what "weighed in" meant, but, happy that the long wait was nearing an end, lathered ourselves with Muskol and began unloading the truck. We were too green to know that we could have driven the truck to the dock, and so all of the load was carried, to the bemusement of the dock hand, who simply shook his head, and began to weigh each article. Then he totaled the weights, turned to us and said, "You guys are way under weight. No problem." Then he took his clipboard, and strode off towards the lodge. We followed.

In very close to the forty minutes promised, Bart was at the lodge door. We had not heard him land. "Let's go." We were at once refreshed. We followed Bart to the dock at nearly a run. The large side door of the Beaver was already open, and Bart stashed each article aboard, in a specific order, as we handed them up. Finally, he attached a cargo net to hooks built into the airplane's framework to restrain the cargo from reaching the rear seat, should some *unfortunate incident* occur. Then, he climbed into the left front seat and said, "Two of you in the back seat and one up here." We obeyed.

"Put your seat belts on. Nice day, not bumpy, but put 'em on anyway." The remaining three in our party would follow upon Bart's return.

None of us knew quite what to expect. All had flown before, but aboard commercial airliners and passenger charters, well-appointed and comfortable cabins, with attention to cosmetic detail. The veteran Beaver was none of that. The airplane had been recently painted, and the exterior looked brand new. But the cabin interior was a shock. Paint was peeling on the instrument panel, which no longer contained a full complement of instruments, the headliner was ragged and torn in several places from the loading of awkward freight, and the seats were stained and threadbare. The windows were still transparent, but clouded from exposure to ultraviolet light. The windshield bore the remains of many insects. A Loran-C navigation receiver was crudely attached to the instrument panel with hardware store shelf brackets. There were two empty engine oil containers on the floor. (The Beaver was designed so that engine oil could be added while in flight.) The bright exterior was a façade. The cabin revealed how many hard hours had been logged. To us, the uninitiated, this was all a bit worrisome.

Most Beavers, like this one, were powered by the Pratt and Whitney R-985 nine cylinder radial engine….a brute of nearly 1000 cubic inch displacement…about 16 liters. I had read about this engine. It had a reputation for ruggedness. It was, literally, bullet proof. Incidents were reported, during WWII, of aircraft powered by these engines bringing pilots home after having had entire cylinders shot off. That recollection made me feel better. At least, until Bart started it.

It fired immediately, but seemed to barely cling to life. The idle was rough and uneven, as if there were something terribly wrong deep inside it. Bart seemed unconcerned. So did Jim. He knew that this was simply the nature of the beast. He did not share that with Butch and me; he just let us worry. I thought that, if this were my engine, it would right now be spread out on the shop floor, and I would *never* trust it to carry me into lonely, rugged wilderness. For what seemed a very long time, Bart idled downwind on the lake, while we listened to that hesitant, halting staccato. Then he turned into the wind, made some trim adjustments, and advanced the throttle. Our ears were assaulted by a deafening, throaty, lusty roar, smooth and strong. And roar is the only word to describe the voice of the Beaver. One need not even look up. The unique, trademark roar unmistakably identifies a DHC-2 overhead.

At an airspeed of 90 mph, and a cruising altitude of 1500 feet, it took a good 30 minutes to reach the destination lake. It was a small lake, perhaps 600 acres. But it was made up of three bays, in an L-shape, with rocky shallows between bays, and a clearly visible rock bar breaking the surface at about the middle of the largest bay. There was no long, open expanse of water. Bart, with a just-another-day-at-the-office air, put the Beaver into a steep dive. There was no sensation of speed, no roller-coaster sense of falling, but tree tops looked frighteningly close to the pontoons. Just as we expected to plunge headlong into these secret waters, Bart leveled the craft and allowed it to settle into the light chop. There was absolutely no sensation of impact. The silken landing was followed by a lumpy, stuttering idle to the dock. But now we understood.

Still some distance from the dock at the outpost camp, Bart switched off the engine, and using the rudders on the pontoons, guided the Beaver in a path parallel to the dock. At the last second, he jumped onto the inboard pontoon, and threw a loop of rope around a cleat affixed to the dock. Then he scampered forward on the pontoon, and snared a second cleat. Leaning into the rope, he brought the Beaver to a perfect stop against the old tires lashed to the logs of the rustic anchorage. We were deeply impressed. How many landings had it taken to hone such a skill?

As we unloaded the gear, I asked Bart, "Is the water here safe to drink?" Bart grinned impishly.

"Tastes just like American beer."

He was clearly anxious to get the gear unloaded. As soon as all of it was on the dock, he said, "Come with me. I'll show you the ropes." He strode to the wall tent that was to be our shelter. "Look here." Level ground was scarce. A deck had been built, the rear side against the grade, the front side made level by posts about five feet high, with a plywood floor and a set of steps to access the door. The underside of the wooden floor, and the posts supporting it, bore unmistakable claw marks The tent had plywood sides extending about 4 feet from the floor, inside the canvas. "Had some bear trouble this spring. Last party in here had to kill one. I don't know what they did with it, but at least they got it out of camp. Now, here's what you do." He opened the door, which was framed by lumber extending upward from the floor. "Anybody know how to use that?" He pointed to a lever action 30-30 rifle leaning against the tent wall.

"Yeah," I said, "at least three of us. But that's a pretty light round to stop a bear."

"Just the point. You don't want to stop it…not here. Do you know how hard it is to drag a bear off into the bush? And you can't leave it here. In three days, you couldn't stand the stink. No, just gut shoot it, and let it run off somewhere else and die."

We couldn't believe what we were hearing. It seemed incredibly cruel. But it also seemed incredibly practical. Never mind that there were multiple violations of law involved. Non-residents may only possess firearms if duly registered; bears were out of season; we were in a no weapons area. And there were probably others. Still, if push came to shove……

"There's a propane stove right there. Here's how you light the pilot light. Have to turn on the tank outside first. No fridge here yet, eh. But there are two big coolers over there, and I'll bring plenty of ice. We hauled all the gear on your flight. Back in about an hour. Good luck!"

We walked down the short, steep trail to the dock with Bart. He removed the rope, and pushed the Beaver away from the dock, leapt onto the pontoon and into the cockpit. In seconds the Beaver was climbing towards the spruce clad ridge beyond the bay. The roar faded and was gone. We looked at each other. It began to sink in that there was no escape from this place except by air. The country was rugged and steep, and the bush was dense and tangled. Overland travel was all but impossible. There were no navigable connecting streams, and anyway, we did not have our faithful canoes. We had no radio. If someone were to be injured, or fell seriously ill……..We had been in the deep bush before, but always with our own way in…and out. Here, we were totally dependent upon others…strangers…upon the weather…and upon a mere machine. It was a sobering thought. One which we wordlessly agreed to ignore.

"Well, let's get the gear put away," someone said. That task was finished long before the now familiar roar of the Beaver was heard, bringing the rest of the party. Bart had indeed brought ice, several hundred pounds of it. It had been frozen in 5 gallon pails, weighing forty pounds each. We struggled up the steep trail with those, and could not fit all of it in the coolers until the chunks had been reduced to chips with a hand axe. Even then, there were a few pounds left over. That was put to good use in Grandpa Ruilman's traditional blessing of those many years ago.

Bart also brought outboard fuel in six five gallon cans. Three boats were drawn up onto the short beach, each with a five horsepower engine. The propellers on all of them were dented and bent, attesting to the shallow rock bars, some of those rock bars in unexpected places. "There are a couple of spare props in the shed", Bart announced, "but they aren't much better than these. Oh, and there's a minnow seine and a minnow trap in there, too." More violations for non-residents. Queried about the best fishing spots and techniques, Bart shrugged. "I don't know, eh. Never fished here."

"Good luck, eh. I'll be back on Tuesday to check on you and I'll bring more ice." Bart once again deftly pushed the Beaver clear of the dock, the starter whinnied briefly, the Pratt sneezed a puff of blue smoke, and lurched into its arrhythmic idle. We were transfixed by how quickly the unburdened Beaver vaulted from the water and was gone. We stood on the dock, shading our eyes, following it to a speck over the horizon. Well, after all, we wanted to be alone. And we were.

"Well', said Tim, "why are we here?". With one mind, the party began to rig fishing tackle, collect necessary gear, fuel the boats, and drag them into the water. Next came the ritual of coaxing the engines to actually run. And, without an inordinate amount of persuasion, all three of them did. Since we had no clue as to the hydrography of this lake, what species inhabited it, or where they were to be found, it was decided that each boat would explore one of the three major bays, and report back to camp an hour before sundown. As we idled away from the dock, Tim shouted an appropriate piece of wisdom: "Watch the rocks!"

Jim and I shared one of the boats and were assigned the bay directly east of the camp. We realized that we had failed miserably at the all-important task of gathering intelligence. Why had we not interrogated our talkative host back at the air base? Surely he would have gone on and on about the details of fishing his secret lake. "Sure he would", agreed Jim, "but how much truth would there have been in it? Would you believe that any more than the rest of those whoppers?"

"Uh….no."

"Well, then, let's start by trolling the shoreline."

"Yeah, at least we'll find out where the rocks are….at low speed."

We selected crankbaits, shallow-running on the shore side of the boat, deep-running on the opposite side. The deep runner occasionally bumped rocks; the other encountered no obstacles, despite our hugging the shoreline as closely as we dared. There were relatively few trees fallen into the water on that shoreline, and snags did not interrupt our progress. Nor did fish. We had covered nearly a mile by now, without a single strike. We were bored, and paying more heed to the scenery than to the fishing. Then, "Oh!" grimaced Jim, "What's THAT?"

"What?"

"My God, don't you smell that?"

"Smell what?"

I raised my head and sniffed the air, expecting to encounter some faint, elusive scent. It was neither faint nor elusive. It was overpowering, and triggered an immediate gag reflex. I swung the boat sharply away from the shore, towards open water. "There!" shouted Jim, "There, by that birch snag." And there, indeed by that birch snag, was the nearly submerged, rotting carcass of a bear.

"Remember what Bart said about those guys killing a bear, and that he didn't know what they did with it? Well, that's what they did with it. They rolled it down the hill into the water and towed it out here with boats. The dirty bastards! Now, we're not gonna drink any water from this lake. We need to find a stream, or a spring."

"Yeah", agreed Jim, "and right now. We don't have any water at camp."

The terrible power of suggestion. I was instantly thirsty. We ceased fishing and began to search for incoming streams. There seemed to be none in that bay. We headed for the north bay, and found Tim and Tom patiently trolling the shoreline, also without success. We told them what we had found, and asked if they had noticed any inflowing streams. They said they had not. This was beginning to look serious. Bart's check flight was four days away, and we had no potable water. "Well, we can always boil the water. It'll be safe that way," Tim's tone was comforting, but not convincing. He hadn't smelled that retching odor nor witnessed that repulsive sight. "Besides," he quipped, "we got plenty of gin."

It was one of Jim's classic, lightning retorts: "Man cannot live by gin alone."

"Tim, you guys search the shoreline of this bay. Sometimes a stream is hidden in brush. Stop every so often and listen for the sound of running water. This lake's not clear enough or cold enough to be spring fed. The water's got to come from somewhere. We're gonna go find Jeff and Butch."

"Yeah, OK."

They immediately departed on their mission. But our engine chose that moment to refuse to start. Excessive application of the choke soon flooded it, but cranking it with the throttle wide open cleared it, and it at last started. It ran for only a few seconds, and again stalled out. A few minutes of head scratching revealed the problem. The air vent on the fuel tank had not been opened. As long as sunlight heated the tank, vapor pressure of the warming gasoline provided sufficient pressure for fuel flow. But now the sun was low in the sky, and the clear air was beginning to chill. The tank contained now enough of a vacuum to resist the engine's fuel pump. Of course. What a stupid, tenderfoot mistake!

That solved, we were about to seek out Jeff and Butch, when shouting from down the bay reversed our intended direction. "Hey! Hey! Down here!" Tim and Tom were standing, waving both arms. The engine started and ran. We made for our comrades as fast as we thought prudent in these unfamiliar, rock strewn waters. Drawing alongside their boat, the obvious question: "You guys find a stream flowin' in?"

"Well…..no. But we found one flowin' out. Right there. That means there HAS to be at least one flowin' in." Unless the lake was spring fed, which we doubted, Tim's logic was unassailable.

"OK. There's none in that east bay, so there has to be one in that bay to the southwest, where Jeff and Butch are. Let's go!" I was much encouraged already. Both boats made for the bay to the southwest, gingerly navigating the rocky bar that spanned the north bay, and then running at full power. We passed the camp and swung wide into the southwest bay, fearful of shallow rocks near the shoreline. Jeff and Butch were casting a promising looking, heavily wooded shoreline, and seemed not only surprised, but mildly irritated that we would approach them at full speed.

"What the hell do you guys think this is, the boat races?" demanded Butch, who had never been a serious candidate for Secretary of State. Butch always said, in uninflected monotone, exactly what he thought. That is what was so great, and so admirable, about him. There was no doubt, no analysis of diplomatic nuances, you always knew exactly what Butch meant. He was refreshing.

Jim and I related what we had found, and the implications of that discovery. Tim and Tom added their findings. And now, the terrible question: "Have you guys seen any streams in this bay?"

"Oh, yeah. There's two of 'em. One over there, by those lily pads, and the other one off on this side. See that little, flat, marshy area right up there? No depth to either one of 'em. We were hopin' there'd be some rapids or scours where we could find some walleyes, but they're just a meander. Fair flow though. We can get water there OK."

"Catch anything?"

"Not even a strike. But we did find a sand bar where there are a lot of minnows. Maybe we can seine some tomorrow. Maybe this place takes live bait. Looks like canned ham for dinner tonight."

The trip was saved. One or another of the boats made a daily excursion to the inflow area to fill a five gallon water container. There may have been an equally dead moose in one of those streams, back up in the bush, but what we did not know did not hurt us.

That evening, sleep was disrupted by a nervous listening for any sound outside the tent. After several hours of reassuring total silence, and weighed down by a sleepless previous night, the party at length descended into slumber. Dawn would have likely come without notice, save for an overachieving woodpecker, who, at first light, began a jackhammer assault on a nearby tree. "Aw, damn it!" muttered Butch, pulling his sleeping bag over his ears. But we were all awake, now, and it was time to begin solving the riddle of Unnamed Lake.

At breakfast, after a review of our total lack of success on the previous day, Tom Wakefield volunteered to seine minnows. The seine stored in the plywood shed required some repairs before it could be used, including the addition of handles, which were fashioned from reasonably straight branches of fallen cedar trees. Restoration of the seine completed, Tom stripped to shorts, and we prepared to go to the sand bar where minnows had been observed. But from the dock, more schools of minnows were sighted, so there was no reason to go elsewhere. Tom waded bravely into the chill water, and netted about a dozen lively shiners. "L…L…Let's see if they work before we get any more", he shivered. It was agreed that we would divide them among the boats and once again try the separate bays. Impromptu bait containers were recruited from among cooking utensils and the dishpan. We set off in three directions.

Jim and I returned to the eastern bay, being careful to remain upwind of, as Jim put it, the "deceased beast". It seemed reasonable that drifting a live shiner along the edge of a water lily patch ought certainly to seduce a northern pike. And we were right. We squandered all four of our shiners on pitifully undersized pike in very short order. Casting the same weed patch produced a few uninspired strikes, but, even as fish-hungry as we were, none even approached an edible size. Two hours of casting the rest of the shoreline, definitely on the shore opposite the "deceased beast", produced nothing.

"Well, Jim, we did it again. It's remote, it's inaccessible, and the fishing is not just bad…it's terrible."

"Yeah. Slow learners. Hey, didn't you say that Mike Shepherd did really well here?"

"No. That's another lake. But I let that used car salesman of an outfitter convince me that this one was even better. This is my fault. Should have stuck with the known quantity. We're not doing anything here. How about a cup of coffee?"

"Well…..why not?"

While we were brewing a pot of coffee, we could hear the engine of another boat approaching from the north. "They smelled the coffee. Either that or they limited out already," Jim observed with pointed sarcasm.

"I really doubt the latter."

But Tim and Tom came, grinning broadly, into the tent holding a stringer from which hung two decent walleyes, of about three pounds each. They reported that the fish had been taken on the rock ridge bisecting the northern bay, but that once they had exhausted their supply of minnows, a grand total of four, all action had ceased.

"Oh, yeah," chortled Tim. "we've got the secret, now. Minnows are the answer, I tell ya. We're gonna go seine up some more right now."

"Who's 'we'?", inquired Tom, knowing what the answer was going to be. "That water's *cold!*"

"Yeah." Tim pondered a moment. "Well….hey…..how about this? We'll take two boats, see, and we'll hold the seine between 'em, and motor along the sand bar, and then up to the beach, right? Nobody has to get wet. And we'll cover more water that way, and we can go fast enough that they can't swim ahead of the seine. I didn't see any rocks or snags on that bar." Ideas that sound good are rarely thought through very thoroughly. That was the case with this one.

We positioned two of the boats side by side. Jim held one handle of the seine, while Tom grasped the other, both in the front of the boats. They lowered the seine into the water, and Tim and I engaged forward gears at idle speed. A few moments forethought would have predicted what was about to happen. The drag on the seine immediately pulled the two boats together, no matter how far to the left and to the right the two engines were steered. Holding the seine amidships did little better. Even held as far aft as possible, the boats were still almost immediately in contact. We tried lashing another branch across the seine's handles to keep it spread. This prevented pulling the boats together, but keeping them on identical courses, at identical speeds, proved impossible. The great experiment had failed. Someone was going to get wet.

Tom had resigned himself to the inevitable, and stripped. Once in the water, he looked up and grinned. "Say, it's not too bad today. Hey, Dad, get in here and help me." Tim reluctantly removed his trousers and waded to the aid of his son. "Wh…what do you mean it's not too bad? It's *freezing!*" Three passes of the seine yielded enough minnows for the day's fishing. Wading, shivering, onto the shallow beach, Tim made an observation.

"Did we ever see so many minnows in one of these lakes? You know what that tells me? There are damn few predator fish. This is not a good sign."

Still, using the minnows over rocky points and bars, four more walleyes, of about the same size as Tim and Tom had produced earlier, were boated by mid-afternoon. It was enough for dinner. And dinner was welcome. We would return to the water as sundown approached; fish activity usually increased as light faded. We were not disappointed; a dozen walleyes were boated that evening, some on white jigheads tipped with chartreuse grubs, as the minnow supply became exhausted. It had not been a great day, or even a good day, but it is never a bad day when one is fishing, especially in such a spectacular, pristine setting.

In rapidly diminishing light, the catch was cleaned on an exposed rock at least a mile from the camp. Offal was disposed of in deep water, and the fillets sealed in plastic bags. Encouraging bears to visit the camp was not in either party's best interest. It was nearly dark as we headed towards the dock. The wind was down, and the lake was a mirror, reflecting a rising moon, fragmented by the upper branches of a statuesque, conical spruce. As if orchestrated, a loon's call cast its haunting echo across the depression cradling the lake. This is what it's about, I thought. It is well and truly worth the effort.

We had eaten earlier, and so the fillets were carefully buried in the ice of one of the coolers, and the lid securely latched. The other cooler was placed atop it, and we sat in the light of the Coleman lantern, sipping a most welcome libation, recounting the events of the day. Tom hoped that the catching of several fish on jigs meant no more immersions in frigid water. Butch opined that it looked as though the weather had been dry for some time, and that perhaps a little rain would improve the fishing. But discussion was short lived, as a pronounced drowsiness overtook the group, and sleeping bags seemed ever more inviting. The uneventful previous night had assuaged the earlier nervousness, and peaceful sleep descended swiftly. All of that was about to change.

Sometime between midnight and dawn, the firewood stacked in a neat pile beneath the tent floor, to keep it dry, came clattering down. Everyone was instantly awake. No one spoke. As we strained to listen, there were scratching, rummaging sounds, and a sharp huffing, as though someone were attempting to clear a foreign object from the nose. I could hear the zipper on Butch's sleeping bag.

"Aw, crap," he muttered through clenched teeth, feeling along the tent wall for the rifle. Tim was on his feet, too, and retrieved a flashlight from his duffel bag. He directed the beam along the tent walls, stopping at the place where the rusting weapon leaned against the canvas, just above the plywood wall. Butch seized it, but then stood motionless. Tim peered out of the screen door. The lake was bathed in bright moonlight, but the tent was shaded by tall birch trees, and the area around it was utterly dark. And still, there came from beneath the tent menacing, scratching sounds, breathing sounds, and sounds of debris being clawed aside.

Tim illuminated as much of the area around the door as he could without opening it….as though that flimsy door could have restrained anything larger than a spaniel. The beam revealed nothing. He went to the windows in the tent walls, with similar results.

"He's…he's under the tent. He's under the damn tent! Come on, everybody up. Let's stomp on the floor."

Irish cloggers could not have made more noise on that tent floor. But, to no avail. Still, the ominous, scratching sounds persisted. With every passing moment, that bear, in our mind's eyes, became larger and more threatening. Those of us with any hunting experience knew that the rifle we had would not stop a charging bear at close range. Those without hunting experience may have been consoled by its presence, but the reality was that it, in this situation, was a fly swatter.

In whispers, we considered options. One option was to open the door, go down the steps, Tim with flashlight, Butch with rifle, illuminate the space under the tent, and, taking advantage of the reloading speed of a lever action, try to achieve lethality by sheer number of rounds. Even with judgment clouded by high stress, that option was immediately rejected. It was unconscionably dangerous, especially in the dark, and, even if successful, we would have a heavy, smelly, bloody carcass to deal with. Tom proposed that, even though the foot stomping had not intimidated the marauder, perhaps a round fired into the air would. It was a low risk alternative, and was agreed upon.

Butch edged open the door and, instead of pointing the muzzle upward, directed it towards the ground, muzzle below the level of the floor. He thumbed back the hammer, and squeezed the trigger. The hammer fell with a metallic click.

"Empty", he hissed, "the damn thing's EMPTY!"

He quickly toggled the action again. It was too dark to see whether a round had been chambered, and if it had not, it meant a frenzied search in the dark for a box of cartridges that we thought we had seen…..*somewhere*. But the trigger produced a bright orange flash and a resounding muzzle blast. Scrambling sounds beneath the floor were clearly directed towards the front of the tent. Tim held the flashlight beam where he thought the intruder would emerge, while Butch chambered a second round, his finger exploring the ejection port to be sure that a cartridge was being fed.

"HAH!" shouted Tim. "There he goes!"

We all felt immensely relieved…. and very, very foolish. Scuttling towards the brush was a fat, bewildered, shell-shocked porcupine! It took a while for nerves to calm, and for us to be able to laugh at ourselves. Butch carefully leaned the rifle back against the tent wall, then turned and addressed us solemnly. "Remember, you guys, there's a live round in the chamber. You hear me? In the chamber."

The rest of the night, and all of the subsequent nights, passed without incident. We saw fit to not relate the matter to Bart when he made his check flight. We could only imagine the objects of derision we would be upon our return to the air base. We could visualize our photographs on the base bulletin board under the banner, "Yanks intimidated by porcupine". We could hear bush pilots sharing the story by radio. Some things are better left unsaid.

Wednesday brought a fitful, peevish, little thunderstorm, which seemed unable to decide where it wanted to rain, across the lake. It was followed by a lethargic cold front that dropped temperatures a few degrees. Fish feeding activity improved, and by the end of the week, was almost up to the standards we were accustomed to in readily accessible, roadside, fifty-yard-carry lakes. But the experience had been excellent. We never saw another human being; we never heard a sound that was man-made, other than those we ourselves made; the setting was magnificent and pristine.

And – frosting on the cake – we would be borne away on the wings of the legend.

In the succeeding three or four years, we flew into other lakes, with other services, one of them to a place called Dyment Lake. The trip to Dyment involved a memorable, and unnerving, episode. It illustrates that I have survived seven plus decades, not by good judgment and wisdom, but often simply by good, old-fashioned, dumb luck.

After another dive-bomber landing, on the taxi in to the dock, we could see that the lake was ringed with promising shoreline, heavily wooded, with abundant weed beds and lilly pad patches. The shorelines were gently sloping on three sides of the lake, with a steep bluff on the remaining side. There was another, L-shaped lake nearby, Top Boot Lake, accessible by foot. A canoe was alleged to be stashed there. The cabin was large for an outpost cabin, and was framed largely of native birch logs. The roof ridge pole was a birch log, at least a foot in diameter at its smallest point. The shelter was a single room, with rustic bunks along one wall. It contained a stove, refrigerator, and lights, all powered by propane. It was roomy and comfortable, and a league above the wall tent at Unnamed Lake.

Dyment is a small lake, weedy and shallow. It harbors a high population of walleyes, also relatively small, but certainly acceptable. The pike population is made up of reasonably large fish, fat and healthy, well fed by an abundance of juvenile walleyes. So abundant is their forage base that they are difficult to seduce with artificial lures. Fishing at Dyment Lake was unremarkable, except for an interesting phenomenon. My fourth son, Andy, discovered that, within a relatively narrow band extending parallel to a rocky point, each evening at about one hour before sunset, a tiny, chartreuse crankbait, trolled within thirty feet of the boat, would produce strike after strike after strike. Casting the same lure produced nothing, but it was impossible to troll ten yards without hooking a thick shouldered 15 inch walleye. No other style or color of lure had any effect whatever. Even live night crawlers were ineffective. It was a puzzlement.

Assured that we could meet our grocery needs via Andy's discovery, the quest turned to elusive northern pike. And they proved indeed elusive. Andy and I decided that an expedition to Top Boot Lake was in order. Armed with the outfitter's hand drawn map, and a simple compass, we set out for Top Boot. The course led first through a sticky, mucky swamp, then up a steep, forested hillside. It was still, humid and hot that day, and sweat soon rinsed away our insect repellent. It had to be re-applied every fifteen minutes, or so. But, at length, we could see an opening ahead, and knew that we were only about sixty yards from the lake.

The shoreline was marshy, and we were forced to slog through it to find the canoe, said to be tied to a tree. It was nearly invisible under a low cedar, but it was, after an increasingly impatient search, located. But there were no paddles to be found. How typical, we thought. We should have known better than to believe the outfitter. By now, we had almost established an immutable law of the universe: *No hike-in lake canoe has paddles.* And Corollary One: *No hike-in lake boat has oars.* Of course, there is Corollary Two: *No hike-in lake outboard (if any) propeller has all of its blades.*

We hacked poles from saplings with pocket knives, but, even hugging the shore, the water was too deep for poles to be effective. And so, we cut cedar saplings, stripped the lower branches, and left the upper branches intact. These were, in effect, ragged brooms, and served to propel us, imprecisely, around Top Boot Lake. The fishing was very good, but having no means to clean or to transport fish, it was catch-and-release.

The temperature and humidity continued to rise. It was becoming oppressive, a summer day in the Everglades, complete with the same hordes of mosquitoes. We sought fishing spots in the shade, rather than where the fish were. We drank water almost non-stop. Then, Andy looked up. "Hey. Look at that." Just over the horizon was a black edge. "It's gonna storm," he said, "let's get back."

By the time we had returned the canoe to its tether beneath the cedar tree, the storm front appeared no nearer. On the trail back to Dyment, a few raindrops fell from a small, isolated cloud, more gray than black. But the heat felt as though it were enveloping us in a giant, inverted cup, gradually constricting around us. Our canteens were empty as we reached Dyment, and we eagerly refilled them. The motion of the boat created at least a breath of air moving over us, though not a leaf stirred on the forested banks. The other boat came into view around the point. We steered for it. "You guys better get in. There's gonna be a storm."

The sun was still shining, though muted by the humid sky, and the black edge of the front could not be seen from the basin of Dyment Lake. Our comrades looked at us quizzically. "What?"

Where the Gulls Are

"Not kidding. You can't see it from here, but it looks bad."

Before the boats were docked, a chill breeze had arisen. It felt good after the oppressive heat, but its intensity was increasing alarmingly. Before we were inside the cabin, leaves and small branches were in horizontal flight at the water's edge. It was not easy to close the door. Then came the rain, torrential and nearly parallel to the ground. It pounded the cabin walls like a fire hose. Debris clattered against the windward wall like machine gun fire. The boats at the dock were being pummeled against the timbers, and their impacts could be heard even above the howl of the wind. And still, the intensity of the wind continued to build. The worst was yet to come.

We stared, transfixed, as uprooted trees, some of them not small, tumbled end over end along the shoreline. Full gasoline cans, weighing thirty-five pounds, were being rolled along the beach. Then we heard a creaking, shattering sound, windward of the cabin, and a large birch tree, fifty feet high, toppled across the cabin roof.

The structure shuddered, but did not collapse. The birch ridge pole had been assaulted by a trunk of equal size, and had not yielded. It had bowed, but not broken. The roof had not been breached. It leaked a bit, but not seriously. In minutes, the wind abated. The rain continued for another hour. It was over. There were no casualties but for frayed nerves and wide-eyed stares.

We decided that the cost/benefit ratio between fly-ins and our previous mode, in terms of the quality of fishing, was, at best, a break-even. For the next four years, our circle of Joes reverted to paddle-and-carry adventures. Then, I happened upon a book with a fascinating title: *"Trespassing in God's Country"*, and subtitled: *"Sixty Years of Flying in Northern Canada"*, published by Treeline Publishing, in Fairfield, Iowa. It had been written by George Theriault, a pioneer in wilderness aviation. It is a wonderful read, the narrative beginning in the 1930's. Whether or not it is still available, I do not know. The cover is a centered photograph of Mr. Theriault, filleting knife in hand, holding a lake trout, in the foreground, with a classic DHC-2 Beaver in the background. The rest of the cover backdrop consisted of a topographic map. On that map were places we had actually been. This was familiar territory. Of course, he had been there sixty years earlier, but a connection was established. Little did I know, gaping at that cover, that future fishing trips would be made aboard that very Beaver.

Two of George Theriault's sons operate flying services. We met one of them, John, at a stateside boat show. It was uncanny. He was the very image of his father's photos in the book. This was a thoroughbred lineage. We immediately scheduled a trip, and have flown with no one else until John's retirement. John Theriault pilots a Beaver with total, utter mastery. And he shares his fishing knowledge of his outpost lakes freely. His advice has never failed to produce abundant fish in the fifteen years, now, that we have annually placed, with total confidence, our gear and ourselves aboard his blue and white Beaver.

Each of those embarkations, banking the faithful Beaver's nose into a different direction, is a story unto itself, enough adventures to fill at least another book. Every destination was a secluded refuge for the soul, an unspoiled place of utterly black and totally silent nights, perforated only by the occasional cry of a loon, and by blue water, green forest days, when sunlight dappled wavelets with fragments of gold, or rain danced little crystal explosions on the surface . Our neighbors were river otters and ospreys, snowshoe hares and gulls, pine squirrels and ravens, moose and eagles, beavers and bold, curious whiskey jacks. We, and foraging bears, like all suspicious neighbors, nervously avoided one another.

The legendary DHC-2 Beaver has delivered us to lakes, and to rivers, and to lakes connected by rivers, in late springs, with the forest erupting bright chartreuse, in midsummers of dark, deep green, and in scarlet/gold autumns. Occasionally, the latter would treat us to brilliant, unearthly, aurora borealis displays. Depending upon venue, catches might include northern pike, whitefish, walleyes, smallmouth bass, perch, and, in deeper waters, an occasional burbot. Fishing was always good, often great, and sometimes, fantastic. In fishing, there is no such thing as sure-fire success, but we came to believe that this approach was as close as was reasonable to ever expect.

Joe is always conscious of the cost effectiveness of his once-a year; that's what makes him Joe. And there is no question that a fly-in costs more than a paddle-and-carry. But for most Joes, his once-a-year lasts a week. We came to realize that the fly-in approach saved a lot of priceless fishing hours, that we were spending a lot of time paddling, carrying and camping that could have been spent fishing. And there is another factor. What is the value of total isolation and pristine surroundings? What should be the price of a ticket to the world as it might have been ten millennia past? Where can you buy a front row seat to a concert of total, utter, perfect silence?

And besides, *there is just something about a Beaver.……..*

Chapter 13
Chasing Sunsets
California Crying Trout

To every Joe who grew up on "the morning side of the mountain" – in this case, the Rocky Mountains – there is a fascination, an allure, about something called "the west". It is a land "glorified in song and fable", a land where heroes and legends were born – or were, at least, invented. It is a land vast, and (relatively) open. Some of it was, until as little as a century ago, still a wild frontier. Unfortunately, most of what the folks from the right side of the country knew of the left side of the country came from the likes of Zane Gray, Louis L'Amour and, of course, from Hollywood.

The latter was especially influential. And it was not so much the stories or the actors – it was the *scenery*. Even in the old, black-and-white films, the locations were magnificent. There was the hero, in a brief respite from his arduous pursuit of evil-doers, drinking, right beside his horse, from a pool in a pure, crystalline stream flowing over time-polished boulders, from snow-capped mountains in the background. The hero was lost to every Joe in the audience. They were staring at that pool to catch a glimpse of a fish slurping a mayfly, or hapless grasshopper, because the Joes knew that there most assuredly *had* to be fat, native trout in so comely a pool.

The advent of color photography took the image of the west to a whole new level. Now the spectacular gold of the aspens, shimmering on the slopes cradling a foothills stream, came to vibrant life. The colors of the walls of a canyon were no longer shades of gray, but red and brown and gold and black and a hundred other colors with no names. Ireland is known as the country of "a hundred shades of green", but so, now, with this technology, was the American west. Each conifer, each deciduous tree, each grass, each shrub, cast upon the screen its own signature "shade of green". There are many examples in the genre, but perhaps none better than in the opening scenes in the John Wayne classic, *"Rooster Cogburn"*. Forget the plot. Forget the actors. Look at that country. Look at those streams!

And then, of course, there is *"A River Ran Through It"*. Good guys and bad guys? Of course. There has to be a social plot. But mostly, it's about trout fishing – in the west. And about lessons. Well worth a look.

Four decades ago, I got a call one evening, in mid-summer, from Tim Wakefield. "Hey," he said, "Jack and I are planning a trip out to Wyoming… do a little trout fishing. Want to go?" Jack was one of Tim's older brothers, and I knew that their father lived in Casper. I also knew that they had fished there before. This sounded like a guided tour.

"Well….yeah….sure." I could already see lofty peaks, their snow caps fathering cold, clear streams that whispered over gravel banks and crashed over boulder rapids into languid pools, then lazily swirled along undercut banks, beneath which lurked fat, hungry trout. I could feel the cold water on my waders gradually chilling my legs. I could look up and see a tent pitched on a shallow knoll just above the stream, where, at dusk, a campfire would be grilling trout and brewing coffee. After dark, I could see a wide, gin-clear sky, ablaze with stars. I could see………..."What? Oh….uh…. yeah, I'm listening."

"Let's meet tomorrow night at my place and put a plan together. Eight o'clock. Can you make it?"

"I'll be there."

At the time, Jack, Tim and I all worked for the same company, Tim and

I in engineering, Jack in sales. And he was good. Jack was one of those people who could sell five dollar bills for six ninety-eight. I should have taken that into account when Jack was describing the incredible trout fishing at the "places we know about". In the course of the meeting, the subject of transportation came up. "Well," Jack said, "company policy just changed. I can use my company car for personal use now. Let's take it, and not put the miles on our own cars. It's about 2500 miles out there and back."

"What is it?"

"It's a Ford four door. Small V-8. Good trunk space."

"Are we gonna be able to get all our camping gear in it?"

"Well….about that….Tim's gonna rent a Nimrod fold-up camper."

"Does that car have a hitch?"

"No. I can rent one of those, too."

"Wait a minute. I thought we'd have to back-pack into these places."

"Nah. Drive right to 'em." An image shattered.

"Well, listen. What do I need? I've got an old fly rod that I use for bluegills, but it's probably not good enough for……."

"Oh, we use spinning tackle. You don't need flies. We catch 'em on worms and cheese marshmallows." Another image shattered.

"OK," interjected Tim, "let's get down to the serious stuff: food and drinks."

The rest of the meeting was devoted to mundane logistics; a departure time and a meeting place were agreed upon, and the assembly was adjourned.

It was, as Frank Miller would have put it, 0-dark-thirty when we set out for Casper, Wyoming, on a warm, clear morning. Even though it was daylight–rich midsummer, we were in the middle of Indiana before it was truly light. And we did not stop, except for fuel, until darkness was almost complete….in Bridgeport, Nebraska. There was a small campground there, and we erected the fold-out and slept until daybreak. Not wanting to unpack cooking gear, we sought breakfast in Bridgeport, a thoroughly pleasant town.

Folks are up early in middle America; a local eating establishment began serving breakfast at 4 am. The grocery opened at 6. There was farm machinery clanking through town as soon as there was light sufficient for safety. Telltale flashes of an arc welder illuminated the windows of the International Harvester dealer halfway down the block. Jack pointed out the window. "Look at that. That's what this country's about." Somehow, not being a part of the productive workforce, even for a few days, seemed to carry with it, that morning in Bridgeport, Nebraska, a certain sense of culpability. We got over it.

The great plains were largely behind us as we left Bridgeport, and the "small V-8" in Jack's car began to seem a bit winded, even though the fold-up camper weighed no more than half a ton. By late morning, we were in Casper, where I had expected to meet Mr. Wakefield, and gain some valuable local intelligence. But Jack never left the main road, and soon we were outside of town, crossing some dry and desolate terrain. Vegetation was sparse, and little of it was green. "Jack, how come we didn't stop and see your Dad?"

"Oh, didn't you know? He died last year."

"No, I didn't know. I'm really sorry." This was awkward. I should have known, probably did, and, worst of all, forgot. The only sensible thing to do was to escape back into the present. "Well, do you know where to go…. what to do?"

"Sure. Don't worry".

At some nondescript point, a lane – that is, two tire tracks - left the road toward the southeast. Jack came to a stop and looked at Tim. Tim nodded, and Jack swung off the road onto a sage brush flat, then followed the pair of tracks for what seemed a tediously long distance. The surface was surprisingly smooth and level, and a speed of 15 to 20 miles per hour was reasonably comfortable. Off to the left and to the right, an occasional pronghorn antelope would stare at us from several hundred yards distance, unconcerned….as long as we kept moving. Then, ahead, almost at the limit of vision, a gate barred the trail.

"Yeah, right, Jack" I thought. *"You know where you're going. Now we're gonna have to turn around and go all the way back to……..*" But Jack just kept driving. He stopped a few feet short of the gate, and sat silently, waiting for the dust cloud, which had stalked us since leaving the road, to swirl by. As it cleared, a low house and several outbuildings appeared. The gate was the only portal in a barbed wire fence that seemed to stretch to the horizon in both directions, containing sheep….which also seemed to extend to the horizon. Jack opened the gate carefully, made sure that it was securely closed behind him, and walked toward the house. Before he reached it, the door opened and a tall, lean man strode briskly toward Jack. This was not a "mosey" or a "saunter". This was a purposeful, get-off-my-land stride. Jack pointed to himself, and then to the vehicle, ending with a gesture suggesting going over a hill and down the other side, off to the man's left. The man shook his head, and pointed in a slightly different direction. Then he drew a horizontal half-circle in the air, and made a palms-down motion, like someone smoothing a table cloth. He and Jack were laughing and nodding; they shook hands and parted. All appeared to be well.

Jack was barely inside the vehicle when Tim began to probe. "What did he say?"

"Well, he said that we'd never get that camper down the way we used to go. Wheels are too small. But he said if we follow that shallow swale over there, we can get down to the water without so many big rocks. Mostly dirt and gravel. He said there's one really sharp hairpin bend, and a nice flat rock face at the bottom where we can easy level up the trailer. He said we'll have to be sure to get out of there quick if a big rain comes up, though. That swale floods."

"What did he say about the fishing?"

"He said some of the hands have been catchin' a few. Now, get out and open that gate and be sure it's closed and latched after I get through."

And so began the final approach to Pathfinder Reservoir. The swale was just as Jack had related. The rock face was indeed flat, but not perfectly level. Nor did we try to level the camper. Jack wisely insisted that the car be parked facing the swale and that the trailer be left on the hitch. "We can pull it out of here folded out if we absolutely have to. A storm can come up pretty fast. I just hope it's not at night."

The site was perhaps forty feet above the surface of the lake. "Damn it, Jack," Tim said, "It's muddy. Look at that." It did not seem muddy to me. I could see the bottom at least four feet down, and made that observation. "No," Tim shook his head, "it should be as clear as well water. This is no good."

Jack sought to put the best possible face on the situation. "Aw, it'll be fine. I've seen it murkier than this."

"Oh, yeah? When?"

"We were here with Dad that time. It was, oh, four or five years ago. We caught a bunch of trout. Don't you remember?"

"No."

"Well, anyway, just look at that. You can see forty miles. Did you ever see air so clear?"

Jack was right. I had truly never seen air so clear. It is ageless wisdom that beauty is in the eye of the beholder. To these beholders, accustomed to an entirely different landscape, the panorama was stunning, if for no other reason, because there was simply so much of it. It was barren and austere, magnificently open, and had about it a unique, in-your-face, hard-edged beauty. Fishing, to restate the obvious, takes one to beautiful places…….. of every kind.

It was, admittedly, difficult to stop staring, but at length the suggestion was made that tackle be readied and that we get about the business of capturing some fresh trout for dinner. Tim lingered a bit at the edge of the rock shelf, staring at the water, likely silently cursing its turbidity. Jack and I were nearly back to the camper, where the tackle was stored, when we heard Tim shout. "Hey! Hey – come over here. Look at that!"

We hurried back. Tim's tone sounded as if he had seen the Loch Ness Monster, or some equally unlikely apparition.

"Look at what?"

"See that stone slab right there? The white one? Follow it on down. It ends in a sort of ledge. About twenty feet further out…isn't that a school of fish?"

There were, in fact, some barely discernable dark shapes where Tim was pointing, but they could have been anything. It was impossible to tell whether these objects were resting on the bottom, or were suspended. The outlines of the shapes were vague, but they did appear to have a length much greater than their width or their depth – just as a fish would have. There was a very light ripple on the surface, making resolution of the objects all the more difficult. We watched for locomotion, that characteristic which positively separates the animate from the inanimate. The ripple could easily mask small motion, but we saw no gross motion on the part of any of the objects, whatever they were.

"Well, let's go," muttered Jack. "You're seein' fish because you *want* to see fish."

"Oh, yeah?" Tim picked up a tennis ball sized stone and lofted it in the direction of the submerged ledge. "Let's just see!"

The stone missed the target by a good forty feet, falling short on the shore side. "Aw, hell, Tim," began Jack, "that doesn't prove anyth……….they're gone! Let's go!"

There was no frenzied rush to rig tackle and climb down to the water. We knew that it would take some time for that school to recover from the Neanderthal air raid. We had stopped in the town of Glendo to obtain fishing licenses, worms and cheese marshmallows, as well as bread, lunch meat and soft drinks. We paused for a leisurely snack while assembling tackle, and then began a descent over a boulder field toward the water's edge. Midlanders are acclimated to near-sea-level air pressure. Elevation here was only about 6000 feet, but even the minor exertion of scrambling down the boulder field left us breathing heavily. We were at water level, now, and but a short hike from the rock structure that ended in the submerged ledge. Twelve hundred miles behind us; just a few yards left ahead.

I watched the experienced Wakefield brothers rig with a light sinker at the end of the monofilament line, a hook about a foot above it and another hook a foot above the first, and did the same. Nothing fancy; classic bottom rig. They baited one hook with a worm, the other with a cheese marshmallow. I did that, too. Something wasn't right, here. This was not my image, albeit vicariously acquired from the printed page and the silver screen, of western trout fishing. But, after all, Tim and Jack had done this before, and apparently successfully. Stick with what works.

All three casts settled to the bottom just beyond the ledge. All of us made the lines as taut as the ¼ ounce sinkers would allow. And then, there is that agonizing, anticipatory watch, that coiled-spring notch in the flow of time, when instant reaction to a barely perceptible strike is the difference between success and failure. How long can one maintain that hair-trigger state of alert? How long before the rod is rested upon a rock, and a consciousness of the brilliance of the sun and of the radiation being reflected from the white rocks behind seizes the mind? It was not long.

Our thermometer indicated mid-nineties, but it was not uncomfortable. We would have expected to be sweat-soaked, but were not. There was, though, a strange sense of heatless roasting of exposed skin. The rays of the sun, unimpeded by moisture, and traversing a mile less of the lowest, and therefore densest, atmosphere felt, fortunately, different. We were alerted. Sleeves were rolled down, and Tim returned to camp for sun screen. It was too late. By evening, we were all a shade or two on the pink side.

Shortly after Tim's return, Jack's rod, cradled between two rocks, twitched violently. He waited tensely, and upon the next deflection of the rod tip, executed a brisk hook-set. The fish was clearly not large, nor had we expected it to be. Their experience had been that fourteen to sixteen inch trout were the norm for these waters. Still, the fish resisted stubbornly. Jack worked it over to a place on the shoreline where a large rock made a shallow and smooth entry into the water. There, he beached the fish. His grin collapsed into a disgusted frown. "Look at that! Nothin' but a droop-snooted mud sucker!"

There are a number of varieties of suckers, and we did not bother to make a detailed identification. It was likely a longnose sucker, or some hybrid thereof. It was not a bad fish; seventeen or so inches long and about two pounds, but the species suffers poor public image – no doubt mostly due to its name. The flesh is of high quality, but very bony, and it is therefore not a popular food fish. There was no convincing Tim and Jack that we should dine on sucker, at least, not here in trout country.

Before dusk, we had landed three more fish, virtually identical to the first, but not a single trout. We decided that climbing the boulder field before total darkness was wise, and upon completing that breathless task, set about to gather firewood. There was none in the vicinity, at least not within reasonable walking distance. So, dinner was prepared on a faithful, battered, old Coleman stove. As soon as the sun had set, the temperature fell rapidly, and we gathered up the blackened, dented coffee pot and sat on the bunks in the camper. Jack and Tim debated the reasons why no trout had been taken that day, and what could be done tomorrow to improve our success rate. It was concluded that a change of venue to the headwaters of the reservoir, the North Platte River, would be the most promising alternative. Listening to their reminiscences of past trout bonanzas, at this very place, I stretched out on the bunk. And then it was dawn.

It was a classic Joe breakfast. The coffee was strong, hot and fresh. It went downhill from there. There was some lunchmeat left over from the prior day's noon snack. It was unidentified, but seemed to be a loaf of some kind. At least, there seemed to be particles of meat of various sizes, colors and textures in it. Slices of it were fried in a venerable, high mileage skillet, on the Coleman stove, and eggs broken over the slices. It was not eggs benedict, but with enough salt, pepper and Tabasco sauce.......

Within less than an hour, we departed for our new location. On the map, it was not far away. But to get there over land required a long detour around some formidable pieces of topography, and it was nearly noon before we had parked the vehicles on a shallow bluff overlooking the North Platte. Tim was even less happy with the turbidity here, but water clarity appeared to me to be about the same as it had been at the site we had just left. Maybe I just didn't understand trout. No. That's misleading. The fact is that I *did* not understand trout. I *do* not understand trout. I will *never* understand trout.

We cautiously picked our way to the water's edge. It would have been easy to fall on that descent, and there was absolutely nothing soft to land on. I was disappointed that this would not be a wading venue. My cherished image of trout fishing, derived, of course, from print and film, was that one practiced that art while wading. But here, banks were steep, rocks were slippery, and the maximum advantage that wading would have provided, in extending casting distance from shore, was no more than five or six feet. So, with the same bottom rigs as on the previous day, replete with red worms and cheese marshmallows, we set our traps for trout.

There was current here – moving water - and that produced action. We landed a number of nice fish that afternoon…..none of them trout. By the time shadow had embraced the river valley, the stringer was still empty, as I could not persuade the Wakefield brothers that suckers were fine – if inconvenient – table fare. Over a disappointing dinner of some pre-packaged rice dish, it was concluded that yet another change of venue was necessary. Tomorrow we would move to Seminoe Reservoir. We had become nomads, motorized, twentieth century equivalents of Bedoin tribesmen, wandering the desert…… in search of the elusive trout.

Again, we retreated, with the pot of hot and fragrant fresh coffee, into the camper, and sat, in the warm and friendly light of a kerosene lantern – we did not wish to consume the Coleman fuel that powered our stove – recounting the events of the past several days. "I thought you guys knew where the trout were," I began, "but so far, we got nothing but……"

"Wait a minute," interjected Tim, "we've been catching trout. You just didn't recognize the species. Very rare. Introduced here from California. These are California Crying Trout. Notice how sad they look, long faces all down and forlorn. Frowning all the time. "

The reference was not lost on me. I had the album, a 33 1/3 rpm vinyl disk – the CD of a half century past – of comedian Jonathan Winters doing a spoof of the media covering the presidential campaign of 1964. In it, a reporter "interviews" various segments of the American population, all played by Winters: there was Sally Sweetwater, typical American housewife; there was Lance Lovegard, the flaming liberal; there was Tick Bitterford, the rock-ribbed conservative; there was Elwood P Suggins, blue-collar Midwesterner; there was outrageous senior citizen, Maudie Frickert. And one of the interviewees was a Native American, Chief Crying Trout. This was, of course, long before the days of pandemic political correctness.

"Oh. Well, forgive me. How could I ever have doubted you?"

"That's more like it. A little respect, if you please."

The morning sun bored intrusively through the canvas walls of the camper. With the vents having been closed against the evening chill, the interior became uncomfortably warm very quickly. There was ample incentive to be outdoors, on the shady side of the camper, as quickly as possible, attending to an abbreviated breakfast of coffee and oatmeal. Within less than an hour, another overland expedition was in progress, following a faint, tire-track trail across a sage brush flat. At some point, which had no distinguishing feature whatsoever, a dust cloud appeared in the distance. As the two vehicles closed, it was apparent that one or the other would have to yield the trail. Both did, and pulled to a stop, side by side. The pick-up truck beside us bore the logo of the State of Wyoming, and the driver was uniformed. As soon as the dust had blown by, both driver side windows were opened.

" 'Morning, men. Where are ya…….Oh, I guess I should tell ya…I'm the wildlife officer for this county…..where ya bound for?"

"Well, we been fishin' Pathfinder. No luck for trout, so we're gonna give Seminoe a try."

"Aw, I hate to tell ya this……..I see from your plates you come a long way …..but there's nothin' bein' caught at Seminoe, either. Just came from there. I was at Alcova yesterday. Same story."

"Why is that? What's wrong?"

"Dunno. Just happens sometimes."

"Well, if you were us, where would you go?"

"It's half way across the state, but I was talkin' to one of the officers over near Shoshoni yesterday, and they're catchin' good walleye in the Bighorn River below Boysen Dam. Just about everybody gettin' limits. If ya decide to go over there, be careful about where ya fish. Some of that country is on the Wind River Reservation, and ya need a tribal permit besides your Wyoming license."

"So, that's where you'd go?"

"If I hadna used up my vacation time on an elk hunt, I'd be there right now."

He was pulling away when Jack shouted, "Did you get an elk?"

The answer was a barely audible, "Nope."

In seconds, a road map of Wyoming was spread out across the hood. "Where the hell is Boysen Dam?"

"Wait a minute," said Tim, "something wrong with that story. The Bighorn's in Montana. That's where Custer....."

"Nah," corrected Jack, " that's the *Little* Bighorn."

"Hey! There's Shoshoni. It's gotta be somewhere around....there it is! Boysen Reservoir!"

I observed that it was "pretty far away for a day trip".

"Who says it's a day trip? And this is Wyoming," Jack reminded me. "*Everything* is far away". And it did seem so. It was a long way between towns, crossroads, and even houses. There was some discussion, but in the end, the consensus was that walleyes beat California crying trout, even though they were not the target species of a very long trip. Besides, we would see some country that none of us had seen before, and that is never a bad thing. And so, again westbound, we set out for Boysen Dam, chasing the sunset, not knowing what to expect, and not expecting what we found.

The distance was but a little over one hundred miles, and was an easy run across arid and largely flat terrain. What grades we encountered were not steep, and altitude decreased by about one thousand feet in the course of the journey. We all, including Jack's engine, were breathing a bit easier. It was a lonely stretch; we saw far more antelopes than people. There were interesting place names; my favorite was Poison Creek. There was, at one point, a village limit sign post....but no village....at least, none visible. Much of it was, at least in 1967, open range, and we were detained to allow road crossing by a stream of sheep that seemed endless. Tim suspected that the sheep were being run in a great loop. He claimed he had seen the same animal pass three times. At length, the brown scrub gave way to lush, green crop fields, irrigated by the waters of Boysen Reservoir. We were in Shoshoni.

A road led north from the town of Shoshoni, generally following the eastern shore of Boysen Reservoir, and then following the Bighorn River below Boysen Dam. The functions of the dam were to provide water for irrigation and to generate hydro power, by detaining the combined flows of the Wind River and the Bighorn River watersheds, a total of about 7700 square miles. Even in dry country, that is a great deal of water. In the April/June season, Boysen may receive an inflow of 845,000 cubic feet per second! But from a fisherman's point of view, the key feature was power generation. To generate power, there must be flow, and flow in the tailwaters of a dam almost always means feeding, especially if that flow is intermittent. And it was indeed intermittent. As we passed the dam, we could see that the river below exhibited little current. This venue was beginning to look very favorable.

The road map indicated a state park on the east side of the river, immediately downstream from the dam. There was a camping area between the road and the canyon, and we pulled into it. There were no gates, no signs indicating that any sort of permit was required, and we parked the camper and set it up, on the principle that it was easier to ask forgiveness than permission. The campground was all but deserted, and was definitely primitive. But it had the one essential feature. There was a well. There was one other vehicle in the campground when we arrived, a pick-up truck with a camper body, and we parked a very respectful distance from it. Little did we imagine that before this adventure was over, we would become well acquainted with the occupant.

The crest of the dam stood about 150 feet above the stream bed. On the downstream side, the canyon was narrow and steep. The walls of the canyon had been buttressed with a rip-rap of huge boulders, to prevent erosion, and getting to the water's edge appeared to be a daunting task, athletic and dangerous. But we could see two widely separated fishermen at the waterline, so there was no doubt that the climb was not impossible, just difficult. We noticed that they did not seem to be fishing. Rods were leaned against rocks, and one was eating a sandwich, the other smoking a cigarette. This seemed inconsistent with what we had been told. If "almost everybody is catching limits", why weren't these two guys fishing? Were we, once again, a day late? Was the officer's story a pure fabrication, worked upon gullible easterners? Our eager anticipation began to dissolve. There was no hurry to rig tackle and scale the rip-rap. We lethargically prepared some lunch. Unknowable to us, the next few hours would utterly banish lethargy.

It was a short distance to the face of the dam, and we decided to have a closer look. Downstream of the exhaust of the power turbines, for several hundred yards, the stream banks had been lined with rip-rap of even larger boulders, heavy enough to withstand the high velocity flows, but extending up the slope only six or eight feet. The canyon walls were shallower here than further downstream. And they were deserted. This looked like a promising place to fish…so long as a careful vigilance was maintained regarding the opening of the generator flumes. We planned to rig our tackle and return to this spot, in a good position to fish the generator tailwaters – if and when they were turned on, and in as good a position as any if they were not. But, there was no hurry. It was still mid-afternoon, and we assumed that generation would not begin until nearly dark, when power demand for lighting and cooking increased. That assumption proved to be incorrect.

We reasoned that we could fish with the bottom rigs until the generators were activated, but after that, lures that were effective in high current conditions would be necessary: jigs, spoons, and heavy, sinking crankbaits. We so armed ourselves. We filled canteens at the well, and strapped them on. This climate seemed to be a very thirsty place. Then we returned, at a leisurely pace, to the site chosen but an hour earlier. It was not as we had left it.

The rocks near water level were nearly shoulder to shoulder with anglers. We did not know where they had come from. We had seen no vehicles. To compound the mystery, they were not fishing. They were simply standing, rods in hand, chatting and laughing. Then came the sound of a siren from upstream. Still, there was not a line cast toward the river, only a shuffling of feet and a motion of arms reminiscent of a batter awaiting a pitch. The water near the face of the dam began to swirl and then to organize itself into a defined flow, building velocity until its path and position were unmistakable. The low hum of the generators could be heard above the sound of the rushing water. Almost in unison, rods were raised and lures strenuously cast, as the flow did not follow the bank, but coursed towards mid-stream. There were few hook-ups initially, but within minutes, almost every cast with enough distance to reach fast water produced a strike. We watched all this in awe from the top of the slope. Then, someone said, "Are we still here?"

The headlong descent was little more than a scarcely controlled fall. It was by virtue of good fortune, and the flexibility of youthful joints, that there were no injuries among us, or broken tackle. There was a limited distance of productive water. Too close to the dam the outflow was unfishable, and too far from it the outflow spread across the stream bed and slowed. The fish were obviously feeding only in the fast water. Trying very hard to be mindful of fishing courtesy, we looked for the widest spaces between anglers. But the folks already in place recognized the situation and spread out to make room for us, and not begrudgingly, but with nods and smiles and greetings. Joes…. every one of them.

With soaring anticipation, we cast 3/8 ounce jigs dressed with white grubs, by far the most productive walleye lure of my experience, as far across the current as we could, being careful to time our casts so as not to interfere with our neighbors. The current quickly swept retrieves downstream, so each fisherman cast upstream, immediately following his downstream neighbor's upstream cast. Without direction or organization, it worked beautifully. There were tangles only when a hooked fish disrupted the cadence, and surprisingly few instances of that. There were walleyes constantly being hoisted onto the boulders on both sides of us, but none of the three of us had hooked a fish. Jack looked at me and shook his head. "How do you spell 'jinx'?"

I reached into my pocket to find a grub tail in a darker color. Everyone seemed to be using brown or maroon lures. Next to me was a stocky fellow with the sun-withered face of someone rarely under a roof. He had taken three nice walleyes in as many minutes, and certainly must have noticed that I had not. He stepped closer to me. " No, not that". He pointed to the grub I was about to attach. "Here's what y'need." He held up a jighead shaped like a flattened bullet, dressed with a deer hair tail, all of it a deep rust color. "All them ornery fish'll take. I tried everything. This here's what works. There's a guy in that truck camper up there makes 'em. Name's Red Dale."

"Well, thanks, Red."

"No…not me…..him." He jerked a thumb towards the campground.

We scrambled up the slope as quickly as thin, hot air would allow. Just as the man had said, Red Dale was there, seated under an awning, humming to himself and painting jig heads. "Howdy," he grinned, "reckon somebody told you about my 'Red Dale Specials'. Aint that right? Well, they're three for four dollars. How many you want?"

"Uh….give us a dozen."

"What color? This here one's the most popular. Can't make 'em fast enough." He held up an exact duplicate of the one the man on the rocks had shown me.

"Nine of those and three white ones." I had to know whether it was shape or color.

"OK, boys. Good luck to ya."

The climb down to the rip-rap was slightly more disciplined this time, but only slightly. This was a phenomenon, and we did not know how long it would last. We returned to the spots we had vacated. The man who had given me the advice about Red Dale was packing up his gear. "Is the party over?" I asked, with ill-concealed anxiety in my voice.

"Nah, but I'm limited out and I sure could use a cold beer. See ya."

Mr. Dale's lures were magic. A cast long enough to reach the far side of the flow, where the fish seemed to be concentrated, produced a hook-up every time. Landing a fish, however, was not so easy. The near side stream bed was shallow and full of large rocks, and walleyes have a tendency to sound. We found that standing a bit further up the slope made for a steeper line angle, and reduced snagging. The waterline rip-rap of very large boulders provided another obstacle. It was very difficult to safely reach the water's edge to grip a fish or to use a conventional landing net. We observed that most people used a heavy leader five or six feet long and simply muscled the fish over the boulders. A few were equipped with very long-handled nets. We had neither. We lost a number of fish to both obstacles. Six of our nine maroon versions of the Red Dale Special remain at the bottom of the Bighorn River. But no matter. We had plenty of fish. We could now afford to experiment.

I attached the white version of the Red Dale Special. It was identical, except for color, but was far less effective. The number of fishermen had decreased markedly by now, and we were able to move up and down the bank. Except for the region of strong flow, there was no action – on any lure. But return to the current, with the rusty maroon Dale, and action was immediate. We did not land any walleyes of trophy size, nor did we see any landed. But this was one of those incongruous experiences – a walleye bonanza in a desert canyon – that will keep fishing fever forever incurable.

The bonanza ended as quickly as it had begun. Abruptly, the hum of the generators fell silent, the outflow slowed to a low level, and the very next cast, and all that followed it, were fruitless. We, and the few fishermen that remained, abandoned the canyon. Trudging back to our campsite, we stopped to visit with Red Dale, whom we now considered the Wizard of Boysen. He told us that, since his retirement, he and his wife winter in Arizona, but, come spring, wander the fishing holes of the western states, doing a little fishing and a lot of lure making. "Pays some of the expenses, anyways," he grinned, "and we get to see a lot of great country and meet a lot of good people."

"What is there about this Special of yours that makes it work so well here when nothing else does?" This was not idle conversation. Jack's tone was serious.

Red leaned back in the lawn chair. "To tell ya the truth, I don't know. I just used it here a few years ago and it really caught 'em….but only when the dam's runnin'. Maybe that current stirs up some little critter from the rocks that it looks like….or moves like. Boys, I'd tell ya if I knew. I really would."

"Does it work this well everywhere?"

"Well, I aint *been* everywhere. Oh, yeah, it works other places, but nothin' like here…..here an' a few other cricks within a hundred miles or so. But always below dams. Don't know why."

We invited Red and Mrs Dale, who sat smiling, but wordless, throughout our visit, to join us for fine Kentucky bourbon and a dinner of fresh walleye. Red declined, saying that they had a lot of packing to do, as they were leaving at first light for Montana. "Aw, damn it," Red grumbled, "me and Mom got to be up with the chickens. Reckon that's why I hate chickens."

Before we left, we replenished our supply of Specials, wished the Dales a safe and pleasant journey, and thanked them for the information. We prepared the evening meal gently. Ice from the cooler was dropped gently into the bourbon, so as not to bruise it. Rice was gently steamed so that it did not become mushy. Walleye was gently sautéed so that it remained tender and moist. We cooked outdoors, but dined in the camper because of the wind, which, confined by the narrow canyon, whistled vigorously and constantly through the cottonwood trees sustained by the waters of the Bighorn. Wind River Valley was indeed an appropriate name for the region. Before the night had ended, Tim and I had been forced to lash the camper to a nearby cottonwood tree to prevent its being tumbled into the canyon.

The after dinner debate centered upon the question of whether we should stay at Boysen, with a virtually assured supply of walleyes, or should press on, chasing sunsets, further west – specifically, to Jenny Lake, in Grand Tetons National Park. It was famous for trout, and Tim held that the mission of the trip had not been accomplished. It had been to catch trout, not walleyes, and that we had failed to do so. I took an opposite position, and quoted Frank Miller: "Never leave fish to find fish." Jack was the tie-breaker. At dawn, we departed for a day at Jenny Lake, leaving the camper at Boysen. The Dales were already gone.

Jack had been right. Everything is far away. Jenny Lake was no exception. We reached it well after mid-day, and found that, without a boat or a canoe, it was very difficult to fish. Having neither, and running out of daylight, we drove into Jackson and impersonated tourists for much longer than I could stand. We arrived back at Boysen just as the sun was executing its usual transition in the western sky. The low humidity, and the winds of the west, bearing aloft incredibly fine particles of dust, create sunsets of indescribable beauty. The western horizon transforms itself from blinding gold, which dissolves to orange, and then to pink, and then to red, and finally, to a deep, dark, tranquil scarlet. This was the spectacle that welcomed us back to Boysen. We were glad to be there.

When we awoke the next morning, there was a faint sound on the wind that snapped everyone awake. It was a familiar sound, one that is made by a fluorescent light or an electric motor, widely known as "sixty cycle hum". Tim sat up. "Hey! The dam's running."

"In the morning?"

"Yeah. Listen."

There was no discussion. Minimal clothing, minimal tackle and maximum speed towards the river, reckless descent to the water and frenzied casting. In my haste, I had tied on a white Red Dale Special, and decided to use it, despite the experience of the day before yesterday. To my amazement, the first cast produced a strong strike, and a heavy fish. Swimming with the current, the fish was unstoppable, but at the end of the swift flow distance, it could be turned. It could run up-current with surprising speed, once charging directly into the turbines' outflow. It could not sustain that flow, and performed another dizzying down-current run. Nearby anglers saw what was happening, and stopped fishing to watch and to clear the water. This was clearly not a walleye. The man to my right nodded, spat tobacco juice on a rock, and gave me a thumbs-up. "Big brown." he shouted. I did not want to lose a German brown trout of the apparent size of this one. This would be a trophy. This would be an over-the-mantle trout. Fishing is full of surprises.

I backed up onto the slope to gain the advantage of a steep line angle, trying to avoid the shallow, rocky bottom close to the bank. A man with a long-handled net scrambled to the water's edge and signaled me to bring the fish to the rocks. After several attempts, he got the fish into the net, and tried to raise it from the water. The net handle bent dangerously, but the man had a look of triumph on his face. He held it aloft, looked closely, and his expression became one of disappointment. The fish was not a "big brown". It was big…but a faded yellow. It was a common carp. No, that is not fair. It was an <u>un</u>common carp, as strong and as game a fish as I had yet encountered. The man with the net asked if I wanted it. I told him that I did not, and that he was welcome to it. He touched the brim of his hat and placed it beside his cooler. It would not fit inside.

Tim and Jack landed a number of fine walleyes that day, and I did, in fact, catch a brown trout. Not an over-the-mantle trout, but a decent one. It was the sole trout caught on the trip. The Wakefield brothers strictly admonished me to not complain about the trout fishing trip. "You caught a trout. Now, shut up."

That day happened to be the Fourth of July. That evening, we toasted George and Ben and Tom and any of the other founding fathers whose names we could remember. Jack apologized for not remembering sooner the Native American Fish Dance, which, he said, had been taught to him in a dream by a princess known as "The Bird Woman". Had he used it earlier, he said, we would have caught numerous trout. He explained that to perform it, one must be in a trance-like state, and that this had been the first opportunity. He demonstrated the dance and then sat down on his bunk. "That's very tiring," he said.

Time had run out. Like all Joes, we had other bells to answer….and soon. With the dawn, we would be eastbound, leaving this magnificently open, wonderfully lonely country. We had seen spectacular places, met friendly, colorful people, learned a few things, and even caught a few fish.

I don't have an over-the-mantle trout. I have something better. I have behind-the-eyebrows memories.

Chapter 14
A Dose of Salt
Landlubbers Learn Lessons

Otto Perry, whom you met in Chapter 10, went each February to Gulf Shores, Alabama, where, he said, it was still October. Temperatures were in the fifties and sixties, and most days were sunny. He didn't fish there; he and his wife spent their days walking the beach and frequenting the many tourist attractions, restaurants, museums and the like. Their stays were usually two weeks, a respite from the cold and gray of Midwestern Februaries. One year, circa 1990, I questioned him about fishing opportunities in that area. He said that he didn't know first hand, but that there were a lot charter boats and tackle shops in the area, so that there must be a substantial amount of sport fishing done. I asked where he had stayed, and he gave me the name of a real estate rental agency. It was a start.

Later that winter, my company got an order from a customer based in Bay Minette, Alabama. One of the project engineers assigned to follow the project lived on Mobile Bay……. and he was a fisherman. He was a cornucopia of information, and, as is always the case it seems, his accounts of the quality of fishing in the area were glowing. Out on the artificial reefs, he said, there were red snappers, vermillion snappers, Lane snappers and groupers of many species, as well as triggerfish and amberjacks. Trolling over the reefs produced dorado and king mackerel. Trolling further inshore, there were bull redfish and spanish mackerel. And, he went on, bluefish and spanish mackerel could be taken trolling just beyond the first breaking wave on the beach. There were offshore oil and gas rigs, he said, that were virtual fish magnets, some of them within Mobile bay, in sheltered waters. He gave me the names of places to stay, and recommended that we stay in Orange Beach, Alabama, where Perdido Pass would give us access to both the open ocean and to sheltered Perdido Bay. "If the wind comes up," he warned, "you won't want to take a twenty-footer out on the Gulf." How prophetic.

Old sayings become <u>old</u> sayings because they are true. "The grass is always greener…." is a perfect example. A scant few hours away, the Lake Erie walleye phenomenon, with limits of large walleyes caught within hours, sometimes minutes, was in full swing. Norris, and other TVA lakes, were teeming with trophy stripers. And, in the opposite direction, but no further distant than Orange Beach, John Theriault's blue and white Beaver stood poised to levitate us to fishing fantasy-land. And we would not have to tow a 5000 pound boat. But memories of Green Turtle Key danced in my head. Logic be damned, I could smell the sea.

We had fished the Gulf before, in Apalachicola Bay. We were armed, then, only with a seventeen foot Grumman center console aluminum boat, and were at least wise enough to not venture more than a few miles offshore. But the sea floor is shallow there, and to reach good fishing waters would have required runs of many miles, so we did not give that area a fair chance. We boated a few flounder and small rays, but largely stayed in the river, upstream of tidewater, catching crappies and bass.

But now we had the heavy, seaworthy Grady-White, bought for the vicious, unpredictable, boat-pummeling chop of Lake Erie. And it had acquitted itself well, there. As Jim Santangelo said, when we had re-trailered the boat after being caught in a violent storm, unpredicted by the National Weather Service, whose channel we constantly monitor, "Well, we got wet, but we didn't get dead."

I proposed the idea of a trip to the Gulf to Jim, prepared to recite stories from Green Turtle Key, and episodes on Lake Erie in which the Grady had proven its mettle. I had lists of the locations of artificial reefs and oil rigs. I had brochures from agents representing properties with dockage. I didn't need any of that. Jim's answer was his classic.

"Well……. why not?"

We offered inclusion to the rest of the circle. My youngest son, Tom, had the same response as had Jim. No one else was able to get away. Tom called me and said, 'Dad, I've never fished salt water before, except from the beach. What do I need and what do I need to know?"

"I don't know any more about it than you do. Bring whatever salt water tackle you have, and your pike rod for fishing the bay. We'll do our homework, read what we can, ask around, and learn as we go……like always."

My customer/informant suggested that, while fishing for king mackerel would be better later on, as the water warmed, early May was a very good compromise for a wider range of species, and for greater comfort. "In June", he said, "it gets pretty toasty out there. In the summer, I only fish at night." And so it was that we planned the trip for the first week of May. Now, by our Midwestern standards, on the Gulf coast, early May *is* summer. Temperatures are in the seventies and eighties, everything is green and blooming, corn is knee high, and the uniform of the day is T-shirt and shorts. The evening we departed the Ohio Valley, there was a frost. I was very tired of being cold.

Jim's Diesel Suburban could cruise 450 miles, even towing a heavy boat, between refuelings. So, when we opened the doors in lower Alabama, we were treated to a soft, moist morning, a welcome change from the chill, wee-hours fuel stop in north Georgia. We reasoned that marina fuel costs would be higher than those on the highway, so we filled the Grady's tank. It thirstily swallowed 62 gallons of gasoline, and not regular unleaded. It had more expensive tastes. But, at least we had aboard the full complement of 80 gallons, enough for 160 miles of cruising range. Big bore, two stroke engines are not fuel efficient. That is the price of high power per unit weight. We thought that we had enough fuel for the week. We would learn that we did not. We would learn many things.

We found the office of the rental agency, but learned that it would not open for another three hours. So we provisioned at a nearby supermarket, and then sought out a local tackle shop, there hoping to gather some intelligence on where to go, what to use, and when. It was a Saturday morning, and the shop was crowded. We tried to listen in on the various conversations between staff and customers to glean what information we could. But, to us, most of it seemed a foreign language, a cryptic code.

"Yeah, did OK yesterday on the pipes, but the beeliners were small. Got a couple of bulls trollin', though. You got any cigars? I'm gonna try Lillian today."

"Only frozen."

"Well….OK. Gimme five pounds."

"Been to the tanks? Leon said they're doin' pretty good out there."

"Prob'ly tomorrow. See ya, Jerry."

We would have understood as much of that conversation had it been in Chinese. We wandered the aisles, ears up. With few exceptions, the tackle displayed was as foreign to us as the language. It was not like the tackle shops in the Outer Banks, oriented to surf fishing. Some of this tackle was serious, blue water equipment, large and heavy. Some was intended for inshore, bay fishing, sizes and styles we could relate to. But most of it was intended for reef fishing, heavy sinkers and strong hooks, attached to braided, stainless steel leaders that looked like aircraft control cables. We were clearly out of our league.

It was time to do some serious pride swallowing. When the crowd had thinned a bit, we walked to the counter to apply for fishing licenses. Because the licenses were non-resident, the woman behind the counter already knew that we were outsiders. "Look, ma'am, we've never been here before. We don't know anything. Where should we go, what should we use, and how should we use it, to catch a few fish?"

She chuckled and smiled. "Y'all got a boat?"

"Yeah. Twenty foot Grady."

"That'll be enough, less'n the wind comes up strong. Now, this map shows the reefs and fish havens. Just get on one of 'em – you can see 'em on a fish finder – you got a fish finder?"

"Yeah."

"Well, just about ever'thing in the ocean'll take shrimp or squid. Just drop a bottom rig. If the wind's down, just drift across it. Otherwise, you have to anchor. Now here, on the back of this map are the Loran co-ordinates of the fish havens. Easy to find. You got Loran?"

"No, ma'am." At that time we were not so equipped.

"Well, y'all just gonna have to do it the old fashioned way, map and compass, an' correct for wind and tide. My husband aint got Loran, either. Says he never needed it before and he don't need it now. 'Course, he was born and raised here."

That *would* make a difference.

We bought frozen shrimp and frozen squid in little tubs, the size of a pint ice cream container. We had no idea how fast, once a structure holding fish is found, such a container is emptied. It did not take more than one day's experience to teach us to buy bait in five pound boxes.

The rental agency's office was open by now, and we registered, got directions to the condo we had rented, and were on our way along the beach road connecting Gulf Shores to Orange Beach. This was the antithesis of the approach to a fishing site *on Beavers' wings.* The road, except for a stretch occupied by a state park, was lined with high rise, beach front hotels and condos, restaurants, shops, and tourist traps of all descriptions. Traffic was reminiscent of rush hour in a major city. Perhaps we had expected Orange Beach to be a quaint and quiet fishing village, with weathered wooden cottages, and nets strung out to dry, something that Norman Rockwell might have painted. It was not. Good fishing venue; not quaint and quiet.

We found the condo complex easily; we also found that it had no launch ramp. We were directed back west along the beach road to a really excellent public ramp at the western end of Cotton Bayou. It had the right slope, the right depth, ample maneuvering room, and was well sheltered, no matter the wind direction. I was anxious to get the hull wet. As far as we knew, this boat had never been in salt water before. We had purchased it, used, from a boat dealer near Lake Erie, who maintained that the previous owner had only used it from June through August, as he was a school teacher, and used it only on the lake. (Let's see, how does that go? "A little old lady only drove it to church on Sunday.") But, in any case, there was no evidence of the corrosive effects of salt water on the exposed hardware. We would remedy that.

Jim is accomplished at trailer handling. He deftly backed the trailer into the water, stopping short of the hull floating free, until I had the engine started and warm. We had learned that the hard way. Then, seeing my thumbs-up signal in the mirror, he inched backward until the hull was clear, waited until I had engaged reverse, and then he drew the trailer clear. Tom and I idled out of the no wake zone. Salt water is slightly denser than fresh water. The hull floats higher and the propeller encounters more inertia against which to thrust. We discovered that the Grady would run about 10% faster than in fresh water. We also discovered that we did not know the vagaries of the channel, and very nearly went aground on a sand bar. We subsequently proceeded at a more cautious pace.

The condo came with a boat slip, but the slips were not marked. We reasoned that a slip without mooring lines left on the mooring posts was unclaimed, and tied off at one of them. Jim was rinsing down the trailer with fresh water, as the trailer was fabricated from painted carbon steel. We did not realize, at the time, that we had, with that single immersion in salt water, set in motion a long-term, but terminal, sequence of corrosion. It ultimately took the life of that trailer. It should have been a clue that the parking lot at the ramp contained not a single trailer that was not either galvanized steel or aluminum. Jim parked the trailer, and we unloaded our gear. The unit we had rented was on the third floor, and the prospect of carrying everything up three flights of stairs was mildly unpleasant. But Jim discovered that there was an elevator……and a baggage cart. We had, I thought, achieved a new low. Fish camp with an elevator!

By the time everything was stowed, the sun was well west of its mid-afternoon position. We decided that we would not venture out of the inlet, but would use what daylight remained to catch, at least, a dinner of pan fish in the bay. We had one of those not-for- navigation, touristy maps of the inshore waters – the kind with the fish species icons and the chart of baits and methods – the ubiquitous kind titled "Fishing the (fill in the blank) Area, sold in every bait shop in the civilized world. The really amazing thing was that we actually believed it.

Using the prescribed methods in the prescribed places proved completely futile. The two tubs each of shrimp and squid were iced down in a cooler, and we thought that was a good thing, as it looked as though they would last the week. The tide was falling, and so was the sun. Recalling the sandbar upon which we had nearly grounded earlier, I was not anxious to navigate unfamiliar shallow water in the dark. Besides, we were all fatigued from the overnight drive. There were no objections to the suggestion that we pack it in. Before the Grady reached the slip, navigation lights were necessary. The day had ended too soon…….as fishing days will.

Attention turned to dinner. Tom was peering into the refrigerator. "Well, there's overconfidence for you. The only meat we bought was a ham hock to cook with collards. We always caught enough fish to eat…..until now.

We have potatoes and carrots and onions, collard greens, milk, eggs, butter, cornmeal, pasta. Rats! I was looking forward to seafood."

"And so, you shall have it," intoned Jim, rising to his feet and retrieving the bait cooler. "Calimari. Yes, an old Italian favorite."

"Wait a minute," Tom enjoined, "we're not gonna eat that squid."

"Calimari." corrected Jim. "If you eat it, it's calamari. It's only squid if you bait with it."

"Oh, no, we're not." Tom took one of the tubs and looked carefully at it. His skeptical expression softened. "Well, there are cooking instructions on the container, so, I guess it's fit….."

"Gimme that", grinned Jim, "and mix me a martini, while I perform some Italian magic."

And that he did. The pasta with calamari sauce was outstanding. We had eaten the bait.

The morning snuck up behind us and took us by surprise. Our sleep-deprived bodies weren't ready for it. They mounted a determined defense, but knew it would win. It enlisted the aid of an arrogant mockingbird on the balcony rail, who recited his entire repertoire, over and over. Resistance was futile. Somebody made coffee.

We had an off-shore hydrographic map, of apparently good quality, that the lady at the tackle shop had recommended. It showed the reefs and fish havens to about twenty-five miles south of the beach, along with their Loran-C co-ordinates, useless to us. But it had a compass rosette, corrected to local magnetic variation, and a scale of distance in both statute and nautical miles. We had a tide table, and we could get wind direction and speed from the NOAA weather channel on the marine radio in the boat. The previous owner had equipped the Grady with a navigation grade, gimbaled compass, and a speedometer. We had a watch with a sweep second hand, all of the tools needed for dead reckoning navigation. At breakfast, we plotted a course to the nearest fish haven.

The morning was bright and warm, with a light southeasterly wind, so light that compensation for it would be minimal. Once beyond the pass, tidal current was also very small. A buoy about a mile offshore served as a fixed reference, and from it we began to time the distance, cruising at twenty miles per hour at the calculated heading. But when the time it should have taken expired, sonar showed no variation in the depth of the featureless bottom, no structure, and, of course, no fish. Confident that we had to be at least close to the target, we began a grid search, watching the sonar screen, idling due north for about 200 yards, then turning east for 50 yards and then due south for 200 yards. Nothing. We decided to return to the starting point and do a westward search. But where WAS the starting point? It was then that we realized that we were short an inexpensive, but crucial, piece of gear: a small marker buoy that would serve as a fixed reference. Another lesson learned.

From what we guessed was close to the search starting point, the first northward leg showed a variation in depth of about four feet, and an irregular bottom. A few yards further, and the screen began to show the characteristic arch-shaped echoes of fish. We had missed the southeast corner of the fish haven by only about 100 yards, about ½ of 1% error, in that distance. But, of course, wind and sea conditions had been ideal. And, there was always the possibility that we had just been very lucky.

Given the conditions, we decided to drift. The wind would carry us over the center of the fish haven. We had not replaced the squid, in our haste to get lines in the water, so shrimp was the only choice. Tom had rigged his surf rod, with the same bottom rig he had used in previous beach outings, while we had been underway. (We would soon learn that surf rods are extremely unhandy for bottom fishing from a boat.) Before either Jim or I could get bait in the water, Tom stood up and placed one foot against the gunwale. "Hey! I got one! And…and…it's BIG….REALLY big."

From the arch of the rod, and the hiss of line slashing the water, it was clear that this was no two pound, or twenty pound, fish. He had set the reel drag at near the breaking strength of the 17 pound test line he was using, and this fish was stripping it at will. But it was a full spool, on a fairly large capacity spinning reel….at least 200 yards. About 100 yards off the port beam, the fish broke water, somersaulting five or six feet above the surface.

"What is it Dad?"

"Can't tell, but it's not a deep bodied fish….more cylindrical."

"Going around the bow!"

This was why we chose a center console configuration boat. Before it was over, Tom had made many full circuit trips around its periphery. But at this point, the battle became a stand-off, line going in neither direction. Tom was beginning to perspire heavily.

"If you're not taking any line, it means he's having to spend energy. Just keep that line tight. He can't do it forever."

"Me either!"

Shortly, the fish tired of that game, and made a strong dash off the starboard bow.

"Almost out….almost out of line", Tom gasped. "you'll have to follow him!"

I was about to start the engine, when the line fell slack.

Tom shook his head. "Lost him!"

"Maybe not! Keep crankin'!"

As Tom recovered line, the line direction gradually changed from the starboard bow direction towards the starboard quarter, as if a strong current were sweeping the slack, broken line westward. But, there was no current.

"Still on! Still on! Be ready!"

Tom scrambled aft to the transom. He had the savvy to keep the rod tip high, and now the awkwardly long surf rod was an advantage, offering great shock absorption. And he was to need it. When the line came taut, the yardage he had recovered disappeared in a few seconds. When the run stopped, the spool on his reel was visible. Another dash, and the contest would be over. Seventeen pound line would not hold this fish. But another stand-off followed. Tom sat down in the helm seat, braced the butt of the rod against it, and held on. After a few minutes, he began to pump the rod to recover line, a few yards at a time. The fish was moving again, in a wide arc to port. Tom followed it, leaning against the console, then climbing onto the forward deck, then to the port side again, gradually recovering line. He was, at least for the moment, winning.

Tom was becoming exhausted, but so was this fish. The spirals around the boat continued, but in ever decreasing radius. At about fifty yards, the fish surfaced briefly. It appeared to be five or six feet long, dark in color, but did not remain visible long enough to be identified. Jim had dug out a booklet we had received with our licenses, with pictures and descriptions of local species, along with information about size and bag limits. "Not a king mackerel," he mumbled, "maybe a cobia? Not a dorado, either. Says amber jacks don't get that long. Need a better look."

"Might never get it', Tom said, "he's gone under the boat!" Again, the long surf rod was an advantage. Tom was able to swing it over the stern, avoiding the propeller, and was lifting hard, the rod arched deeply, its tip almost in the water. By feet and by inches, the fish was surrendering depth. We peered intently into the water, trying to follow the line to whatever was affixed to the other end of it. Finally, a blurred, dark shape appeared, then sounded again, and that sequence was repeated a half dozen times before a definable view was possible.

"Look at that blunt nose. That's a shark!"

"What kind?"

Jim was staring at the booklet. "Boy, I don't know. There's a lot of 'em that look pretty much alike. I think it's this one here…the black tipped shark. Look at those fins. See? Just like this picture."

"There are a lot of protected species. How about this one?'

"No. Not that I can tell. It's not on this list here."

Throughout this debate, Tom was leaning into the rod, keeping pressure on the fish. He was clearly reaching the limit of his endurance. "Make up your minds", he pleaded, "either boat this thing or cut it loose. I'm worn out."

Jim had retrieved another book from the console. "Hey, this other book says black tips are good to eat."

"Your fish, Tom. What do you want to do?"

"I never ate shark. Let's try it. Where's your gaff hook?"

"Uh….we don't have a gaff hook."

It was time to take charge of the situation; ignorance has never deterred me. "OK. Jim, grab one of those mooring lines in that starboard hatch, there, and we'll get a loop around its tail, tie it off to one of the aft cleats, and tow it in." Bad idea. Really bad idea. First of all, lassoing a shark's tail is like trying to put waders on a wildcat, but we finally accomplished it. Secondly, towing the beast at any speed over idle threatened to rip the aft cleat off the boat, and we had thirteen miles to go…..at about one mile per hour. It was clear that the fish had to be put aboard the boat, an even worse idea.

Now, folklore has it that if you tow a shark backwards in the water, it will drown. That is probably true, and you likely need tow it no further than Morocco or Sweden. We have empirical evidence that one mile is not enough. The terrible illusion is that it *appears* to be enough. The fish we dragged over the gunwale and placed on the deck seemed to be, as the Munchkin coroner had famously put it, "really quite sincerely dead". Prodding it produced no response, whatever. We set a course for the buoy, and brought the Grady up on plane. The day was perfect, light chop on the sea, mid-seventies, cloudless, soft blue skies….and suddenly a violently thrashing shark all over the deck, the forward end with a large number of very unfriendly teeth, the aft end capable of bone-breaking blows. We drifted for what seemed a very long time, all three of us standing on the gunwales, clinging to the T-top frame – fortunately fabricated of very substantial stainless steel tubing. It was, after all, merely a question of time. The thrashing abated, and we proceeded back to our dockage. It had been an experience.

It was mid-day, most of the boats were elsewhere, and the fish cleaning station on the dock was deserted. Once hefted onto the cleaning table, the fish looked smaller than it had in the water, as all fish do. We had means neither to weigh it, nor measure it, but it was longer than the width of the deck at the transom, and that distance is sixty-six inches, so it was well over the minimum length requirement. We were greatly encouraged: the very first fish. What would the rest of the week bring, as we became more properly equipped, and began to learn the waters? As it turned out, the rest of the week saw many nice fish come over the transom, but nothing like this one. In fact, in the subsequent years of fishing that area, with great success, our circle has never boated its equal. Beginners' luck.

Cleaning a shark is not a task for the faint of heart….or stomach. Knowing no better, we decided to cut it into steaks, on the theory that the skin, which strongly resisted removal, would be easily dealt with after grilling the steaks. Slicing the carcass into steaks proved more difficult than expected, as well. Jim saved the day. He had, under the seat of his truck, a pruning saw, and it was able to cut through the cartilaginous spine, though not without considerable effort. It was a messy business, and the steaks were a bit ragged, but they grilled well enough….after we learned to marinate them in buttermilk to remove the pronounced ammonia flavor. All in all, quite edible….. "but it aint swordfish".

Trolling the beaches produced "snapper", or "tailor", bluefish and spanish mackerel, but not every day. Some days the schools were there, and some days they were not. When they were present, they were exactly where we had been told: just beyond the first breaking wave in the surf. We observed that while a number of boats were trolling the beaches, none of them seemed to be working the outer edge of the surf, as we were, and we were catching fish. We learned, very nearly the hard way, that a helmsman not paying strict and constant attention, could in seconds find his boat on its side on the beach. It was a risky occupation for another reason. An engine failure could immediately result in the same fate.

So, we kept an anchor at the ready. If that engine so much as hic-cupped, the anchor was instantly overboard on the seaward side. We've been "getting by with it" for years, now.

We learned, from that encyclopedia of local fishing intelligence, the tackle shop, that the lure of choice was something called a spanish mackerel rig. We midlanders had never seen anything like it. It consisted simply of a length of fairly heavy monofilament leader, about three feet, with a hook attached every six inches or so, and a snap hook at the end. The hooks were dressed with short pieces of plastic straws of various colors. It looked to us more like something one would hang on a Christmas tree than drag through the water. But when a small, bright, silver spoon was attached to the snap hook, and it was deployed at, to us, an insanely high trolling speed, it was very effective. On a few fortunate occasions, we happened upon a school of bluefish in blitz mode. Two lines, each with two or three feisty bluefish attached, in a rolling, yawing boat trolling the edge of disaster, make for an interesting time.

Our first venture to a serious reef, rather than to a relatively close-in fish haven, was, let us say, *instructive*. The sea was relatively placid that morning, with a southwest wind at 8 to10 mph. The sky was clear, NWS predicted no rain or increase in wind speed. Conditions were good. We plotted a course from the buoy to a reef called, on the map, Lillian Bridge, the rubble from the demolition of a bridge near the town of Lillian, Alabama. (Aha. So that's what he meant by, "I'm gonna try Lillian today".) We did not know the area that this reef covered. Let us assume that the bridge was 60 feet wide and 1000 feet long, 60,000 square feet, as it had stood. Let's assume that it was dumped covering the same area, about an acre and a half. If that is so, and I have no evidence to suggest that it is, then, by dead reckoning, we are attempting to find a typical suburban lot, 245 feet by 245 feet, about thirteen miles away. Just one degree error in heading, at that distance, is 1167 feet. This was not going to be easy.

After arriving at what we thought was the site, it took two hours of grid search before sonar revealed a slight change in depth, and another half hour before fish echoes appeared. And they were highly concentrated. It took another forty minutes of anchoring and re-anchoring, tying together every scrap of rope aboard – the anchor line was not long enough – before the boat was finally located over the fish. But it was worth the effort. It was impossible to get bait to the bottom. Every drop caught a fish. Most of them were small, grunts, undersized red snappers, vermillion snappers, aka beeliners (Aha!), and pesky remora, the "pilotfish" that attach themselves to sharks. But, there was the occasional keeper red snapper, good sized vermillion, and rod-bending triggerfish. We had bought five pounds of squid, and exhausted them quickly. By the time the bait was gone, we had a decent catch of reef fish. It had been furious action. We were delighted.

It was clear, blue water here, and we had noticed schools of large fish cruising by the boat at no more than 10 feet below the surface. They appeared to be amber jacks, but did not respond to any bait or lure cast to them. We had also seen several sharks cruise by, but wanted no more of that. We decided to troll king mackerel rigs on the way back to the buoy, but had no success until we were perhaps a mile south of the buoy, no more than two miles from shore. There, Jim hooked a heavy, very fast fish. It streaked across the surface, its silver body easily visible in the sun, took all of the line on the reel, and broke off.

"What was that, Jim?"

"I don't know. Big king I guess. Let's get in. I gotta get to the tackle place before they close. I need some more serious line."

We also acquired 200 feet of heavy anchor line, a gaff hook, and a marker buoy, and we resupplied with squid and shrimp. I noticed, in the bait freezer, a box marked "cigar minnows". (Aha!) We were beginning to learn the language. Lillian was not a cigar-chomping lady friend, after all. Then, we had a transom well full of fish to clean, assisted by a raucous flock of sea birds, which we thought to be laughing gulls, who appeared out of nowhere as soon as we took up positions at the cleaning bench, and by a bold, great blue heron who stood patiently eight or ten feet away on the dock. He assumed, apparently from experience, that he was entitled to a handout, which, of course, he got. Offal from the cleaned fish were thrown into the water, (unless intercepted, as most were, by these remarkably agile birds), where small fish and crabs assure that nothing, absolutely nothing, goes to waste. It was nearly dark before the fish cleaning task was complete, and as the sun departed the horizon to the west, there was no red sky.

We were tired. It had been a long and interesting day, and before a wonderful dinner of perfectly fresh fish had been eaten, the rest packed and frozen, and things put in order, midnight had passed. We missed the dawn by two hours; we did not know whether the morning sky had been red. But we knew that the weather channel on the VHF marine radio in the boat did not convey a cheerful message: "….occasional rain, northwest winds 15 to 20 knots, and afternoon thunderstorms." At the dock, the sky was overcast, but not ominously black, the wind seemed gentle enough, perhaps 5 to 8 knots, and there was but a light chop on bay waters as we made our way towards the pass. We decided to troll the beach for bluefish and spanish mackerel, never allowing ourselves more than two miles from the pass….. just in case the weather channel had been correct. And it had been.

We were well east of the pass, close to two miles, and without a single strike, when the soft, moist breeze suddenly rose to a chill, ugly wind. We were sheltered by the land mass, and did not encounter rough seas, but the message of that wind was clear. This time, for once, we had the good sense to listen, and turned into the pass. The west jetty of the inlet was sheltered from the wind, and we anchored there, hoping to engage a black drum or a sheepshead. That effort was not rewarded, but the rain, which had begun on the way to the pass, was not objectionable, and it was not unpleasant to remain there, sheltered from the wind, and to at least be on the water – fish or no fish.

I thought back to the salt water fishing advice given me by Frank Miller: "Don't bother to fish in any wind with a "w" in it." Now that I thought about it, that had been true on the Outer Banks, in the Florida Keys, and in the Bahamas. And yet, there was Grandpa Ruilman's wisdom: "Wind from the west, fish bite the best; wind from the east, fish bite the least." Must one of my trusted mentors be wrong? Not at all; totally different venues, a thousand miles apart. Then, to the west, we heard the ominous rumble. "Guys, we're out of here!"

The thunderstorm's approach was incredibly rapid. It seemed most inconsistent with the movement of the weather system as a whole. It was clear that we would not reach dockage before it overtook us. In a thunderstorm, the safest place to be is inside a shelter. That lacking, the idea is to not be the highest point in the vicinity and to not be the best electrical path to ground. For those purposes, it is hard to beat being under a big, steel bridge, and that is exactly where we headed, all six throttles open. No guarantees, mind you, but damned good odds. The tidal outflow was strong, and it was not easy to secure an anchorage under the bridge. By the time the anchor was set, rain was pelting down with a fury, and lightning kept the sodden sky illuminated almost constantly. But we were safe, or, at least, we so convinced ourselves. There was nothing to do but to fish.

The strong current required heavy sinkers, at least four ounces. Even then, when they engaged the bottom, the line formed a good thirty degree angle with the vertical. Sonar showed an irregular bottom, obviously rocky, and a surprising number of fish echoes, not large, but many. But there was no action. It was true that the echoes were from directly beneath the transom, and that our lines were down-current far enough that they might not have been among the fish. We tried dropping the heavy sinkers up-current, but even when line angles were vertical, there was no response. On the reefs and fish havens, dropping squid or shrimp into such echoes produced instant strikes. What was going on here?

The sound of thunder trailed off to the southeast. The rain decreased in intensity to a steady, but gentle, shower, and the sky brightened a bit. Someone had a strike. Then another of us. Thereafter, it was again impossible to get bait to the bottom. The fish were small, mostly blue grunts, now and then a sheepshead, but they were certainly of edible size, for the most part. We kept enough for dinner, not knowing whether we would have any further chance to fish that day. And we did not. Between storms, we made for our dockage, as weather conditions turned worse. Still, it had been a great day. As Jim had said of the storm on Lake Erie, "We got wet, but we didn't get dead." That always makes for a great day on the water. Or anywhere else.

The next day was cloudless and bright, but there was a cool northeasterly breeze of about 12 knots. The sea was certainly not smooth, but the waves of two to three feet were not so intimidating that we abandoned the idea of going back to Lillian Bridge. We were surprised that the ride was not more uncomfortable. We were accustomed to very slow and bumpy progress in "two-to-three's" on Lake Erie. But here, the wavelength was much longer, and the boat-bashing much less severe. Nevertheless, about half way to destination, we decided to look for a closer reef. Not starting from a fixed point would make navigation by dead reckoning all the more difficult. But we were still within easy sight of land, and by triangulating from fixed points on the map, could roughly pinpoint our location. And "roughly" was indeed the appropriate descriptor.

The map offered us few options. The nearest reef to our position was called Kelly Pipes. (Aha!) So, that's what the man meant by, "..did OK on the pipes". An inexact heading from an inexact position leads to an inexact destination. It took us hours to find the reef, finally resorting to following hydrographic contours of constant depth. Sonar had become our navigation instrument. But when we finally found the reef, the sonar screen lit up with fish echoes. The man had been right. The beeliners, another name for vermillion snappers, were small; only a small percentage were worth keeping. But they were legion. They, large blue grunts, trigger fish, and the ubiquitous remoras soon ran us out of bait. It was still early, despite our wanderings in search of the reef, and we decided to troll back to the buoy, again using king mackerel rigs. This was not based upon any advice, or upon our own knowledge, it was simply what we had available.

Recovering the anchor proved no mean feat. It had apparently become lodged in the submarine debris of the reef, and it took a great deal of coaxing, pulling from every point on the compass, to finally free it. The heavy steel shank was badly bent, but it was repairable…..if there happened to be a blacksmith shop nearby. The marker buoy proved also unequal to the task. It was about the size of a five pound dumbbell, with line wrapped around the middle, connected to a heavy sinker. Tossed overboard, it spun as the sinker fell, and if the length of the line was appropriate, marked the spot where the sinker had encountered the bottom. It was colored blaze orange, and was highly visible….on a calm surface. In three foot seas, we were never able to find it again. The marker buoy now carried as standard equipment on the Grady is 18 inches long and 10 inches in diameter. Spy satellites always know where we are.

We had not trolled 50 yards when Jim hooked a very respectable fish, fast and strong. We were hopeful that it was a nice king mackerel, but I doubted that. I had seen this particular fighting style before, in the Bahamas. I could almost hear Joe Sawyer screaming, "Leave it in the water, dom ye." The adversary had to be a dorado – dolphin fish – aka mahi-mahi. Jim handled it skillfully, never applying too much pressure, but never allowing the fish to rest. And our new gaff was put to good use. It turned out to not be so large as it seemed at first – fish never are – but was a magnificently colored cow dorado, perhaps seven or eight pounds. "Well," I said, "ol' Joe Sawyer said they're always in schools. Let's troll over this reef again, right here." And so we did, for at least an hour. We never had the second strike.

In our circle, there is no such thing as "my fish", except for purposes of photography. All fish brought over the gunwales are "our fish", equally shared, for as we all know, in the same place, using the same baits, with identical techniques, luck is the arbiter of whose hook a given fish attacks. My share of that dorado was never cooked. It was eaten as sashimi, and not artfully carved into floral designs. It was eaten in a chunk…..like a beefsteak. Cold. A fish of that ilk is always iced down immediately. I am sure that the broiled dorado was excellent. But no trade.

Finally, the weather drove us into Perdido Bay, as winds made the sea imprudent for a twenty foot boat. The bay was a whole new environment. The Intracoastal Waterway crossed it, with a channel dredged to a depth suitable for ocean-going tugs, and large private vessels. This artificial depth presented fishing opportunities. Outside the marked channels, depth was shallow and uncertain, as each year's storms altered the bottom. We thought that perhaps, like Croatan Sound, in the Outer Banks of North Carolina, the edges of dredged channels would yield flounder. We found that, in fact, they did. But the flounder were small, not of legal size. We discovered, again by accident, a far better resource, a strong and determined fighter, excellent table fare, and plentiful. I am somewhat loathe to expose the apparently well-kept secret of this under-appreciated species, but accuracy in reporting dictates that I must. We spent a wonderful afternoon in the company of the gafftopsail catfish, a marine catfish, easily as tasty as a freshwater channel catfish, but on average, much larger. Somehow, they seem to be distained by locals. We did not understand that, but we applauded it.

Once, on a later visit, on an usually cold and windy afternoon, we were accosted by the local wildlife officer, in a remote cove in the bay. "What're y'all fishin' for back in here?"

"Sail cats."

"How y'all know about that?" he asked, looking at the Ohio registration on our boat.

"Caught 'em before. Good eatin' and a hell of a fight."

"For my money, best tastin' fish in the ocean. Now, right over there, in that channel back to those docks, is a good place. I'm not gonna ask for your licenses. Out-of-staters always got 'em. Good luck to ya."

He was right about the channel. Southern hospitality.

And there was another interesting facet of these fish. They are heavily enveloped in a layer of thick slime. The amount, and not the presence, was the remarkable aspect of it. All fish are protected by a slippery mucus coating, but the gafftopsail catfish (sail cat, for short) had what seemed a gross – in every sense of the word – oversupply of it. And it was difficult to wash off after handling one of them. Now, for several months prior to the trip, Jim had been battling a problem with the skin on his hands. After a long winter in dry, artificial heat, his hands were deeply and painfully cracked, despite the best efforts of the medical community. He was worried that he would be vulnerable to infection from the countless microbes, unknown to his immune system, in the marine environment. Instead, after a few days of catching and handling sail cats, his hands were healing nicely. Upon his return, he reported this phenomenon to his physician. Jim had expected skepticism, or, at least, surprise. "Sure," said the good doctor, "fish slime is full of a variety of natural anti-biotics, and you happened to hit the right one."

We also learned, the <u>very</u> hard way, that another species of marine catfish known as the "hardhead", smaller than sailcats, but very widely distributed, is equipped with extremely sharp fins, loaded with a potent venom. Carelessness, or more correctly, lack of extreme caution, in handling them can lead to excruciatingly painful wounds, and even temporary local paralysis. After receiving a fairly deep puncture in my right palm, in addition to the pain, my right hand refused to do what I asked it to do for about an hour. We discovered that rubbing wound sites with sail cat slime reduced, and shortened, the pain of hardhead "accidents".

It was our practice to scrub down the boat each evening with fresh water, and not only to reduce corrosion. The interior was usually spattered with blood, squid ink, and bait fragments. Gaffing a fish too large to net is a messy business, and spanish mackerel, even when cleanly hooked in the jaw, seem to bleed just for practice. So it was that, putting away the brushes and hose, I was engaged in conversation one evening by a resident of the condo complex. He pointed to a veranda overlooking the docks.

"I been watchin'", he said, "y'all boys been catchin' some fish."

"Yeah. But we haven't been able to connect with many king mackerel. Got only one, so far."

"How you been goin' after 'em?"

"Trollin' with king rigs."

"Nah. Just go out about a mile off the beach and drift with live pinfish. Hook 'em through both lips and just let 'em swim….no sinkers or anything. Kings'll be migratin' through here this time of year. The pinfish gotta be live. Dead ones won't work."

"Hate to ask this, but…….what's a pinfish?"

The man regarded me as though I had just emerged from an alien spaceship. "Why," he said, "those little stripe-itty fellas that hang around these dock posts and rock piles and things. You want 'em about this big. Just take a little hook an' a bobber an' a tiny piece o' squid tentacle. Easy."

"OK. Hey, thanks a lot."

Later that evening, well after dark, Jim asked, "Hey, did you switch off the batteries in the boat?"

I had been distracted from the routine procedure by the conversation about pinfish. "No. Better go do it."

The docks were well lighted, and there was a powerful floodlight at one corner, a few feet off the water, directed downward. It had attracted a swarm of small fish. I was wondering whether they were pinfish and, if so, whether this might be the ideal place to collect a few, when they erupted from the water in a shower, as a bright silver flash appeared momentarily in the cone of light. Every few minutes, the baitfish would be scattered by another brief flash of silver, then re-collect under the light. The batteries were forgotten; I retrieved my light rod from the boat and selected a slowly sinking crankbait that I thought resembled the baitfish. This looked like a sure thing.

The only way to cast across the orb of light was to cling precariously to the end of an adjoining boat slip. There were mooring lines and other obstructions in the way, and it became apparent that trying to cast beyond the cone of light, and to retrieve through it, was impractical. I was reduced to the inelegant technique of dropping the lure directly into the light's beam, letting it sink, and twitching it upwards. This disturbed the swarm, but they gathered again. I had repeated this process unsuccessfully a dozen times, and was ready to abandon the effort, when the periodic silver flash was accompanied by a violent strike.

There is an old saying that failing to plan is planning to fail. One of my business partners was fond of it. I had failed to consider how I might handle a large fish on light line in this minefield of obstructions. I had also failed to think about, in the unlikely event that a fish could be brought to the surface, how it might be landed; I did not bring the landing net from the boat. But there is yet another old saying: I'd rather be lucky than good. And I was lucky. That fish did not dash for the sanctuary of the structure under the docks, but out into the open water of the bayou. And, at length, after stubborn resistance, it was indeed brought to surface beside the dock. It was a very nice speckled sea trout, about four pounds, too heavy to try to lift onto the dock with 6 pound test line. I lay, face down, on the dock, but could still not reach the water, as the tide was out. My plan had been to grasp the fish under the gill covers, a very risky maneuver with the front set of treble hooks still exposed. The tide had likely spared me a painful injury. But the problem of landing the fish remained. What do I do now?

I could not leave the site; I had to make do with what was within reach. There was nothing in my pockets of any use, but there was a multi-tool on my belt. Perhaps, by using the pliers feature, I could grip the fish's jaw. The lowering water level made that plan unworkable. There happened to be a boat moored in the next slip, and the tag end of a mooring line was gently waving in the tidal flow, almost a rod length out. It took several tries, but by allowing the fish some slack – never a good idea – it was possible to get the rod tip under the mooring line and coax it down the rod and into hand. Raising the fish to the surface, so that its head and the lure were exposed, after a frustrating dozen or so attempts, the lure's front hooks finally embedded into the rope, and the fish was hoisted onto the dock. Then came the equally frustrating business of getting the hooks out of the mooring line. But the fish was landed. It should not have been, by all odds, but every once in a while, by the quirkiest of means, one experiences undeserved good fortune. When it goes the other way, as it usually does, we refer to that as "paying your dues".

Baked trout makes a fine breakfast.

We intended to put to use the instruction we had received, and went down to the dock equipped, we thought, to catch pinfish. It was not nearly so easy as had been represented. They attacked the squid tentacles voraciously, but proved difficult to hook with the smallest hooks we had, which were the number six Aberdeens we used for Lake Erie perch. It took an hour to collect six or eight pinfish, and we set out for the pass. This time, free advice turned out to be worth every cent we had paid for it. Long, boring hours of drifting resulted in no action except for the occasional freight train strike followed by a complete stripping of a spool full of 30 pound test line and a loud snap as it gave way. Undoubtedly large sharks, we concluded. This was not working.

Someone suggested that we go back to trolling, but parallel to the beach, and about a mile out. There were certainly no objections to a change in tactics. Opting to troll in a westward direction first, it was easy to keep track of position by landmarks easily visible on the shoreline. We agreed that we would turn back eastward after two miles, then troll for four miles. We were using deep-running lures that occasionally contacted the bottom, which was, in that area, about thirty feet deep. But the bottom was relatively featureless and contacts with the bottom were infrequent and, so far, snagless. But just short of the two mile turn-around point, the drag clutch on Tom's reel hissed angrily. He seized the rod from the holder, and said, dejectedly, "I'm hung up."

"OK. We're about to turn around anyway." I shifted to neutral while Jim and I recovered our lines. The boat slowed to a stop, but the out-paying of Tom's line did not.

"This boat's not moving. Whadaya got there, another damn shark?"

"I…I don't think so. Acts more like…like a striper….or a REALLY big white perch."

"OK. You know what to do. I'm gonna get a drink of water, and watch."

The contest between an angler and a fish equal to, or greater than, the strength of his equipment, in unobstructed water, lies somewhere between chess and wrestling. It is a game of both body and mind. Strength, endurance and reflexes matter, but anticipation of the adversary's moves wins the day. Perhaps, in that sense, it is more accurately compared to an aerial dogfight between two evenly matched aircraft, and two equally skilled pilots. Whatever analogy one might choose, it is interesting to watch the contest unfold. Ten pound line can land a fifty pound fish, and a five pound fish can break ten pound line. Everything depends upon a branch of physics called *mechanics*, and how well the angler manages to deny the fish the advantage of *momentum*.

Whatever species was at the other end of that line, it was strong, but not unusually fast. Its runs were long, but when it turned towards the boat, it was not fast enough to over-run Tom's ability to recover line and to avoid slack. It never had the opportunity to exploit slack line so as to create a shock load on the tackle. Tom saw to that. *"Damn,"* I thought, *"the kid's good!"* Not that bringing it to boat was easy. It took a good twenty minutes. As soon as it became visible, the copper color and the pronounced spot near the tail told us that it was a redfish. We had caught five and six pound redfish on the Outer Banks, where they are called puppy drum, but nothing like this!

"My God," exclaimed Jim, "look at the SIZE of it!"

I was fumbling in the port side rod rack for the gaff hook.

"No. No. You can't kill that fish," Jim was thumbing through the regulations. "There's a slot limit, 16 to 26 inches, and that fish is four feet long!"

"Well, I'm not gonna just cut the line," Tom objected, "That's a twenty-six dollar lure."

"Let's try the net."

The net in question is deformed to this day by the weight of that fish, but it got the brute aboard, where the hooks were carefully removed, and the length measured. It was not four feet long, "only" thirty-nine inches. It was gently released, and immediately sounded.

"Well, we can't keep 'em, but it's great fishin'."

"Yeah. Let's troll that stretch again."

By late afternoon, we had released two more redfish, so obviously over the slot limit that we hadn't even bothered to measure them. The scale we had on board was limited to twenty pounds, and so, was useless. We returned to the beach to catch a dinner of bluefish and spanish mackerel, which was accomplished without difficulty. What an incredible day. But the surprises of the day were not over.

Dinner clean-up had been completed and we were waiting for the drier to complete its cycle, as we had felt the need to launder some very sweaty and bloody garments, which had become too aromatic, even for us. Jim was browsing the regulations yet again, while Tom and I were staring listlessly at the Weather Channel. "Hey. HEY! Look at this." Jim was jabbing his finger at a page as if it were a typewriter keyboard. "Down here…down here, it says you can keep one redfish over the slot limit per day. We could have kept all those fish!"

"What?"

"Yeah. Right there. See?"

"You know what this means, don't you?"

"Well, yeah, it says right here that………."

"It means that, now that we know this, we'll never hook another one."

And, by that trip's end, we never did. But we certainly did on subsequent trips.

Over time, our knowledge got upgraded, with each successive visit, and so did our equipment. Dead reckoning navigation may be soul-satisfying, but it is too time consuming. The Grady became outfitted with Loran-C, which still required some skill to employ. And then, with total surrender of self respect, with GPS. I hate GPS. It requires no skill, no geometry, no judgment, just follow the arrow on the display. But it is fast, reliable, and extremely accurate. Any greenhorn can easily find any reef whose co-ordinates are published……in longitude and latitude, not in the mysterious and esoteric "grid repetition intervals" of Loran-C. I hate GPS, but I use it. We are, after all, there to fish, not to engage in an exercise in Euclidian mathematics.

And then, there was Charlie. One excursion to the gulf involved Jim, myself, and Charlie Gay……which he most assuredly was not. Charlie is one of those personalities that infuses any environment with laughter and the unexpected. He was not, as he accused Jim and I of being, "hard core" with regard to fishing. Charlie was more at home in a cocktail lounge, where he usually became the impromptu floor show, than in a boat. But he had paid his dues at Cape Hatteras, standing in ice water, in 35F temperatures, and in a 20 knot wind, in pursuit of bluefish. We had assured Charlie that the weather would be warm, and that he would not have to get wet. The latter may have been an exaggeration.

There were high winds, and thunderstorms in progress, the day we arrived; we were not able to do much more than to launch the boat and secure it in its slip. After a rather extended happy hour, and a dinner unfortunately not involving seafood, we busied ourselves rigging tackle for the next day, in the hope that the weather would clear by dawn. Charlie could stand it no longer. "Where's the night life around here?"

"Oh, there's plenty to do at night. First, we clean fish. Then we swab down the boat. Then, we cook dinner and do dishes. Then, we pack and freeze the fish. Then, we repair tackle and pack lunch for the next day. Then, we have a nightcap and go to bed. And before you know it, it's 5 o'clock and time to get up."

Charlie just stared at us. "You…you guys are serious!"

"Yep."

"OK. Well, give me the keys to the truck. I think I'll explore the neighborhood."

"Uh……..listen, Charlie, nothin' personal, but that truck is the only way we have to get that boat back home. Anything happens to it, we can't just rent a car or book a flight. And….you know…. like they say, alcohol and Diesel fuel don't mix. But, hey, over there on the fridge is one of those magnet things with some cab company's number on it…..take you anywhere you want."

"Damn, you guys *are* hard core. Five o'clock? You mean, like, in the *morning?*"

"Yeah. Right before breakfast."

Charlie did not take personal offense, and was in the kitchen a bit before five, making coffee. Fortified with steaming mugs of it, we climbed the stairs of the condo building to look at sea conditions. The wind was down, the sky was lightly overcast, and there were large swells rolling from the south, creating a thundering surf, but there were no whitecaps. The wind was no longer driving the sea. We concluded that conditions were right for calming, and decided to check again after breakfast. An hour later, the swells had not diminished, but we convinced ourselves that they had, and thought that, at least, we should cruise out to the entrance to the pass for a closer look. Charlie said that he had been susceptible to *mal de mere* in the past and thought that he would remain ashore. He was, perhaps, wiser than we. Fools rush in…..

The tidal outflow from the north and the swells rolling from the south created a sort of standing breaker at the mouth of the pass. To midlanders, it looked like a mountain. I throttled back to idle speed, and approached it with caution. Another boat, of local registry and of about the same size, overtook and passed us to port. The closer to the outlet of the pass, the rougher the water, and they slowed as they approached the breaker. Then we heard that unmistakable sound, even above the noise of the surf, of air rushing through abruptly opened throttles. No one who survived the hot-rod/muscle car era of the 50's and 60's will ever forget that sound.

They were actually driving the boat up the wall of water. They crested it easily, and were gone; we could see them occasionally, on the tops of swells, heading south.

"Jim, did you see their engine? What was it?'

"Merc two hundred, I think. Maybe a two twenty-five."

"Well, what do you think? We only have a hundred and fifty."

"I don't know. If we can't climb it, there's no backin' down on the throttle. We'd go abeam of it and get swamped. And that's not the worst of it. Next stop is those rocks on the jetty."

I had turned the boat around, idling up current in the tidal flow. Another boat, not dissimilar to the first, passed us to the east and continued to cruise, without slowing down, toward that menacing barrier to the sea. They were talking and laughing, seemingly oblivious to their impending doom. Their boat was outboard powered, and by an engine smaller than ours…a ninety horsepower Honda. We watched in horror as they drove directly into the breaker……….and disappeared over the other side.

I looked at Jim. He said, "Well…..why not?"

That intimidating menace proved to be no menace at all. The only menace was our own abysmal ignorance. The engine rocketed the boat up the slope, and I had not the good sense to close the throttles as the top was approached. As a result, when the boat began to pitch over, I looked over the port gunwale…….and did not see water. The boat had been launched, and was momentarily airborne. That ended with a violent impact. But nothing seemed to be damaged, so far as we could tell, and we found ourselves being gently lifted and lowered by the swells. At their crests, one could see the entire horizon. In their troughs, the only things visible in any direction were slopes of gray-blue water. Unlike breaking waves, the swells seemed benign…even friendly.

We decided to troll the beach, but well outside the first breaking wave. The surf would not be forgiving today. We immediately began to engage spanish mackerel. They were unusually large. Some we had to inspect closely, looking at the lateral line, to be sure that they were not undersized king mackerel. It was a bonanza. Within an hour, we had all we wanted to clean, even given the fact that spanish mackerel clean quickly and easily.

The fish were off-loaded at the dock adjacent to the cleaning station, and the boat later tied off at its slip. Jim went to the condo to fetch a container for the fillets.

"Charlie, you should've come with us. We really got into the spanish out there."

"I was watchin' you guys with binoculars. You'd completely disappear in the waves and then come back to where I could see the whole boat. It was really rough."

"No. It was a ride on a merry-go-round pony. What do mean we disappeared? The top on that boat is eight feet above the water line."

"Yeah. That's exactly what I mean."

While we were cleaning the catch of Spanish mackerel, the ever-thoughtful Charlie brought us each a cold beer. "What's the plan for the rest of the day?"

"Too late to go out to a reef. Can't run more than 8 or 10 (mph) in those swells. Let's get some live shrimp and see if we can catch some trout in the cove."

The day ended with a few disappointingly small trout, but a nice catch of whiting, congregated at the edge of a shallow drop-off. These are not an impressive sport fish, but become quite impressive when sauteed in butter.

By the following morning, the sea had calmed to a wave height of about one foot, there was a very light south wind, a purple-blue sky, an unusually brilliant sun, and the National Weather Service marine forecast was totally reassuring. We set out for a sunken ship of WWII vintage. Given the distance, it was a small target, but now we were equipped with GPS; the only unknown was the accuracy of the co-ordinates given on the map. But when the GPS read-out said that DTG (distance to go) was zero, sonar showed nothing. Using that point as reference – we called it "electronic zero" – a grid search soon revealed a sonar image of the wreck. It was fairly small in extent, but the structure rose a considerable distance from the bottom. Here we deployed the marker buoy, to aid in anchoring over it. The wind had come up a bit, but was still gentle. Nevertheless, it took four tries to get an anchor, at the end of 250 feet of line, positioned to put the boat over the wreck. There was one disquieting aspect to the sonar display: no fish echoes.

Charlie had an explanation: "They're all in their staterooms!"

Classic Charlie. But it appeared that he was right. The first line to the bottom immediately produced a legal size red snapper. With three lines, each offering two baited hooks, in the water, the sonar screen filled with fish echoes. The bite was on. We went to progressively heavier sinkers in an effort to get bait to the bottom fast enough to avoid remoras, higher in the water column. The action was furious, and then, suddenly, stopped. The sonar echoes disappeared, but the screen showed that the structure was still there. We had not drifted out of position. Something else was going on.

Charlie was standing on the forward deck, staring at the anchor line, following it down from white to progressively deeper blue shades until it disappeared. 'Hey! I can see at least twenty feet of line, and there's bunch of big fish down there, about as far down as I can see!"

Looking over the gunwale, on the side away from the sun, we could see them, almost at the limit of visibility. I switched to a large jigging spoon, and could see it in their midst, but it elicited no response. Jim tried his king mackerel rig with the same lack of interest on the part of whatever these fish were. The school was moving slowly, from south to north, and in a few minutes, was gone.

"OK. The next time somebody catches one of those small brown grunts, don't throw it back. I'm gonna put a live fish down at about fifteen feet, and see what happens if another school comes by."

It took twenty minutes or so before the fish on the wreck showed any interest in bait, but eventually they did, and I soon had a baitfish. It was rigged on a surf rod, the length of which tended to keep it away from the boat, the rod extending from one of the trolling rod holders that served as a poor man's outrigger. The reel drag was set loose to avoid shock loading. We went back to bottom fishing. Again, after about an hour, the bottom action abruptly stopped. Charlie called back over his shoulder, "Here they come again!" We watched as the school of fish swam at a leisurely pace past the boat. What came to mind was the lettering I had once seen on somebody's tee shirt: "On a still night, I can hear the fish laughing."

"Well, I guess live bait wasn't the ans………………..WHOA!" The surf rod in the holder arched violently, tip and first two guides in the water. Struggling to get the rod handle out of the holder, I regretted having set the drag so loose. I could picture that fish tying knots around pieces of a rusty, steel ship. But the fish did not sound; it streaked off to the north. I tightened the drag as much as I dared, as the spool had only fifty or seventy five yards remaining. Somehow, once an angler has encountered a few fish, he can tell the difference between a heavy fish and a strong fish, even though the tension in the line may be the same. This was no hundreds-of-pounds leviathan; this was an athlete.

Fish on, it is sometimes hard to remember the fundamentals: never try to force a fish stronger than your tackle; never allow the fish to apply the impulse-momentum principle; never let the fish rest. The latter, of course, means that the angler is never allowed to rest, either. Before this contest was decided, a little rest would have been welcome.

The fish brought over the transom was a 30" amber jack. We continued that technique, and each of us boated two, of identical size, that day. In mid-afternoon, during one of those periods in which the reef fish had disappeared, Charlie was once again on lookout duty on the forward deck, eagerly anticipating the appearance of a school of amber jacks. He turned and shouted, "Here comes a big….uh…..looks like a shark."

Moment of decision: remove the lines and miss a potential amber jack, or leave them in the water and risk having to deal with another shark? We opted to leave them. In seconds I had a fish on. There was no doubt as to its identity. I resisted futilely as it ran out all of the spool of line and snapped it without so much as slowing down. "Damn, Charlie, how big *was* that shark?"

The answer was vintage Charlie. "Oh…… I'd say……..about the size of a '64 Pontiac!"

In almost twenty years, now, of annual pilgrimages to the Alabama coast, operating from several different bases, we have learned a lot – mostly, what not to do. But there is one thing I have never learned to do, despite expert instruction: throw a cast net. Third world urchins seem to have no problem whatever in projecting that net into a perfect circle, but I cannot master it. And it is not for lack of hours of practice and focused effort. I could never play a violin either, much to my parents' chagrin. There seem to be certain brain-muscle co-ordinations for which I am simply not wired.

The Gulf coast, of whatever state, offers Joe a smorgasbord of fishing opportunities, and is, as Charlie so aptly put it, "cost effective". Three or four anglers, sharing food, fuel and lodging costs, can enjoy a week or two of outstanding fishing quite reasonably. Part of the fascination is that there is always something to learn, so many are the species, so varied the tactics, and so fickle the winds and the currents.

But the greater part of the fascination is the sea itself. It is a wonderful experience to stand on the forward deck, scan the entire horizon, and to see absolutely nothing but that perfect line separating two shades of brilliant blue. Of course, one can do the same on the Great Lakes, but the sea is somehow different. There is an innate awareness of the enormity of it, the primitive nature of it, the geological seniority of it. I have seen many boats which have, attached to a bulkhead or console, a plaque containing a brief, and appropriate, prayer:

"Oh, Lord, thy sea is so great,

And my boat is so small."

Chapter 15
A Fish Named Sauger
Big Time on the Big O

Let me tell you a story of a river, of many rivers, for this story is but one example of what has happened on many of America's great river systems in the past five or six decades. This is a success story, not only about fishing success, but about fishery success. Such stories are rare enough, but even more unusual, this is an *environmental* success story. It is not that environmental successes don't happen, they do. But they seem to attract little media attention. The attention goes to environmental disasters, alleged disasters, rumors of disasters, and predictions of disasters yet to come. There was an early twentieth century saying in the newspaper business to the effect that, "Good news isn't news. Bad news is news." And contemporary electronic journalist Gloria Borger reminds that the principle still applies: "…..for the press, good news is not news."

It is 1950. I am sitting in a high school classroom. The subject is biology, and the teacher, Mr. Stoughton, is ahead of his time. The US economy is booming. The rest of the industrialized world has not yet recovered from the devastation of WWII, leaving America the world's powerhouse of production. Factories, mills, and mines are humming at capacity, farm fields are becoming subdivisions by the millions of acres, all with little thought being given to unintended side effects. But Mr. Stoughton was among the avant garde of an embryonic movement called *environmentalism*.

"You are sitting here today between two bodies of water," he said, "Lake Erie and the Ohio River, which are both dead. They have been poisoned forever. They can never recover." And he was right that they had been poisoned. My father had grown up, in the very early years of the twentieth century, literally on the banks of the Ohio River. He told stories of swimming, canoeing and fishing in that stream that seemed unbelievable. Catches of bass, white perch, catfish and jack salmon, virtually whenever the family needed fish for the table, and stories of the enormous catfish caught by men equipped with heavy salt water tackle, fishing from wooden boats propelled by two or three oarsmen. Some of those fish, he said, were "bigger than me."

Now, in 1950, that river was an industrial and municipal sewer. It was almost devoid of life. Nothing lived in it except creatures which could tolerate the most egregious pollution, and very few of those. Swimming in it was unthinkable. It was clinically dead.

But Mr. Stoughton had violated an ancient philosophical maxim: never say never. Enter ORSANCO, the newly formed Ohio River Sanitation Commission, a co-operative effort of states bordering the river. Armed with authority conferred by those states, it set out, with little fanfare, and far too little recognition, even to this day, to clean up the river. It was a Herculean task, taking decades. Gradually, the ranks swelled with other agencies taking up the banner, from county building inspectors to the United States Coast Guard. And the task was accomplished. To be sure, the Ohio River is not an idyllic stream flowing through unspoiled wilderness. It is a commercial waterway, sweeping past major cities, and bordered by industrial facilities and extensive agriculture. It is a highway to throbbing Diesel towboats, navigating long strings of barges of coal, petroleum and chemicals. Near the mid-point of its length, there is a sign: "More tons of freight pass this point each day than pass through the Suez and Panama canals combined." The river is alive with commercial traffic.

And it is *full* of fish. Nature has an incredible capacity to heal. Of course, the river is not in "like new" condition; it is not as it was when the Declaration of Independence was signed. That will take a little longer. The silt and sand of its bottom still harbor "durable" contaminants, like mercury and PCB's. Zealous public health agencies warn against consumption of bottom feeding species, and over-consumption of any species. That is their job. Here is the irony. I have a booklet published by the Province of Ontario. It warns against consumption of some species, and in some cases, all species, from certain lakes and streams in the province. I know some of those lakes and streams. They are in watersheds with absolutely NO human activity or habitation. There are no factories, there are no mines, there are no farms, there are no houses. The contaminants are natural – in a totally pristine wilderness. One cannot help but wonder how many parts per million of mercury contaminated the Ohio River on the day that the passengers of the Mayflower came ashore.

A few months ago, I was casting for stripers in the tailwaters of a dam on the Ohio. The angler to my left hooked a big fish, and the rest of us retreated to give him clearance. After a long and exhausting struggle, he brought to the rocks a 39 pound blue catfish. As is the custom among the anglers who are the "regulars" at that site, he weighed it, photographed it, and released it. To my far right was an older gentleman ("older" is an arrogance on my part, I have passed three quarters of a century). He was not casting large spoons like the rest of us. He was hunkered on the rocks, bait fishing. (Folks in this region do not squat – they hunker.) I saw him look intently at that big blue cat, but I paid no further attention. The man to my left had another strike, and landed a much smaller catfish, this one a channel cat, of about eight pounds. The fellow to my right waved at him as he was about to release the fish, and shouted, "Kin ah have that'n?"

"Sure."

The fish was delivered to the supplicant. I could stand it no longer. I walked over to the man. I had read the published warnings. "Excuse me, but are you gonna eat that fish?"

"Wal, yeah. I lived along this river all mah life. I love catfish."

"How many do you eat….like in a week?"

"Oh, ah eat 'em two, three times a week. An' ah don't hold back, neither. Ah'll eat a big ol' skillet o' catfish fer a meal."

"Well….uh…if you don't mind me askin', how old are you?"

"Ah'm eighty-fav".

Most of our circle ignored the big river, our impressions of it having been formed in the 1950's and 1960's. Instead, we made long treks elsewhere. Then, one cold, misty November Saturday, in the mid-1970's, Tim

Wakefield, Mike Shepherd and I were bow hunting for deer in the hills north of a town called Franklin Furnace, where Mike knew a landowner. We had not so much as seen a deer, although there were abundant tracks and rubs, and by mid afternoon, we were cold, wet and hungry. Our consensus was that hunting at dusk was not likely to be any better than it had been at daybreak, and we set out for home. Now, a vehicle heater cannot be compared to a crackling fire of hardwood logs in a stone hearth, but it was indeed deeply appreciated that day. By the time we had reached the main road, US 52, we were again conscious of having toes. The road passes very close to Greenup Dam, and with the trees leafless, we could see the parking area near the dam. It was jammed with vehicles.

"What's going on over there?' Tim asked.

"I don't know. Let's go see."

As we swung into the parking area, two men were lowering a cooler into the trunk of a car. They had closed the trunk lid and were unlocking the doors as we reached them. I lowered the window. "What's …what's going on?"

The response was one of those what-planet-are-you-from looks, then, "Sauger are runnin'." I suspect that they, too, were cold and wet, because, without another word, they climbed inside and started the engine. We took their parking spot and walked closer to the water. Fishermen were shoulder to shoulder, casting the tailwaters. Hook-ups were frequent, and a good number of very nice fish were being landed. The late autumn river was not the stained, brownish color we had expected. It was green, and clear enough to see hooked fish still several feet below the surface. A young fellow of about twelve years old came up the walkway towards us dragging a stringer bearing a limit catch of fat, healthy sauger. He was wearing only a sweatshirt, jeans and a ball cap. "Pretty chilly out there today," Tim observed to him.

"Aw, once you get to catchin' sauger, it ain't cold anymore." He grinned.

"Yeah, w…w…well *I'm* cold," Mike chattered, "let's go."

"OK, but I know where I'm gonna be next weekend."

There was no significant sauger run the following weekend. We knew that was the case before even wetting a line; the parking area was nearly deserted. Fishing is like that. But Tim and I did catch a few sauger, well below bragging size, and two very nice smallmouth bass. It was a "bluebird day", the kind anglers routinely hate, deep blue cloudless sky, crisply cold and energetically breezy. Higher up on the hillsides, there were numerous oaks, which retain their leaves well into winter. The late afternoon sun, now far to the south, approaching the winter solstice, was more red than gold; it painted those russet oak leaves the warm color of the very last coals of an evening campfire. It was actually beautiful here. But as if to remind us of where we were, the massive engines of a tow boat rumbled from the locks on the opposite bank. We had missed the bonanza, but it had been a wonderful day of fishing. Thus were we re-introduced to an old neighbor, the mighty Ohio, affectionately referred to in these parts as "the Big O".

And it had been nothing short of resurrected, brought back from the dead by the diligent efforts of ORSANCO and a host of other agencies from state and federal governments. To be sure, one cannot drink its untreated water, and, like the highways on land, this liquid thoroughfare is littered with the trash of the uncaring. And it still responds to rain events as it always has, becoming "too thin to plow and too thick to drink". But it was alive again, and not clinging tenuously to life, but thriving.

In the 1985 season, Jim Santangelo and I decided to log our catches by species. Here is the list: channel catfish, blue catfish, flathead (shovelhead) catfish, largemouth bass, smallmouth bass, Kentucky spotted bass, bluegill, sunfish, crappie, rock bass (Uncle Herman's "loudmouth bass"), skipjacks, shad (by cast net), longnose gar, stripers, wipers (hybrids), white bass, carp, quillback suckers, bowfin (dogfish), sauger, walleyes, saugeyes, white perch (freshwater drum), and one hapless paddlefish which got tangled in a bottom rig. That paddlefish was not entirely unlucky. It had avoided the hooks, and was released healthy..... but somewhat out of sorts. I have often wished that Mr. Stoughton, a half century deceased, could have been there.

The Ohio was certainly not the only river undergoing rebirth in those times. In the mid 1970's, I was on a technical support mission in the Bucksport, Maine plant of the St Regis Paper Company. The plant used process water taken from the Penobscot River, and returned its effluents to that river. The process engineer I was working with was a Maine native, and was a fisherman. Our discussion about how best to refinish paper mill rolls concluded, he said, in that wonderful "down east" accent, "Come heah, I want to show ya somethin'." I followed him out onto a concrete deck at the water's edge. A large effluent pipe was pouring a huge stream of waste water into the Penobscot. He took from the corner of the guard rail a broomstick which had a laboratory beaker in a wire harness at one end. He lowered the beaker into the effluent stream, drew it back, detached it from the harness and held it up for me to see. It was perfectly clear. Then he grinned at me and drank the entire beaker.

"The watah we put back in the rivah is cleanah than the watah we take out," he announced with obvious pride, "and may I say, much cleanah. The othah mills on the Penobscot are doin' the same thing. We're cleanin' her up."

"How's the fishing in the Penobscot?"

"Comin' back. Comin' back strong."

Having been re-acquainted with our neighbor, we visited it often. It was learning new water, as if it had been a fishing venue a thousand miles away. As in any water, there were productive spots and unproductive spots, and these changed with season. We listened and learned. We watched and learned. We read and learned. We experimented and learned. It offered four season fishing, when it was fishable, and for the hardy – or deranged – winter fishing was often the best of all. High water often limits its fishable days. But on the other hand, flowing between steep banks and high hills, wind does not limit fishability as it would on a large lake. There are virtually no ice fishing opportunities, as the river has frozen over only twice in my lifetime….so far. And even in those years, flowing water and changing levels made the ice exceedingly dangerous.

And there are other hazards. Boat fishermen must be alert to commercial traffic, to barely visible, water-logged trees, and to other boaters who may not be practicing the best of seamanship, particularly when in the company of adult beverages. Jim Santangelo and I were very nearly rammed one evening, anchored no more than 30 feet from shore over a submerged wing dam, by a large cruiser whose occupants were obviously "partying". Wading fishermen need to keep in mind that last week's sand bar may have been re-sculpted by current into a deep hole, or that a tangled piece of broken anchor line lies in wait to ensnare an unwary foot. The grand old girl demands respect.

We learned that techniques and tackle were not the same as those used in fishing the smaller tributaries. Broken tackle and lost fish taught us that, when fishing areas harboring shovelhead and blue catfish, surf tackle was far more practical than the standard freshwater gear. Holding a bottom rig in heavy current requires heavy sinkers, and rods stout enough to handle them. Fishing dam tailwaters for stripers and hybrids requires not only surf tackle, but the skill to cast heavy lures long distances, accurately.

We learned that, for some species and locations, bank fishing was effective; for others, wading was the best approach; for still others, only a boat would provide access. (Boats are prohibited in some of the best fishing venues, particularly near navigation dams, for reasons of safety). And while there are numerous public access points along the river, launch ramps, parks and the like, bank fishing access along much of the river is limited by private property. And so, the land accessible hotspots tend to be shoulder-to-shoulder, and the boat accessible hotspots tend to attract considerable flotillas, when "the bite is on".

The hotspots are exactly where Joe would expect. Most of the river species are benthic, seeking food and structure. Hotspots include dam tailwaters, lock wings, remnants of old dams, submerged by the high level navigation dams, sand bars, rock bars, bridge and other piers, tributary mouths, and in winter, the warm water discharges of power plants, or other facilities using river water for cooling. Which of these sites will be productive on a given day depends upon season, species, water level and turbidity, light conditions and weather. But, except for the dog days of summer, the warm water discharges seem to be highly popular, sometimes resulting in heated competition for "a place to stand".

In recent times, enviropolitical lobbies have coerced the use of cooling towers, rather than using river water to cool heat exchangers. That certainly did no favor to the fish. The warm water discharges extend the seasonal growth cycle of phytoplankton, attracting hordes of forage fish, which feed predator fish. I recall attending one of the many public hearings held in connection with the permitting process for the Zimmer Power Station, in Moscow, Ohio. I heard the arguments presented for the use of cooling towers – a much more expensive solution – complete with elaborate isothermal diagrams showing the effect on water temperatures downstream of the proposed discharge. At any significant distance – feet, not miles – the temperature differences on that chart were fractions of a degree. It was argued that this would have a negative effect upon aquatic life. The other plants along the river, using river-cooled heat exchangers, seemed not to have had a negative effect on aquatic life, quite the opposite. In the end, the regulators mandated cooling towers. I was bemused by all of this.

Anglers on the Big O are a very diverse slice of society. One chilly November morning, I was wading waist deep next to a utility company lineman, a retired gunnery sergeant, a surgeon, a railroad worker, and the mayor of a municipality. And that group included three different races. There are no social, economic or racial boundaries between people standing in ice water.

One meets interesting folk. One gorgeous spring day in early May, Jim Santangelo and I were trolling a shoal on an inside bend, and had caught two very nice stripers, and several freshwater drum over ten pounds, on shallow running crankbaits. The shoal was only four to six feet deep and snags were frequent. Freeing one of them allowed a small boat that had been trolling behind us to close to within less than fifty yards. In it were a man and his very, very pregnant wife. Jim and I were just back under way when she hooked a fish, and it was obviously a large fish. The man shut down the engine, while she battled the lunker. We retrieved our lines and likewise shut down to watch, curious as to what she had engaged. Drifting a bit closer together, I shouted to the man, "What is it?"

"We're fishin' for walleye," he shouted back, "with night crawler harnesses."

"That's one heck of a walleye."

"Yeah!" he grinned.

She had considerable skill, but she was struggling, twisting and turning, and I had frightening visions of becoming involved in an on-water emergency delivery, in not the most sterile environment. Finally, she had the fish nearly to the boat, and the man stood with a landing net, peering into the water. "Damn," he muttered, "nothin' but an ol' white perch. I'll just cut the line."

"You do," she hissed through clenched teeth, "and we're divorced!"

The man struggled to net the fish, and we could see why she had taken such a firm position. That fish weighed, at very least, twenty pounds. Bragging rights.

The Big O is like everywhere else in that it has its species-specific groups of anglers. There is the bass group, the striper/hybrid group, the catfish group, the sauger group, and the targets-of-opportunity group, to which our circle, by and large, belongs. But just as everyone is Irish on St Patrick's Day, come late fall, everyone is a sauger fisherman. Despite historical legend, and despite the Disney film and TV series about Davy Crockett, Mike Fink is *not* the King of the River. The King of the River is a fish named sauger.

Talk about sauger fishing very far from one of the valleys of the great mid-American river systems, and, even from dedicated anglers, you will draw blank stares, quizzical looks, and suspicion of hoax. I was telling a fellow angler, at the fish cleaning bench on Cotton Bayou, on the Gulf coast, how much I enjoyed sauger fishing. He told me that he and his brother liked unicorn hunting equally well. He said they had bagged three last season - before he walked away, shaking his head.

Webster's New Collegiate Dictionary defines the word as follows: "sauger\ sog-er\ n [origin unknown] : a pike-perch (*Stizostedion (sometimes Sander) canadense*) similar to the walleye, but smaller; *also*: WALLEYE".

Webster is wrong; the origin is not unknown. Here it is, on the absolute authority of my Prussian grandfather: German settlers were attracted to the Ohio valley because it so resembled the river valleys of the Fatherland. There were no dams on the river in those times – the mid-1800's – and there were rapids. The early settlers observed fish struggling upstream through those rapids in the fall of the year, and assumed that they were the salmon of their Old World experience. Since these fish were much smaller than mature salmon, the settlers concluded that they were young male salmon, or jacks. That is how the sauger became popularly known in the Ohio valley as a "jack salmon", a term still on the menus of river valley restaurants to this day. (Commercial trade in sauger is prohibited today, and so the "jack salmon" delivered to your table is really a walleye.) The settlers noticed that these "jack salmon" were often light and tentative biters, especially on live minnows, and so they called the fish *sauger* – the German word for a suckling animal.

The sauger is a member of family percidae - the yellow perch family.

Relatives range from the tiny johnny darter, minnow sized, to the European zander, weighing up to 44 pounds. Sauger are typically smaller than walleyes. The world record is 17pounds, twelve ounces, but a three or four pound specimen is considered a very good fish, and many run in the one to two pound range. By contrast, the world record walleye is 25 pounds, and walleye of five to eight pounds are considered very good fish, though many walleye in the 1 ½ to 2 pound class have found their way to a dinner table. The saugeye, a hybrid of walleye and sauger, is midway in size between the two. Sauger prefer streams to lakes and reservoirs, while walleye prefer the latter. Sauger tolerate more turbid water, and warmer water, and have been successfully introduced where walleye stocking has failed. All three species inhabit the Big O, but sauger outnumber their two cousins by a huge margin.

Sauger, saugeye, walleye and zander are of the same general shape, elongated, cylindrical and streamlined. All are clearly designed for predation, with deep tails, thick, muscular bodies, large fins and pronounced, needle sharp, inward curving fangs. Of that group, the teeth of the sauger are perhaps the most intimidating, being larger, relative to body size, than those of the others. All of them have very large eyes, with great light-gathering ability, and therefore, tend to be active in low light conditions. This is perhaps why sauger fishermen hate bluebird days. The sauger, on bluebird days, are in the deepest, darkest places they can find….and will stay there.

Coloration varies with location in all four species, but in general, sauger tend to be darker and exhibit large black blotches, not unexpected for a fish that frequents deep, turbid water. Walleyes are more uniform in color, whatever color the location dictates. Zander have perch-like vertical bars. Sauger have black spots on the membrane between the spines of the dorsal fin; walleyes do not. Any given saugeye may look like a sauger, look like a walleye, or anything in between. There <u>are</u> positive means to identify a saugeye…..known only to biologists and game wardens.

If beauty is in the eye of the beholder, then flavor must be in his or her mouth. But there seems to be a universal consensus: sauger are *good*. Most of the anglers encountered on the Big O are catch and release practitioners….. until sauger season. My wife was a fish hater. She had a sweatshirt bearing a logo showing a fish in a circle, with a diagonal bar through it – the international "no fish" symbol. I would bring home fresh red snapper from the Gulf, immediately iced and twelve hours in transit. She would hold her nose. Fresh walleye, or even yellow perch, swimming four hours earlier in Lake Erie – same response. But sauger from the Big O she would eat with great gusto. Sauger season was the only time she actually encouraged me to go fishing. It would be 25 degrees, wind howling…… "You look stressed. You've been working too hard. Let's see….I know! You should go fishing. Have a good time!"… pushing me out the door.

Our early sauger outings were tentative, bank-based affairs, usually joining the throng casting dam tailwaters. Due to inexperience, our circle had limited success, but those around us usually did very well indeed. This was a puzzle. We were using the same lures, in the same places, at the same times, and being thoroughly outfished. The overwhelmingly preferred lures were ¼ ounce and 3/8 ounce round-head jigs. The popular color combinations were white or chartreuse heads dressed with white, chartreuse, or fluorescent yellow, grub tails. Some anglers tipped jigs, whether with or without grub tails, with live minnows. We tried all of those combinations with virtually no effect upon our success ratio. Clearly, as is so often the case, there was more to this than met the eye.

These river bank gatherings were like country church socials – everybody knew everybody else. But we were not yet parishioners. It is not that we were shunned as outsiders, everyone was friendly, courteous and hospitable. "Come on over here by our fire and warm up a little." Or, "I got a pot o' hot coffee here. Like some?" But there was no one who offered, "Look buddy, I know what yer doin' wrong. All you gotta do is…." And I do not think that was because anyone wanted to limit our catch – there seemed to be plenty of sauger when a bite was on – I think it was for fear of offending the "newbies" by saying, in effect, "I'm smarter than you." Based upon that theory, I devised a plan of action.

There was one individual who seemed to virtually *live* at the tailwaters. He was there every time I climbed down the bank, and he was usually still there when I left. And he caught sauger. He would cull his stringer, replacing smaller fish with larger fish, and always had a limit catch of 16" to 18" sauger, usually with one or two larger than that. He was a very pleasant fellow, with a round, freckled face, and a deep, eastern Kentucky drawl. I made it a point to fish near him whenever possible. He never failed to greet me with a big grin and a "Hey!" when I arrived or to wish me well when I left. We laughed and joked as we fished, and built up a bit of a relationship. When I felt it was safe, I waded over next to him and said,

"I notice you're hookin' three or four fish to every one of mine. And a lot of these other guys are, too. What am I doin' wrong?"

"Oooh, you haint doin' nothin' wrong. See, it's a-knowin' the bottom. Rat straight out ther, the bottom's smooth. Them saugers, they lak rocks. Hahd under 'em, 'special when hit's brat out. See over yonder….how thet current runs past thet little eddy? Ther's whur they lak to hahd in them rocks a-waitin' fer a shad that's all dizzy from goin' through them gates. Y' got to be able to cast thet fur, 'n' then let yer jig sink to just off 'n the bottom. Too fur, 'n' yer snagged up. Not fur enough, 'n' you haint a-gonna get no strak. Rat over ther's a shalla rock bar. Snag up ever' time. Tell ya what y'need to do. Come down here when they haint no bat on, and nobody's here. Go up 'n' down the rocks a-castin', an' let yer jig sink. You're a-gonna lose some jigs, but y' got to learn the bottom. Haint no other way. That's what I done."

It's called paying your dues. I left a lot of jigs on the floor of that classroom. But eventually, the nuances of river bed terrain and current, what weight jig to use, how long to let it sink, and what speed of retrieve would keep it in the strike zone, began to form a mental picture. It is a complex picture because water level, current, and light conditions constantly change. The next season, my catch rate was as good as anybody's. My mentor, God bless him, had been absolutely right….I mean rat.

The sauger season on the Big O has no official, legal, opening day. For practical purposes, the sauger season opens on Halloween and closes on Easter, give or take a few weeks either way. Sauger can be caught any time, but outside of the "season", they are widely spread. The observations of the German settlers were correct. Sauger move upstream in autumn to spawn. Continuing up-current until obstructed by a navigation dam, they winter fairly well concentrated in the pool below the dam, until the spawn is completed in early spring. Then, they disperse throughout the pools between dams, some of which are over 100 miles long. The reason sauger will seem to have disappeared during the summer months is a matter of the math. Let us say that dam A is 125 miles upstream from dam B. Let us say that during the "season", 100,000 sauger have collected in the mile or so below dam A. Let us also say that the river averages 600 yards wide between A and B. When those sauger disperse in the spring, their average concentration will be 3.6 fish per acre, as opposed to a "season" average concentration of 458 fish per acre. The numbers are "what-if" numbers, but the principle is valid. That's why sauger fishing is a cold weather business......and it ain't for sissies.

It was on New Year's Eve a few years ago that I decided, with strong encouragement from my wife, to go sauger fishing. It was a nasty morning, with snow flurries being hurried along by a dagger-pointed wind from the west. I got to the tailwaters before daylight, expecting, because it was mid-week and most unpleasant weather, to find few anglers. The rocky grade down to water level was becoming snow-covered, and a treacherous descent in the dark. I hadn't noticed how many vehicles were at the site, but I found the water's edge almost shoulder to shoulder. One of the regulars, a fellow named Sam, recognized me. "Hey, Bob! They're right out there, man," he said, pointing. Another voice came from the dark: "Hell, they're everywhere!"

It was a genuine, bona fide, lick-your-chops bonanza. The snowflakes felt like number 8 shot on your face, and even if you could successfully finesse a ¼ ounce jig with gloves on, the gloves were soon soaked. Woe to him who lost a fish to a break-off or a lost a jig to a snag. Fingers were too numb to tie a clinch knot in six pound test line, and most of us resorted ingloriously to half a dozen granny knots to attach a new one. Fang wounds sustained in unhooking a fish bled, but did not hurt. Water froze in the rod guides, and it was necessary to periodically dunk the rod in the river to thaw them. Water lapping the rocks at the water's edge froze, making retreating to land to repair tackle or to stringer a fish a very risky business. It was a dull, gray daylight, now, and surprisingly, the bite continued. The chill of the water had soaked through my waders, and I was shivering uncontrollably. It was wonderful!

It was also unusual. It was much more likely that one would have endured those same conditions to catch some, a few, or perhaps no, sauger. As the saying goes, "Been there, done that." One day may produce outstanding action and the next, with water and weather conditions identical, may be very slow. But in general, given decent water level conditions, if one is willing to brave the cold and the dark, night-time winter sauger fishing in the tailwaters is usually not without reward.

One winter, a couple of years ago, Tim Wakefield and I decided that some fresh sauger would be a welcome change from beef, pork, and venison, and even from pike, catfish, snappers, redfish and lake perch frozen the previous summer. I called Tim on Christmas Eve. It was about 34 degrees and raining, and the forecast called for three more days of the same.

"Merry Christmas. Let's catch some sauger day after tomorrow."

"Are you nuts?"

"You've always known that I am. Be here about five."

"OK."

It was well before daylight when we half-walked, half-slid to the water's edge at the tailwaters. We were, as usual, not alone. A dozen or so anglers had preceded us. It looked like a village meeting of Inuits, dressed in heavy parkas and exhaling steam. Two fishermen were gathering their gear and holding limit stringers of thick-shouldered sauger. "Take our spot," one of them said, "cast a little to the left. They're really in there. We got here about 2 o'clock. Must've landed near fifty. A lot of 'em small, though. Kept ten each of the good ones. Good luck." We fumbled in the confined beams of cap lights to tie on 3/8 ounce jig heads, giving us more distance, but greater risk of snags. We took up positions where our predecessors had been, and casted "a little to the left". Knowledge of the bottom was of no benefit here. It was too dark to know exactly where we were, or to see where the lure had fallen. Wherever it was, it was greeted by a solid strike. Could this be another………nah. One may not dare to think such a thing. Bonanzas are rare.

Tim and I had each captured three or four decent fish by the time the eastern sky had begun to brighten. The rain had slowed to a persistent, light drizzle, and the wind remained calm. The river water was warmer than the air, and a mist obscured the river. Visibility was perhaps forty or fifty yards. Despite the chill, there was a tranquil softness that hid everything except the immediate time and the immediate place. There is a strange sort of peace that envelops the isolated right-here-and-right-now. But as the sunrise proceeded, the cloud cover thinned, and the mist glowed ever brighter, our large-eyed quarry retreated to deeper water and the bite was over.

And then, the following season, Rodney Null and I relived that morning almost precisely. Except for the exact date, and the rain, it was total déjà vu. As we reached the water's edge, in total darkness, departing anglers bequeathed us their standing room. It was too dark to know exactly where we were, or to see where a cast entered the water. Our fingers were too numb to tie clinch knots. We caught several nice sauger. There was a white-out caused by river mist. As soon as that mist became bright, the party was over. It was uncanny, and a little spooky. Would that one could depend upon that kind of consistency on the Big O. The opposite is true.

Rod is a member of our loosely defined circle, and a welcome fishing companion. Rod is a professor of mathematics by occupation, but, as Rod will tell you, "only because I need the money." Were that not so, Rod would leave the water but occasionally, and then only to hunt or to shoot sporting clays. Now, every outing, whether a day trip, a week-end camp, or some extended safari to a distant and exotic fishing site, has associated with it mundane chores. Gathering wood, packing, bailing a bilge, washing dishes…..a long list could easily be drawn up. Those chores and Rod are hypergolic, a jargon term used in rocket technology to describe fuel components which react upon contact with one another. When Rod and an undone chore come into contact, there is an instant reaction. No third party ignition is required. None of us ever say, "Hey, Rod, how about……", because it will have already been done. And, on long drives, long cruises, or long paddles, Rod keeps the brain awake with questions like, "If we could drive this truck at the speed of light, would the headlights still work?" or, "What is the duration of a fall into a bottomless pit?" or, "How would you determine the diameter of the Earth with only a steel tape and a plumb bob?" And Rod was a godsend when he and I were involved in a sauger fishing incident so terrifying that nightmares of it persist. But that story comes later.

Jim Santangelo seldom went to the tailwaters with us, or to sites where wading was the order of the day. He had knee problems (since repaired), and scrambling over steep rock banks was very painful, as well as dangerous, for him. So Jim fished primarily from a boat. Early on, before the Grady-White, we had a 17 foot Grumman center console, powered by a faithful, little, 3 cylinder, 70 horsepower engine. It was perfect for fishing the Big O. Draft was shallow, the hull weighed only about 850 pounds, and if a recovery to the trailer went somewhat awry, the two of us could muscle the hull into position. It would troll all day on six gallons of fuel, and if the battery failed, it could be manually started with the cord provided under the cowl. We actually did that……just to be sure that we could. Yet, it was seaworthy enough to be safe in the wakes of large power boats and commercial traffic, and, in fairly flat water, would run 30 knots. A lot of fish, from the Great Lakes to the Florida Keys, came over the gunwales of that Grumman. And no matter how far beyond reasonable expectations we pushed that little boat, it never failed to bring us home. Alive.

One Sunday afternoon in late January, Jim and I were both infected with nearly terminal cases of cabin fever. It was not terribly cold, low forties, but the typical Ohio Valley winter shade of gray. As we were attaching the trailer to the hitch, Jim looked across the trailer tongue at me and said, "You know, this is crazy."

"Yes. It is. What's your point? A sane person would sit by the fire, sip twelve year old Scotch, and tell tall tales. Wouldn't you rather go make some tall tales?"

"Well…… why not?"

Before we had even gotten to the launch ramp, we could see from the road that the river was a few feet above pool stage, and deeply stained. To add to bad omens, there was a strong west wind inciting the river's surface into two foot whitecaps – or, more correctly – browncaps. "Let's find a place to turn around," I said.

"What…you're goin' home?"

"No. We're gonna need minnows today. That water's really murky."

Equipped with three dozen fathead minnows, we returned to the ramp, and launched. The run upstream was not uncomfortable, running downwind at a bit over wind speed. We found the spot that I thought might be promising, a small cove separating a shallow beach from a deep, rocky shore. There was not a single boat in the area. The current was too strong to drift, and we anchored. Now, that damp wind was cold indeed, and I turned my back to it to fish. We were both using bottom rigs, with two hooks baited with fathead minnows, lip hooked. Twenty minutes passed and there was not the slightest tremor in either line. Jim reeled his rig into the boat. "Bait check", he mumbled. A half minute or so after he returned the bait to the water, his rod tip twitched, and he hooked and landed an average sauger. In the next half hour, he caught several more, and also lost a number of minnows to bites that did not end in a hook-up. All this time, I might as well have had my bait in the boat. By the time Jim had exhausted the minnow supply, he had boated ten sauger, I had not had so much as a nibble, and it was getting dark. There were no lights at the launch ramp, and so I ran – perhaps faster than prudent – upwind. I was miserably cold. For some reason, Jim didn't seem to mind!

Whether in autumn, winter or early spring, the most popular boat fishing technique was jigging. The reason is a very practical one. With a number of boats clustered together (remember the nucleation effect?), casting lures becomes somewhat dangerous. Stationary bottom rigs were used, of course, but most anglers subscribed to the theory that sauger, preying on disoriented baitfish, strike on the fall of the prey item. So, the standard practice was to briskly lift the lure off the bottom, and then allow it to fall at its natural rate of descent. According to the theory, the strike would occur at, or near, the end of the fall, and the sudden upward lift of the rod tip would set the hook. Never having been down near the bottom to observe what was actually going on, I cannot attest to that, but it was a technique that seemed to work very well indeed. Jigs, and especially jigs tipped with minnows, were effective. But our experience was that spoons, and spoon-like lures, worked even better. In a less-than-scientific experiment, it seemed that a heavy, flat spoon, like a Hopkins, was more effective than a lighter spoon, like a Johnson or a Daredevle. This was counter-intuitive. The more "fluttery" spoon should have been a better simulation of a wounded or disoriented baitfish. Fishing is full of surprises.

And it did not seem that this observation was an anomaly. We could repeat the experiment on every trip and get the same general results. We noticed that the commercially available lures all exhibited a less-than-perfect characteristic: they were not predictable in the path of the fall. In trying to present the lure as close to the bottom as possible, over a very uneven rocky bottom, this unpredictability led to many snags. And if we had learned anything, it was that usually – not always – sauger preferred to be very close to the shelter of large, river bed rocks. We needed a *mission specific* jigging lure. Poring over tackle catalogs without success, we were finally driven to take the advice of Dr Seuss's (original) Grinch: "If I can't find a reindeer, I'll make one instead."

Fifty-five years in the manufacturing industry has some residual advantages. It took a few evenings in the company of a small universal milling machine, and a number of false starts, but I soon had some crude tooling with which to make a prototype. We could not wait to test it. But by now it was late winter. The Big O was high and muddy, and it began to look as though it would not be until the next fall that a fair test could be made. Then, in early April, there was an unusual period of dry weather, the river cleared and returned to near-pool level. Even if the sauger were already dispersed, we reasoned, we could still test the free-fall characteristics of this truly ugly prototype lure.

When we arrived on site, we were amazed to find a large group of boats in the usual spots. We had to settle for a less than ideal anchorage. Jim rigged with the commercial spoon that had been the most successful of all of those we had tried. I tied on the ugly prototype. The prototype, over the course of the next few hours, enjoyed a four to one strike rate advantage. But, remembering Jim's one-sided success rate on the above outing, that may have had nothing to do with the prototype lure. So we traded lures. Now, Jim was hooking about four times more fish than I was. We limited out, rushed home, and made twelve more.

These were distributed among members of the circle, who used them for everything from lake trout in Quetico to spanish mackerel in the Gulf. If I am going sauger fishing, they are like the American Express card – I don't leave home without them. I have no idea why they work so well. They are very simple; the design was driven not by any particular insight, but primarily by the equipment I had. And, no, they are not for sale. I am retired. I want to fish, not manufacture lures.

It does not happen every year. But sometimes, on one of those pleasant, mid-October days, with the sun still warm on your back, the tannin incense of drying leaves in the air, and the hills along the river gaudy with the colors of deciduous trees dozing off, when there should not yet be, there will be a sauger run. It is not fair. The discomfort index is not nearly high enough for the sauger fishing to be good. But it *is* good. This is one of those unexpected and undeserved blessings that every Joe experiences. This is why he pays his dues, in the cold and in the rain and in high wind and in unsuccessful frustration. Here, and now, the green water bears discarded leaves, from yet green, to yellow, to gold, to red, to black, and slashing through the water between them is a tiny nylon filament. At its end, there is a golden-bronze, black mottled sauger, with its great, liquid eyes and its tall, spotted dorsal fin. Rare indeed are those moments when everything is perfect. This was one of them. Jim and I limited out in what seemed a very short time. But we could not bear to leave the river, despite having a substantial fish-cleaning task ahead of us. We trolled for hybrids and languidly drifted the rocky banks, casting for bass. We caught none of either………just as we had hoped.

No image recording system, electronic or otherwise, yet devised can capture such a day. They are limited to the visual and the audible. But the human brain can indelibly store away not only the sights and the sounds, but the aromas, the warmth of the sun, the gentle pressure of a light breeze on the skin, the surge of a hooked fish, sounding for the haven of the limestone slabs on the ancient river bed. There is an old saying: "Cameras don't lie" (unless, of course, they are digital). But they certainly do not "tell the whole truth".

On balance, sauger fishing action seems proportional to the discomfort index, a loosely defined number taking into account air temperature, precipitation rate, wind velocity, humidity, sun radiation intensity, and any other discomfort-causing effect not cited here. The discomfort index peaks in the winter. So does the sauger fishing. A great sauger bite on a pleasant day is not impossible….it's just damned unlikely.

It was not such a pleasant day, the Sunday after Thanksgiving, when my son, Lee, Rod Null, and I launched the Grady in the Big O. The temperature was in the upper forties, but a steady, cold rain, slanted by a west wind, fell from a charcoal colored sky. The primary objective was not even fishing, but to test whether a stubborn hull leak, which I had been pursuing for months, had finally been repaired. Nevertheless, we were armed with those ugly jigging lures which, by now, we referred to as "Marvels". The run to the tailwaters, in a center console boat, was wet and chill, but, once anchored, the discomfort index was bearable. It would be necessary to remain stationary in the water for several hours to test whether the hull repair had been successful; it had never leaked while underway.

The first and the second anchorages had produced no action, but the third site showed clouds of baitfish on the sonar screen, extending downward through the water column all the way to the bottom. We began immediately to hook sauger, and not the slender jacks, but thick, heavy females, and about every tenth fish was a three to five pound walleye. There were hybrid stripers in the mix, and strong, aggressive white perch, as well. Running the bilge pump to determine whether water had entered the hull was forgotten. The persistent rain was forgotten. The damp, bone-chilling wind was forgotten. All attention was focused upon keeping hooked fish out of the bottom rubble, which painted a picture on the sonar screen resembling a profile of the Alps. And we were, for the most part, succeeding.

Lee had been fishing from the bow, unhooking fish and sliding them down the wet deck for me to corral and place into the transom well, at a frequency so great that I scarcely had time to fish. Rod was at the starboard gunwale, and happily, was stowing his fish without my intervention. Lee had lost a battle to a fish which had successfully gotten into the rocks, and came aft to tie on another Marvel. "How many do we have? Are we close to limiting out?"

"I don't know. I don't think so. Why?"

"I don't feel so good." He forced a sodden grin. "Ah…I'll be OK."

He went back to his station at the bow. Rod looked at me and twisted his head to the side with a questioning frown. The two of them had been friends since college days, and Rod knew how to read him. They had been involved in some on-the-edge outdoor adventures in their younger days, and both of them were disinclined to give up….on anything. I did not like the look I saw on Rod's face. But, the fish were biting.

In minutes, Lee came back to the helm. "Dad, you gotta get me out of here. I'm in trouble." His face was ashen, and for Lee to want to leave a bite like this said that the situation was indeed serious.

"What's wrong?"

"Chest pains. In my arm and shoulder. Pulse fluttering."

Rod was already pulling the anchor. Without help from the engine, against the current, he was struggling, but the anchor was in the boat before I had the engine started. I advanced the throttle, and the J150 coughed and stalled. *"Not now! Oh, dear God, not now!"* I thought. But it fired immediately and we picked our way through the group of boats faster than I would ordinarily have thought prudent….or courteous. The rain had intensified, and visibility was very low heading upwind. The windshield over the console was opaque with rain splatter, and looking to the side of it was little better. Rod had taken Lee's cell phone out of the water proof pouch and already had a 911 operator engaged. "EMTs will meet us at the ramp," Rod shouted in my ear, over the noise of the engine and the rain, "They say time is important!"

I thrust the throttle against the firewall, and trimmed the tabs and the engine tilt to get maximum speed. The tachometer indicated 5500 rpm. I could see absolutely nothing ahead. "Rod! Watch the bank to starboard. I'll watch port. Let's try to keep her about a third of the way to the Kentucky side!" I knew that there were submerged trees and navigation buoys on the Ohio side and that barges normally favored the Kentucky side of midstream. We could only hope that there was no floating debris in our path. A modest 4 inch limb would easily punch through the hull at 40 knots. I would normally never run the river at anything much over twenty, with perfect visibility. But there were no options, now.

The banks seemed to be passing in slow motion. The tachometer needle had not moved and the wake pattern had not changed, but the time between the bank landmarks, that I knew well, seemed grossly extended. Lee's face was more pale now, and he seemed to be gasping for breath. Rod bent over him, then straightened and with teeth clenched, gave his head a half shake. Cold now seized me from the inside. And then, our deepest dread became a nightmare of reality.

Something impacted the hull. The boat shuddered with the first impact, and then there was a second. The helm wheel ripped at my hands, as whatever the object was hit the propeller. All that I could visualize was a punctured hull and a helpless, powerless boat sinking in frigid water with my stricken son unable even to fight for his life. I was too paralyzed to take action of any kind. But the engine was still running! It was vibrating slightly, but the tach needle hadn't moved. The hull was still on plane. Had I been in full possession of reason, I would have known that the second impact meant that the first had not penetrated the hull, and that the propeller contact meant that the object was likely now astern. Whatever damage there was could be addressed later. If that boat were sinking, it would sink as close to the dock as I could get it, and if necessary, I would run it aground short of the dock. That throttle would remain open just as long as the carburetor intakes were above water. Reason was returning.

Rod had been maintaining contact with the 911 operator. "They're at the ramp!" Then, "They can see us!"

Out of the gray curtain, piercing red strobe lights dimly flickered, then brightened. We swung to starboard, and I made what could only be charitably described as "a hard landing" at the dock. Rod was already on the dock with a mooring line. We hustled Lee to the paramedics and a waiting gurney. They hoisted him into the vehicle and closed the door. Rod and I secured the boat, and noticed that steam was pouring from the engine's cooling water exhaust port. "Think we hurt it?" Rod asked.

"Don't care, now!"

We returned to the ambulance. A young paramedic opened the door. He was smiling, a very good sign. "Well, it doesn't look like a classic heart attack. His pulse is high, but pretty steady. We're gonna take him to the ER, you know, find out what's going on. He said you were really slayin' 'em out there. Always happens when I'm on duty. Call the hospital in a couple of hours."

"Yeah, OK. Hey, thanks, guys."

"It's what we do," he shrugged.

Rod and I re-trailered the boat and went to clean fish. The engine started and ran normally. It seemed no worse for its heavy exertion. One propeller blade was nicked and bent. There was an ugly black abrasion on the hull, but no real damage. It turned out that Lee did have a heart abnormality, now being treated. There are no limitations on his activities, but he is a bit nervous about fishing with Rod and me.

He says we drive boats much too fast.

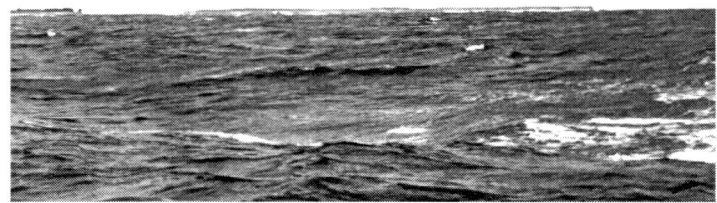

Chapter 16
The Sweet Sea
Renaissance

Here is another rescue story. It involves Mr. Stoughton's second case in point: the body of water that the early French explorers referred to as "The Sweet Sea". It is bordered by four states and two nations, and lies in the watershed flow path of huge cities and massive industry. And just as that astute teacher had said, by 1950, it had been poisoned. And while the level of poisoning was never totally fatal to aquatic life, the Sweet Sea was indeed in very poor health. There is the infamous incident in which one of its major tributaries actually caught fire. It remained one of America's great inland seas, but it was no longer sweet.

The renaissance of Lake Erie parallels the story of the Ohio River. Long and diligent efforts by the bordering states, the Province of Ontario, and of the national governments of the United States and Canada, working in concert – remarkable in itself – gradually ransomed the life and health of the lake. But somehow, it seemed more than a restoration. By the late 1970's, the aquatic life of the lake was more than well; it was flourishing. It had, in less than three decades, become an outstanding fishery. There was a school of thought, among some of the "old-timers" on the lake, that it was actually better than it had *ever* been. Thus began that golden age that Al Lindner and associates, in their wonderful book, "*Walleye Wisdom*" referred to as "The Lake Erie Phenomenon."

Where the Gulls Are

And phenomenon it was! Our circle had heard about the incredible walleye fishing in Lake Erie, and had discounted it out of hand. "Yeah, right." We all had been taught that the lake was dead. It wasn't until we had seen first-hand what had happened on the Big O that we began to say, grudgingly, "Well, maybe." Then, at a family gathering, a distant in-law, Dale, was going on at great length about his own experiences, limiting out with walleyes – BIG walleyes – virtually every time he put his boat in the water, and often in less than two hours. I took one of my sons aside. "Too much beer," I scoffed.

"Dad', he reminded me, "Dale doesn't drink."

"Oh. Well, then, let's gather intelligence."

We questioned – no, we interrogated – him as to all details. Where do you launch? How do you get there? Where do you stay? Where are the hotspots? What bait or lures do you use? Where do you get them? When are the best times? He was completely open; information flowed from him like a fire hose. "Wait a minute," he said, "I'll get a map and show you. It's right here in the car." While he retrieved the map, I retrieved a note pad. It was more information, and coming faster, than I could remember.

"Hey, listen, I'll take you with me next trip. I'm going back in four weeks. I'll be out of town 'til then."

"Uh…. thanks, but I'll be there *Saturday!*"

The gathering lasted until late evening. I called Jim Santangelo anyway, and roused him from bed. The phone rang a long time before a sleepy, and a bit cranky, voice answered. "Uh…hel….hello?"

"Hey, Jim! It's Bob. Listen, here's what I just found out."

As I related what I had learned, Jim's drowsiness disappeared. He questioned me as to whether I really believed what I had been told, pointing out that we had heard such songs before, and had chased many a wild goose. I reassured him that I did believe it, and he reminded me that I had said that before, too. But, before the conversation ended, Jim said, "Well….. why not? What time do you want to leave?"

"Three thirty."

"Three thirty???? Well…… OK. Can I go to sleep, now?"

Even though it was mid-June, it was still very dark at 3:30, as we fumbled in the gloom to get the little Grumman secured to the hitch of our then only tow vehicle: a 1975 International Harvester crew cab pick-up, with an eight foot bed and a gargantuan 176 inch wheel base. It was the "Contractor's Special", a no-frills, stripped-down unit with no power steering, no air conditioning, no radio, vinyl bench seats, and a four speed manual. It had a fuel capacity of 48 gallons, and needed every drop.

It was a beast to handle, but it would tow anything not built on a reinforced foundation, gross overkill for an 850 pound boat. I have shoulder problems to this day that may very well be the result of repetitive motion injury in fifteen years of steering that monster. Backing a relatively short trailer down a launch ramp was a sweaty exercise in frustration. But, it did develop one's upper body strength......and one's vocabulary.

Every Joe knows that there is another fundamental law of the universe: boat trailer lights never work, at least, not all at the same time. That was, of course, the case. Another twenty minutes were spent clearing bulbs of corrosion. Then, Jim remembered that the trailer wheel bearings had not been lubricated in a while, and that was attended to. By about 4:20, the expedition was finally launched. "I guess we should have said 2:30," I observed. "Pfff", said Jim.

We found the East Harbor State Park campground exactly as we had been directed. But this was a week-end in early June, and the campground - largest state park campground in the entire state - was full. We decided to drive around to the Catawba State Park launch ramp, and worry about a place to sleep later. There were walleye out there, just waiting for us. The launch ramp parking lot was full, as well, and we were forced to back the empty trailer into the edge of the brush in an overflow area. There were four usable ramps at Catawba, but we waited in a line of vehicles for nearly an hour, anyway. "Do you believe this? It must be as good as they say," I remarked to Jim.

"Either that, or P. T. Barnum was right."

We were finally afloat. The ramp was well sheltered by a concrete pier/breakwater, forming a protected lagoon. That lagoon was full of boats, a full spectrum of anything that could be trailered, from 24 foot cruisers to 14 foot jon boats, and with just that wide a spectrum of seamanship skills. It reminded me of that chaotic scene at Amity harbor in the movie *"Jaws"*.

Thankfully, it was a calm day – winds from the west at five to seven miles per hour. We would learn that those conditions were not exactly the norm, an understatement of almost criminal proportions. We gingerly picked our way between boats and finally got into more open water. The wind may have been calm, but the wakes of boats, accelerating at full throttle, as soon as clear of the no-wake zone, created nasty cross-chop. I did not envy those in smaller boats. The Grumman was only 17 feet in length, and was light in weight, but it had deep freeboard. We felt pretty secure in it. Ignorance is indeed bliss.

We had no Loran, and this was before the advent of civilian GPS, nor did we have a speedometer for dead reckoning navigation. But we had installed a high quality compass and a mid-range sonar. If all else fails, we reasoned, just head south. There has to be land there, somewhere. But visibility was excellent; the haze of late summer had not yet set in, and we could easily see the landmarks that Dale had described.

"Now, listen," he had said, "It's easy. Just imagine a line between Green Island – see? right here – and the cooling tower at the power plant – right there. Get on that line and drift. That's all." But as we approached Green Island, it appeared that there was no room to drift. There were boats everywhere. It truly did look as if one could have walked the imaginary line Dale had described, from boat to boat. At the southern edge of the flotilla, we turned west, into the wind, ran about three miles, then slithered into the center of the pack.

The boats were not so close together as they had looked from a distance, but were close enough that inter-boat conversations could be easily held without much shouting. Since our boat was lighter than average, it drifted faster than average, requiring frequent repositioning to avoid contact with other boats. This could usually be accomplished by paddle, without resorting to an engine start. Sometimes, we would drift to within a distance that I thought would be an objectionable encroachment, but the folks in the other boat would smile and wave. It was a festival out there…a party. Every boat we could observe was bringing walleye aboard with regularity. There was laughter and chatter in every direction, and whooping, if an unusually large fish was boated. It was nearly impossible to scan the drifting raft of boats, with the naked eye, and not see at least one bent rod and tight line, at any given time. It simply defied belief.

We rigged with the lure that Dale had recommended, a front-weighted spinner with the trade name, Erie Dearie, tipped with a night crawler. Dale had not detailed the depth at which the lure should be presented, so we simply cast upwind and allowed the lure to sink to whatever depth it would. In less than three minutes, Jim had a strike – not an aggressive, ton-of-bricks strike, but a gentle, intermittent tugging. Jim set the hook, but there was no resistance. "Couldn't have gotten that whole 'crawler that fast," he muttered to himself, and left the lure in place. Almost immediately, the tugging resumed, and then became a light drag, as if the hook had snagged a large leaf. The drag became heavier and heavier. Again to himself: "Must've picked up some weeds or something…." But when he began his retrieve, to clear whatever debris he had encountered, his rod suddenly doubled. Responsibility belonged to a five pound walleye.

Jim had to net his fish one-handed, because before he had wrestled it to the boat, I had a fish on. It was not as large as Jim's, but certainly not a cull. Over the next several hours, we hooked a large walleye every ten minutes or so. The limit on walleye was then six, and by then, we, and most of the boats in the raft, were strictly catch-and-release. Dale had been as truthful as an Eagle Scout. But even here, seeing it, being part of it, it was almost impossible to believe. We were greenhorns, with no skills and no experience in this venue, and hooking fish after fish after fish. We asked the boat next to us whether this was a unique day – a bonanza day. "Oh," he said, "maybe just a little better than usual. Wind's just the right speed. But almost any time the wind'll let ya get out here and drift, it's pretty much like this. 'Course, later in the summer, the schools'll spread out to the east and north, but yeah, it's like this while they're here."

I reminded Jim that we had no place to sleep, twelve big fish to clean, and nowhere to clean them. We decided to leave early, beat the mob at the ramp, and allow plenty of time to find lodging. We left the raft of boats early, but the rest of that plan did not work out well. We would learn that there was *always* a mob at the ramp, every ramp, at least on days when the lake was marginally benign enough that fishing was not life-threatening. We waited a long time just to drop Jim off at the dock so that he could go get the truck and wait in line. There were boats tied off all along the breakwater, so that there was no choice but to hold position at idle in the lagoon. Finally, I anchored, so that I could shut down the engine. While waiting….. and waiting….. and waiting, I asked myself this question:

"*This fishing is fantastic….like nothing I have ever seen, but is it worth all of this?*"

And then, I answered myself: "*Damned right it is!*"

Now, if you ever have an afternoon with nothing to do, and you would like to have a few laughs, pack a picnic lunch and go to your local boat ramp. The weather should be very pleasant, and it is well if the fish are biting, because those conditions will bring out the less serious, and less experienced, fishermen and boaters. You will see things that make the Three Stooges look like a Shakespearian troupe. So it was at Catawba ramp that day. A 24 foot cuddy cabin boat, with three tan skinned, but white haired, fishermen aboard would wait for their fourth partner to back a triple axle trailer into the water to exactly the right depth. Then the helmsman would align the boat, blip the throttle but once, and the boat was re-trailered, and off the ramp in less than twenty seconds. Next would be a much smaller boat, more attuned to partying than to fishing, waxed and polished, and with a stereo boom box at full volume. The vehicle driver would back the trailer into the dock rails several times, back it in to total submergence, and then draw it back out much too far. The helmsman would make a number of attempts to stab the trailer with the boat, and at length, would jump into the water – well, he was wearing shorts and a flowered shirt, anyway – and hitch the winch rope to the bow ring, guiding the boat up onto the trailer manually, while the driver, unhappy to be wet, cranked the winch handle. It took thirty minutes.

Jim was extraordinarily talented at backing boat trailers, even with the ungainly I-H. When it was his turn, in one graceful maneuver, the trailer was at precisely the right depth. My job was easy: align, power the boat onto the trailer, and keep the throttle about one quarter open until Jim had drawn the trailer clear of the water, then shut down and wait until he had reached a tie-down area. Jim *always* made my job easy. On-lookers think that a quick, clean recovery is the skill of the helmsman. It is not. The key skill is at the wheel of the tow vehicle.

Our next task was to find a place to stay, and, even more immediate, find a place to clean fish. We were to find every campground, public or private, full, and a no vacancy sign on every motel or camp. We drove south, away from the lake, as far as Fremont. There was "no room at the inn." But we had a large cooler aboard the truck, and buried the fish in ice, at least temporarily preserving them. We had not started this odyssey with both truck tanks full, and were beginning to run low. We came across a large truck stop, and refueled. We decided to eat dinner there, and so, I pulled the rig into an empty space behind two eighteen wheelers at the rear edge of the lot, so as not to occupy a space that a big rig could use.

After dinner, sipping coffee, I said to Jim, "You know what? Everything is here. There are restroom facilities, we can get breakfast, we're not tyin' up a big truck parking space, and we can get more ice in the morning. Sure, we're twenty miles from the lake, but it looks like this is the best we're gonna do. Let's just stay here."

"Where do we sleep?"

"That's an eight foot bed. We put all the stuff in the first two feet and on the seats. Bed's got a cap over it. We brought sleeping bags and air mattresses anyway."

"Well……why not?"

And so, we were lulled to sleep by the hammering idle of two very large Diesel engines. The sound was loud and monotonous, but strangely soothing. In fact, when one of them left, shortly before dawn, the sudden quiet woke me.

Recognizing that we were twenty miles from the lake and that the launch ramps would again be crowded, we abandoned the idea of a sit-down breakfast, and bought donuts and coffee to go, as well as another bag of ice, which was dumped over the fish in the cooler. It was still dark, but as we approached the lake, traffic became heavy with vehicles towing boats, and, at the lake, approaches to boat ramps were bumper to bumper. It was a stampede, a gold rush, a frenzy. Waiting in line in the launch ramp parking lot, we counted license plates from thirteen different states…..and one of them was Colorado! We had never seen anything like it. This "dead" lake had become the Super Bowl of angling.

Once in the water and out of the chaotic lagoon, we came to a heading of zero degrees – due north. The wind was again benign, and we were able to run on plane. In minutes, the boats were visible, this time further west than on the previous day. We had no accurate count; it was a large number – perhaps hundreds. And it was certainly likely that this was not the only flotilla of boats over a school of walleyes in the western basin of Lake Erie. It was simply the first one that we encountered. There was no reason to search further. We joined the group and began to drift, using the same technique as had worked so well a day earlier. It worked again. We had boated a limit of fine walleyes by noon, and decided that we had better head for home, where at least we had a place to clean these fish and those already iced down in the cooler. Thus ended our first foray into the walleye glory days of Lake Erie. It would certainly not be the last.

We had learned some lessons: 1. The stories we had heard, which seemed too good to be true, *were* true. 2. It was a very crowded venue, and we would need to be prepared for that. Lodging facilities, restaurants, and bait shops were overwhelmed on week-ends, and bringing supplies of food, bait and sometimes even fuel, was a wise strategy. Making lodging reservations well in advance was not as practical a matter as it might have seemed. The demand being as great as it was, many establishments did not accept reservations. And then there was the problem that a reservation, upon which a non-refundable deposit had been paid in advance, might well have been for days on which the wind precluded fishing, as it often did. Having had two very calm days as the sum total of our experience, we had not yet learned that particular lesson. But we soon would, and as always, the hard way.

Having been exposed to this angling Eldorado, we returned as frequently as our schedules allowed. On the very next visit, we were able to secure a campsite at East Harbor State Park. There is a launch ramp at the campground, in a sheltered bay, connected to the lake by a channel between two rock jetties. Finding an open campsite on a Saturday morning surprised us, and even more surprising was the fact that there was no long line at the ramp. Rejoicing at our good fortune, Jim and I turned the bow of the Grumman towards the channel. There was considerable boat traffic in the channel, mostly larger craft, many of them charter boats, and we took our place in line. As we approached the open lake, we could see that boats some distance away from the jetties were pitching noticeably……. very noticeably. But once again, ignorance was bliss.

The wind was from the southwest, and therefore, the south shore of the lake was somewhat sheltered. As we proceeded northward, we were forced to reduce speed, reduce speed again, and finally to run at just over idle in order to avoid violent impacts to the hull. In another hundred yards, we were both drenched, and that while running with a quartering sea. It seemed prudent to reverse direction, just to see how difficult returning to the channel was going to be. And the answer was: "very". Aha! So this was why there was space at the campground and no line at the ramp!

We learned that we were desperately under-equipped for a mere fifteen mile per hour wind on a large and relatively shallow lake. The boat was taking a little water over the gunwales and being pounded mercilessly. Finally, by turning directly into the wind and seeking the shelter of the south shore, then following the shore eastward to the channel, we arrived in calmer water without serious incident. We were wet, and more than a little concerned…..no, concerned is not the word. Scared is the word. But then, I suppose that "scared" precedes "learning" in most situations in our lives.

A light-weight, seventeen foot boat is definitely not an all-weather fishing platform on Lake Erie. It was uncomfortably rough-riding even in a light chop, and traveling any distance in waves over two feet was nearly unbearable. Once on site, and drifting, that boat was stable and pleasant, but getting there was, for the most part, a grit-your-teeth-and-hang-on business. And yet, we had many a highly successful day of walleye fishing aboard the Grumman, as long as wind was carefully monitored and treated with suspicion and distrust. And in those days, before electronic access to weather forecasts was available for just about any location on the planet, NOAA weather radio was limited to the locale in question, and by the time the locale was reached, for someone coming from hundreds of miles away, it was too late. There were a number of occasions on which we towed the boat to the lake…..and promptly turned around and towed it back, a 480 mile round trip. There had to be a better way.

We resorted to calling the National Weather Service office in Cleveland, on a number which played the recorded forecast continuously. Apparently, this was no unique discovery on our part, for as time went on, the line was increasingly busy, and the service was finally discontinued. But even armed with a forecast a few minutes old upon departure, most anglers traveling any distance to the lake found that conditions had often changed by the time their boat was in the water. Even today, despite the advances in meteorology, sophisticated computer modeling, and the rest, wind forecasting is not a precise business. We found that there was no substitute for "go and look." So powerful was the allure of the Eldorado days of Lake

Erie walleye fishing that boats, of whatever size, were frequently pushed to, and sometimes beyond, their reasonable limits.

Sometimes, the treacherous, unpredictable winds of Lake Erie are the angler's friend. It is common knowledge that calm conditions do not favor walleye feeding activity; you need what is referred to as "a walleye chop". And a wind that thwarts your going fishing where you would like to go is not necessarily your enemy. One bright, sunny, June morning, a dreaded bluebird day, my son, Jeff, and I set out from East Harbor for Green Island, where we had enjoyed great fishing the previous evening. But the north wind was up a bit that morning, and we realized that the trip out to Green Island would be a long, wet and harsh cruise. We had sought some relief from the pounding in the lee of South Bass Island. We were just off Starve Island when Jeff said, "Hey, Dad, instead of getting beat to death as soon as we clear South Bass, let's see if we can find some smallmouth bass in these rocks around Starve Island."

"That's a good enough excuse for me."

We had no live bait but night crawlers. They were a total failure; fresh water drum, here referred to, you will recall, as "sheepshead", inhaled the night crawlers as soon as they hit the water. "Well," Jeff said, "I'm going to a jighead tipped with one of these plastic craws." He held up a plastic grub that looked more like an octopus than a crawfish, but it was, at least, crawfish colored. On the very first cast, he immediately hooked a heavy fish. But something was wrong, here. That fish did not exhibit smallmouth bass speed. Nor did it ever leave the water, as a bronzeback would almost certainly have done in four or five feet of depth.

"What've you got there?"

Jeff did not answer, he simply made a bleating sound, indicating that he expected another sheepshead – this time, larger. This fish was stripping line against the drag clutch, and if it could get into the stone shards which ringed Starve Island, it would be gone. But it shied from the shallows and sounded, going under the boat and southward towards deeper, open water. The contest was decided at that point, but not over. As Jeff worked the fish to the boat, and could, at last, see it, he whooped, "Whoa! Get the net! It's a big walleye!" And indeed it was. We had no scale aboard, but had a steel tape, and the fish measured 30 ½ inches.

It should not have been there in four feet of water, in the middle of a bright day, on the south side of the islands. It should have been in thirty feet of water, at least two miles from any shoreline, in the dim light, near the bottom. And, amazingly, it was not alone. We caught eight more in the next two hours, the smallest of which had a length of 24 inches. And then, suddenly, it was over. In the next several visits to the lake, we always stopped at Starve Island, just to see if that day had been an anomaly. We never caught another walleye there.

The charter business was booming in those Eldorado days. Rod Null took a job as first mate on a 26 foot Stamas, in the summer of 1984. In case that sounds like a dream summer job for a student who likes to fish, consider the typical day: up at 5 AM to have the boat ready by 7, with fuel, bait and tackle aboard and shipshape. For the person who, at the end of the day, had to scrub down the boat, nightcrawlers were a problem. The fine black bedding in which they were kept made a streaky mess of deck, walls and gunwales. So, one of the things that Rod would do each morning was to remove the 'crawlers from their packages, rinse them, and then bury them in finely cracked ice. He says that they kept well and made his scrub-down chores much easier.

The Captain, Ron Cree, paid close attention to customer relations. With him, an eight hour charter was not dock-to-dock, but a full eight hours on station, and so the boat rarely was moored before 5PM. Then there was clean-up, fish cleaning, and other chores, until about 7:30. So, the duty cycle was a 14½ hour day, seven days per week…..unless limited by weather. At about 7:30, a group of charter captains would meet for dinner, each evening, in a different, pre-agreed-upon local restaurant. It was there that the real information was exchanged…….never via VHF radio, in spite of the elaborate codes that were devised to hide true locations, methods and results.

It was in late July that a party of regular clients booked a multi- day charter. There were twelve in the party, more than one boat could accommodate, so Captain Cree teamed with another captain. The first morning, both boats began to catch walleyes immediately, drifting south of Kelly's Island. But they were disappointingly small, and so, Cree asked his clients whether they would like to buy Canadian fishing licenses, as the schools of larger walleyes had migrated north, into Canadian waters. The clients agreed, and, when properly documented, the party headed for North Harbor

Shoal. The average depth in the area was about eighteen feet, but there were a series of humps, some rising from the bottom to a depth of only about five feet. Drifting over the humps from northwest to southeast, a distance of only about 150 yards, fifteen walleyes were taken on the first drift, the smallest of which was 25 inches in length. The boat was allowed to drift well off the humps before returning, under power, via a wide swing to open water, to the drift starting point. But after the second perfect drift, another boat, of about forty feet in length, motored across the humps and the fishing completely shut down. Boat traffic over a school of walleyes in 30 feet of water is one thing, over a school in five feet is quite another.

Rod reminisced that, for the most part, the clients were "good folks". But one occasion nearly led to an ugly situation. A company had rewarded six of its employees with an all-expense charter trip. These were not necessarily serious fishermen. They had established a "biggest walleye" pool, with an ante of $25 each, making the "pot" $150. About mid-day, one of them, call him George, landed a seven pound walleye. Fifteen minutes later, another big fish was hooked, and it displayed walleye characteristics. George slipped up, with a concealed fillet knife, and, pretending to assist in landing the fish, cut the line. It took both captain and mate to prevent violence.

One day, in line with the growing tourism brought about by the walleye phenomenon, a group of state dignitaries, including the then Governor, Richard Celeste, were scheduled for a day of walleye fishing aboard charter boats, conscripted by the local Chamber of Commerce, or an organization of like intent. Most of the captains were not overjoyed with this public relations "free ride" anyway, and when the appointed day carried with it a forecast of five to seven foot seas, the predominant attitude was "aint goin'." Finally the sponsors prevailed upon the captain of the largest boat, and he reluctantly took a party to the nearest location that offered any chance whatever of landing a walleye. As soon as one small walleye was aboard, "it was photo-op time and back to the dock". Lake Erie wind is no respecter of rank…….or anything else.

There are many places which call themselves "The Walleye Capital of the World", but during those days, Lake Erie certainly seemed to have valid claim to the title. A walleye "culture" began to spring up along Ohio's north coast. A local winery began to produce a Riesling style wine called "Walleye White". The city of Port Clinton hosts a New Years Eve street festival in which a 600 pound fiberglass walleye, named Wylie, descends at midnight while revelers sing "Hang on Wylie" to the tune of "Hang on Sloopy", which just happens to be the official state rock song. There were, and are, caps and tee shirts and coffee mugs, and a host of other items emblazoned with the image of the marble-eyed benefactor of the area's commerce. Supply increased to meet demand, and new lodging and eating establishments, and other businesses attuned to the needs of visiting anglers sprang up. But beneath it all was an unspoken worry.

Jim gave it voice one afternoon, on a drift northwest of Rattlesnake Island. "You know, I wonder how long this can go on. I mean, look at this. There have to be a hundred or more boats out here. Every one of 'em's got at least two guys in it , some of 'em four or five or more. And nobody leaves without six walleyes. We been doin' this for four years now, and it was goin' on long before we knew about it. And it's every day. Let's say an average of three guys. OK? That's eighteen fish per boat. That's eighteen hundred fish per day….and that's just for this bunch of boats. If you start the season in mid-may and it only goes to the first of August, that's ten weeks. OK, now, let's say half the days are too windy. That leaves thirty-five days. That's ….uh…..uh…63,000 fish, right? And let's say there are at least four of these rafts in just the western basin. Now that's ….uh…about a quarter million fish a year. How long can ya keep takin' a quarter million apex predators out of here before somethin' gets out of whack?"

I did not know how realistic Jim's numbers were, but the question was valid. Sure, it was a big, fertile lake, but each year fishing pressure increased, and each year angler success seemed undiminished. How long could this surreal harvest be sustained? "Well," I said to Jim, "if you look at just the economic value of the walleye fishery to this area, you know your question gets a lot of serious thought down in Columbus. I haven't got time to worry about it right now. I got a fish on!"

By now, the brutal pounding of Lake Erie's short wavelength chop had caused severe damage to the Grumman. Rivets were missing and two ribs in the hull, heavy channel sections of aircraft aluminum, were broken. Jim could not believe it. "If anybody knows how to build a strong aluminum structure, it should be those guys. They've been building carrier-based fighters for forty years. Do you have any idea of the G-forces involved in a carrier landing?" I did not, but I knew that this light boat was no match for the Sweet Sea. The following winter, we bought the Grady-White.

Where the Gulls Are

And the following summer, we learned that it was not an all-weather Erie platform, either. Nothing is.

As each summer wore on, walleye fishing usually tapered off. The fish moved east into the deeper central basin and north of the Canadian border, into the cooler waters flowing from Lake Huron via the St Clair and Detroit rivers, and the schools became less densely packed. The walleye fishing wasn't over, but the *easy* walleye fishing was over. From our launch points, the walleye hotspots were long runs – slow and uncomfortable under anything but low wind conditions – and low wind conditions were usually not good walleye fishing. But Lake Erie offered some other very attractive options: smallmouth bass and yellow perch. The former has long been considered the premier, pound-for-pound freshwater game fish; the latter is considered by some – and I am among them – to be the ultimate seafood. Of course, as long as there are at least two fishermen on the planet, and it doesn't take more than two, there will be differences of opinion, and perhaps, uncharacteristic of this gentlemanly lot, arguments……. sometimes with raised voices and inferences of canine ancestry.

Fishing for perch – or "perch jerking", as it is condescendingly referred to by those in quest of larger, sport fish – peaks in late autumn, but good perch fishing can be found as early as August, usually in deep water, over marl bottom. Excellent catches can be made in the spring as well, usually in April. Perch can be caught all year, of course. "Good" perch fishing usually only means that the fish are concentrated in fairly dense schools. Every hot dog vender knows that his sales will be brisker on a crowded sidewalk. Larger perch are often hooked during what would ordinarily be considered "the walleye season" by anglers drifting or trolling for walleyes with lures tipped with nightcrawlers, but they are certainly not hooked one after another. A good perch bite should be like swatting mosquitoes….. in a deep bush swamp….at sundown….in June….after a rain: non-stop action.

Perch are not sought after because of their speed or strength, but simply because they are so damned good! Their flesh is firm, yet tender, and their subtle flavor is………well, how do you describe flavor? What is chocolate, or coffee, or twelve year old Islay single malt Scotch whiskey in the written word? Perhaps the best description is that I would not trade a plate of lake perch, sautéed gently in garlic butter, for Maine lobster, yellow tail snapper, mahi mahi, toro tuna sashimi or (forgive me, Wylie) walleye. And, no, not even for sauger.

In almost everything, there is theory – what ought to happen – and then there is practice – what actually does happen. Our circle's experiences have been that perch are often not where they are supposed to be, when they are supposed to be there. It was in July. Rod Null had relatives who owned a cabin on Middle Bass Island. It was accessible only by boat, either your own, or the ferry. The ferry dock was far from the cabin, and we had no land transport…..and a lot of gear to carry. So, the Grady was loaded like a freighter; it was difficult to find deck space to stand. Rod had a huge cooler full of minnows, oxygenated by an air pump, with its batteries. He also had another cooler full of dry ice to keep the water, in the first cooler, cool. And then there was all of the usual gear: clothing, sleeping bags, air mattresses, food, utensils, and tackle. To add interest to the day, a northwest wind was sprinting from Manitoba, across Michigan, and right down our throats. We had often joked that the wide open, center console Grady was "a rainsuit boat….even on a clear day". That observation was entirely without humor that morning.

Even at 15 miles per hour, well under planing speed, the four foot chop was drenching the boat with every wave. It was a self-bailing hull design, but there were places at which water could enter the hull: the opening for the anchor rope, the rod holder openings, the opening in the deck under the console, where steering, throttle, and electrical cables entered the console, and the opening where those same cables exited the hull and connected to the engine. By the time we were approaching Middle Bass Island, the boat's response to the helm had become sluggish, and I knew that there was a lot of water in the bilge. No problem, I thought, we'll just pump it out. I flipped on the bilge pump switch, and looked over the starboard gunwale to observe the outflow stream. There was none. Then, the words no one ever wants to hear the helmsman say: "Uh-oh!"

"Rod! How deep is that little harbor by the cabin?"

"With the lake down like it is, I'd say about a foot and a half to two feet."

"We're not gonna make it with water in the hull. We draw a foot and a half with a dry bilge. Move as much of this stuff as far forward as you can, and sit as far out on the bow as you can. Maybe we can get the transom well deck up out of the water so I can open the access port and see why this bilge pump isn't workin'."

One of the problems with that boat was that the deck of the transom well was below the water line…….and the inspection port accessing the bilge pump and the wash-down pump was in the transom well deck. So, while the main deck was self-bailing, the transom well was not, unless the hull were on plane, impossible that day. In the lee of Middle Bass Island, moving the load forward was accomplished, and the inspection port was opened. The problem was obvious; the impellor housing on the bilge pump was split, and the pump was happily pumping 1000 gallons per hour….. right back into the bilge.

"Just stay as far forward as you can. I'm gonna try to hold the housing together to pump out the bilge before we go into that shallow channel." It took twenty minutes to pump out the bilge. That's 330 gallons of water, or about 2600 pounds. With the bow low, the bilge dry, and the engine tilted up, we successfully negotiated the narrow channel leading to the private basin serving cabin owners on that part of the island. Leaving the boat front-heavy, we semi-secured the pump housing with that greatest of all emergency repair tools – except for duct tape – baling wire! At least, it now pumped a little more water overboard than it pumped back into the hull.

The wind denied our hopes of going walleye fishing that afternoon. Rod suggested that, rather than standing on the island watching the wind blow, we venture along the sheltered shore of Middle Bass and traverse the short distance to Ballast Island, and there, shelter on the lee side and fish for perch. There was little hope of finding perch in that shallow water at this season, but anything beat being confined to shore. So, we scooped about four dozen minnows out of Rod's ventilated, refrigerated cooler, and made for Ballast Island. Unless squarely in the lee of Ballast Island, the seventeen pound Danforth anchor would not hold, no matter how much rope was paid out. But once it was secured, in twenty-two feet of water, we began to catch perch. It was soon clear that the four dozen minnows, thought to be a wasteful overkill, were being used up at a high rate. We began to cut the tiny emerald shiners into halves, then thirds. The tiniest fragment of minnow would attract a bite. Just as the very last shiner was used, we had limited out.

The wind mellowed overnight. The next morning we supplied ourselves with about twice as many minnows, and returned to the same spot. In just the first two hours, we caught.........nothing. We finally caught some perch that day, exactly where we – or anyone – would have expected: in forty feet of water, northeast of Kelly's Island. Why they were where they were on the previous day, we have not a clue. That is the fascination, and the frustration, of perch fishing.

It was the first week-end in November, and it was a glorious autumn day. Lake Erie, and for that matter, most fishing venues, are wonderful places to be on a fine autumn day. The sky was crisp and clear, an almost purple blue. The air was cool, but not cold, and the shores were spectacular, not with the yellows, reds, and golds of early autumn, but with the rich russets and maroons of those trees "made of sterner stuff." The wind was a friendly, docile, five to eight knots. Jim Santangelo and I were on the water by 10 am, having secured a campsite at the now nearly deserted East Harbor State Park. My recollection is that there were three other parties in the entire park. Facilities were shut down. There was no water, no showers, no anything. There were no dogs barking, no children screaming, no radios playing. It was my favorite time of year.

Jim and I fished every one of our favorite, never-fail perch spots. In a full day of fishing, we had caught not a single fish. But we had burned a lot of fuel. We kept shaking our heads. "This can't be happening. It's a dream!"

"It's a nightmare. But we'll wake up in a minute."

A dinner of fried Spam and packaged Spanish rice, cooked over a battered, rusty Coleman stove, tasted pretty good. We were just cleaning up when the rain started. Retreating into the bed of the now also battered and rusty International crew cab, the rain drummed on the cap over the bed with some vigor. The sound of rain on a tent is soothing; it is good. The sound of rain on a tin cabin roof is better. But the sound of rain on a metal pick-up truck cap is best of all. It is closer, more intimate. It is an arm's length from your nose.

Morning dawned cold, gray and wet. Rain was still falling, and the wind was up. Jim and I decided to give it up and tow the boat home. Rather than break out all the cooking gear, we decided to eat breakfast at some restaurant out on the main road. Being warm, dry, and full makes one unreasonably willing to brave the cold and the wet. We decided that, since we were here, we might as well put the boat back in the water, and at least test whether fishing was still so incredibly bad. As we made our way from the ramp to the channel, the rain slacked off a bit, but the wind had no such inclination. As we got to the end of the jetty, swells of four to five feet greeted us. We turned downwind and anchored not 50 yards from the end of the Jetty. "Twenty minutes. If we don't catch anything in twenty minutes, we're gone,"

"OK".

In twenty minutes, we had nineteen perch, in two hours, one hundred perch, the limit in those days for two anglers. Why such a pronounced difference from one day to the next? Weather conditions were entirely different. Was that all there was to it? We didn't know. We don't know now. We will likely never know. And that is the beauty of it.

Even in the peak days of the walleye bonanza, we noticed anglers who paid absolutely no attention to the marble-eyed fish which had achieved such rock-star celebrity. These, instead, patiently worked the island shores and the mainland limestone cliffs and rock banks for smallmouth bass. The lake is a legendary bronzeback fishery, and has been for at least a century. The lake's predominant islands all have the word "bass" in their names, and for good reason. Why, then, the overwhelming popularity of the walleye? It is because the smallmouth bass is not so easily taken. It is a finicky feeder, a rock-seeking adversary, and routinely goes airborne to get hook-shedding slack in an angler's line.

It was one of those days, one of those perfect October days, so beautiful that justice demands no fish be caught. Fortunately, in fishing, there is no justice. It was not yet a beautiful day when Jim and I launched at Mazurik ramp. The wind was a dead calm, and yes, it was Lake Erie. We checked the map. Or, at least, we thought so. We could not see it for the fog. By now, we had GPS, and set a course for the "humps" east of Kelly's Island. Once out of the launch ramp basin, the body of water was appropriately named. Erie was indeed eerie. The fog was dense enough that seeing a boat forty yards away was impossible. Every sixty seconds, we shut down the engine to listen for other boats. There were none. Jim was leaning on the forward rail, peering over the bow, looking for floating debris. He suddenly threw his arms out horizontally. "Whoa! Whoa! Whoa!"

The sonar, transducer at the transom, showed a depth of over six feet, but

Jim was shouting at me, "It's two feet deep up here!" We had expected to cross the shallow rock bar extending southeast from Kelly's Island, but it should have been five or six feet deep. Then it sank in. A GPS route is a straight line. It does not care what may be in the way. And in the way were several hundred thousand tons of rocks. We backed out southward, very carefully, and then moved eastward about a mile. We then re-engaged the original target – the humps – and proceeded, very cautiously.

By the time we had reached the electronic target – thought to be the humps – the fog was beginning to burn off. The shoreline of Kelly's Island was distractingly spectacular. The autumn colors were in full array. It was almost enough to make one forget the mission…..but not quite. A south wind had begun to blow, very softly, and we began a very gentle drift to the north. We had been able to acquire, by visiting a number of bait stores, a half dozen, five inch long, golden shiners. These were presented on a simple, single hook, bottom rig. The first one had hardly touched bottom when it was seized by a four pound smallmouth bass, who told us that he could not only swim, but fly. No other fish in fresh water….**NO** other fish in fresh water…..possesses the spirit of a smallmouth bass. If that statement incites a debate, that was my intent.

By the time all six shiners were expended, we had but two smallmouth bass. But together, they weighed over seven pounds. Other lures, including those that closely mimicked a golden shiner, were of no use. Even the tube jigs, closely resembling a round goby, so effective in Lake St Clair, produced no response, even though smallmouth bass feed heavily on that alien invader. We spent the rest of the day on perch and did fairly well. The key point is that the Sweet Sea is not a one dimensional walleye habitat.

Over time, the Lake Erie walleye fishery returned to a more sensible, more sustainable level. It is still a premier walleye lake, maybe the best there is, but it is not the Eldorado it once was. Nevertheless, the allure remains. In February of 2009, 130, or so, walleye anglers were rescued from an ice floe on Lake Erie, which had separated from shore ice. The fact that there was a crack in the ice was known to these anglers, who crossed it using a wooden pallet. As the crack widened, the US Coast Guard, and local authorities, rescued all but one, using airboats and helicopters. It had been a frightening, narrow, escape. The very next day, to the chagrin of first responders, the ice was again filled with walleye anglers! It is irresistible. It is an addiction..

And what of the infamous, inflammable Cuyahoga River? It is today an outstanding steelhead trout fishery, with smallmouth bass and northern pike as bonuses….frosting on the cake. Lake Erie is alive, and well, and living in Ontario…. and Ohio…... and Michigan…. and Pennsylvania….. and New York.

Catching a limit of large Lake Erie walleyes is not the slam dunk of the 1980's. It requires skill, knowledge, favorable conditions, and, of course, good fortune. It is challenging again.

And I am glad.

Chapter 17
Pa-hay-okee
Fishing the Edge

Pa-hay-okee, meaning "grassy water", was the term the Seminoles used to describe the vast area of south Florida now referred to as The Everglades. Everglades National Park has well defined boundaries, but the Everglades eco-region boundaries extend far beyond those of the Park, and are not universally agreed upon. For example, the World Wildlife Fund for Nature includes Lake Okeechobee as part of the Everglades. The National Wildlife Federation defines the Everglades region as beginning as far north as Orlando. Some define the region as beginning south of Lake Okeechobee. The region is unique in that the boundary between fresh and salt water is not so well defined as in the mouth of a river or even an estuarine delta. Here, the River of Grass is what hydrologists call a "sheetflow", very wide, very slow, and very shallow, delivering fresh water into the sea over a large front. This wide edge creates unique fishing opportunities, and is itself ill-defined, changing, often quickly, with weather conditions, especially rainfall.

We're going fishing with Joe at both ends of Pa-hay-okee: Lake Okeechobee, and the Florida Bay region. Tim Wakefield and Frank Miller, by now, familiar names, will be our companions, Tim in fresh water, Frank in salt.

The following was written in longhand by Tim Wakefield in 1971 and is transcribed <u>exactly</u> as written. We join the group as they arrive at Uncle Joe's Fish Camp, after a white-knuckled tow of a twenty foot airboat, hand built by Tim and Al Smith, through a snowstorm in north Georgia.

Okeechobee Chronicle

We finally pulled up in front of a small block building with minnow tanks in front, a huge water oak towering above the building, a dim light outside and a light inside. I thought to myself, this must be Uncle Joe's. We went inside and Al introduced us to Richard, one of Uncle Joe's sons, who now ran the camp. He told us that we'd be staying in number five and walked back to our cabin with us. Richard was a tall, lean, sunburned chap of about thirty that didn't have too much to say. Our cabin wasn't the Ritz but it had the necessities, a combo stove, frig and sink unit, two double beds, a table and chairs, a TV and a john. What else could man want? We had a night cap, odd manned for the lone bed and settled in for a night's sleep.

We awoke about 8:00 and without getting out of bed could tell that there was a definite chill to the air. Bob got up and started breakfast and it wasn't long before the gas stove burners had our little bungalow warm as toast. In fact Al wanted to turn the air conditioner on. This was a standing joke as Al had bet me that we would use the air conditioner before the week was over and I said we wouldn't. We'd agreed to let Bob decide when we needed it. I felt this was a good bet becuase I knew that Bob didn't cater to any fancities when on a vacation and would resist using the damn air conditioner if he could!

The aroma of freshly brewed coffee and frying bacon got to me and I had to get up. I threw my clothes on and decided to go outside to see if the orange trees that Al said were behind our bungalow were for real. When I opened the door I realized how chilly it really was. Later we found out that it had been 25 degrees earlier that morning! As I walked around our cabin I suddenly became aware of the lazy serene atmosphere of Uncle Joe's. It wasn't the stark silence of the Canadian backwoods but kind of a do your own thing take it easy feeling and that was exactly what I was yearning for. Sure enough, there were the orange trees, laden with beauties. I picked an armload and went back inside. The freshly squeezed orange juice, bacon, eggs and coffee set well with all of us. We decided to drive into Clewiston to launch the boat and one of us would bring the car and trailer back and the other two bring the boat back the canal.

Clewiston was a combination ranching, tourist and retirement community, clean and typically Florida. Al and I launched the boat and had a little trouble getting the engine fired. She finally caught and we chugged away from the ramp. We motored thru the flood gates in the dike. These are closed during a hurricane to prohibit the waters from Lake Okeechobee flooding Clewiston as had happened years ago. Once into the lake, we took a hard left and started down the canal to our camp.

The Corps of Army Engineers had built the canal and dike and it was an inland waterway that went east-west all the way across the state. It was about 15 miles to Uncle Joe's. The Lycoming seemed to be running a little rough. I wondered if the choke was stuck. Al stopped and I walked back and manually actuated it a few times. He restarted it and this time it sounded good. Oil pressure and temp and cylinder head temp were all normal. We were breezing along at 40 mph easily. In no time we were at camp and tied up at Uncle Joe's dock. Bob had just gotten there himself. We gassed the boat and had Sam get us some big shiners, as we were ready to fish!

With the airboat, Al had planned on being able to head due north from the dock and cut across the swamp to get to Moonshine Bay for the good fishing. Uncle Joe's was located at the Y where two canals joined. One was the old canal going out to the lake, about a five mile jaunt and the other was the newer canal going to Clewiston one way and Moorehaven the other. In the past, Al said it was a good hour's trip to go to Moonshine Bay via the canal and the lake. Moonshine Bay was a body of water 5 by 10 miles across that laid amidst the swamp land and was accessible from Okeechobee via a passage through the swamp grass. Al figured that we could cut the trip time to 15 minutes if we could head cross country with the airboat. Sam advised us not to try it, as the lake was about 3 feet lower than normal and many rocks were exposed in the swamp grass. We took his advice and decided to try the old route.

We headed out the canal toward the lake and felt the chill of the air. We were all bundled up like Eskimos but were ready to fish. The unmuffled sound of the engine was deafening and we couldn't talk to each other at all. When we got to the lake, many small boats were anchored at the inlet to the canal, fishing for crappie. We weren't after that small stuff so we headed north along the western shore of the lake. We tried anchoring and fishing into the needle grass along the shore with no luck. The engine seemed to be running worse the further we went so we decided to find some pepper grass beds and fish them rather than try to get into Moonshine.

We had no luck in the pepper grass either. Each time we started the engine to move to another bed, it was harder to start. I climbed to the rear of the boat to check it out. By now my hearing was so numb that the noise made little difference. By feeling the exhaust pipes, it was apparent that we were running on 3 cylinders! I said that we had better head back because if we lost another cylinder, we'd be in trouble. Two cylinders and 15 miles out would be bad news! Most of the lake was shallow enough that one could walk to shore but that was a long ways from being back at camp. Late in the afternoon we decided to head back.

Al had trouble starting the engine. When it finally started, it blubbered badly and wouldn't come up to speed. We chugged slowly, keeping our fingers crossed, all the way back to the canal. It was obvious that the beast was flooding but we were afraid to shut her down for fear she wouldn't restart. Once we were in the canal I decided to experiment around. I asked Bob for the channel lock pliers out of the tool box. I went back to the engine and pinched the fuel hose leading up from the 24 gallon tank to the fuel pump. By doing this I was able to periodically lean out the engine and get it to run good in spurts. We finally made it back to the dock. We all had one thing in mind, get out of that damned boat and get some chow and an orange blossom, mainly an orange blossom.

The noise from the Lycoming and the Florida son had taken its toll on us and we were all beat. We decided to use one of Uncle Joe's wooden boats and our 10 HP engine the next day. That evening we just relaxed and planned our strategy for the next day. At about 9:00 pm, Al and I mosied up to the camp office to catch any gossip about the day's fishing. One had to do a lot of talking to gain any real info about how people were doing. Like all fishermen, everyone was pretty tight lipped about where they were fishing and what they were catching. An old weather beaten, white bearded guide took people out to fish each day and apparently he'd done fairly well. He claimed that the only place to catch them was right in the pepper grass! This was like fishing in a barrel of snags and Al said that in the past they had only fished the edges of the pepper grass. Al added that the guide was a cocky son of a bitch, inferring that he only half believed him. In any case we decided to give the pepper grass theory a try tomorrow.

Tuesday morning we were up at dawn. My sun burn from the day before was killing me and I felt like hell. This was a vacation so I decided to sleep late. Al and Bob decided to give it a try anyway so they took off. Later I concluded that the high sound level of the airboat the previous day was what had really made me sick. That morning as my hearing came back I started to feel pretty *chipper. Walsh-Healy* [29CFR 1910 – The Occupational Safety and Health Act] *would never have passed that darned air boat! I got up about 10:00 and ate breakfast and walked up to the dock.*

The air was finally beginning to warm up and felt quite pleasant. Uncle Joe's dock at 10 am was the most peaceful sight in the world. The blue sky, the Spanish moss and the lazy canal combined to make it a paradise. Sam was gassing motors, bailing boats, etc. around the dock. I watched quite a few people come in from the morning's fishing and none of them had many fish. I asked Sam where Prince was. Prince was a legend that Al had built up during the 1100 mile trip from Cincy. Apparently Prince was an old negro that worked at Uncle Joe's and had the ability to go to sleep any where at any time. Al claimed that he would frequently fall asleep in the middle of a sentence!

According to Sam, Prince was at home with a broken leg. The boys, Sam and Richard have an old van truck that they use to haul motors and gear in from the camp office to the dock, a distance of about 150 yards. The dock is on top of the levee, an elevation of about 40 feet above the flat caneland that the camp sits in. The drive going up to the dock is quite steep. Sam tells it that Prince was driving the truck from the dock to the office and fell asleep coming down the hill, the truck ran off the road, turned over, threw Prince out and broke his leg! Consequently, he was at home recovering. I was saddened to hear this. Number one for Prince's sake and number two, I wasn't going to get a chance to meet this legendary character. O' well, there'd be another time. Al said that it took him 10 years before he could understand what Prince was saying anyhow so I guess that one year won't hurt! Apparently Prince's negro draw was so thick and lubricated that it frequently was mistaken for a squeaky barn door.

About 1:00 Al and Bob returned. They had fished the pepper grass with little luck. We discussed our strategy over lunch and an orange blossom. We decided to fish the canal that evening for crappies.

After a pleasant afternoon nap, we got up about 4:00 and went up to the office and bought 3 doz. crappie minnows. Crappies, like most other fish, require their own technique for fishing. About 1 – 1 ½" shiner minnows are used. One fishes with a a small float and a very light line about 18" below the surface. Crappie's mouths are very tender and a sudden jerk on the line seldom sets the hook. A steady ever increasing pull is used to hook them.

We gassed our boat, got our gear together and motored across the canal to a little inlet about 100 yards from Uncle Joe's dock. We all fished for crappie and Bob *put out another line dead on the bottom for catfish. We'd bought some Spam to use for this. Undoubtedly, Spam is the best catfish bait going. We had fair luck with the crappies but Bob was getting one bite after another on his dead line. He was having trouble landing them but what a fight! Something was giving him fits! Al and I sat back and watched and enjoyed the spectacular sun set as the retiring sun painted the sky a beautiful red and purple. By night fall we had a fair string of crappies and a few catfish.*

Bob had spotted a restaurant in Clewiston with $1.98 and all the catfish you can eat so we decided to give it a try. The place was owned by a guide who had every kind of fish, bird and animal you can imagine mounted on the walls and ceiling of the restaurant. After consuming our fair share of catfish, we agreed unanimously that it was the greatest fish eating going, bar none! This may be argued about by connoisseur's of fine seafood, etc, but I've eaten my share of lobster, flounder, swordfish......and I'll have to agree that nothing beats freshly caught and filleted catfish. Unquestionably it's name is quite common and its looks quite ugly but fixed properly it can tickle the palate till hek won't have it!

We drove back to the cabin and flipped on the TV. We had no sound, so that one coild carry on a conversation and watch TV at the same time. It turned out to be quite handy that way. We had a night cap and decided to hit the pepper grass again tomorrow.

As usual, we were up at dawn again. I went outside to pick some oranges and noticed that the breeze was warmer now. This was the Florida our winterized bodies had yearned for. The smell of orange blossoms and a warm southerly breeze. I truly think that fishermen would come here if Lake Okeechobee had but two fish in it. As we sipped our after breakfast coffee Bob decided to put on a pot of his famous camp beans. These beans had become a tradition on every trip and I'd eaten them from Wyoming to Pennsylvania and from Tennessee to Ontario and Florida wasn't going to be an exception. The trick was to make up a huge pot of beans and any time anybody took a whim to, he start em cookin and et some. After three or four days with plenty of bacon, ham hocks, pepper and onions they'd really get good. In Pennsylvania last year we cooked a pot for 7 days and each day they got better.

We drove up to the dock and loaded our gear into the boat. Sam had her all gassed and ready to go. I thought to myself, he must get up about 5:00 AM and he seldom leaves the dock before 9:00 PM. Of course he's his own boss and that makes a difference. The water was like glass and we motored out the canal. The sun was just coming up and was painting the most beautiful purple and red sunrise that one could imagine. The early morning boat ride out the canal was the high point of our trip each day. The waterfoul was abundant along the canal. White egrets were everywhere. The snake birds were perched high atop the cypress trees with their wings spread in handsome fashion. After their swim they have to dry their wings before they can take another dip. Unlike ducks, they have little natural oil on their feathers.

When we got into the lake we decided to follow the channel marker bouys straight out until we found a good pepper grass bed. We went out about a mile and then veered to the right, smack dab into a big bed of pepper grass. We baited up and immediately started to get action. We had poor luck in landing any as the grass was so thick and as soon as you'd get a bite they'd dive deep into the grass. We caught a few small bass, 2 – 3 #, and were constantly plagued with catching bowfins or dogfish as they're called. A hell of a good fight but you can't eat them so they're the curse of the Okeechobee bass fishermen.

About 10:00 the action quit. We drifted lazily through the grass beds and just soaked up the sun. Out in that vast expanse of lake with the warm sun training its rays on you, one can just lay back, prop his feet up and shut out every worldly thought about anything he's ever thought of. Boy, you talk about shutting down all systems, that's it!

Occasionally someone would mumble something about the stress and strain of this lightning pace life we were living or sing a few bars of our song "You can't go to Sleep in a Pepper Grass bed". Other than that, things were pretty peaceful. Once in a great while a Sea Gull would badger us for a handout but that was about it. We studied such things as the damping effect of the pepper grass upon the waves, the average time a snake bird stays underwater, etc. About 1:30 we decided to head back for lunch.

Motoring out of the grass beds was always difficult because the motor had to be lifted and the prop cleaned every 20 yds. or so. As Bob repeatedly lifted the motor and cleaned the prop, Al and I both agreed that it would be tough if we hadn't hired this Cuban guide. With that, our "Cuban Guide" immediately went on strike. He manifested his stubbornness by sitting down and propping his feet up and then smiled and lit up a big black Marsh Wheeling cigar. After much coaxing, we finally got going again and headed back to camp.

Going down the canal we passed the usual armamda of "Geritol generation" *crappie fishermen that didn't dare venture out into the big pond. This seemed strange to me because as big as Okeechobee is, 750 SQ. miles, in most places it isn't over your head. Al tells the story about the jockey that came down with them one year and had his motor quit when he was out about ¼ mile. He politely stepped out of the boat and waded to shore with the boat in tow!*

We arrived back at the dock about noon. It was getting hotter than hell and we listened to Sam for a while as he moaned about the tough life he had. We sympathized and secretly wondered how we could trade places with him. We left the gear in the boat and drove over to the cabin for some lunch. We were running short on orange blossom fixins so we had to break into Al's private stock that he'd bought to take back to Cincy.

For lunch we deep fried crappies that we'd caught the night before and saved the bass for supper. Al had brought a deep frier along for the fish and inspite of Bob and my razzings about the citified contrivances, it proved to be a God send for cooking fish. We finished lunch with our daily argument about whether to turn the air conditioner on. The no's won. Bob and I couldn't bare the thought of closing the cabin up and depriving ourselves of that fresh cypress breeze that was blowing.

Again that evening we hit the crappies and cats in the canal with good luck. After supper we strolled up to the fish cleaning table to survey the day's action. This was a meeting place each night where everyone surveyed everyone elses catches during the cleaning process. Uncle Joe had large freezers that one could store his fish in until he was ready to head home and they were located here also.

Bob and I noticed that the party that the cocky guide, who Al disliked, had taken out that day had a fine catch. Not too many but most were 8 – 10 pounds in size and that's some bass! Early that morning we had seen him head way out in the lake toward Clewiston harbor. Apparently the big ones must still be out quite a ways. We stored this bit of data in the back of our minds for future reference.

It was just about dark and we noticed that the sky to the east had an orange glow to it. We walked to the top of the levee for a better look. By the time we got there the sky was really aglow and we realized what was going on. A cane field in the direction of Clewiston was being burnt. This was frequently done at night so that roads could be blocked. We dashed back to the cabin, grabbed our cameras and took off in the direction of the fire in the truck. We didn't get as close as we wished but we did get some good flicks of the spectacle.

When we got back to camp, Al said that he wanted to show us something. We walked up on the levee near the boat dock and there was a pick up truck parked next to the light pole with an electrical cord plugged into a box on the pole and running in the window of the truck. Asleep, curled up on the seat, with an electric heater going full tilt was Uncle Joe! He'd come out to spend the night by the dock with his boats. Apparently some boat steeling had been going on and Uncle Joe wasn't about to be had. Al said philosophically, that there was 80 year old Uncle Joe curled up in the front seat of that truck, the happiest man in the world. Why? Because he was doing what he wanted to do and wasn't bothering anyone in the process. We had to agree enviously.

Thursday morning over flapjacks, orange juice and coffee we planned our strategy for the day. We mutually agreed that we had to get further out in the lake to hit the big ones. Apparently the spawn was late this year and they just hadn't come in yet. The previous cold snaps probably caused this.

After motoring out the canal we decided to follow the channel markers as we had the day before but this time we'd go further out. We went a good 3 or 4 miles this time and then started to look for the the familiar oil slick look of a pepper grass bed. Bob said he thought he saw one about 50 yards off our port. We swung the boat in that direction and as we got closer we could all see that it was a big bed! Excitedly but with restraint we all readied our gear as we throttled back and coasted in so as to do as little spooking as necessary. By now we were whispering and frantically baiting up with 5" shiners. Shit, if this isn't the place, then it doesn't exist.

Al had his line in the water for 30 seconds and the water exploded! He had a biggie. He hollered to me to get the net! I said [word deleted] I haven't got my line in the water yet! When he got it near the boat I had a difficult time maneuvering the net under it. Finally I was able to and I hoisted out our first good size bass. He was a beast! Probably 6 pounds with a low slung belly like a C-119. About that time Bob got a strike and hollered for me to get the net. I protested but really didn't mind since we were finally getting some action! This continued for about 45 minutes during which we netted more bass than we had the previous 4 days. Things had slowed down so we decided to move to another bed we had spotted. Pulling up the bass laden stringers tangled in pepper grass was a chore, but obviously no one complained!

We coasted into the new bed just as we had the last and the action started all over again. By now we had developed quite a following of sea gulls who immediately grabbed up any stray piece of bait in the water. We'd bet each other how long it would take for a gull to grab a piece of bait when we threw it overboard. Usually it was just a few seconds.

We fished this bed till about 1:00 in the afternoon. Our stringers were heavily laiden and we were getting hungry so we decided to call it a day. As we motored back to Uncle Joe's we had the contented feeling of success and triumph that can only come from filling a stringer as we had done.

It was a pleasantly warm southern afternoon at Uncle Joe's camp. The humid pungent odor of the swamp lands and cane fields seemed to act as a tranquilizer to one's conscience mind. I would ask myself, "Does Uncle Joe need any extra help around this place?" I'm sure there's some menial task I could perform for a few dollars a day. Oh how sweet it would be. Then one's mind returns to the task at hand of unloading the boat & getting some lunch.

We had an extra round of orange blossoms today. After lunch we all napped for a spell. That hot sun had taken its toll on us. About 4:00 we got up and cleaned the durnedest batch of bass you've ever seen. That evening we fished the canal and took our usual share of crappie and catfish out. We cooked the catfish for supper and figured we'd bring most of the bass home to Cincy.

That night around the cleaning table it appeared that some of the others had fair luck also but none better than ours.

Friday morning at breakfast we all had the same solemn mood. No one had to tell anyone else that this was our last day. Tomorrow we'd be heading home. That day, we cherished each moment. We appreciated a little more the beauty of our boatride out of the canal with the sky in its regal display of color and natures birds and flowers showing off all their beauty. Our Friday success was every bit as good as it was Thursday. We fished most of the same beds all morning. We called it quits about noon because we had to take Al's airboat down the canal to Clewiston to Uncle Joe's marina.

When we arrived back at the camp, we left our gear in the boat so we could do a little canal fishing later in the afternoon. Bob and Al took the airboat down the canal to Clewiston. I drove the Travelall down and met them at the ramp with the trailer. We took a few pictures of Al next to his boat as a kind of momento to remember the beast by. Al and I both had many hours of sweat put into her. He was leaving the boat with Sam, Uncle Joe's son, to sell for him, as we had little use for it in Cincinnati.

That evening after fishing, we ate fish, grits and beans till it wouldn't quit, all washed down with copious amounts of spiritus fermenti.

We mosied up to the cleaning tables to see what the action had been. It obviously was picking up. Quite a few people had fair strings but none better than ours. We packed the truck as much as we could that night. Before we hit the sack we sipped a cool one and recalled the events of the past week. The sound of the breeze slithering through the cypress trees beckoned us to stay and not to leave. We knew it was almost over.

The next morning we awoke about 7:00, ate breakfast and hit the road. As we drove down the gravel next to the levy and cane fields each of us secretly knew that someday when the snow was ablow up north, that he'd return to Uncle Joe's.

By late morning we were into the big citrus country of central Florida. This time we were able to photograph the rolling miles and miles and miles of citrus groves. We stopped at one grove and each of us bought a bushel each of grapefruit and oranges to take home to family and friends. What on earth could anybody do with so many oranges I wondered, looking at truckload after truckload? The rest of the day we had good weather and drove steadily to northern Georgia where we spent the night. The sun and the rest had done us wonders! Nothing seemed to matter too much.

Sunday morning we hit the road early. Signs of winter were beginning to show as we drove north. The robins along the roadside were disappearing and the landscape was becoming more and more barren. By the time we reached Cincinnati that afternoon, Uncle Joe's was just a memory. It was great to be home again inspite of the winter! Maybe I'll just jot down a few notes about Uncle Joe's so I don't forget. How could I?

(End of Chronicle)

As Tim had predicted, we did return to Uncle Joe's many times. And we did get to meet the legendary Prince. There were some interchanges between Al Smith and Prince that were priceless. One morning, on our way to the boat, we met Prince. "Well, how are you this morning, Prince?" Al asked.

"Oh, Mista Smif, I aint too good. My brother died, and I had t' call all eleben o' my brothers and sisters, and spen' all that money on long distance, an' then I had t' make the buryin' arrangements, an' git me a preacher, an' fin' places fer all of 'em t' sleep. 'Course….it coulda bin worse."

"What do you mean, Prince?"

"Coulda bin me."

And it was Prince who gifted us with perhaps the greatest piece of fishing wisdom we would ever receive. One mid-day, after a totally fruitless morning of bass fishing, we pulled the boat up alongside Prince's residence, a small bungalow built atop poles driven into the swamp. "Hey Prince," Al called out, "are you in there?" Prince came out onto the landing.

"Prince, what's the secret to catchin' these bass? We're not doin' any good at all."

Prince stroked his chin. "Well, Mista Smif, they ain't but one way I knows t' do it. You gots t' keep y' bait in the watee."

A Salty Slice of 'Glades

By Frank Miller

(The following is a word-for-word transcription of a "sittin' by the fire, just listenin'" conversation with Frank)

"Everglades National Park is comprised of most of Florida Bay. Florida Bay is the body of water that is between the Florida Keys and the mainland, and the major part of it is Monroe County. That's the part that extends north into mainland Florida, and most of that part of mainland Monroe County is part of Everglades Park. The Park itself is comprised, a great deal, of fresh water, and runs basically a few yards to a fourth of a mile on the Gulf side of Florida, bay side of the Keys, from Key Largo down to approximately Isla Morada, up to the area of Chokoloskee/Everglade City, and then turns inland and goes up into the mainland.

That geographical area, that portion of it, the mainland portion of it, was deeded over to a man named Henry Flagler. Now, Henry Flagler was a railroad magnate; he developed the Florida East Coast Railway, and he is the guy who developed the 'Railroad That Went to Sea'. It went from Miami Homestead to Key West."

"Oh, yeah, I remember that."

"Well, it lasted about three years before a hurricane totally blew it out. The Governor of Florida at that time promised Henry Flagler that he would deed to him X number of acres of Florida land to develop if he completed that railroad. Well, Henry did. He completed it, but the Governor, when it came to it, found out that he didn't have any (main) land to deed to Henry Flagler. So, he deeded, I'm going to say, 180,000 acres of swamp. I don't want you to hold me to that."

"Okay."

"But a huge tract of land in the Florida Everglades. Henry decided, well, I'm gonna develop that land, so…..there are still some vestiges of his development there. He dug a canal from….uh….approximately halfway down that highway that goes from Florida City down to Flamingo that went westward for about thirty miles, then it turned to the south and joined the Gulf of Mexico. He was going to drain that land and develop it with hotels, and homes and civic centers, et cetera, et cetera.

"That canal was dug in the nineteen twenties and I read a very interesting book on the subject by a gentleman that worked on one of the dredge boats. The canal actually is still there, but it's all overgrown with mangroves and so forth. You actually have been in a small portion of it. We went up a water way called East Cape Canal when you were here; we went up a small finger creek whereupon we got our push pole stuck in a muddy bottom and broke it off."

"I remember that, yeah."

"Back there, I believe….and I know I've seen it several times, lying up on a mud bank, was a huge crocodile."

"I remember that…very well. That's where I asked you, 'What happens if I fall out of the boat?', and you said, 'Don't fall out of the boat'."

"That bigger straight body of water, when it was dug by Henry Flagler's bunch, was thirty feet wide. It's now probably a quarter of a mile wide, as the constant tidal flow washes the mud away and washes it back into a body of water called Lake Ingraham, which has a very narrow channel that runs from one end to the other, and the rest of it is mud flats at low tide.

"Okay, that's a little bit of the history of the boundaries of the fort. Flamingo itself was a commercial fishing village and was otherwise a base for people who……did not like society – murderers, bankrobbers, et cetera, et cetera."

"I didn't know that!"

"In the early days of that era, in the teens and twenties, women's hats were adorned with white plumage."

"Oh, yeah. Yeah."

"Well, that came from egrets in that area of the Everglades –now Everglades Park – and to which they nearly wiped out the egret population there. But if you wander around enough in the Park, particularly east of Flamingo, you find remnants of old docks from an island here and from the mainland there….and these were old homesteads of people that *really* wanted to be away from society.

"That road, in those days, going down there, you and I traveled it, it's a wide paved road now, but in those days it was a mud road virtually impassable in the rainy season. So, again, the commercial fishermen and the full time residents lived there, summer and winter. In the summertime, the mosquito population is just so horrendous that it's mind-boggling, until….until you see it. They burned pine knots and what have you inside the house to chase the mosquitoes. Until…I'm reading a book about the area…the screens were so dirty and filthy with smoke and residue that it was unbelievable. That was the only way they could tolerate the mosquitoes.

"Everglades National Park was formed in 1947 in the administration of one infamous Harry S. Truman. And in which commercial fishing was to be phased out and did, in fact, take place. Not all at once, in one day....I don't remember exactly when the last fishing was allowed."

"You mean, in the Park waters?"

"Yeah."

"Okay"

"You can find......in the stone crab season....you can find the Park boundaries exactly, because the crab boys come right up to the boundaries and you can see the trap markers in both directions when the stone crab season is on. So, that's kind of a very broad thumbnail of......"

"Well, how...how far back up into the Park is the water salty?"

"Oh...not too far. I can't answer that honestly, but as you drive down that road to Flamingo, particularly.....you don't probably remember, but for a great portion of the distance, all you see is grassy flats with isolated hammocks of trees both near the road and at a distance. As you get down....oh.....probably within five miles of Florida Bay and Flamingo, you'll gradually notice that the undergrowth or overgrowth is right up to the road....the mangrove growth. And that would be where the salt starts. I'm guessing five miles plus or minus....on that end. As you go up towards the Chokoloskee area, there are...there are numerous creeks and waterways that go back up into the mainland that are all salt and brackish and I can't tell ya how far that goes back into there....I'm not real familiar with that end of the Park. Uh....I haven't spent that much time up on that end. Uh...but that kind of describes the Park and what goes on up in there.

"I've read a couple of books that were really interesting......the activities..... the poaching.....well, there were really two books. One was written by a commercial alligator hunter, who is still alive...or he was a couple of years ago, and his name was Glenn Thompson. He lived in Homestead City. He would go hitch a.....hook a ride partway down the road to Flamingo. He would take off on foot and take with him one single shot 22 rifle, camping gear, ie, a pup tent of some kind, something to wrap himself up in, and he'd be gone for two weeks. He'd take along some salt and lard, and lard cans, and he would hunt alligators by shinin' 'em. He would put on a carbide miner's cap, on his head, and walk the edge of the waterways and when he spied the red eyes, he'd plink 'em between the eyeballs, pull 'em up on dry land. He'd shoot as many as he could overnight and then go back in the daytime and skin 'em and roll the hides up, and……this guy started out as a teenager doin' this.……roll up the hides and put'em in the lard cans. However big a lard can was in those days, I don't know. Then, when he had all he could carry or all he could do, he'd slog back to the road and wait for somebody to come along and pick him up. And he made a living doing that, until the Park came into being. He tried to still do that, but they put the heat on him to the point where he couldn't make a living doin' it. He had to stop.

"And….the topography of that area down there has changed drastically, since the twenties. Oh, drastically. There…..at that time, as described in his book, you could go……there's a marina over on Biscayne Bay at the south end called Black Point. You could go by dugout canoe from the Black Point area all the way to Cape Sable, Cape Sable being twenty miles, I guess, west of Flamingo…..all by dugout canoe. And now, it's all farm fields, dry as a bone, and in the summer, in the rainy season, uh, you can cover maybe a third to a half of that distance, in some kind of a shallow draft canoe or boat….kayak maybe. So, drainage for development and for human population has changed…I'll call it the topography….there's probably a better word to describe it, hydrology or whatever, of that area. A tremendous amount. As here, where we're living right now……uh….. even in Miami there are a couple of areas that I had to drive through when I was cleaning swimming pools that in heavy, heavy summer rains were impassable. There were houses that were virtual islands. But that's way far off the subject.

"Let me get into a little……I'll tell a couple of fishing stories."

"Okay."

"We'll digress as necessary. Let's see. The southwest tip of Florida is called Cape Sable. It's comprised of East Cape, Middle Cape, and Northwest Cape. Middle Cape is a beautiful beachy area and it protrudes the furthest into the Gulf of Mexico, and the tidal currents swirl around that point of land….a hook shaped point of land that's constantly changing shape based on storms and strong tidal currents and so forth. Great place to camp. Terrific place to camp, as long as you don't get a south or a northwest wind. In that case you're in deep trouble. You get swamped and you got a problem. Our fishing club, The South Florida Sport Fishermen, had numerous camp-outs there, and we'd pick a weekend, in the non-buggy season, basically middle fall or middle spring, hoping to avoid the cold fronts of winter, because that's when, in the cold fronts of winter the wind starts....it's normally a southeast wind....and when the cold front gets into lower Florida, the wind starts to clock around to the south and then the southwest and uh-oh, that's a bad direction. And as the front gets closer it goes to west and then northwest, and the wind strength picks up drastically as the front passes over. And, you may get a cold rain with it, but at least you're gonna get wind and cooler, if not kind of chilly, temperatures.

So, we would camp there…uh…sometime in the fall or spring, sometimes twice…..the club. One trip, my partner and I….I had at the time a fourteen foot aluminum boat with a twenty five horse Johnson motor on it…..and it was a pretty good little fishing boat. I built a casting deck on the front and the back and we could stand up and fish and pole it around. But we were the last ones to pull into camp, and just as we were about to pull up on the sand, he and I made one last cast, and we both hooked up with *nice* trout. Hah! That current swirling around that point there at Middle Cape was a great hangout for fish because it would swirl baitfish around it and crabs and shrimp and you name it, and it was a great place to fish. Well, we commenced to catch trout after trout after trout, and guys on the beach were all flabbergasted….they were already sittin' back with a campfire goin' and..and sipping some medicine, as Tim says…. rum and coke….and they saw us catchin' fish, and pretty soon there's twenty five guys on the beach, all whalin' trout. Nice spotted sea trout, and they were all sayin' 'what will we do with 'em all?', but….."

"What were you catchin' 'em on?"

"Just artificials. Just little jig heads with a rubber tail on 'em. Didn't need any live bait. And this was …..ah…..1982. The trout population isn't quite what it used to be, although it's still good in spots. You need to know where to go. I had a particular spot that was shown to me by two old time Flamingo fishermen…..they didn't need the money…at all…they were two pilots…..but they would go down there and whale trout and fill up a huge cooler with 'em, then sell 'em on the way home. Which went directly against my….I….I don't believe….I don't like the idea of amateur fishermen selling fish."

"Well, that's illegal isn't it?"

"Of course. But there are plenty of local markets and restaurants that will buy fish from ya. Yeah, my best friend in that club….he was a welder by trade….he loved to fish, he loved owning boats, he always had a decent boat, but he felt he had to catch enough fish to pay for his gas bill and expenses on the trip, otherwise he's takin' money away from the house or the family. Ah, we never got into serious arguments about it. He knows how I am and I know how he is and we're still good friends. Well, anyway, we caught a load of trout that afternoon in about an hour before they moved on and shut off. We went ashore and commenced to have a little medicine ourselves….went to bed…..well, we had some dinner. The outing director would arrange to have whatever we were gonna have….probably steaks and baked potatoes on the grill. He wouldn't fish much. He'd bring in most of the stuff and arrange for other people to bring in the rest of it.

"So, about 2 o'clock, I woke up and went down to the beach where the boat was docked, and all I could see was a furry behind stickin' up………my forward casting deck had a little lift-up hatch so I could store my anchor in there, and some other stuff and cooking supplies, there's the butt end of a coon stickin' up out of there. There was a frying pan laying on the seat of the boat, so I grabbed that up and whacked him on the behind, and he came up out of that hole like HOLY…. But that area is run over with raccoons, you have to……I've seen 'em get into a cooler that was tied shut."

"Oh, I know. They can pick a combination lock!"

"Oh, absolutely. They're incredible. They…..One time we stayed in some cottages that were there in Flamingo at the park. When I went out on Sunday morning….we thought we might fish a little bit on Sunday morning….when I went out, the boat was so deep in raccoon crap that I just told my partner, 'Forget it. We're goin' home'. It was just…..just…. oh, it was awful.

"So, anyway, that's not a too humorous a story. But we did manage to have one of….probably the best day of trout fishing there, although Rosie and I were there one afternoon….just fishing. She kept me absolutely busy just taking trout off her hook, and I think we had some shrimp and we were fishing shrimp, but anyway, I didn't get to fish at all! So much fun catching trout. They were there in the same place…..one after the other. Now we're only allowed to keep four, but there was no limit in those days, and that was in the early 80's…..late 70's. Times have changed. Everywhere, I guess."

"Yeah."

"But…..in 1984, on the 20th of August, a friend of mine, well, two friends, and I took off on my 23 foot Seacraft center console boat. Bill McCauley and another guy……I….I can't remember his name. Maybe it'll come to me before we finish. McCauley is a walking, talking fishing encyclopedia. You'll see why I say that in a couple of minutes. He had come by three sets of Loran numbers, from another friend. GPS wasn't invented yet….well, it was invented but it was not in civilian use. So, we had three sets of Loran numbers, a hump out in the Gulf of Mexico, a derelict barge about seven miles further out and a little pile of rocks about 15 miles northeast of that, so we hooked up the Seacraft on the trailer and drug it over to Everglades City, put it in the water and launched off out into the Gulf, went to the first set of numbers and couldn't catch a grunt, even.

"Well, went on down to the barge, put out some chum and we did get some mangrove snappers up behind the boat very briefly, but didn't catch a thing, and so we went to look for the thing called the rock pile….it's off of Shark River…..uh……which is the western terminus of Whitewater Bay, a large body of water in the Park. You and I spent some time in the eastern end of Whitewater Bay. But, the rock pile is a pile of ballast rock……or a barge load of ballast rock which was being transported from someplace down to build the Florida East Coast Railway in the twenties, and the barge upset and left this huge pile of boulders in fourteen feet of water. We ran the Loran numbers and found the rock pile and we could see it not far under the surface. We figured out the current, anchored up and put some chum out to catch some…. hopefully, to catch some nice big mangrove snappers, and around…..around us swam a school of permit, a very prized game fish further down in the keys, and in Biscayne Bay.

"The permit…..this school of permit was probably a third of an acre in size. All out of the same mold. They were all about seven to eight pounds. Now, a good permit runs bigger than that……a permit that gives you a terrific fight. But every time……they had never seen humans before, I don't think. Every time that school would swim within casting distance, we'd throw over into 'em and everybody would hook up. Who knows? We started out with maybe twelve pound tackle and then went down to eight pound tackle, and then six pound tackle. I had a four pound rod with me ……and there was also a huge resident population of barracuda layin' over the top of this rock pile. I got tired of catchin' permit, and I thought, I will catch me a barracuda. And I reached for what we called a tube lure, which is a piece of surgical tubing with a piece of wire….some strong wire cable strung up through it with a double hook at the end and another double hook in the middle, and a sinker in the front to give it a little weight and ability to sink. I tied that on my four pound rig, and spied a suitable size barracuda, and flung it out, and naturally, the biggest barracuda in the bunch jumped on the thing and inhaled it.

"At some time after that, we finally got him to the boat. I don't know….. twenty minutes….half an hour. And barracuda are interesting. Most of the time when they fight on light tackle like that, they're dead by the time you get 'em to the boat. I had no idea that wouldn't happen, but anyway, we got him to the boat, and lifted him in, and Mr McCauley says, 'I think that's a world record'. And I thought to myself, how in the world would he ever know that that's a world record. The International Game Fishing Association record book is about an inch thick. It contains records from all over the world. He said 'I think that's a world record', and I said, 'Aw McCauley, you're crazy.' He said, 'Yeah, think it is. You better save it and we'll get it weighed tomorrow'. So, we weighed it on my hand-held scale and it was a little over thirty pounds. On four pound tackle. And in order to certify….to be certified, you have to save your terminal rig and thirty feet of your line and send that to IGFA. And lo and behold, it all passed, and I got a world record out of that. It lasted about six months before somebody beat it. Actually, we didn't have much ice. By the time I got the fish to a weigh station the next day, he lost a pound. It might still be a good record if he hadn't dehydrated and lost so much weight.

"We finished our fun with the permit and the barracuda, and so forth, and headed back to Chokoloskee, got there about five o'clock, and commenced to put the boat back up on the trailer. We were using a ramp that was way out of the way, so we were the only boat that was there and ……when did I say that was?……….oh, yeah, that was '84, and the Seacraft was only four years old….bright and shiny new. It didn't look like it does now. But, off a little distance in the parking lot was a Ford pick-up truck with tinted windows <u>all</u> round, and there was a woman by the running board talkin' to the driver and they talked and intently watched us load the boat on the trailer and stow our gear so it wouldn't blow out on the way back to Miami, and finally she walks over to us and says, 'That sure is a nice boat'.

"'Thank you, that's great.'

"'Have any luck?'

'Well, yeah, we went to a place and we caught a bunch of permit'………….. and we told her our fishing story, and she says, 'Oh. Well, that *sure is* a nice boat. Where you boys from?'

"'We're from Miami'.

"'Ooohh.'

"We chatted for a while and finally she said, 'Have a nice day', and she walked back over to that pick-up truck, and had a few words and the truck drove away and she disappeared, and we didn't pay much attention………but we loaded our gear up and off we went.

"Well. They were scoutin' us out. They were just absolutely sure that we were federal drug agents. Sometime a little after that I was in a doctor's office…. I'm not sure of the time, maybe six months or a year, and I'm in a doctor's office reading, and there's this story about a big drug bust in Everglades City/Chokoloskee. The feds cordoned off the town and arrested *everybody* in the town, for drugs. Well, you could tell who the drug runners were. There were fine, nice houses and fine, nice boats, with radars on 'em and so forth. The good ol' boys, for years, could go out and meet the mother ship in the Gulf of Mexico and run in, and the revenuers – so to speak – couldn't follow 'em, 'cause the good ol' boys knew that area, and the water up in that end of the Park is laced with oyster bars. If you don't know exactly where you're goin', you're gonna rip the bottom of the boat out. And these guys would scurry around through these oyster bars and up through mangrove passes, and leave the revenuers high and dry behind 'em. And they got away with that for years, until the feds finally…. somehow….got enough information and were able to….to….oh, arrest half the town. That was incred…...and I'm readin' this and I'm thinkin' HOLY SMOKES….it was scary what that woman was doin', and those two people in that truck. Those guys in that truck, they were watchin' us and they thought we were….bad guys.

"OK. That's pretty much…...that was a scary situation, in reflection.

Nowadays, it's totally above board……I don't think there's any drugs……oh, maybe a few drugs come in that way, but they know what's goin' on. The locals all turned into……. the ones that were left……and when they got out of prison and came back to town….. they became fishing guides and there are a couple of big airboat tour operators there, and they turned to above board businesses."

"As far as you know."

"As far as I know. It's still a well-known fishing area. That's a <u>whole</u> different ecosystem…..it's a different ecosphere than down toward Flamingo.

"Now. Running from Chokoloskee to Flamingo is a phenomenon called the Wilderness Waterway. And the National Park Service has mapped out a trail down through the inlet…..mangrove waterways…. that runs almost all the way inshore. And you can start at one end and run all the way down to the other end, or you can run halfway down and come back. So, the club planned a trip in 1985, in the fall, running the Wilderness Waterway. Those of us that could get our wives to drive our trailers home launched at Chokoloskee, and sent the wives home with the trailers and told 'em that we would call Sunday morning from Flamingo and they could come fetch us. The ones that couldn't make that arrangement were gonna leave out of Flamingo and meet us at a halfway point called Highland Beach…….it's roughly halfway between Flamingo and Chokoloskee, beachy area, great place to camp, again, if you don't get a southwest or northwest wind.

"Well, the fella that was supposed to co-ordinate the outing went out there on Thursday and he camped at Highland Beach Thursday night, had the camp all set up and he had a little generator and a little chain saw to cut some firewood, and so forth. And we….those of us that could, arrived at Chokoloskee bright and early Saturday morning, launched the boats, and we were getting set up with co-ordination, buying bait and whatever supplies we needed, and a cold front – first cold front of the year – went through. Of course! And it rained for fifteen or twenty minutes, and got a little cold. The wind started to blow, which wasn't gonna be much of a problem because we were gonna be on the inland waterway. The wind came around to the southwest and then to the northwest, and started to blow pretty good. So be it for camping on Highland Beach!

"Well, the co-ordinator, a guy named Ralph Galliano, who, at one point was a commercial fisherman in Alaska………..made good money…..

until he wore himself out doing offshore fishing in Alaska………anyway, he says, 'Huh-uh. We can't do this.' So, he picked up all the stuff and moved up to a campsite that was on…..was squarely on the Wilderness Waterway, hoping that we would intercept him and come ashore there and camp out. Well, the waterways were mere yards wide, some of it spread out into a half mile open lake or whatnot, but there was a trail marked by the Park Service, and so forth. True enough, we all ended up there at Ralph's campsite, got up on land, built a big fire.

"One of the highlights of this outing was going to be an item called Jungle Juice. A form of medicine. Hah, hah, hah…..white rum, dark rum, coconut milk, I don't know what all was in it, but it was lethal. Absolutely lethal.

"Now, this is rambling on a little bit, but the other contingent…..they didn't have rides….they all left out of Flamingo and came up through Whitewater Bay, and they got to a point where this Wilderness Waterway had to traverse an eight to ten mile stretch of open water along the Gulf shore. So, they got to a little camp site, because the wind was blowin', it was raining, and they knew they weren't gonna be able to go out into the Gulf in small boats. Oh…..this campsite was called Mosquito Creek. And, uh-oh, woe is me, we had all the dinner supplies…the steaks, the baked potatoes, the salad, and the Jungle Juice with us. Upstream there, ten miles, and we're tucked snugly into the campsite, with a big fire goin' and the Jungle Juice is slidin' down oh, so slick, and we just had a wonderful time….. with a big fire, and we cooked those steaks and baked potatoes, and those poor guys just sat down there and shivered. Oh, boy! Oooh, boy!

"This was ostensibly to be a fishing trip. My partner and I caught one skinny trout…he was so skinny, I don't think he'd eaten for a month. I don't know if anybody else caught anything or not. But, next morning, we packed up and headed down the shore, and stumbled on the group that was at Mosquito Creek. And….Oh, brother…. were they happy to see us! We unloaded their share of the steaks and baked potatoes and they built fires and had steaks and baked potatoes and Jungle Juice……they were glad to see <u>that</u>….and we went on our way…..down to Flamingo. I called Rosie, and it took her about an hour and a half, from where we lived at that time, it took about an hour and a half to get down there and bring the trailer. We got the boat on the trailer, and the group from Mosquito Creek campsite commenced to show up.

" And here they came! Zig-zaggin' across the flats, blowin' mud….they didn't have any idea where they were going or what they were doing, they were all blind as bats, Jungle Juice had all been consumed, and….they pulled up to the boat ramp, and half of 'em ran up onto the ramp itself. One fella, Rick, got his boat on the trailer…..we'd been watchin' him, comin' across the flats blowin' a big muddy rooster tail…..now, today, of course, that would land him in jail…..the Park Service does not like you mowin' their grass! Noooooooh! And suddenly he blew a rooster tail thirty feet high and ground to a halt. He was high and dry in the mud. Well, the tide came up a little bit, and he got off and he got his boat on the trailer. The rest of their trailers were parked there already, so they left to go home.

"We left and we were halfway up the highway toward Homestead, and woe is me, everybody's pulled off on the side of the road, the Park ranger was there…..no, the Park ranger was not there, yet. Rick's boat was facing the wrong way, off the trailer, over in the freshwater swamp, and the boys were getting' him backed down to where his trailer was kind of aimed toward the boat, and they all got ahold of the gunwales and on the ropes, and they pulled it out and got it up on the trailer and Rick got it into the right direction *just* as the Park ranger pulled up. And he wanted to know what happened.

"'Nothin', officer, everything's cool.'

"'Well, I see tire tracks in my grass, here. What're you guys gonna do about that?'

"'Oh, I don't know who made those, officer'.

"Anyway, Rick went on his way and the officer went on his way, shaking his head. He didn't know what to do.

"So, another humorous story – humorous to an extent – no date attached, but it was pretty far after these trips, I invited another gentleman with me to go down to Flamingo, and we left out of Flamingo and we went up into Snake Bight Channel, where you and I fished for two days, I think, tryin' to stay out of the wind. We got in there and fished for a while. This day was a nice, hot, calm day; we had left out of my house pretty early, O-dark-thirty. I was a little bleary-eyed, and we didn't do well there, so, I said, 'Let's go on out to the east and see what we can scare up'. So we went bustin' out of the Snake Bight Channel, and I meant to hook a hard left, and proceed up another marked channel called Tin Can Channel. I don't know why it's called Tin Can Channel…..maybe it's littered with beer cans…..but somehow, I missed the turn. I continued on about another hundred yards before I realized what I had done, and the engine began to scream and blow mud, and we ground to a halt.

"I shut it off and tilted the motor up out of the water, and John said, 'Well, can we get the boat turned around and push it back to deep water?' I said, 'I don't know. I don't think so, but I'll try.' So, I took my clothes off and got into the water which is something you really, *really* don't want to do, because you sink up to your crotch in ucky gray mud, and after you get out of the water, the little critters that are in that mud start to bite on ya….you have a terrible, itchy….well anyway, I had to display some kind of effort so John didn't think I was just gonna let him sit there til high tide comes, which was three to four hours hence. The boat wouldn't move. Didn't think it would. So, I got back in the boat and got a rag out, wipin' off, and washin' off, tryin' to get that mud off and get it out of my crotch so I wouldn't die of misery. I did pretty good, got dressed and said to John, 'Might as well lay down and take a nap, 'cause we aint goin' <u>anywhere</u>.'

"So, we laid down on the deck and had a little snooze, and I commenced to hear a radio talking, and I sat up and looked, and off about a hundred yards, in the deep water was the Park ranger in his boat. And he's talkin' about this boat that's up in the mud, and he wants to give us a ticket, and it would have been an expensive ticket. He kept wavin' at us to come over and I kept wavin' to him, you come over to us, we can't go there. The water was two or three inches deep, yet, and he sat out there and idled and fussed and fumed and groused, and messed around for an hour, waitin' for us to float out. I wouldn't have floated if I could, because I didn't want him to catch us. He finally gave up. We were within a mile of Flamingo, and he went on his way and went back to headquarters. And by and by the water came up and we floated out of there, and started the motor and went the other way!"

"What would he have given you a ticket for?"

"Oh. I don't know what their term for it would be, but it would be for churning up….destroying the grass beds…… disturbing the bottom. That's a real…..these days it's even worse. A real no-no. In the old days, the guy, McCauley, first taught me to fish the flats down there, and he said, 'Now, here's how you do this. We'll pick a flat out and we'll go run it, and if we see a redfish, we'll come around and start poling to within casting distance.' Well, when you run a flat you leave a prop trail down through the grass, and that's not politically or any other way acceptable these days. And now, they've got some small, shallow water boats where they can chase you in the shallow water.

"Considering, they…what the Park Service calls a management plan, supposed to be re-written every ten or fifteen years. They're considering making these areas off limits to motor boats. You have to either pole or use an electric trolling motor. To get from the Keys….a lot of guides in the Keys bring people all the way over from the Keys, but they have to traverse large areas of shallow flats to get there, and they use trails marked with PVC pipes and so forth. They're not official Coast and Geodetic or Park Service channel markers, but they're marked. Those guys all know the way by heart anyway. But they'll be….if they….the areas they want to close down will be areas with less than three feet of water. It's a big boondoggle and the guys are all fightin' it. It'll severely impact their fishing and their income if they have to live with that restriction. Individuals are fighting it because it's always been Flamingo and you could always go where you wanted to go, and the heck with it. But the Park Service being the Park Service, when they get a wild hair, look out.

"They haven't come out with a final issue of that management plan yet, but it'll be out almost any day. I've participated in two or three meetings where the individual users, guides, and so forth could come in and express their views. Most of those views didn't get much consideration."

"That's always the case. Public input is rarely listened to."

"As is always the case. I miss goin' down there since we moved upstate. You never knew what you might see. You might see a big flock of roseate spoonbills wading the flats, you know, swishin' their bills for food, or you might see a great big crocodile, like you and I saw. A friend of mine…… we went up that same creek….I think it was that same creek, if not, it was another one very close to it……it was very, very muddy water, and he threw his jig up against the bank and got a hook-up. It turned out to be about a six foot alligator, and the alligator went the other way and we didn't know what it was……we thought it was a huge fish, until he finally raised his head up and snorted, and I guess he bit the line off, or broke it. We didn't see anything of him after that. But you never did know what you were gonna see. Uh…in addition to occasionally catching a fish!

"I enjoyed poling the flats, and fishing for tailing redfish and sight fishing for 'em. That was a lot of fun, especially on a glassy calm morning, and to spot a tail…you know…off in the distance. That was sight casting, accuracy casting, with a little Johnson spoon or a spoon with a little chunk of cut mullet on it. Mc Cauley and I…..one of the first trips I went down there with him, we went east a few miles and got into a bight called Rankin Bight, and it was shortly after we'd had a tropical storm threat, a lot of fresh water came down and we…..going down into the opening of that bight there was a huge school of redfish….right….right along it, so we each caught a redfish out of that, and we went on in, and the school came in there and dispersed. And we spent the rest of the day. A tail here and two tails over there…..we'd pole to the closest one, catch another redfish and on and on and on. We had a heck of a day.

"You can only keep one redfish now. But that was a political settlement with the commercial interests. A guy in New Orleans, Paul Prudhomme, you may have heard the name, came up with blackened redfish. So, the big redfish are in schools and they're out in the Gulf, and the commercials got to goin' out there with airplanes and spotting the big schools of reds, and the boats would come out there and circle 'em with nets and catch 'em all and send 'em off to hither and yon, to be cooked up as blackened redfish. Well, big redfish are not good to eat, coarse and fishy and so forth. But Paul Prudhomme could mask that in his blistering hot pepper recipe until you couldn't tell whether it was fish or fowl. So, the commercial interests nearly wiped out the redfish population in the northern Gulf and on down all the way south.

"Finally, the Coastal Conservation Association, which formerly was the Florida Conservation Association, combined with Alabama, Mississippi, Louisiana and so forth, they mounted an effort in the Florida legislature to ban gill netting, and redfish netting period. But to get that through they had to agree that the recreational fisherman could only take one fish. So, before the population was totally decimated, they went for it. So, that's what it is today in Florida. I don't know what….how many fish you're allowed to keep in Alabama. Is there a limit on 'em?"

"Oh, yeah, yeah. You can keep three, but there's a slot limit. I don't remember exactly, but I think it was between sixteen or maybe eighteen inches and twenty eight inches, but you could keep one per day over the maximum slot limit."

"Okay. We're only allowed one……but that's OK.

You know, as I sit here and I talk , I have a mental picture of those places, and how enjoyable they were, and are, and I don't think I was able to adequately convey that to you."

"Yeah, you were, but you well know, Frank, that no words, no camera, can capture those experiences. You gotta be there."

"Yep. A pair of bald eagles floatin' around over your head………ah, it just goes on."

Chapter 18
Meeting the Natives
Lions and tigers and BEARS, Oh, my!

Apologies to Frank Baum for purloining his famous line from "*The Wizard of Oz*". It seemed appropriate. Wherever Joe goes fishing, there are native creatures, and they are not always benign little Munchkins. Native creatures cause very, very few angler fatalities each year, and of course Joe does not wish to be one of those few. On the other hand, a lot of trips are made very uncomfortable, and sometimes totally ruined, by unfortunate interactions with native creatures. As always, there is no substitute for local intelligence gathering. Knowing what's out there to "bite you, stab you or sting you" is a great help in avoiding an encounter with "unfriendlies". Avoidance is to be preferred, because the subsequent steps, encounter tactics and damage control, may be far more unpleasant than avoidance. Joe needs to be prepared for all three. The time-honored Boy Scout motto, "Be Prepared", is good advice.

Most fishing trip fatalities/injuries have nothing to do with native creatures. The number one cause of angler fatality is drowning. Then, there are hook impalements, burns, including sunburn, falls, cuts and impact wounds. Can't blame the critters for those. Most are the result of poor angler judgment. Here is a text-book example, as related by eye-witness, Bob Kroger.

Walter Robowski was a man possessing clearly above average intelligence. He held a key position with one of the world's largest companies. Walter loved to fish, and he loved the outdoors. He was one of those pitch-in-and-get-it-done individuals so welcome at a fish camp. Walter's company was a primary customer of our company, and so, Walter was along on a canoe trip deep into Northern Ontario. And it was going very well, indeed. Fishing was excellent, the weather was spectacular, there had been no equipment failures. It was shaping up to be the perfect trip. Then, one day, the party decided to stop for a shore lunch.

Under Walter's canoe seat was a waterproof bag containing a bag of coffee, salt, pepper, some biscuits and a large can of pork and beans. Under Bob Kroger's seat, at the other end of the canoe, was a canvas bag housing cooking utensils. Bob removed it, built a fire, and went to clean four fat, bronze walleyes, the typical color for walleyes from heavily tannin-stained water. Walter remained in the canoe seat. He removed the can of pork and beans from the bag, and reached into his pocket to retrieve a multi-bladed knife, one of the blades a can opener. The commercial sized can, intended for restaurants, defied the pocket-knife can opener. Walter fixed a disgusted gaze upon the tool for a moment, then thrust it back into his pocket.

Walter had another implement that he reckoned was equal to the task. On his belt was a large knife – not a typical hunting, or skinning, knife, with the curved section near the point. This was a straight-bladed, heavy-shanked knife, resembling a miniature bayonet. Walter placed the can on the canoe seat, between his legs, and clamped it with his thighs. Then, seizing the handle of the knife with both hands, he began to stab at the edge of the can with the point of the mini-bayonet. You already know what was going to happen. And it did. Had it not been for the alertness of the pilot of a bush plane to the smoke of a distress fire, Walter's tenure upon this earth would have been much shorter.

Joe's fishing universe is likely to be the North American continent. On that continent are three distinct classes of native creatures: nuisance, serious, and life-threatening. The nuisance class includes such ubiquitous pests as mosquitoes, black flies, leeches and other small, biting or stinging creatures. They can be life-threatening because of the transmission of disease, although they generally are not. But they can certainly make a fishing trip a miserable experience for the unprepared.

The serious class includes such creatures as scorpions, snakes, spiders, jellyfish, and others, which are equipped with toxin-injecting features. Any creature which injects anything into the human body is a threat because of allergic reaction, but some of these creatures inject neurotoxins which are, allergic or not - to understate - no fun at all.

The life-threatening class, oddly enough, is the least likely class to cause Joe harm. The reason is simple. One of the least likely manufactured products to cause human injury is, of all things, the chain saw. It is so dramatically and obviously dangerous that it is treated with caution and respect. The same is true of the life threatening class of native creatures. Creatures like sharks, alligators and bears are large, and dramatically and obviously dangerous, and all humans, with certain idiot exceptions, treat them with respect and caution.

Joe's encounter with this class is most likely to be with a bear, and for the following reasons. We know where sharks are. They are in the water, mostly salt, occasionally fresh, but always in the water. Alligators are also in, or near, water. Encountering a shark or an alligator totally unexpectedly only happens if you have not done your homework. But bears are another matter, and they range over some of the most fishable areas of North America. And they can turn up anywhere. A few decades ago there was a country comedian, not from the South or from the West, but from New England, specifically, Maine, named Marshall Dodge. He told a story involving a Maine guide and his party of clients, also from Maine. It went something like this.

The guide and the clients were hiking in to a remote cabin in the backwoods of northern Maine. The cabin had not yet been used in the current season, and so the trail had to be cleared of deadfalls, wood had to be cut, minor damage to the roof had to be repaired…..all the usual. Once inside, the place had to be swept out, contents dusted, and dishes and utensils washed. Water was needed.

Guide: "You, theah, Chaw-ley. Take this heah bucket and go on down that othah trail. Theah's a spring down theah. Bring us back some nice, fresh watah foah drinking an' cleanin' up."

Charlie: "How fer down theah is it?"

Guide: "Oh, just a hop, skip an' a jump."

Charlie: "Theah's no bears down that way is theah?"

Guide: "Nevah seen one".

Charlie (reluctantly): "Well…..all right."

In less than one minute, there was the sound of crashing through the brush, and Charlie burst through the door, ashen and trembling, pointing behind him.

Charlie: "Theah….theah was a beah…standin', standin' up to his belly….right….right….right in the middle o' that spring!"

Guide: "Well, now Chaw-ley, calm down. Why, that beah was just as scared of you as you was of him."

Charlie: "Oh, well, then. That watah wouldn't a been fittin' to drink, no how."

Dodge's tale is amusing, but it is fiction. Fact is stranger, as the old saying goes, than fiction, as Tim Wakefield's unnerving experience, first alluded to in Chapter 7, demonstrates.

It was mid-summer and we were camped in our familiar deep-woods site – the one with terrific wind shelter, and more than abundant mosquitoes – the site of the infamous peat fire. There were only the two of us, with one canoe. That canoe is akin to life itself. Without it, getting out of the bush would be exceedingly difficult, given the rough terrain, dense undergrowth and marsh areas bottomed with soft, deep muck. But we were not concerned with those depressing matters. Fishing was excellent, and as we carefully tied off the precious canoe in a small, well-sheltered cove, we realized that we had more fish than we could eat. We decided to save one northern pike, of about six pounds, for breakfast, as it was alive and in excellent condition. We left it stringered to the center thwart of the canoe, hung our damp life jackets on the overhanging branches to dry, and made for camp and dinner.

There was nothing remarkable about the passage of the night. We slept well, and woke refreshed to a pleasant, cool, sun-dappled morning with the hushed whisper of a not-quite-awake summer breeze nudging at the spruce boughs. A breeze in an evergreen forest does not sound like a breeze in a deciduous forest. A breeze makes deciduous trees chatter and laugh; it makes evergreens whisper and hiss. It was pleasant to remain in our sleeping bags a few minutes just to listen to the gossiping spruce. At length, the idea of hot coffee, and that pike, baked with butter in a foil purse, overwhelmed the subtle appreciation of morning wind-song, and we yawned, stretched, donned boots, and insect repellent, and started a fire.

"Well", yawned Tim, "I'll paddle over to the rock and clean that pike. I will expect fresh coffee when I get back."

"OK. You want it hot, too?"

"That'd be nice."

Tim disappeared down the trail toward the cove. I filled the coffee pot with water and poured in a carelessly estimated amount of coffee. I was placing it on the fire when I heard Tim.

"Hey! Hey! Get down here! Right now!"

The tone was not one summoning me to see an unusual bird or rare mammal. This was a distress call. The distance was less than fifty yards. I was there in seconds. The canoe was capsized, floating upside down. All of our gear was on the bottom of the cove, fortunately only about two feet deep. There were scratch marks in the hull of the canoe, not seriously damaging it. But there was a deep dent in one side. The pike was gone; the stringer chain broken. But most ominous, Tim's life jacket had been thoroughly shredded. Not shredded as in a search for food. Maliciously, purposefully shredded.

Mine was unmolested.

It was not a total disaster. We got wet and cold doing it, but we retrieved our gear from the bottom of the cove. Using a rounded boulder and a hand axe as body-work tools, we pounded out the dent in the canoe. It was otherwise unharmed. The wind was blowing into the cove, and so we were able to recover the paddles without much difficulty. We had a spare life jacket in the tent. We changed our clothes and hung the wet items on a rope between two trees near the tent. Before noon, we had recovered, and were ready to go fishing, as we had lost our breakfast to the marauder. The coffee had long since boiled over and was a total loss. So, we heated some water and ate instant oatmeal. The repulsiveness of instant oatmeal is inversely proportional to how hungry one is.

While fishing, we reviewed the incident we had just experienced, and concluded that the odor of the fish, even though submerged and alive, was the attractant that had brought the bear to the site. We resolved to be more careful in the future, and to leave no fish, dead or alive, anywhere near the camp or the cove. We could not explain the fact that one life jacket was shredded, with what certainly appeared to be malice, while the other was untouched. We chalked it up to a random, anomalous event. It wasn't.

It did not take long to boat enough fish for a good meal, and, the staying power of instant oatmeal being what it is, there was early consensus that lunch would be a very fine idea. We also concluded that cleaning the fish far from camp would be wise. Finding a place to stand, or kneel, with some crude surface available on which to fillet fish, was not easy. The shoreline alternated between dense, impenetrable brush and jagged rocks. We were aware of a small, barren, rocky island in the approximate center of the lake; it was a mile and a half away, and not on the way back to camp. But we found, crossing a shallow bay, a large granite boulder, whose top was a foot or so above lake level. It served our purpose nicely. A bowline knot in the stern line of the canoe, slipped over one ankle, served to keep the craft from drifting away, and the paddle blades served as workable, if not entirely stable, filleting boards. In minutes we were stroking towards camp with four thick, translucent fillets, and with hearty appetites.

In the cove at the campsite, we removed all the gear from the canoe, and intentionally capsized it to remove any odor remaining from having transported the fish. We hauled it up onto the deadfall along the bank and inverted it, leaving it there to dry. Satisfied that we had done all that should have been done, we walked up the trail to the tent site. Rounding a bend in the trail, I could see my garments drying on the impromptu clothesline…..but Tim's were not there. As we got closer, we could see that they were spread over an area about fifty feet in diameter, and that they were torn into small strips. Even more alarming, the tent was ripped in the corner where Tim slept, and his sleeping bag had been torn, but not totally destroyed. Nothing of mine had been disturbed in the least.

Thoughts of lunch were forgotten. As quickly as we could possibly do so, camp was struck, and we were on our way to that small, barren, rocky island. It was terribly exposed, had no firewood, no soil into which to drive a tent stake, no good harborage for the canoe, and no level site for the tent. But it was a long enough swim from the mainland to overcome that bear's unexplainable malice towards Tim, and we were thereafter undisturbed.

Rod Null, a regular member of our circle – you met him in Chapter 15 – is married to an admirable woman named Beth Basista. She is a professor of physics, by occupation, at a well regarded Midwestern university. By avocation, she is a nature photographer who has done some spectacular work. But most important, she's an angler. Her photography is spectacular partly because many of the scenes are of very remote and inaccessible places, reachable only on foot. And so, several times each year, she and Rod hike into seldom visited places. Naturally, Rod, in addition to bearing camera gear, is never without fishing tackle. This has lead, over time, to some interesting adventures. What follows are Rod's and Beth's separate accounts of exactly the same incident. They are reproduced exactly as originally written.

As the saying goes, ladies first.

Bear Story- Her version.

My husband and I enjoy going to the Canadian Rockies for summer vacations. I'm a semi-professional photographer, and the photographic opportunities are outstanding. I love the photography, he loves the fishing, and we both love the hiking. I can be fairly obsessive about getting as much photographically out of our trips and my husband is incredibly supportive and patient, frequently having to stop every hundred yards on a trail and wait for me to take pictures. If I don't want to endure comments all year about how our trips are "only" about photography, I allocate time on these trips for exclusively fishing. A few years ago, we spent 5 days in Jasper dedicated almost totally to fishing- I only took pictures 3 times, which is quite a feat if you've ever visited this beautiful area.

Jasper has many good fishing spots, and one of our favorites is about a 3 mile hike from the road with only a small altitude change. It is frequented by mountain bikers, horse riders, and the occasional hiker. It's a pretty little lake, with a small island in the middle and a resident population of loons to try to steal your fish. There is nothing photographically spectacular about it, so I don't even bring a camera I have to admit, though, that when the fish are biting here, it is really enjoyable fishing. Decent sized rainbows populate the lake, and they fight like crazy, as well as being very tasty for dinner.

This year on our second day in Jasper, we hiked back to fish. The fish were leaping out of the water, and we anticipated some good fishing. However, we couldn't cast far enough to get to the most active fish, and weren't catching anything. We worked our way around the lake trying to reach the active fish. We had our hearts set on trout dinner, so my husband decided to wade out to the island and see if he could catch some fish from there. He took off his boots and socks and rolled up his pants and walked about 75 ft out. I tried fishing from shore, but there was a lot of dead wood in the water and I didn't want to lose any lures, so I finally just sat down and watched my husband fish. While waiting, I kept thinking that this was partial payback for all the times that he had waited for me while I took pictures. He was somewhat entertaining- you could tell the water was really cold by the way he had waded- his walked like his legs were wood (later I found out that all the muscle he had gained hiking cramped up due to the cold). You could tell that the island wasn't much of one and that he didn't really want to step on it- later I found out it was mostly loon poop. Within a few minutes of getting out there, he caught a medium sized rainbow and I gestured for him to stay out there until he'd caught his limit- 2 fish for dinner. While waiting for him to catch his second fish, I heard some larger animal breaking brush behind me. I got a bit paranoid since this is bear country, and moved toward the trail so I could at least see behind me. I heard the noise several more times, then my husband got his second fish and waded back toward shore. We left and on the way out, stopped at the first place so I could try to catch some fish too. The fish were really hitting at this time, so I immediately got two. Even though I asked him not to kill the second one, so I could keep fishing, he killed it and then said I couldn't fish any more since I'd gotten a limit. This ticked me off, since I know that catch and release is the way a lot of fishing is done in protected areas, and I didn't see the difference in catching and releasing before or after a limit. Probably some weird fisherman code of honor that I suspect only applies to women who are fishing after their husbands have caught their limit.

The next day, we decided to go back and fish at the same lake. We were going to stay in a lodge on Bow Lake near Banff, and hoped to catch some fish for the chef to cook up for us. It was a beautiful Sunday morning, and no one was around except the loons, an eagle, and us. We had just started putting our lures on (ok- he put mine on, but honestly, if you only do this 2-3 times each year, it's hard to remember how to do it!) when a mom moose and two baby calves burst from the trees across the lake and ran into the lake toward the island my husband had fished from the day before. The mom moose was really disturbed- she was stomping and snorting and had gone far enough out into the lake that the babies just had their noses above water. I softly told my husband that there were only two things that could make the moose do this- a bear or a mountain lion, when out of the trees stormed a medium sized grizzly into the water after the moose. He got within 15 ft of them, and would have had to swim to reach them. You could just see his frustration. I immediately started packing our things up to leave and whispered to my husband "let's go". He whispered back "Shh- they haven't seen us yet". My first thoughts were: "wasn't that the time that you want to get away from a grizzly? Why would you wait until it saw you? "

In spite of this common sense thought, I stayed and watched the bear, very frustrated, get out of the water and pace back and forth on the shore, then run back into the water until he would have had to swim, then get out of the water and pace. Once again, I tried to communicate quietly to my husband that we should leave and once again I got the inane response "Shhh- they haven't seen us yet". After pacing in frustration on the shore, the bear then went into the woods and we couldn't see him anymore.

This made me really nervous and I watched the mom moose and where she was watching the woods by the lake. As she started to look back toward our side of the lake where the trail curved around the lake, I tried one more time to convince my husband that staying here was not a good idea. "Rod- we need to leave NOW!" I couldn't believe it when I got once again the "shh- they haven't seen us" response. All the while, the mom moose continues to look at the woods toward our side of the lake. My husband must have seen the look on my face, because he climbed up the bank to the trail to look for the bear and called softly down " there's no bear on this side". Whether he could see the bear or not, I climbed up the bank and was going to leave- with our without my husband. What stopped me was the thought that if the bear was now on our side of the lake and approached us, it was probably best to do the same things the moose did- get in the lake and go far enough out that the bear would have to swim to get you. Of course, it would have been a lot simpler to leave way back when the bear was on the other side of the lake when its attention was on with the moose.

Just then, the mom moose relaxed and lead the babies to the island and then to the far shore. The calves were high stepping and gallivanting in the water and you could just see them thinking "we got away- we got away!" To me, moose had always been slightly more interesting than elk or deer, but these babies had personality just oozing out of them.

Since the mom had relaxed,, I figured the bear must gone away so it was ok to fish. So, we stayed and fished, both reflecting on what we had seen. I did have to endure comments from my husband about not having the camera for the one time he really wanted some pictures! Fishing was slow, so an hour later we decided to go look for prints where the bear had come out of the woods. We walked down the trail about 50 ft and just before it turned to follow the lake, we found fresh bear tracks pointed toward where we had been fishing. We followed the tracks back to where the bear had gone into the water. This confirmed for me that the mom moose had been tracking the bear around the lake and the bear must have seen my husband on the trail and decided to take off. I couldn' t help but think once again that we should have left the minute the bear showed up, but I didn't say anything because I was grateful that the bear had not come up behind us while we were on the shore and we didn't have to try out the theory that the bear wouldn't have followed us further than it could walk in the water. I have never seen a bear hunting in the wild- only on nature programs on TV. I'll never forget what I saw- it was incredible, but scared the proverbial crap out of me. My husband each time in telling the story always comments that if this had happened one day earlier he would have been out on the island and would have literally had the crap scared out of him. I frequently make comments about the wisdom of listening to your spouse.

We went back to our original fishing spot and the fish were just getting active about two hours after the bear scenario when two ladies with a sheeshy-poof dog (the ones that you want to punt kick to see how far they will go and how Doppler shifted high frequency barks sound) came up the trail and asked us if we had seen any bears. We briefly told them what we had seen and recommended that perhaps they might not want to continue, especially with a bear bait dog. Some mountain bikers then rode up and we listened in amusement as the ladies relayed to the bikers that a grizzly had attacked and killed a bull moose just a half hour ago. We were going to interrupt and correct them, but the fish were really biting and we just wanted them all to leave. As more people came up, the story got immensely more embellished as it was relayed from one person to the next. I thought one positive outcome of all this would be that the story would get back to the park rangers, and they would close the trail due to bear activity- more fish for us! We eventually caught some very nice sized fish (mine were the biggest) and enjoyed a wonderful dinner cooked by a chef at the lodge on Bow Lake.

And his version……

Having had the pleasure of many a camping/fishing trip in the forest of Ontario, I can relate numerous encounters with black bears. They range from a brief glimpse of a fleeting bear to sitting, ok some might say cowering, in a tent while a marauding bear ransacked the camp site. Though black bears can be a nuisance and potentially threatening animal, I love seeing them. It makes me feel like I am in the wilds. Take that feelings, in magnum doses, throw in an enormous amount of awe and respect along with the sudden primordial reminder your brain provides that you can serve a role other than "consumer" in the food chain and you have my best description of encountering a grizzle back in the woods with no one else around for miles.

It was towards the end of an indulgently long vacation, our fifth year in a row of going to Alberta and British Colombia. Beth and I have fallen in love with the, deservedly, famous parks of the Canadian Rockies and the lesser know Selkirks. Banff, Yoho, Kootenay, Jasper, and Glacier offer an array of spectacular scenery from mountains and glaciers to wildflowers and of course animals. We were spending three nights in Jasper after two weeks of day hikes in the other parks. I was particularly looking forward to this part of the trip because it afforded the best opportunity for me to get in some fishing around the hiking and photography we had been focusing on to that point.

On our first day, a slight drizzle and the prospect of a fresh trout dinner, convinced Beth to put the camera away and indulge my fishing craving. A short drive and we were at a trailhead we had visited a number of times before. A leisurely 2.5 mile hike leads to a beautiful small lake that is residence to a good population of rainbow trout in the 10 to 17inch range. The trout were active that day slashing at some type of insect on the surface, but just out of casting range. The lake is perhaps 3 casts wide and 5 casts long. I realize that a cast is not a very standard unit of measure, but you get the idea. After a frustrating hour of trying from one side a short hike to the opposite side of the lake only compounded the torment. Finally I could stand it no longer, took off my hiking boots, zipped off the legs of the pants and started wading towards a small island that I thought would surely put me in range of those darn trout. After 100 plus miles of hiking my "flatlander" legs were as toned as they will ever be and immersing them in the very cold water produced instant debilitating muscle cramps. Despite this and sinking 3 to 5 inches in the grease like silt of the bottom I forged on to the island which consisted of 3 big rocks, 2 square feet of gravel and 8 square feet of loon guano. It worked. After a little finagling with lure selection I finally started to catch some fish. Feisty jumping rainbows are a bunch of fun. Beth on the other hand was stranded back on the shore and pantomimed that something large was rustling in the brush near her. I had seen fresh moose tracks on the shore and assumed that was the source of the noise. We have been around plenty of moose and I was not particularly concerned. I knew she was bored perhaps even envious watching me catch fish so I reluctantly headed back. We went back to our starting spot and the fish had actually moved in closer. Beth caught several fish in quick succession. In the heat of the moment, I quickly killed our limit, not realizing she would have enjoyed spending more time fishing.

We headed back to the car and Beth explained she was a bit upset that just when the fishing got good we had to stop. Being the selfless companion that I am, I vowed we would return the next morning. I know…. when do we get to the BEAR story?

Fast forward 16 hours, it is about 7:30am the following morning and we are the first and only car at the trail head. Other than no rain it is a carbon copy of the prior morning. Slate gray skies slight breeze and wonderfully cool. Perfect for a nice morning hike and, of course, fishing. We make it back to the lake in record time and are pleased to see trout slashing sporadically on the surface around the lake, even within casting range. I started to assemble the rods and rig them for fishing when we got the first indications that this would not be a boring day. About a third of the way around the lake, let's say about 150 yards across the water, there is considerable crashing through the bushes followed shortly by the appearance of a cow moose with two calves in tow. They hit the edge of the lake and with no hesitation dive into the lake wading at a frantic pace towards deeper water. The cow is vocalizing more than I have ever heard a moose do before. Having been around big game I knew something was up and started to say to Beth "they must have been spooked by a hiker or it could have been…" she cut my sentence short with the exclamation, "It's a bear!" I glanced back to where the moose had emerged from cover and there had appeared a beautiful, very agitated, male grizzly with a deep brown coat. He did a couple of back and forth paces at the waters edge and then dove in and headed at flank speed toward the trio of moose.

This is where Beth's version of the events probably differs a bit from mine. I am in awe of what is unfolding before us. I did a conscious assessment of the situation. Our proximity to the animals is getting a might close but they don't swim too fast and the bear is, shall we say, very focused on moose for lunch. I even checked the prevailing breeze, which was slightly rippling the surface of the water, it was a cross wind so I related to Beth, "they haven't seen us and they aren't going to scent us." She was, I won't say panicking, but she was preparing for a rapid egress from the area. I am not that smart, having never had cable television, the National Geographic channel had never come in with the degree of clarity unfolding before us. I wanted to watch ever moment. Despite her best judgment Beth decides to stay as well. The moose head for the small island that I was standing on, catching trout, not 24 hours before! I would later contemplate, what in the hell I might have done had I been out there at the same time.

The moose had chosen their escape route wisely, the cow leads the calves to deeper and deeper water and their long slender legs make them much faster waders/swimmers than the bear. The bear is loosing ground and knows it. About the time the moose reach the small island the bear turns around and heads back to shore. Beth is still lobbying for leaving immediately and I am still in disagreement. This is really exciting and I don't feel we are in imminent danger. The bear reaches shore and does some very animated pacing back and forth then disappears into the brush. The cow has stopped the almost hysterical vocalization and I am thinking all of the action is over. We can't see the bear but the cow sure as heck can see or hear the bear because her gaze is locked on what is surly the bear moving in the cover. And then her head starts to pivot like the needle of a compass tracking the bear's movement, which seems to be around the perimeter of the lake along the trail towards US! UH OH maybe Beth's prudent suggestion of getting out while the getting was good wasn't so bad after all? Too late now, time for a backup plan, with a close encounter with a grizzly, whose blood is up shall we say, impending in the next minute or two, I surveyed the available trees for climbing. No good there, all way too small. So I decided on the moose plan. With backpacks shed, I think we can fair at least as well in the lake as the moose did, so I tell Beth to prepare for a morning swim and I moved to a place where I had a good line of sight down the trail and brush to see the bear coming from 30 or 40 yards away. Plenty of time to dive into the water should the need arise, right? Well it did not come to that. The cows head continued to pivot around until just shy of where I thought it was going to get to be a really REALLY good bear story and stopped. Things gradually deescalated, the moose calmed down and continued on across the lake. Upon reaching shallower water the calves pranced about as if celebrating their survival. With no sign of the bear after awhile, Beth and I started to fish and it was fantastic. We even witnessed an osprey take a 15in rainbow not 40 feet from us. It was all the bird could do to get off the water with that fish. After a couple of hours had passed with no sign of the bear and the moose long gone, since no one had been down the trail as yet, I suggested we go and look at the tracks created by our earlier visitors. And so we started around the lake on the hiking trail. As clear as could be, the first tracks we encountered started about 50 yards down the trail, just out of my earlier field of view. Why the bear had pulled up short, I can not be certain, did he just give up the chase or my feeling is that he caught our scent at that point and decided to back off. Seeing those tracks and putting a hand down into one for a size comparison, noting with no small interest the distance the claws extend beyond the pads, sure got the hackles on the back of my neck up again.

I'm not sure we did everything right during this bear encounter but I was more than delighted with the outcomes as were the moose. I do hope the bear found lunch elsewhere that day.

An interesting side note, when the first group of other hikers showed up around midday we related, without substantial embellishment, our earlier encounter. Which they then related to the next group that came by and so on, each successive telling of the tale was not subject to the same restraint on embellishment. When we packed up and left for the day I believe the story was on its 5th version, involved a pack of grizzlies a dead bull moose and happened a scant 30 minutes ago.

In Chapter 11, *The Land of Kah weh-teh-kon,* another incident involving an ursine visitor to our fishing camp is mentioned. It was the end of the day, and the group had just eaten a fine dinner prepared by Jim Reese. It may have been the ultimate in the mixing of cultures: smallmouth bass satay. Now cooking with peanut butter in bear country is not very wise. I recalled later that Bert Sear, a bear hunting guide in the Algoma District of Ontario, used nothing but peanut butter, mixed with water and boiled over an alcohol stove affixed to a tree, to attract bears. He had said that it would call in bears from as far away as five miles, downwind. And, unfortunately for us, he was right.

Our fire was always built in a fire ring of stones at the water's edge, so that water was readily available should a fire become too…..enthusiastic. There was a fallen log on the landward side of the fire forming a perfect bench. All of us were seated on it.

Jeff walked over to the fire, retrieved the coffee pot, and returned to the log to refill cups. As he leaned over to refill mine, he froze.

"Dad," he whispered, " there's a bear about ten feet behind you. Don't make any sudden moves."

"OK". Then, in a stage whisper, "Guys, there's a bear close behind me. Very slowly, get up and walk to the canoes. Grab the food bags on the way. Get out in the lake. Don't look and don't run."

The bear stood in one spot and watched all of that happen. From the water, we watched the bear pillage the camp. The tent was some distance from the dining site, but the bear explored it anyway. Things in camp were scattered, but not really damaged. The only casualty was a plastic water container, which will never hold water again. However frightening it might have been at the time, it ended well.

The overwhelming majority of such incidents do end well. There is a down side to that. Given enough exposures to such encounters, one begins to believe that all such incidents will end well. It is a very dangerous complacency.

A later chapter, *61°N, 146°W,* deals with our circle's first trip to Alaska.

Where the Gulls Are

The following incident took place on a later trip, to the same general area, and is somewhat out of sequence, but clearly belongs in this chapter. This is the story of an encounter I do not wish ever to repeat. I live today not by virtue of intelligence or good judgment, but by virtue of dumb luck. It is said that "The Lord protects fools and drunks". I live as proof.

Jim Santangelo and I had caught and released three or four dozen pink and chum salmon that morning, had kept a few for dinner in case the other boat, bearing my brother, Lee, and Jim's cousin, Richard, had not done well at halibut fishing, which was their quest for the day. They were in open water in Prince William Sound, as it was an almost windless day, while Jim and I were determined to find silver salmon, the main run of which had not yet quite begun. We were cruising the shoreline, exploring each freshwater stream entering the Sound. All of them were alive with pinks and chums, but we had not seen a silver. The bay was narrowing into a channel with steep gravel banks on either side, at about a forty-five degree slope. A great deal of the gravel bank was exposed, as the tide was nearing its ebb. Ahead we could see a steep set of rapids – almost, but not quite, a waterfall, and at its base, the unmistakable metallic flash of large silver salmon, struggling to ascend the cataract. Eureka!

In our haste to fish the pool immediately below the rapids, we took scarce note, only a quick photo, of one of two black bear cubs on the gravel bank. And they, in reciprocity, seemed to take scarce note of us, even though the channel was no more than 100 feet wide at that point. Ahead was a snag below a level spot on the bank, where a tree root had apparently torn loose from the bank and had been washed away by an unusually strong spring run-off, at one time or another. We decided to tie the boat off at the snag. Jim would fish from it. He had a painful knee injury that precluded his scrambling out of the boat and up the steep bank.

A large spruce tree, its roots above the high tide line, had freshly fallen towards the stream, about half way between the boat and the base of the rapids. Its upper branches were short of the water by about five feet, and I could easily walk between it and the water to reach the target pool, without entering the water and disturbing the school of silver salmon stacked up there. Further up the rapids, the slope of the stream bed became less steep, and in it was a lone black bear, feeding there on the salmon which had made it past the initial cataract, not at all an uncommon sight for that time and place. The bear was about 200 yards upstream from the base of the rapids, and I gave it no further attention.

Without great difficulty, I reached the pool below the rapids and began to cast, my attention riveted to that pool, which seemed to be almost all salmon and very little water. These fish were large and powerful, but I could not seem to get a solid hookset. Three or four slipped the hook before I was finally fast to a gleaming, silver torpedo. The fish was strong, turned downstream, and in two or three seconds had stripped enough twelve pound test line to be well past where Jim sat, casting from the boat. I could envision our becoming tangled in a three way struggle, which the salmon was certain to win. I could not alert Jim because of the noise of the rapids, so I opened the bail of the spinning reel. It was a counter-intuitive maneuver, but it worked.

The salmon, no longer opposing a restraining force, stopped briefly, then turned back upstream – in the direction the instinct of the spawning season drove it. I had to be very careful to retrieve slack, but not to exert any force on the fish, which would trigger it to again turn against the direction of that force. Unlike the downstream dash, the upstream return was leisurely, and wandered back and forth across the stream, frequently pausing. I would allow it to get back upstream of me and resume the fight, repeating the slack line ploy if necessary. We had gone the whole week without landing a silver salmon, and I was not about to lose this one.

Meanwhile, without my notice, the tide had turned. Tides at this latitude are very significant, producing, depending upon location, very swift flows and water level changes in double digits, measured in feet. The water exiting the rapids was still clear, fresh, and swift-flowing seaward, as the tide rose, but the stream bed was filling, and the upper branches of the fallen spruce, behind me, downstream, were now nearly awash. I was not even vaguely aware of any of this. My attention was sharply focused upon a fish weighing at least half again the rated strength of my line, a fish I was absolutely determined to bring to hand. I had lost "situational awareness", a lapse which often exacts heavy penalty.

There is a familiar saying: "Time flies when you're having fun." And certainly it does. That salmon and I were attached for a much longer time than it seemed. By the time it was on the gravel bank, after several unsuccessful attempts to grasp it under a gill cover – I had left the landing net with Jim – the upper end of the spruce was submerged, and with it, my escape route. The only alternative now was to struggle through the thick and tangled branches, slow, but doable. I tied a short piece of quarter inch rope around the jaw of the fish, and stood to find a place to tie it off, so that the hard-won prize would not wriggle back into the water as I pursued yet another. I took a deep breath and looked around. I noticed that the feeding bear was no longer in the rapids. It was on the stream bank fifty yards away…and approaching. Then I remembered those cubs. This was not good.

I had not removed my PFD when I left the boat. I remember thinking that it was not Kevlar body armor, but it was at least something. I struggled to try to remember the rules for dealing with a bear in a very personal manner. All I could summon up was: "never run". That is a very hard rule to follow in such circumstances, but not in this one; there *was* nowhere to run. The alternatives were to back slowly into the spruce branches and to try to get through them without turning my back on the bear, or to dive into the stream and allow it to carry me downstream to the boat, hopefully kept afloat, despite flooded waders, by the PFD. Climbing the bank to get around the roots of the spruce was out of the question. The bush there was impenetrable. There were no good alternatives. I remember wondering how I could ever have allowed myself to get into this situation……and how I was ever going to get out of it.

I decided that the better of two bad options was the stream. The boat was close enough, and the stream swift enough, that, even though that water was ice only a few miles back, hypothermia would not be an issue. I wished that I had tied that fish a bit further from me, though I doubted that food had anything to do with the bear's approach. It could not be hungry. I had seen it eat several very large salmon in the rapids. The motive had to be the cubs. But where were they? The worst possible action would be to move towards them. The bear stopped at about thirty yards, and swung her head from side to side, sniffing and staring. I could not dive into the stream from where I stood. I had to move.

I recall thinking that choosing the right direction might well be, literally, a life-and-death decision. *Where were those cubs?* I did not know where the cubs were, but I knew where they weren't. They were not with her. I remember, even at the time, being surprised at how calmly the decision was made to walk directly towards the bear.

I was not really terribly amazed, but I was terribly relieved, to see her turn and amble off into the bush. I seized the fish and my rod and tore through the branches of that spruce like a chain saw. Jim, who was blocked from view of the entire incident by the spruce could not imagine what I was doing when I threw a fish and a rod at him, untied the boat and pushed it into midstream. "What the hell are you doing……..?"

It is a marvel of the human mind's survival algorithm that somehow, focus is maintained until the real, physical crisis is over. It was then that disabling panic set in. Incoherence and trembling are most unbecoming at a fish camp.

Chapter 19
61°N, 146°W
Yes, Virginia, There is a Salmon Claus

The chapter title is the latitude/longitude, rounded to the nearest degree, of a truly fantastic fishing venue, rivaling, or perhaps surpassing, any we had experienced. Admittedly, for most Joes, particularly midlanders, it is, likely, due to distance and cost, one of those once-in-a- lifetime trips. For us, it was a twice-in-a-lifetime…at least, so far. After the first experience, it was nearly impossible to not return.

The first visit is described, in highly abbreviated, grammatically shameful form, as a verbatim transcription of notes taken in a less-than-waterproof pocket notebook. The narrative is not complete, some of it made illegible by water damage. If you are going to fish this area of Alaska, in September, you are absolutely, positively, going to get wet, one way or another. Most of it survived the rain, the spray, and the wader leakage, and provides at least a hint, a whiff, of the experience. First experiences are usually the best experiences. The eyes, the ears, the nostrils, and especially the mind, are wide open.

By way of explanation, the group, on both visits, consisted of Jim Santangelo, a regular in our circle, my brother, Lee, and Dick Santangelo, Jim's cousin and a classmate of Lee's in med school. This quartet began fishing together nearly 45 years ago, and now know instinctively when to duck someone's backcast.

*The following is a **verbatim** transcription of notes taken on site*

Saturday.

It is a bright, orange-golden dawn in Cincinnati. Except for a few patches of fog in the river valley, it is crystalline. DL Flight 457 is on time. No problems at baggage check or security. This is too good.

We are in Seattle. The flight was on time. The America West concourse is not far from Delta. Bright and sunny. America West is on time The plane is not full. There is a cloud cover most of the way, but it is far below. The landing at Anchorage is on time. Dick and Lee need to recheck their baggage on to Cordova. It's all there. The recheck to ERA goes without a hitch. It's too good.

We have two hours. The Anchorage airport is not large, but very busy. Lots of connections to Asia, and regionals to all over Alaska. Drizzling rain. 25Kt winds from the south.

I feel lousy. Neck sore, congested. Maybe some virus or sinus infection. I'll be OK. Nothing a couple of martinis won't fix.

We're in a "Cheers" copy bar. Dick notices everybody in here – all men – are either in fishing clothes or oil field coveralls. We're the only ones without beards.

We're in the ERA gate area. There are Swearingens and twin Otters, a venerable Convair 580, and the queen herself, a DC-3, parked outside. Jim and I say a little prayer: please let it be the '3.

But it isn't. It's the 580. Oh, well. Almost as good. The two turbo-props pull the old bird quickly into the overcast. We can see nothing. We break out of the clouds at only a few hundred feet. The Copper River delta south of Cordova is a huge tidal flat with glacial streams of thick gray water, the color of Portland cement, flowing into the sound. Makes an Ohio River flood look like a mountain spring. Miles of mud.

Cordova airport is built on this flat. The runways are long, but the airport is small. The passenger terminal building is an industrial steel warehouse. Crowded. Hardly room to walk. We elbow our way to baggage claim. It's all here! My rod case is damaged, but the rods are OK. Alaska Wilderness Outfitters is here to meet us. Clockwork. It's too good.

We ride to town with one of their guys. Nice fellow, but knows, or pretends to know, nothing. We pump him for info but get little. We pull into the lot at The Reluctant Fisherman Inn, which is on the harbor. He says that "It's 700 slips, and all the boats are here".

"Why?"

"No salmon….uh….well, not enough to justify going out".

We're looking out of the window of our room, watching the rain fall in wind-driven torrents. Dick has a local magazine that says Cordova gets about 100" of rain per year, and September is the wettest month! There's a sea otter swimming in the marina, eating clams. They're bigger than I thought. 2 or 3 times the size of a beaver.

We go to dinner at the Inn. Crowded. Takes forever. Conversation around us is gloomy. There hasn't been a silver salmon run this year. Limit has been lowered to one per day.

We check the weather forecast. Rain next 5 days. Small craft warning posted for tomorrow.

All of a sudden, not too good.

We go to bed. AWO is to meet us at 9:30 tomorrow morning.

Sunday.

Wind howled all night. Heavy rain. Daylight is 7a local time. We go to breakfast. Long faces everywhere. Visibility is under one mile. Still pouring and blowing.

Back in room. Watching the harbor. Waitress said locals are still waiting for the silvers, but they're already two weeks late. Not a boat has left a slip. Planes are grounded. Dick got a call from AWO. We're on hold until at least 10a, but told to be ready. Wind still fierce. Tide coming in. Tides here are 11 feet.

I feel a lot better. Sinuses still plugged, but much better.

Visibility improving slightly. Still not good enough to fly. I watch a guy on the dock check his mooring lines and then run back to shelter. Better review the GPS manual. We may need it.

It is noon. At about 10 o'clock, AWO called to tell us to hold until noon. Just called again. Will re-evaluate the weather at 2p. Still raining very hard.

2 pm. AWO called. Be ready in 15 minutes. Still can't fly. Going by boat. Sea is <u>rough</u>. Should be some ride.

Still raining. Get fishing licenses at AWO and prepare to go to the dock. Tom, AWO's guy, says, "It looks like we might be flying you guys in after all". I don't see how. Ceiling is still only halfway up the mountains, but the sky is a little brighter and the rain has slowed to a drizzle.

Back in AWO's Suburban. In about 2 miles we turn onto a gravel causeway between two lakes. On the left is a Cessna and a beautiful old DeHavilland Beaver, idling. The stuttering clippity-clop of the radial's idle is one beautiful sound.

We help Tom load the Beaver. Besides our gear – and we're all over the 50 lb weight limit - we put aboard two coolers full of ice, a Johnson 15, 15 gallons of fuel, a hundred lb tank of propane, and some miscellaneous packages.

The wind, still howling at 20Kts, pushes the Beaver away from the dock. How small the Cessna looks beside it! We taxi a long way down the lake. Tom finally turns her into the wind, and cracks the throttle – not open, just advanced. Then firewall.

Deafening noise, but the Beaver doesn't accelerate very fast. Tom rocks the yoke to break it loose. Now the floats are planing and we gain a little more speed. Causeway coming up fast. Tom doesn't look worried. Good sign. At the last moment, the old Beaver breaks free, clears the causeway and climbs leisurely.

Tom levels at 700 feet. The mountains around Cordova go to 3500 feet – and you can't see them! We fly over the town of Cordova and out over the sound. Tom hugs the coastline, then banks northeast into Sheep Bay.

We are literally flying up a fjord. High rock walls on both sides that disappear into the clouds. East of us is a non-descript island. Tom banks sharply and eases the Beaver toward the sea. It all looks the same to us. The shores are steep and spruce clad.

The floats touch down in a calm bay…imperceptibly. Tom has done this before. We taxi into a tiny cove, and there is the wannigan. We're here.

Tom apologizes for not helping us get settled, but says he wants to get out while he can. We unload onto the front deck of the wannigan, he pushes the Beaver clear, cranks the engine, and is gone. This time, the Beaver lifts quickly and climbs briskly.

It is dark gray, raining again. The mountains are extremely rugged, almost vertical. The boats are full of water from the 7" of rain. There is no way out of here. We've done this before, but suddenly, we feel pretty much alone.

Get the boats ready. It's already late afternoon. Put the stuff inside. Worry about order later. Rig the rods. Life jackets, fuel. Come on, you guys, we're burning daylight.

We head up the bay. We troll. We cast the shorelines. We have no idea what we're doing. Jim and I rely on our most accurate fishing guides: gulls. We notice a flock of them in a small cove, standing in the water, not diving. But their calls are definitely the characteristic feeding call. Ah ha!

The cove turns out to be the mouth of a small stream. We see salmon – not coho, but chum and pinks. Thousands and thousands of them. We catch three before darkness closes on us. They are strong and determined fighters, but only 5 or 6 pounds. That's OK. This is what it's about.

We are not far from the wannigan, but the shoreline is full of inlets and islands. The tide keeps altering the landscape. It all looks alike, but none looks familiar. The map Tom gave us is in the wannigan. It's getting darker very fast.

The wannigan is in a small, L-shaped cove, not visible from anywhere else. Damn! That last salmon took 20 minutes to land. Wish we had those minutes back.

There's a cabin on an island in mid-channel. Cursed it before. We wanted to be here alone. But it saves us now. Nobody about. It's deserted. No lights, but we remember: that cabin is just opposite our cove.

The twilight is almost gone. Hard to fillet a fish in this light. Good thing that they're large. That's easier. We are wet and chilled. But we have more than enough salmon for dinner. Boy, is it ever martini time.

First time we've looked, really looked, at the wannigan. It is literally a small chalet on floats. Two stories, four bedrooms. Kitchen with a counter. There's a propane fridge, stove, even a flash boiler for hot water. Fresh water comes from two plastic barrel "cisterns" on brackets each side of the structure, supplied by roof gutters. With 100" of rain a year – that doesn't count snow – this works great. There's a deck fore and aft, and a gas grill! We are used to tents. This is a palace.

Dick is making a marinade for the salmon. He brought fresh herbs and spices. Andy gave us a jar of fresh Red Pelican mustard. Jim brought McIlhenny's tabasco sauce. Marinade smells good.

Grilled minutes-old salmon is magnificent. Fish market and restaurant salmon is – well – not like this.

Clean up. Slug some coffee. Bed. Still raining. Wind still gusting. Not as bad. Turn off the propane valve. Lantern mantle goes dark. It is totally, utterly, completely dark. I stumble into the kitchen, look through all the windows. Every direction. No light anywhere – not even the faintest starlight seeping through the clouds. No silhouette of the shoreline. Dark.

<u>Monday.</u>

It's still dark. Use my flashlight to check my watch. It's 8:30 "real time", but 4:30 here. How soon does it get light? I know where the salmon are!

At first glimmer, somebody's making coffee. Dick and Lee are already up. Dick, our chef in residence, is making french toast. Coffee's perking in an old-time, real, by-God percolator. Smells good.

Still raining. Nobody cares. Took a long time to bail out the boats yesterday. They're full of rain water again. Yeah, it's rain water. Doesn't taste salty. Dick and Lee cut off a plastic jug to bail with. Jim and I drag our boat on to the deck and pull the transom plugs. All this is taking forever. Let's go!

Wide open throttle. AWO's Johnson 15's don't seem so fast this morning.

The mouth of the small, unnamed stream is alive with chum salmon and pink salmon. One on every cast. They are so thick, most are snagged before one has a chance to strike at the lure. Some are injured from the battle to get here. But many are in perfect condition. We keep only these. A fish on all the time!

The chum salmon we hook are 10 to 15 lbs. Their runs are lightning, a bullet in the water. Many are in the air eight or nine times. The pinks are not spectacular fighters; they are dogged, determined, enormous stamina. They never give up, they never seem to tire. This is incredible!

We keep only 12 salmon, half our possession limit. By high tide, we are tired. Let's go back, clean these fish and go after halibut. We don't want to end up with too many salmon in possession. And tomorrow's another day.

Twelve salmon fillet out into a lot of fish. We use a portion of the dock that is stashed on the rear deck as a table. It's only a foot high but that's better than cleaning 'em on the floor.

Salmon eggs fall thru the cracks between the boards and onto the deck. They'll smell in a couple of days.

Rain down to a drizzle. Wind down too. Sky brighter. Bag the fillets. In the cooler. We're off after halibut.

None of us has ever even seen a halibut in real life, but Tom showed us where the halibut tackle is. And it's obviously for very heavy fish. 80 lb test line, Penn 309's, hooks that belong on a small crane, this tells us that halibut must be really, really big.

Freezer contains herring – whole ones. Tom said to use 1/3 to ½ herring per hook. He's marked the spots on the map. They're close. We ought to have a couple by dark.

Tom said, "Now, don't get discouraged about halibut fishing." But I am. It's raining again. Hard. Wind is blowing too. It's cold. Haven't had a bite except for some small fish that steal the herring. It's soft, and these huge hooks tear loose easily. Still, all the rods are rigged with them. Must be right.

Lee and Dick have drifted with the tidal outflow pretty far out into the bay. It's getting a little choppy. Worried a little. Let's go out and see how bad it is.

Not as bad as it looks. These little boats are tunnel hulled. Good for shallow water, but handle terribly. They're stable, though.

We're beside their boat. They're grinning. Lee holds up a big halibut. Looks like a flounder on steroids. I guess it at 20 to 25 lbs. Maybe more. I can't curl it with either arm, and I can easily curl 25. They've got some flounders, too. Nice ones. Well.

It's getting dark. No more cleaning fish in the dark. Let's go.

Dick's the chef in residence. I'm the fish butcher. Not that everyone doesn't help with all the chores, it's just that somehow everything falls into its niche.

Halibut makes four gorgeous fillets. Lee is making from-scratch home fries. We're grilling salmon to reduce our in-possession number.

Great meal. Tired. Kill the lights. No one even says goodnight.

Tuesday.

It's daylight. Way into daylight. No sun on the trees outside, but it's not raining. Shirt, shoes. Dick's already looking out the front window. "Look!

Sun on the glacier". The peaks are sunlit and spectacular, but the glacier is a brilliant blue-white.

While we admire the mountains – first time we've seen them – we hear wolves. With binoculars we see them running across a low meadow about two miles away.

Scan the peaks across Sheep Bay with the glasses. Dall sheep. They're tiny specks, even through the binocs. But they're real. They move across meadows that are at least 60 degrees with the horizontal as casually as we walk on this deck.

The leftover hash browns, some green pepper, crumbled bacon, onion, eggs, dry milk, we have some serious scrambled eggs. Not so great a hurry today. We are beginning to see the world around us as being so unbelievable that we're…well…not believing it while we're actually looking at it. Almost too much to grasp. No postcard ever photographed could touch this. And we're actually, really here.

We're going to Sahlin Lagoon today. Tom said there were salmon and Dolly Vardin trout, but to be sure we got in with the high tide and out before the low.

Jim and I are entering the inlet to Sahlin Lagoon. It's high tide by the tide table, but the flow is like a whitewater river. The bottom is shallow and strewn with large boulders. Engine is tilted up to shallow-drive position, so I can't get much thrust. This is getting out of control. We're alone in here. This is not my boat. This water is so cold, you'd only last….. "No!" I shouted to Jim. "We're getting out of here."

The boat responds to steering, but is being swept along faster than the steering maneuvers. It is sideways in the current. More power only cavitates the prop. The inlet is narrowing and speeding up. There are wakes created by boulders. Throat dry.

There's a turn up ahead, should create a backwater eddy. It does. Ease into it. Get the boat headed up tide. Barely makes headway against the current. We're out.

Near the inlet, Koppen Creek flows into the Lagoon. It is ice cold, melting from a glacier not two miles away. It is also full of salmon. We beach the boat in a clump of weeds and start to cast. First cast hooks a chum that screams the drag clutch for a good 75 yards. It goes on and on. We become very selective. We keep only the biggest and the best. 95% released.

Dick and Lee join us. This is incredible. This is too easy. It's like an unending bluefish blitz. The brochures were right. This IS the fisherman's paradise. How many do we want? 12 more? OK. This one. Not that one. Not that one. This one's OK.

Tide's beginning to ebb. Let's get out of here.

The sun is shining now, most of the time, with short periods of cloud cover.

We clean salmon, eat lunch. Go after halibut. Jim's got one. About the same size as Lee's. Flounder, rock cod, Dick even comes up with a red snapper.

We seem to spend most of the day cleaning fish. Tom made a check flight today and told us that we could ship home twice our daily limit. That's 48 salmon and 8 halibut. Now we get serious.

Wednesday.

Sun is over the mountain. We're looking down the cove. Water is flat. The usual sea otters are pounding clam shells on their chests, noisily slurping the clams, and diving again. A huge flock of gulls is at rest on a gravel bar about 1000 yards away. Once in a while, a straggler pink salmon swims by.

Dick and Lee decide to dig some clams after breakfast. They had collected about a quart of small ones on Monday evening, and Dick had made a great Italian delicacy with them as an appetizer. So, why not some more.... bigger this time?

Jim and I had fished the gravel bar where the gulls were, so we knew there were clams there. This won't take long. We'll wait and all go to Sahlin Lagoon together, timing it so the tide is slack.

Here they come. It took long, but they have a lot of clams. No big ones.

We go out with the boat, meet them halfway. We'll wait at the Lagoon entrance. No, they say, they're going to Sahlin Falls, try to climb up to the first pool for trout.

Inlet not nearly so violent this time. Timed it right. As we enter the lagoon, we see that it is full of seals. We don't know what kind. Gulls, geese, eagles, otters. This is a party. Something's going on!

A few casts tell us that It's not trout. At the northeastern end of the lagoon, the Sheep River flows into salt water. At the edge of the fresh water, there is a sharp line separating the green, plankton-laden sea water from the cold, crystal clear water of the Sheep River. All of the clear water is crowded with salmon. Not a single fish is in the salt water. The stream itself is so glutted with fish that it is difficult to wade.

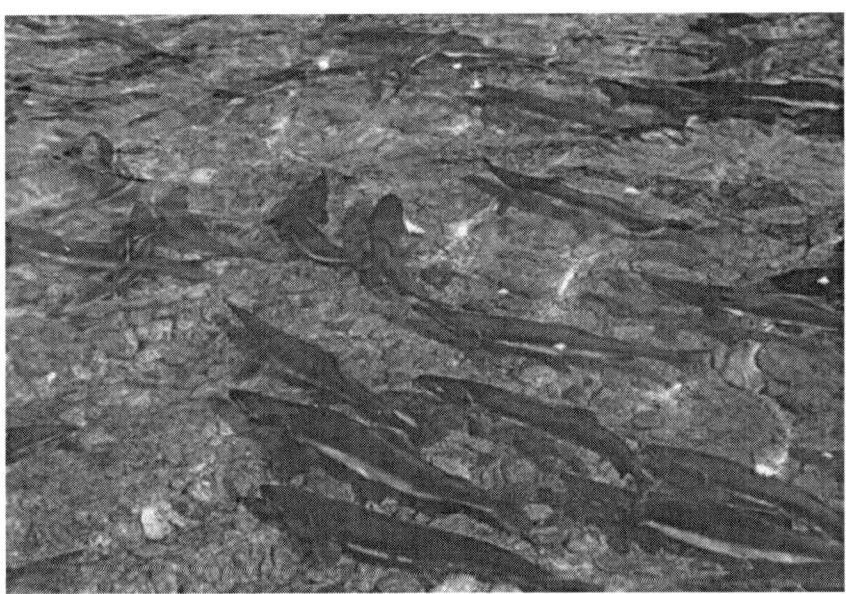

As an experiment, because Tom had said there were Dolly Vardin in this lagoon, I cast a Blue Fox Vibrax into the salt water at the edge line. Can't see it. Too murky. Hit something. It's moving. Closer. I see it's a salmon carcass. Coming in.

Hook pulls out. 8 ½ foot carbon fiber salmon rod stores a lot of energy. Vibrax is now a bullet. Duck behind my rod hand. Something stings my hand. Expect splash as the Vibrax falls into the water. Never comes. Uh-oh.

Two points of the treble are buried – one in the hand, one in the base of the little finger. Decide I don't want to leave. Too much effort to get here, too many fish. I'll just jerk the hooks out. Pain not too bad. I know it will be, if I rip the hooks out, but worth the price. One comes out, the other won't. Don't know if I can force myself to pull hard enough – pulled really hard already - or if the barb is hung up on a tendon or something. Better get the docs. (They're both pediatricians, but kids get hooked, too.) Don't want permanent damage.

Tide still up. Easy to get out of the passage. Dick and Lee are at the waterfall, getting out of their boat. Glad we caught them before they started their climb. They follow us back.

Dick had charge of the med kit. He's prepared. Has all the tools needed. Even has Lidocaine. Strange, but it doesn't hurt very much anyhow. They photograph it. Weird. My friends debate the best methods, discuss infection risk. Beginning to not like this. Can't help but laugh. "Are we having fun, yet?"

Dick has something called a "Kelly Clamp"…sort of a wimpy needle-nosed pliers, but clean. Pulls <u>hard</u> on the hook, but it won't come out. Don't feel it thanks to Lidocaine. Another debate. Jim has a pair of heavy duty side cutters. Decide to push the point through, then cut off the hook, holding the barb so it can't back into the flesh. Come on, guys. Hooks don't back up. Dick has a hard time pushing the point through the skin. Brand new hook, too. Finally through. Jim's cutters are heavy duty, but thick. Getting them on the shank of the hook puts a lot of tension on the hook. Boy, am I glad I can't feel any of this!

Cutter won't cut the hook. Fumble with my left hand down inside my waders for my Leatherman tool. Hand it to them. "Try this". Cuts hook easily. They push it out. Done.

We finish the dressing with duct tape to make it water proof. Tide's still high enough to get to Koppen Creek. We go fishing.

Sun is out now. It is actually hot. Remove life jacket and shirt. Think about it, put life jacket back on. Here we are, fishing in glacial waters, in our undershirts.

Where the Gulls Are

It's the same as before. A salmon hook-up on every cast. We're very, very selective now. Only the biggest and the best go into the boat.

We're not paying attention. The tide is falling fast. Somebody looks up and sees a boat stranded on the gravel. We have to carry, then drag, the boats several hundred yards. Wind is up. One foot chop. Cloud cover. Dark.

Back to the fish-cleaning table. Then out on the bay for halibut. Fish are active. Jim winches in a nice flounder. Now he has another hard strike. This fish doesn't sound, it surfaces! We can't believe it. It's a silver salmon, a coho, taking a herring at 125 feet! Maybe this signals the start of the run. The fish is definitely ocean-run coloration, not spawning coloration. Still……

Jim's got another big fish. This time, a ling cod. Regs say they must be handled by hand and must be 35" to keep. It is. Easily. But we release it gently. Don't even measure it. We don't need a fish that scarce. Sea getting rougher.

The other boat has done well, too. Back to the cleaning table. Lee has a 40" halibut. About 18" wide. And some flounder. I'm trying to fillet fish with a waterproof glove on my right hand. Very clumsy.

Having this grill is wonderful. We eat salmon again. Pushing our limit.

Not much talk after dinner. Everyone's exhausted. But the sky is clear, now. We look for the northern lights. Only a luminescence in the north sky. Nobody lasts very long.

<u>Thursday</u>

Tide is just about bottoming out as we finish breakfast. Good time to go for halibut.

Morning is reasonably clear. Sun is on the peaks, but the whole bay is still in shadow. A little chill, maybe 50 or 55 degrees. Not a whisper of a breeze. Dead calm. Bay is mirror smooth.

There is little activity. No otters, no seals, no birds. Once the engines are shut down, there is no sound at all. Eerie, weird silence.

No surprise that fishing is dead, too. We spend two hours without a strike, and catch several small flounders in the next hour, as the tide begins to flow in. Pointless.

We give it up, clean fish, prepare to go to Sahlin Lagoon with a rising tide so that we can stay a few hours.

Sunny weather makes the trip through the pass a little less intimidating. Good visibility lets us avoid the boulders. It's a milk run.

We're inside now. The lagoon is about a half mile long, a quarter mile wide. Looks like any of a hundred small lakes in Quetico, except that it's salt water. As yesterday, the lagoon is full of seals and birds. The mouth of Sheep River is still full of salmon.

Dick has made a fish count to know how many we can keep. We intentionally undershoot it in case the silvers should show up.

Dick and Lee wade upstream to look for trout pools, but the river is so full of salmon that it is impossible to fish for trout.

Jim and I realize that the tide is beginning to recede. Time to get out. We move our boat a little off shore, then go to get theirs, which is tied off upstream a bit. Have to drag it over some shallows, tie it off further out. Holler for Dick and Lee. Probably can't hear us for noise of the stream.

We don't want to spend the night in this lagoon. If we don't get out soon, that's what we'll have to do.

Here they come. Not carrying any trout.

We're out of the pass in plenty of time. Head for the halibut spots. Tom said to fish two hours either side of the tide change for halibut, but we're beginning to see a pattern. Evening is always better than morning. Calm sea is no good, especially on bright days.

But now there's a little ripple on the water and it's clouding over again. Maybe this is the day for a really big halibut. I get another 40 incher, and we collect some nice flounder, rock cod. Lee catches a red snapper. Nice one.

Getting dark. Back to the wannigan. Fish are cleaned in the last minutes of daylight. We recount the day's activities while cooking, but not over dinner. Everyone's busy, then.

No one lingers. Sleep is deep, sound and almost instant.

<u>Friday</u>.

Last day. We want to make it count. A little sun is already on the peaks. Looks like a nice day. Dead calm. No activity. For the first time, we don't see a single creature from the wannigan. Total silence. Ominous, and don't know why.

Go for broke strategy. Jim and I decide to improvise downriggers using the halibut rigs to lower 2 lb lead balls, and fasten the salmon rods' line to them with some breakaway means. Troll deep for silver salmon the only place we've caught one – deep water in the center of the bay. Breakaway means hard to come up with. Finally cut strips of plastic garbage bags. Hard strike will break them – if the line doesn't twist around the lead ball.

Lee and Dick are going after big halibut. Use whole herring, or at least big chunks.

Jerry-rigged downriggers hard to handle in the small boat. Takes two or three tries to get one set. Troll for hours. Catch one small rock cod. Dick and Lee catch some flounders and a rockfish.

We know we can catch more salmon, but we're not really sure we have more than 8 slots open, and we're saving those for silvers....just in case. Decide to fill them with pinks.

Go back to Sahlin Lagoon. Keep only five. Prime condition fish getting scarce – plenty of beat-up, exhausted specimens. Spawn about over, but Sheep River is still clogged with fish. Koppen Creek the same, as is every stream. Never, ever would believe this.

Just beat the tide out of the lagoon. Cloudy now, and breeze picking up. Maybe a repeat of last evening in the halibut spots.

It isn't. Fishing slow. We do catch some prime flounder for dinner, and three rock cod. I try jigging a Hopkins for rock cod on light tackle, but it's too deep. Too much line stretch.

Jim and Dick make a pasta sauce with the fish, and two pounds of spaghetti. What are we gonna do with all of this?

It's gone. We start organizing and packing. Doesn't last long. Do it in the morning. Tom won't be here til 10. Bone tired. Besides, not much enthusiasm for leaving.

Saturday.

We're up at daylight. Nobody says much. Breaking camp is always a sad day. I cook a big stack of pancakes, but nobody's very hungry. "Eat 'em up yum", I say, "we don't know when we'll get a chance to eat today".

Everything's in slow motion, but we still have everything on the deck by a little after 9. We're looking at lowering clouds slowly shrouding the glacier. Not a ripple on the bay. No activity in the water. Weather definitely closing in. Maybe it's a good time to go.

It's still morning, but Tom has the Beaver on the water, not 100 yards away before we hear it. We don't want to hear it.

Clouds are low now. Same 600 foot, touch-the-tree-tops-altitude route back to Cordova. Houses, roads, cars, people. It's over.

It's been an experience full of surprises. We're recounting all the things we didn't know, sitting here in the Cordova airport. Then Jim says, "and we've only seen a tiny, little fraction of it".

I think of a sweatshirt I have at home. The logo is a guy sitting in a boat with a huge tackle box open.

The caption is, "So many lures, so little time".

Where th.

Chapter 20
Taman Negara
Fishing the Sungei of Malaysia

(The following was written by Tim Wakefield in 1975. He was living in Singapore at the time, on work assignment. It recounts a truly once-in-a-lifetime fishing trip. It is transcribed here <u>exactly</u> as written.)

My Singapore neighbor Paulo Petronio actually worked in Malacca, an old Portugese/Malay settlement on the west coast of Malaysia about 100 miles from Singapore. He managed a plant there for Siemen's Electronics and returned to Singapore each weekend to be with his family who resided next door to us. Since he had good communication channels into the Malaysian government he obtained details as to what was involved to go to Taman Negara and by the first of May we'd set the last week of June as a tentative date for the fishing trip. All we needed now were some other willing adventurists to share the cost and as Paulo proclaimed in his great Italian humor, to "help us drink, the more the merrier". With humor like this on a trip it couldn't help being fun! I oft mused that typical humorous easy going Italian Paulo and Siemens, the typically disciplined square cut German electronics firm constituted a rather strange marriage. Practically though, I'm sure Siemens chose him knowing that his temperament was better suited to managing Chinese and Malays than the German temperament which had oft proved rather incompatible with local folk.

During the next month Paulo and I worked hard to find recruits for the trip. As usual, everyone was interested and thought it sounded great but for one reason or another just couldn't swing it. By June first we had two more jungle companions, a German chap that worked with Paulo at Siemen's, Dirk, and another neighbor of mine, Carl Becker, Scotsman cum Australian who'd traveled the far east for 25 years. The die was cast. On the 20th of June Carl and I were to meet Dirk and Paulo in Kuala Lumpur and head off from there.

Around mid June I started preparations for the trip and rapidly came to realize that my outdoor and fishing equipment inventory was zero, all back in the USA. Carl had the same problem so we spent a few days rounding up what we could from the local Singaporean back lane merchants. As it turned out, jungle boots, clothing, water bottles, packs, etc. were no problem, since half the Vietnam war supply stock seemed to be on the shelves of Singapore's Arab street shops. I'm sure that if we'd needed it we could have bought a "Phantom Jet" at rock bottom prices. The fishing gear was standard imported stuff at premium prices but at least we had found some and what was a few extra bucks when it comes to fishing.

The medical regiman for the trip was reviewed carefully as we'd all either had or heard of unpleasant experiences relating to jungle life. A quick check of immunization record showed my Cholera, typhoid and tetanus up to date. I started the six week one pill a day Malaria routine before we left. A gamma globulin shot right where it hurts should provide some added resistance to things such as Hepatitas but we also planned to keep our bodies plied with beverages to kill any foreign germs and bugs. The first aid kit, prepared mainly by my able wife, included everything but a photo of Ben Casey, antiseptics, bandages (or plasters as the British term them), antroviaform for disentary, salt tablets, sugar tablets, burn salve, etc., etc., not to forget six quarts of "real medicine" that Paulo would pick up in K.L. since it was cheaper there.

On the 20th, all our gear stowed in one canvas bag and one back pack each, Carl and I flew from Singapore to K. L. We took off at 11 am and immediately refused the polite stewardess's offer of a cocktail, too early we said. O how our thinking would change on this matter during the next week!

Paulo maneuvered the little Fiat 132 thru the numerous switchbacks like Juan Fangio in real Italian racing fashion. About 50 kilometers east of K. L. lies a small (7000 ft) mountain range that we had to cross on our way to Temerloh and we were now in the midst of it. The road was built by the British in the 40"s and was one tight turn after another but paved fairly well. Near the summit of the ridge we came thru an area where orange and tangerine trees were being cultivated in abundance. I was surprised as I hadn't seen them in Malaysia before. Dirk and Carl were asleep so mentally I helped Paulo weave his way around the mountains, logging lorries and occasional carts drawn by water buffalo. About 5 in the afternoon we pulled into Temerloh, a sleepy little rural center typical of Malaysia, Chinese restaurants, pot holed streets, etc. Paulo had been to the rest house where we had reservations about two years ago and knew he could drive right to it. After touring every road in Temerloh, we submitted and asked directions. It's incredible that people can live in a town 5 miles by 3 miles and have never heard of a place at the other end of town!

The rest house was neat, simple and proper as expected. These rest houses are owned by the government and are spread throughout West Malaysia. Their original use dates back many years and was to provide an overnight stopping place for government officials (mainly British) who were traveling into the hinterland. Today they really weren't necessary but they were a safe place to stay that you knew would be clean, quiet and the food adequate. The place was run by an elderly Chinese who after having served us a few "whiskies" promptly brought out the guest book for us to write in. Customarily guests are supposed to write their comments (usually praise) on the service, rooms, etc. Obviously after two drinks ours would be positive……crafty ole devil.

My bed was of sufficient length but the mosquito canopy was less than 5' long and let little air in so I spent a warm stuffy night in the prenatal position but still woke up refreshed the next morning. We really piled on the praise when we wrote in the guest book the night before because we wanted breakfast at 6:30 and the normal breakfast time was 7:30. We had to meet the boat at Tembeling Station at 10 am and we figured we'd need 3 hours to drive it because the road was reputed to be "very bad" which translated means only passable by army tanks and the most robust water buffalo. We were a little relieved when Mr. Lim, the rest house manager, told us that six months ago the local Sultan of Pahang decided to pay a visit to Jerantut, a town east of Tembeling Station that had to be reached by this same road. Mr.Lim complained that the Sultan paid no taxes but they probably fixed up the road just for him. Malaysia's population is about equal numbers of Chinese and Malays with the remaining 10% a mixture of everything. The Malays hold all government positions and the Chinese control most of the economy. Consequently, there's a perpetual struggle with the government trying every method to bleed the economy and the businesses trying to hold on to every cent they can. About the same thing that's going on in most other countries around the world also.

We were in relatively flat country now and portions of the road had been repaved but an equal number of portions were just terrible. Unlike USA drivers, you'll find by and large that European drivers are either "full brakes or flat out" types. About the time we'd hit 125 kph in fifth gear on the repaved portions we'd have to lean hard on the brakes and go thru a screaming grand prix downshift sequence to avoid shattering the little Fiat on the potholes of the upcoming unrepaired section of road. Obviously after the Sultan's visit work on the road had ceased. Why not? The Sultan wouldn't be back for a few years.

We rolled into Kuala Tembeling about 9:00, not too bad, 2 hours and no blown tires or broken springs, the little Fiat was more durable than I had given it credit for. I know my Ford Cortina would have left a string of parts on that road resembling an aircraft crash scene. It was agreed that we'd buy some fruit here to take with us. Carl got out to make the purchase from a group of roadside stands. He came back empty handed muttering something about "wanted five for a dollar, I offered six, got to teach the buggars a lesson occasionally". Anyhow, that fruit would have sure been good but it seems that Carl could never strike the right bargain so we went without.

Surprisingly the boat was waiting for us at the sleepy little river dock. Ten in the morning in Malaysia is short for "sometime before supper". We dug up the chap in charge. He wanted to see our permit to enter the park so we produced it and explained that it was for five people and the fifth person, Carl's son, would arrive Tuesday and we'd send a boat down for him. Bruce had seriously cut his eye and was having the stitches removed on Monday and would find out then if the doctor would let him come on the trip. If so he'd take a fourteen hour every town stop train from Singapore to Jerantut and taxi to Tembeling. The boat was a 25' dugout with builtup sides resulting in about 10" of freeboard and a 3' beam width. There was a canopy to keep the sun or rain off, two seats, we sat side by side, many many red gas cans and a shiney new Chrysler 25 at the stern. Abdullah, dressed in nicely starched tans, was the park guide who was assigned to us. He operated the boat's motor. His assistant Herodin was the "pole man" in the front of the boat. Later I'd find out what his function was. Quickly our gear was loaded, we got into the boat and set off. I remarked how comfortable the seats were, just plywood but with nice 3" thick pieces of foam. I assumed these doubled as life preservers, how nice I mused. Later I discovered the jerks had used an "open cell" foam the nicest sponge you can imagine. O'well just what you'd expect. Malaysia wouldn't be Malaysia if it weren't this way.

The Sungei Tembeling was just as I expected a tropical river to be, wide, lazy and a bit murky. This was the dry season (relatively) and the river was low and not too swift. The large dugout canoe was heavy but moved pretty fast because of its narrow beam. The jungle was beautiful, cameras clicked at birds, otters, water buffalo, local populas, etc. It was quickly apparent that the Sungei Tembeling was "mainstreet" in this neck of the woods. Dugout canoes, bamboo rafts, anything that'd float could be seen. Every few miles we passed a kampong of thatched huts with people fishing, kids playing, mothers washing in the river, water buffalo, banana and papaya trees, etc. Everyone enjoying themselves and no over-exertion evident. One hour up the river from Kuala Tembeling the lazy sungei displayed a turbulent frothy rapids. When I noticed that Abdullah was heading straight for it I swallowed a lump and thought "My God he's going through that thing!" Before I could react we were going up through the rapids. As we entered Herodin grabbed his long pole and stood up in the bow of the canoe. Because of the boat's low profile and long length the man on the motor couldn't see in front nor could he turn the boat quickly, he could only aim it. Herodin's job was to pole us around the rocks and give occasional hand signals to Abdullah who was busy gunning the engine, throttling it down if he thought hitting a rock was unavoidable and then gunning the engine again to maintain our attitude so the swift water didn't turn us around. After a few sets of these rapids I started to respect these guy's skill. I'd done a fair amount of canoeing but never anything like this! One of their techniques was to get as close to the side of the rapids as possible where a sort of boundary layer of less turbulent water existed, this kept us from being swamped and allowed them to observe submerged rocks more easily. Sometimes this "less turbulent" ribbon was so narrow that I could have stepped right out onto rocks on shore.

What must be the Taman Negara Park Headquarters loomed in the distance. Situated on a fairly high bluff at the confluence of the Sungei Tembeling and the Sungei Tahan were a group of buildings. It had been three hours since we set out and we'd gotten soaked in rapids and dried out three or four times since. Wisely we'd sealed all our gear in plastic bags. The sun was overhead and it was hot and sticky but beautiful, just beautiful, water, trees, hills, birds, animals, what a contrast to Singapore! Parts of the Sungei Tembeling could have been the Little Miami River in Ohio. I felt good and comfortable in this type of country, it was familiar and filled my mind with memories of similar places in the midwest, USA.

The park headquarters consisted of a building to house the employees of higher status. A diesel electric generation hut, the headquarters office, bungalows for guests and a central dining hall. The area was well maintained, flowers, grass cut etc. It was obviously the nucleus of civilization in this part of the bush. We were shown to our rooms that I must admit were more posh than we'd bargained for. Flush toilet, mosquito netting and of course the quaint ever present Somerset Maugham swish-swish ceiling fan. We unloaded our gear, mixed up a little "medicine" and discussed our fishing strategy. The place was so quiet it almost bugged me at first. Only an occasional long drawn out whining buzz of some local jungle insect. According to the guide the closest "good" fishing was three hours further up the river by boat and the "best" fishing was two days beyond that. Now I like to fish but two days was rediculous! Reminded me of the fabled "Wiggly Lake" trout fishing caper that Bob Burroughs and I got hornswaggled into once. Spent better part of the day going down Whiskey Lake, carrying motors, gasoline, etc. up the mountain to Trap Lake, boating across this lake, more carrying and finally arrive at Wiggly Lake, fish for two hours and then head back to make it to camp before dark. I voted for the three hour just "good" fishing. Hell, mother nature determines the best fishing anyhow, you just have to be there at the right time, anywhere. The plan was to head out early next morning, fish the day and spend the night at an outpost cabin and then fish most of the next day before returning to Kuala Tahan, the headquarters.

Bright and early the next morning, our fishing gear all prepared, our city tensions removed by strong doses of medicine the night before, we took off for Perkai. The boats were smaller than the one we'd come up on and could only accommodate two passengers with gear so we had to take two boats (about 14' dugouts) with two guides in each boat. Again the jungle and river life was fascinating and beautiful. The long forgotten childhood feeling triggered by a smell, a sound, a vision, who knows what would ripple through my mind and body. Maybe it was just that unequalled elusive <u>freedom</u> that man so yearns for. Here we were, a combination of "African Queen" and "Deliverance" all together. Sungei Tembeling, vicious in places and docile as a lamb in others. Mammoth trees with their following of parasitic fern like plants shut out the sky in many places. Hills, cliffs, sand bars, damn it could be the "Little Miami". After an hour of this we started up a tributary river, the Sungei Terrengau. The water was crystal clear, too clear for good fishing I thought, and in deep places appeared coal black. We stopped here where there was a small shack and a single lone Malay house. By the time we eased our boat to shore a man, his wife, and gosh knows how many children were there to greet us. I thought wasn't hard to guess what they did all day long. O'well, just my envious mind at work again. Apparently this guy was employed by the Park to watch after the padlocked shed. It contained some outboard motors, cans of gas, etc. Here we exchanged the 25 HP jobs for smaller 10's that would be easier to handle in the smaller river. We also picked up some worn but clean, sheets and mosquito netting. After a brief rest and sip out of the water bottles we were off again.

This was real jungle now. In places the river was only ten feet wide and the treed ceilings of vegetation seldom let the sun in except maybe at high noon. The river had a pretty good flow to it and since this was the dry season I figured it must originate in the higher mountains which were about three days from here. The rapids were getting more and more shallow and just as I was thinking that this sit down boating can't last much longer we ran aground with a grinding sound. Everyone out and push and push and push. And so it went off and on for the next hour or so. At last we made it to the outpost cabin at Perkai. I now realized that Perkai and this little cabin were one and the same. We'd all stripped to swimming trunks and tennis shoes by this stage after wading many rapids. I was taking to this "river rat" life. We decided to dump our gear, eat lunch and go fishing. The cabin's residents were a pack of very unhappy jungle rats. After a delightful chase, return, chase, return bout it looked like we'd finally won. In rat life, having a place like this to yourself must be likened to living in Buckingham Palace.

No wonder they put up such a fight before leaving. The Malays swept the place and put up mosquito netting. Just a roof and bunks but that's all we needed. The night before we left Tembeling we asked the Chinese cook to wrestle up some grub to take with us. We ended up with 24 hardboiled eggs, 24 oven rolls and a mammoth container of Nasi Goreng (Malay fried rice). This made lunch preparation easy, two eggs, two rolls each, O, yes I almost forgot, we did bring a few cans of beer to wash it down with. Stomachs filled, it was time to fish. Where? Omar, the poleman in our boat said the best fishing was three hours upstream. At this Paulo and I both rolled our eyes and laughed. Oh of course, further up, always further up! We decided to settle for something close and soon we pulled to shore at the end of a long still pool at the base of a rapids.

Spoons first as this was touted to be the best. Eventually you learn that everything anybody here tells you has some ulterior motive that benefits the teller and I suspected that only those selling spoons felt they were the best bait. As "Uncle Joe" used to say, "I threw steel till I couldn't piss" A few strikes but that was all. By then the guides were turning up rocks in the rapids and putting something in a can. "Prawns" they said.

Ah yes, crawfish I figured but upon examination they did turn out to be freshwater prawns. Carl, fishing the rapids, was the first to pick up a fish. Local name was unpronounceable but it looked like a saltwater whiting, white and shiney with small scales. "Good eat" said Abdullah. We picked up a few more of these fish about a kati (1¼ lb) each. Really had to feel em bite to hook em. Tried still fishing with a gob of prawns on a big hook. Not much action. Everyone was looking for shade! The four guides were busily engaged in a card game under a large broadleaf bush. Earlier while using spinners, the first time one of us got snagged on a rock one of the guides would dive into the water, grab the line and swim out and retrieve the lure. By golly these guys weren't half bad! I figured by the end of the trip they'd saved us fifty lures because these rivers were "full of wood" as the local talk goes.

Later in the afternoon when the real "heat of the day" had subsided we picked up several more small carp like fish on natural bait again. Nothing spectacular, I knew we weren't yet on to the secret of the "big ones". We drifted the current back toward Perkai. So still that if someone coughed you resented the intrusion on nature's silence. The air was cooling and becoming heavy with moisture. That acrid aroma of decaying jungle vegetation permeated the air. My nostrils took it in deeply, savoring each breath. The smell of the wild, so precious yet so abundant. Birds everywhere, a last bout of squaking and jeering before sundown. A chance to do unbusy things, observe the mist starting to drape the hills, listen to the music of the river, observe the myriad grotesque yet handsome trees that lined the banks, pick out those few trees that grow straight and tall achieving an unshielded face to the sky, the rustle in the trees imagining some jungle children vying for territory or a morsel to eat or a place to spend the night, just soaking up the multi-colored, vary shaped rocks, no heavy thoughts, just passing everything in for what it is. I guess the power, attraction, respect, love of nature by man has its roots in the fact that we can take it all in with little reservation. No noxious fumes to avoid, no excessive noise to filter, no ugliness to rationalize away, no fickle responses. The bow of the dugout grated gently on the sand as we arrived at our cabin, No one lept to get out, no rush, we had a whole week, the jungle's symphony was playing, the day was closing. Someone suggested some medicine, that broke the spell, we piled out, gathered our gear and headed up the bank to our palace in the bush, boy that bunk would be heaven tonight, even if it was a foot too short. Now this is living, plunked down in a chair on the front porch, feet up on the railing, an empty beer can with lid cut out, full of medicine, a view of the silver river at dusk and the moon coming up behind the far hills. I smelled a wood fire and could barely see some smoke rising from where we left the boats. Must be the guides, guess I'll mosey down there, after my medicine, of course. Abdullah was busy cooking the fish we'd given them over a wood fire, some kind of stew with greens from the surroundings, plus fish, smelled fantastic. When I got back to the cabin I was elated at the fact Paulo was fixing our supper. We all knew that if we sat around and drank long enough that Paulo's insatiable appetite would eventually prevail and drive him to fix supper, anyhow he enjoyed it. He and Omar fooled around with this little kerosene stove trying to get some flame. Omar just shook his head, "no work". Eventually we were eating our bush banquet of hardboiled eggs, rolls and nasi goreng. The simplest of foods can satisfy the palate in these surroundings, anything fancy would have been out of place. Dirk was busy shooting time lapse pictures of the moon coming up with his movie camera, very serious and intent about the whole thing. "Das experiment" he announced. Carl was proclaiming his victory about catching the most fish, Paulo and I drank and kept saying "good fishing three hours further up", followed by a series of uncontrolled belly laughs each time. Carl was convinced, and probably correct, that these guys would never show us where the 'big ones' were, that was their domain, not ours.

I slept like the proverbial log that night only waking twice as I recall. I'd hit the sack a little ahead of Carl and when he turned in I heard him stirring and muttering loudly that "Wakefield had taken his bunk!" I chuckled to myself and went back to sleep. When I turned in I noticed that one bunk butted against a large wooden storage box, just right height and position to put my pillow on and thus extend the effective bunk length a foot or so, unfortunately the other bunks didn't include this feature. The only other thing I remembered was a loud dork-dork-dork sound that woke me up.

Never did figure out if it was beast or bird. The next morning we fished the same area and had the same marginal success. We decided to eat lunch, pack the boats and head downstream and fish in the larger Sungei Tembeling close to Kuala Tahan so we could make it back to headquarters before dark in half an hour or so. Dirk wasn't really a fisherman, he'd come to photograph mainly, Carl was a Scotland fly/trout type. As for

Paulo and me, we were becoming convinced that we were going to have to do some nitty gritty plain ole "river fishin".

We switched motors and dumped the mosquito nets at the outpost shack. An hour downstream from there Abdullah brought us to an area I couldn't believe and hadn't noticed on the way up. Here was a white sand beach 150 yards long that rivaled anything that Waikiki or Daytona had to offer. Amazing, this would be perfect for river fishing as the bottom dropped off steeply. While Herodin cut forked branches to hold our rods, we baited with prawns and tossed out "deadline or earth fishing" as it's known in Europe. Soon we were all having strikes but not much luck in landing them.

Abdullah using red worms caught a freshwater prawn that my eyes wouldn't believe! It was 10 inches long! The Malays said the river was full of them and you could only catch them on red worms. We quickly sliced this prawn up and baited with large chunks of the white flesh. This produced results, carp, catfish and….what's Becker got hooked? Carl was intently playing something larger than usual that was putting up a good fight. Within a short while he'd landed it. "Banita" they said, never seen anything like it before. Small head and mouth, large flat silvery body and no tail! Probably seven or eight kati, the best fish so far.

Paulo and I were convinced that we'd turn Carl, the Scottish perfect salmon fly angling elite into a down to earth common ordinary base river fisherman. I hollered to Paulo, what we need are some "chicken guts". Paulo grinned, "Ah yes, entrails very good, use in Italy all the time". Carl sensed we were serious.

The headquarters at Tahan bustled with the usual evening activities. We had a square meal and planned the next day's strategy. Dirk decided to do some hiking and the three of us would boat up the Tembeling again and fish the deep holes with big bait. The electric went off at 11:00 each night, the swishing of the ceiling fan stopped, silence, there's a damn mosquito inside this net with me, wish he'd get his fill soon. The mosquito repellent coils we'd brought had soaked up moisture and kept burning out so we had to rely on the nets. By and large, not too many mosquitos. I awoke to the fan's swish swish again. Must be 6:30, electric's on. Cold shower and dress, these duds are getting a bit rank I noticed, must think about doing something about that, maybe tomorrow, besides, keeps the bugs away. At breakfast we discussed a bad situation, the medicine was running low, never fails, no more café' capacino we concluded, strict rationing from here on, beer whenever possible. The Chinese that ran the eating hall brought our breakfast. I half jokingly asked "How much he'd take for one of the chickens we saw out back?" What for, he querried? Bait I said, the whole chicken, he laughed. Paulo told him that actually we only needed the insides. He thought the chicken might miss his insides so he proposed we buy two chickens, take the entrails and he'd fix the rest for supper that evening. Six dollars each (Malay dollars), a deal. We finished our coffee and another couple eating breakfast nearby stared inquisitively as we were handed a a plastic bag full of fresh 'chicken guts'. Paulo smiled, real fishing now! What, no liver, no gizzard? Back to the kitchen, ah here it is, the guy plucking the birds had them set aside for himself, no doubt. "Best bait" I said as I put them in the bag.

Abdullah and Herodin threaded our dugout thru the rapids with the expertise we'd by then come to expect. A small dousing occasionally but 100% under control. Oh look, otters, someone said. Paulo laughed and gave his standard reply that was becoming a joke. Every time we would see a wild animal Paulo would say, "Ah, we used to have in Italy, no more now, people eat all up". Paulo insists that 99% of all wildlife in Italy has been eradicated because the people eat everything! "Even eating small birds now", he added, snakes too. He and I chatted back and forth, mainly for Carl's amusement, how ripe the entrails would be for bait after they aged in the sun for a few hours. We picked a nice pool and got out onto some large rocks just below a rapids. Paulo showed me the Italian style of threading the entrails onto the hook and up about 12" onto the line and then tying the line and entrails in a knot at the top. They can't get them off this way he explained. After a few bites and no fish, Paulo loudly announced that the contents of the entrails on his hook had been removed by some sly fish. Ah! "A Taman Negara shit sucker" he blurted out. I almost fell into the water laughing, our repertoire had finally reached "ground zero"! Thereafter when things got dull we frequently referred to this mythical cunning fish of the Taman Negara. To foil this creature Paulo now tied a knot at the bottom also. Herodin had something big on, it was staying deep, we coached him not to get impatient, a nice catfish, much like the channel cats, maybe fifteen pounds or so. We fished several pools with pretty good success and ended up on our white sand beach again, primarily because it was on the west bank and the towering jungle foliage provided afternoon shade. I noticed that late in the afternoon that, the Malays, Abdullah and Herodin, always put their sarongs on. Almost all Malays are Muslims and I didn't know if this was of religious significance or not. Obviously in a hot place a sarong is very comfortable as I'd worn a large towel as one occasionally after I'd learned to tie it so it didn't fall off.

Back at headquarters that night Dirk told us of his adventures with the jungle leeches, a tapir he'd photographed from a "high hide" and the large trees he'd seen. The trees sounded unreal and I had to see them before we left. We mused about the "Taman Negara shit suckers". Paulo had to put this into German before we could get a smile from Dirk. The next day we'd boat up the Sungei Tahan to a waterfall and do a little swimming and fishing. During the medicine hour before supper I kept trying to finish a paperback book I'd brought. I was sitting on the porch stretched out, book in hand, medicine close by, watching the "chit chats" catch insects on the ceiling when I heard something rustling the bushes behind me. There stood a 300 pound deer browsing the the shrubs planted around the building. She seemed oblivious to civilization, what little bit there was. She was so close I could almost touch her, a very large doe almost identical to the North American whitetails in all respects but without the white tail. The Chinese cook came out and I discovered that I really could touch her. He petted her head and scratched her ears. Tame as a dog. Apparently she'd grown up from a fawn around the headquarters and had no fear of man. She'd stay in the jungle during the day and each evening thereafter at dusk she'd come into the camp and receive her human affection. I figured she didn't roam too far or surely she'd fall prey to a tiger. We'd been told when we asked that most of the tigers and elephants were further up river, just like the fish, further up! At Perkai we'd seen fresh elephant spore and needless to say it was impressive.

The following morning boating up the Tahan we came across four aboriginals sitting on a log in the water, a mother and three children. They were black skinned with fuzzy hair and very negroid or African looking in features. Actually all the Malaysian, New Guinean, and even Australian aboriginals exhibit these same negroid features. The lighter skinned Malays and Indonesians were obviously later comers that no doubt migrated from China centuries ago and interbred with the aboriginals on a small scale to produce today's Malay/Indonesian race. All the aboriginals we saw seemed almost prehistoric and their simplistic looks provided a glimpse into dark history eons ago, civilization had bypassed them. An hour up the Tahan brought us to the waterfall, small in drop, more of a violently turbulent cascade of rapids. Our guides like the true "children of the bush" that they were, were first into the quiet pool at the base of the falls. I couldn't resist long either, boy that water's cold. A later check on the map revealed that Mt. Tahan (7200 feet) was only fifteen miles north, no wonder the water was so chilly. The locals had discovered a place in the cascade in which the water flowed and dropped thru a two foot wide opening between rocks and there was a rock shelf just below it such that one could stand on the shelf, lean back and be completely engulfed by the rushing water but yet be able to breathe in the downstream void created by his body. It wasn't too cool if you lost your balance and got knocked over frontwards. Nature's super whirlpool bath!

While I was taking my turn at this game I thought, what if a floating log......O, what the hek. We considered fishing the Tehan but concluded big water, big fish and headed back to the larger Tembeling.

We'd barely put our lines in the water when Abdullah tied into a real pole bender. I thought to myself, if he lands that I'm Uncle Remus, in perfect Malay style he was trying to horse it in. Funny thing was that occasionally the fish would let him bring it in close and then at will just turn and dive, slipping that drag so that it sounded like a bird whistling. Rather than play the fish, as we were suggesting, Abdullah just kept tightening the drag. Each run the fish made was more shrill until the inevitable happened, the line broke. I later tested the line and it was at least 25 pound test. Whatever that was we never got a glimpse of it, I'd have given my right arm to have it on my line. The Malays never consider that the fish may get tired, they view it as "either him stronger or me stronger".

Again our luck was just 'fair' and we fished every pool along that stretch of river. Occasionally we wanted to fish in the middle of a deep pool. The guides had an interesting anchor set up for the boat. They'd disappear into the jungle with their Parang and come back with long split pieces from a large diameter vine, then they'd find an appropriate rock, we'd boat to where we wanted to fish, tie vines to the rock, throw it over board and keep splicing on vines til it got to the bottom and secure it to the boat. All pretty standard so far. When we'd leave this spot they'd untie the vine from the boat and tie it to a large diameter piece of bamboo to act as a float. Simple, if we came back the anchor'd be there ready to use again.

That afternoon, fishing at our favorite white sand beach, I was marveling at the quiet of the place. Large hills bordered the river on each side. Occasionally, I'd hear this slow rhythmic whoop, whoop, whoop sound in the air. As it grew louder I'd look to the sky just in time to see a Giant Hornbill in full flight emerge from behind one of the hills a full thousand feet in the air above us, the droning steady beat of his wings producing sound as if he were right next to us. Similarly upon occasion some animal, I believe a monkey because there are numerous gibbons in the area, would eminate a screech from the jungle that contrasted to the perfect silence would startle me to such a point that once I almost dropped my beer. Now that's getting serious, dehydration's nothing to fool around with!

We fished till it was almost dark, piled into the boat and made a full throttle dash downstream in order to preserve what daylight existed for navigating the rapids, until now I know it was just blind luck that we didn't hit a rock on the way back. That night at supper Dirk prowdly showed us his jungle battle scars, leech marks again, that he'd accumulated on his hikes that day. Again he told us about these giant trees he'd seen. That did it, I couldn't believe they were that big, and besides, Dirk was only drinking beer. We decided that since the next day was our last in camp, we'd fish in the morning, meet Dirk for lunch back at the headquarters and then take the trail up some small nearby mountain and return by the trail he'd seen these fabled trees on. That evening we ran completely out of medicine, poor planning, O well, I got my book finished anyhow. Decided to shower before I hit the sack because I didn't think I could stand myself much longer. Afterwards when I reached for my towel I was greeted by a lovely four inch diameter jungle spider who'd chosen my towel as his abode for the night. Never did figure out where that went but before I tucked in my mosquito netting that night I made darn sure we weren't sharing a bed. Thereafter whenever I put my clothes on I gave them a good shake.

We started up the river early the next morning, mist still heavy on the river. This is the time of day that the good Lord made for those who love the wilds. Life just beginning to stir, nothing hectic, an easy going pace, nice and cool, a little humid and ole man sun up there somewhere trying to burn his way thru. You can feel him but can't see him yet. What ever ails ya, the crack of dawn will cure it, hangovers excluded please. Even the river seems a bit more peaceful at day break. We gradually worked our way upstream from pool to pool, savoring each cast and each jungle sight as this was about the last of our fishing on this trip. About noon we reluctantly concluded "that's it" time to head back. We'd picked up our share of fish, nothing fantastic but more importantly we'd shared a new life style that to me was most agreeable. We packed our fishing gear into the boat, I even packed my camera in my back pack, I didn't want anything busy to do on this last trip thru thus beautiful part of the river, I wanted to be free to soak it all up.

Abdullah was easy on the throttle as he picked his way downstream, the current itself gave us plenty of speed. About halfway down to headquarters, I don't even recall what I was doing, probably in some distant daydream, we were about two thirds thru a rapids when the guys in the front pof the boat, I was in a rear seat, hollered "Tigers, get the cameras!" I didn't even look up, somewhere in the back of my mind when I packed the camera I had the feeling I'd need it, simultaneously I cursed and grabbed my backpack, ripped it open frantically, grabbed the camera, tore the cover off and flicked the lens cap into the boat. Damn I thought! I jumped up just in time to see some shapes moving across a rock strewn flat along the shore. Everyone was shouting and Abdullah got the boat over to shore immediately. We ran up onto the rocky area that extended back from shore maybe 100 yards or so to a hill. Nothing. They're gone Carl said, he and I were the only ones with cameras, they've slipped away. I'm not sure I said, I haven't taken my eyes off that hill and I didn't see them go up it. We walked about 25 yards closer to the hill, cameras poised. Everyone agreed, they're gone. Let's throw a rock, I picked one up and let fly. Nothing, O yes, there he is, a massive bounding hulk of wild moved up the slope and stopped short of the jungle undergrowth. I'll never forget that moment, I'd set the light on my camera and gotten off one shot when he turned around and roared! Abdullah or someone said with tension in their voice, he's hungry. I was too excited to be worried, to me it was a roar or growl of anger at being disturbed. I waited for the others to emerge so I could get another shot but finally took another hurried one of this "not to be intimidated master of the jungle" just before he lunged into the undergrowth with bushes shaking and branches crashing in the wake of his hasty flight. Again I cursed myself for not buying that zoom lens before I left Singapore. With a F2.0 and poor contrast at that distance lucky if I'll see anything.

We all stood around dazed trying to reconstruct events. Herodin in the front of the boat had seen them first, three in all, two large and a smaller one. No doubt mother, father and cub. That's the only time a tiger and tigress are seen together, either at courting time or when she's raising a youngster or two. We could see from the wet trails on the rocks leading from the river that they'd apparently swum across at this narrow place and we'd come upon them just as they got out of the water. Paulo, who was the only one with a telephoto lens had not brought his camera this day and said he had seen all three tigers go up the hill. In the confusion I only saw one. Incredible, nobody sees a tiger in the wild, let along three at once. Abdullah later told us that he could count on both hands the number he'd seen in twenty years in the park and he'd never had a visitor with him on any of the occasions. The trip really was over now, nothing could equal this. Now I understood, the Lion is the King of the Jungle but the Ruling Power resides with the Tiger.

When we arrived back at the headquarters of course everyone laughed when we told them, O sure, three tigers, ha, ha. It took some convincing. That afternoon we hiked to the summit of the local mountain. Talk about sweat, whew! On the way back we saw Dirk's trees and he hadn't exaggerated, every bit of fifteen feet in diameter, when taking pictures of the guys standing in front of it I had to think of the giant California Redwoods. We passed by the river and thought it would be a perfect place to strip, deleech and take a cooling dip, so we did just that. I drifted down in the cool current and thought, this has got to be the ultimate in "letting all systems go", not one restriction, reservation, conflict or even serious thought. We arrived back at the headquarters an hour before dusk. A few people there were leaving to go to a high hide nearby to try to photograph animals at a salt lick. We went along but I left the hide after about ten minutes and mosied back, just couldn't get too fired up about the possibility of photographing a wild pig or such. I kind of felt like a kid whose team had just won the state triple A championship and now he was watching a class C knothold baseball game. Interesting, but that's all.

That night we replayed the whole game a dozen times. Our trip down to Kuala Tembeling the next morning was delightful. Photographed some otters and saw a water buffalo calf stuck in the river mud. Carl shouted to Abdullah, "he's stuck", inferring that Abdullah should steer over so we could be of help. Abdullah didn't react. Finally after Carl had shouted twice more, "he's stuck", Abdullah, holding his course straight ahead, smiled and said, "probably". The calf truely was stuck but Abdullah no doubt figured that someone else could take care of it. His remark was typical of the unconcerned life people lived around there.

The trip home was pretty uneventful. The tigers were barely visible on the slides but it didn't really matter. No photo could capture that adrenaline fed emotion, that momentary staring stand of defiance, that gutteral beastly roar of intimidation, that massive yet lightning fast cat hulk lunging up the hill and finally the spectacular crash of the wild thing into the jungle. It's vividly captured in my mind and for that I am thankful, it's enough.

T. Wakefield

Singapore

16 June 1975

Lightning Source UK Ltd.
Milton Keynes UK
UKOW04f1826050215

245736UK00014B/75/P